HEALTH CARE LIBRARIANSHIP AND INFORMATION WORK

SECOND EDITION

HEALTH CARE LIBRARIANSHIP AND INFORMATION WORK

Edited by
Michael Carmel
Director of Library Services, South Thames (West)

Library Association Publishing
London

Published by
Library Association Publishing
7 Ridgmount Street
London WC1E 7AE

First published as *Medical librarianship* 1981
This second edition 1995

British Library Cataloguing in Publication Data
A catalogue record for this book is available from the British Library
ISBN 1-85604-145-X

Typset from authors' disks in 10/13pt Palermo by Library Association Publishing
Printed and made in Great Britain by Bookcraft (Bath) Ltd

❖ Contents

❖ Dedication

Roy Tabor, Wessex Regional Librarian, 1967–90

Roy Tabor was the first regional librarian appointed in the British National Health Service. Throughout his tenure he tirelessly campaigned for library services to be as responsive, effective and efficient as human effort and technology could make them. He led us in exploration of the many issues addressed in this book, whether it be the educational use of audiovisuals, the information needs of health care consumers, or the relevance of health informatics to librarianship. Above all he stressed by precept and example the need to root every library development in the needs of the patient for quality health care. To him this book is dedicated.

❖ Acknowledgements

A book of this nature is a major collaborative effort involving many people doing a lot of work for little or no reward. It is not possible to thank everyone, but I would like to recognize specifically the staff of Library Association Publishing for their support, guidance and tolerance; Barbara Haynes for holding the operation together through many difficulties; and Helen Carmel for her forbearance in the face of disrupted holidays, a lost dining-room and other provocations.

❖ Contributors

Lorraine Bate MA ALA

Present employment: Information Resource Centre Manager, Nuffield Institute for Health, University of Leeds, 1987 to date. Previous employment: Nursing Librarian, Huddersfield Health Authority, 1985–7. Professional interests include European health care information, health information networking, current awareness/SDI, marketing information services.

Andrew Booth BA DipLib ALA

Present employment: Senior Information Officer, Sheffield Centre for Health and Related Research, University of Sheffield. Previous employment: Information Services Manager, Kings Fund Centre, London. Professional interests: purchasing intelligence, information audit, critical appraisal skills, questionnaire and database design.

Sheila Cannell MA ALA

Present employment: Head, Medical Science and Veterinary Libraries Division, Edinburgh University Library, Erskine Medical Library, Edinburgh, 1986 to date. Previous employment: Online Information Development Officer, Glasgow University Library. Assistant Librarian, Biological and Medical Division, Glasgow University Library, 1976–86. Professional interests: staff development, networked information developments, provision of information to scientists and medics.

Michael Carmel BA MS, FLA

Present employment: Director of Library Services, South Thames (West), 1976 to date. Previously worked for Dorset Area Health Authority, University of Nairobi, and Manchester Public Libraries. Edited the previous edition of this book and has published over 50 papers mainly on policy, management and network issues. Professional interests: cooperation. As 1993 Fulbright Research Librarian visited USA for four months to study the NLM's IAIMS and informatics programmes.

Penny Cockerill MLS ALA MIInfSci

Previous employment: Librarian, St Peter's District Health Library,

Chertsey Surrey, 1991–4. Assistant Librarian (Readers Services), St Georges Medical School Library, 1980–5. Information Research Officer, Medical Information Review Panel, British Library Research and Development Department, 1978–80. Professional interests: literature searching, promoting library skills and library profile raising.

Anne Collins BSc MSc ALA

Present employment: Librarian, University of Leeds Medical Library, School of Medicine, 1975 to date. Previous employment: Assistant Librarian, University of Salford, 1970–5. Professional interests include user education and CD-ROM technology.

Rachel Cooke BA MLib ALA

Present employment: Regional Librarian (Contracts and Staff Development), South Thames (West), 1990 to date (a post job-shared with Janet Holman). Previous employment: Librarian, Kingston College of Nursing, 1987–9, District Librarian, St Helier, 1989–90. Master's dissertation on the training needs of library assistants in public libraries.

Robert Gann BA Dip Lib FLA

Present employment: Director, Help for Health Trust, Winchester, Hampshire. Previous employment: Health Information Manager, Wessex Regional Health Authority 1982–92. Professional interests: consumer health information, outcomes and effectiveness, decision making. External examiner, University of Wales Department of Information and Library Studies; Visiting Lecturer, Wessex Institute of Public Health Medicine, University of Southampton.

Susan Gilbert BA MSc ALA

Present employment: Readers' Adviser, St George's Medical School Library, London, 1989 to date. Previous employment: Medical Librarian, St Helier Hospital, Carshalton, Surrey, 1982–9. Professional interests include provision of information to health science professionals, user education and library automation.

Shane Godbolt BA FLA

Present employment: North Thames (West) Regional Librarian, British Postgraduate Medical Federation, London, 1973 to date. Previous employment: Librarian, Charing Cross and Westminster Medical School, London. Professional interests: Editor, *Health libraries review*.

Felicity Grainger MIInfS BSc PhD DipInfSci

Present employment: Medical Sciences Librarian, Glasgow University, 1991 to date. Previous employment: Head of Library and Information Services, Kennedy Institute of Rheumatology, 1980–91. Professional interests: developments in information transfer which allow dissemination of datasets and full-text across networks.

Margaret Haines BA MLS AHIP

Present employment: NHS Library Adviser, Department of Health, Skipton House, London, 1995 to date. Previous employment: Head of Information Resources, King's Fund Centre, 1989–95. Associate Instructor, Faculty of Library and Information Science, University of Toronto, 1988-9. Director of Library Service, Children's Hospital of Eastern Ontario, 1978–88. Professional interests: national information policies, networks, international cooperation, quality management, evidence based health care, consumer health information services.

Janet Holman MA ALA

Present employment: Regional Librarian (Contracts and Staff Development), South Thames (West), 1993 to date (a post job-shared with Rachel Cooke). Previous employment: Librarian, Frances Harrison College of Healthcare, 1990-3. Library adviser, Inner London Education Authority, 1982–90. Professional interests: staff development, including pre-registration training. Library Association Scrutineer.

Peter Morgan MA ALA

Present employment: Senior Under-Librarian (Science and Medicine), Cambridge University Library, and Librarian, Cambridge University Medical Library, Addenbrooke's Hospital, Cambridge, 1975 to date. Previous employment: Assistant Library Officer, Cambridge University Library, 1973–5. Has undertaken consultancies for the British Council in Pakistan and Kuwait. Professional interests: library management; development and integration of electronic information services and training of their users; ethical and legal aspects of health care librarianship.

Sheila Padden MA ALA

Present employment: John Rylands University Library, University of Manchester, 1993 to date. Previous employment: Librarian, North Western Regional Health Authority, 1987–93. Professional interests: health service grey literature and statistics, user education in library skills and CD-ROMs for undergraduates.

Judith Palmer BSc PhD MIInfSc ALA

Present employment: Director of Health Care Libraries in the Oxford Region, 1993 to date. Previous employment: Information Manager and Executive Assistant to the Director of Research, AFRC Institute of Arable Crops Research, Rothamsted Experimental Station, 1988–93. Has worked for the British Council in Zambia, and also has work experience in Zimbabwe and Malawi. Chair of the Health Libraries Group of The Library Association and Chair of the NHS Regional Librarians Group.

Caroline Sawers MSc FLA

Present employment: Regional Librarian (Systems), South Thames (West)

Regional Library Service, 1985 to date. Mrs Sawers obtained her MSc in Information Science at University College London in 1992, and was elected a Fellow of the Library Association in 1993.

Regina Cammy Shakakata BA DipLib

Appointed National Focal Point Librarian for health information in 1991, and acts as liaison officer to HealthNet. On the Board of Studies and the Dean's advisory Committee of the University of Zambia's School of Medicine. Has also been involved in gender and developmental research projects and is a member of the Eastern and Southern African Technology Policy Studies Network.

Margaret C. Stewart BA AKC ALA

Present employment: freelance consultant, 1984 to date. Previous employment has been in medical and audiovisual librarianship at the Royal College of Veterinary Surgeons, British Life Assurance Trust Centre for Health and Medical Education, Coronary Prevention Group, and the Mental After Care Association. Well known for her books on audiovisual materials, she is former Audiovisual Column Editor of *Health libraries review*.

Graham Walton MA BSc FETC ALA

Present employment: Faculty Librarian (Health, Social Work and Education), University of Northumbria at Newcastle, 1994 to date. Previous employment: Faculty Librarian (Social Sciences), Newcastle Polytechnic, 1984–94, Subject Librarian (Health Sciences), Newcastle Polytechnic, 1980–4, Librarian, Highland Health Sciences Library, 1987–9. Professional interests include development of services via networks, curriculum integration of information skills, interface between IT staff and library staff.

Jean Yeoh MEd BA ALA

Present employment: Tutor/Librarian, St Georges Medical School Library, London, 1986 to date. Previous employers have included a variety of academic libraries. Professional interests include user education, learning skills and research into the relationship between information use by trained nurses and patient care.

❖ Acronyms and abbreviations

AAAS	American Association for the Advancement of Science
AAS	African Academy of Science
ACOG	American College of Obstetricians and Gynecologists
AHA	American Hospitals Association
AHEC	Area Health Education Center
AHIP	Academy of Health Information Professionals
AIOPI	Association of Information Officers in the Pharmaceutical Industry
ART	automated request transmission
ASHSL	Association of Scottish Health Service Librarians
ASSIA	*Applied social sciences indexes and abstracts*
ASSIST	Association for Information Management and Technology Staff in the National Health Service
AWHL	Association of Welsh Health Librarians
BDA	British Dental Association
BDS	Bachelor of Dental Surgery
BIDS	Bath Information and Data Services
BLCMP	Birmingham Libraries Cooperative Mechanization Project
BLDSC	British Library Document Supply Centre
BLRDD	British Library Research and Development Department
BM	Bachelor of Medicine
BMA	British Medical Association
BNB	British National Bibliography
BPMF	British Postgraduate Medical Federation
BUFVC	British Universities Film and Video Council
CAB	Citizens' Advice Bureau
CASIAS	current awareness service – individual article supply
CAT	credit, accumulation and transfer

CCU	coronary care unit
CD-ROM	compact disc – read only memory
CHC	community health council
CHI	consumer health information
CHIC	Consumer Health Information Consortium
CHLA	Canadian Health Libraries Association
CINAHL	*Cumulative index to nursing and allied health literature*
CIP	cataloguing in publication
CLIC	Cancer Libraries in Cooperation
CMAZ	Churches Medical Association of Zambia
CME	continuing medical education
CPD	continuing professional development
CPN	community psychiatric nurse
CPSM	Council for Professions Supplementary to Medicine
CURL	Consortium of University Research Libraries
DDS	Doctorate in Dental Surgery
DDSc	Doctorate in Dental Science
DIAL	Disablement Information and Advice Line
DLG	Dental Librarians Group
DHSS	Department of Health and Social Security
DSS	decision support system
EAGLE	European Association of Grey Literature Exploitation
EAHIL	European Association for Health Information and Libraries
ECR	extra-contractual referrals
EDI	electronic data interchange
EN	Enrolled Nurse
ENB	English National Board
ENT	ear, nose and throat
EPR	electronic patient record
ERA	Educational Recording Agency
ESRC	Economic and Social Research Council
EU	European Union
FCA	Fellow of the College of Anaesthetists
FDS	Fellow in Dental Surgery
FHSA	family health services authority
FRCS	Fellow of the Royal College of Surgeons
FTE	full-time equivalent
GMC	General Medical Council

GP	general practitioner
GPFH	general practice fund-holder
HA	Health Authority
HEA	Health Education Authority
HELMIS	Health Management Information Service
HIP	health information plan
HIS	Health Information Service
HLG	Library Association Health Libraries Group
HMIC	Healthcare Management Information Consortium
HMO	Health Maintenance Organization
HMSO	Her Majesty's Stationery Office
HVA	Health Visitors Association
IAIMS	Integrated Advanced Information Management System
ICML	International Congress on Medical Librarianship
IDRC	International Development and Research Centre
IFLA	International Federation of Library Associations
IIS	Institute of Information Scientists
ILL	interlibrary loan
ILLG	Independent London Librarians Group
ILS-LB	Information and Library Services Lead Body
IM&T	information management and technology
IMPI	Information Managers in the Pharmaceutical Industry
InFAH	Information Focus for Allied Health
ION	Interlending Open Systems Project
ISBD	International Standard Bibliographic Description
ISBN	International Standard Book Number
ISDD	Institute for the Study of Drug Dependence
ISI	Institute of Scientific Information
ISSN	International Standard Serial Number
IT	information technology
ITU	intensive therapy unit
IVCA	International Visual Communications Association
JANET	Joint Academic Network
LA	The Library Association
LAN	local-area network
LASER	London and South Eastern Library Region
LDS	License in Dental Surgery

LINC	Library and Information Cooperation Council
MARC	machine readable cataloguing
MARS	Medical Archive Retrieval System
MB BCh	Bachelor of Medicine and Bachelor of Surgery
MB BS	Bachelor of Medicine and Bachelor of Surgery
MeSH	Medical Subject Headings
MGDSRCS	Member in General Dental Surgery of the Royal College of Surgeons
MI	medical informatics
MIDIRS	Midwives Information and Resource Service
MIMS	*Monthly index of medical specialities*
MIWP	Medical Information Working Party
MLA	Medical Library Association
MLSO	medical laboratory scientific officer
MRC	Medical Research Council
MRCGP	Member of the Royal College of General Practitioners
MRCP	Member of the Royal College of Physicians
NGO	non-governmental organization
NHS	National Health Service
NHSME	National Health Service Management Executive
NHSTD	National Health Service Training Directorate
NIH	National Institutes for Health
NLM	National Library of Medicine
NN/LM	National Network of Libraries of Medicine
NSA	National Sound Archive
NTIS	National Technical Information Service
NVQ	National Vocational Qualification
OCLC	Online Computer Library Centre
OCR	optical character recognition
OHE	Office of Health Economics
OMS	Outpatient Medical Record
OPAC	online public access catalogue
OPCS	Office of Population, Censuses and Surveys
PADISNET	Pan Africa Development Information System Network
PAMs	professions allied to medicine
PC	personal computer
PDQ	Physician Data Query

PLCS	Psychiatric Libraries Cooperative Scheme
PMDE	postgraduate medical and dental education
PREP	post-registration education and practice
R&D	research and development
RCM	Royal College of Midwives
RCN	Royal College of Nursing
RCT	randomized controlled trial
RGN	Registered General Nurse
RHA	regional health authority
RHV	Registered Health Visitor
RLG	Regional Librarians Group
RML	Regional Medical Library
RMN	Registered Mental Nurse
RSM	Royal Society of Medicine
SCONUL	Standing Conference of National and University Libraries
SCOPME	Standing Committee for Postgraduate Medical Education
SDI	selective dissemination of information
SHO	senior house officer
SIGLE	*System for information on grey literature in Europe*
SLA	Special Libraries Association
SR	senior registrar
SRIS	Science Reference and Information Service
SUBIS	Sheffield University Biomedical Information Service
SVQ	Scottish Vocational Qualification
TCA	transplant clinician's assistant
UAP	Universal Availability of Publications
UBC	Universal Bibliographic Control
UHSL	University Health Science Librarians
UKCC	United Kingdom Central Council for Nursing, Midwifery and Health Visiting
UMLS	Unified Medical Language System
UMSLG	University Medical School Librarians Group
UNZANET	University of Zambia Network
UTH	University Teaching Hospital (Zambia)
VA	Department of Veterans Affairs
VDU	visual display unit

WAIS	Wide-Area Information Servers
WAN	wide-area network
WHO	World Health Organization
WORM	write once read many times
WRLIS	Wessex Regional Library and Information Service
WWW	World Wide Web
ZANGONET	Zambia Non-governmental Organizations Network
ZFDS	Zambia Flying Doctor Service

1 Introduction: health care and libraries in the 1990s

❖ *Michael Carmel*

The purpose of this book is to help librarians who work in the field of health, and even more to help those, including students, who would like to move into this growing but ever-challenging area. We have not attempted to give all the answers. We have tried rather to provide a sound framework within which individuals can develop their own knowledge, understanding and skills.

The structure of the book is a progression from context (the organization of health care and the professions) to service, resource and management aspects, followed by three descriptive chapters on the state of the art in the contrasting environments of the developed and developing worlds. The final two chapters are concerned with the development of the profession itself – one asking how we shall relate to the new science of health informatics, and one looking at the organization of the profession in the UK.

The theme which, more than any other, unites this book is that of change. Nowhere is this more dramatic than in the structure of health care itself. In this introductory chapter, we shall look at changes in health care, some of their causes, and the consequences and opportunities for library services.

HEALTH CARE IN CRISIS

The management and finance of health care has become a major political issue throughout the developed world, and looks set to remain high on the agenda well into the next century. Although each country has its own problems and approach, the break-up of old values and structures and the resulting disruption are universal. These headlines are just a small selection from the *British medical journal*:

'Italian medical system faces demolition' (10 Oct 1992)
'Doctors furious with German health reforms' (17 Oct 1992)
'AMA starts fighting Clinton's reforms' (9 Oct 1993)
'Health care access under threat in the Netherlands' (13 Nov 1993)
'Australia's health row intensifies' (11 Dec 1993)
'New health minister faces crisis in Israel' (25 June 1994)

Such are the problems in the developed world. Those of the developing world, exacerbated by poverty and war, are far worse. So too are those of the former command economies where adult life expectancy has been falling for the first time in almost 200 years.

DRIVING FORCES

There are three main forces pushing governments of every persuasion into health care reform despite the political risks involved; these are ageing populations, new medical technology, and the growth of consumerism in health. These put a direct strain on existing institutions, and contribute to ever-rising health costs, which now account for a staggering 14% of gross domestic product in the USA. At these levels, health costs put a major strain on any economy, and come directly up against another important trend: the taxpayers', or insurance payers', revolt.

Ageing populations

The population of the European Union (EU) over the age of 65 – pensionable age in most countries – has risen from 5% at the beginning of the 20th century to 20% (and still rising) at its end. The 'greying' of North America has been partly mitigated by large-scale immigration, but Japan is even further down the road than Europe.

Not only do we typically require more health care as we get older, but the pattern of need changes. In particular, there is more emphasis on degenerative diseases of the cardiovascular system, cancers, and bone and joint problems. Equally, recovery from either disease or treatment tends to be slower, and older people may require more emphasis on care than on cure.

Medical progress

The practice of clinical medicine has been transformed in the last 20 years by the discoveries of the biological sciences and by advances in information technology. Totally new treatments have been introduced, some expensive, some cheaper than those previously available, but often offering hope in previously untreatable conditions.

Much of this progress has been made possible by the deeper understanding of both health and disease which has come especially from the sciences of immunology and genetics. At the same time progress in electronics and the use of new imaging technology, as well as the ability of 'big science' to create purpose-designed chemicals, have put whole new armouries of investigative and treatment tools into the hands of clinicians.

Surgery, in particular, has been transformed. At one extreme, previously difficult operative procedures are handled by 'minimal access surgery' and treated on a short stay or even a day-case basis. At the other extreme, advances in anaesthesia and life support systems mean that longer and more heroic surgical operations are possible, treating not only previously untreatable conditions, but also people such as the very young or very old who would once not have been expected to survive.

On the medical side progress has been equally spectacular. Drug treatments have, in some instances, virtually eliminated the need for surgery as well as saving both lives and much pain, as in the case of peptic ulcers.

Of all the ills that afflict mankind, cancer used to be the most feared because it was almost invariably fatal, mysterious, and seemingly inexorable in its progress. Today, although some types are still usually fatal, many cancers are routinely treated with outstanding success by a mixture of surgery, drugs and computerized radiation therapy.

Resurgent diseases

Infectious diseases were thought by many in the 1970s to be all but conquered. The combined efforts of public sanitation, immunization programmes and antibiotic treatments seemed to promise the possibility of a near-disease-free world. The high point of this optimism was reached in 1979 with the announcement of the eradication of smallpox.

The most dramatic setback to this optimism, though not the most serious, has come from the appearance of a new disease, AIDS, for which, at the time of writing, there is still neither cure nor vaccine. At the same time, old diseases like tuberculosis have reappeared in Western cities, and malaria has developed new strains immune to drug treatment.

These setbacks are a reminder that as medical technology moves forward to conquer new areas of ill-health, old problems live on in the background.

The social dimension

As medicine conquers new areas, it often seems that treatments have become more heroic, more expensive, more technological, and perhaps more potentially harmful, or at least painful. With modern medicine there is often a sense of dependency and loss of control which comes up against the demand for more personal control represented by consumerism.

As a result, educated lay opinion is tending to look for more reliable assurance on the efficacy of treatment, and for evidence that the most appropriate therapy is applied in each case. The present emphases on clinical audit and on evidence based practice are two manifestations of the health professions' response to these demands.

As the margins of treatability are pushed ever backwards, whether in terms of type of disease, severity, or the age of the patient, difficult issues arise around equitable access to expensive treatments, for the old as well as the poor. There are also questions about how a world organized on free-market principles can cope with problems which predominantly affect poor countries or individuals.

These are practical as well as ethical issues in a world where diseases are easily and rapidly spread from place to place. This was the original inspiration for the establishment of the World Health Organization (WHO), but today's issues are as much concerned with the research priorities of drug companies as they are with public sanitation.

The role of the hospital in health care is going through changes which may seem paradoxical. Public figures emphasize the need to move care into the community. The increase in day surgery, for example, seems to favour this. Nevertheless, much modern care requires access to centres with technologically sophisticated facilities and round-the-clock support, while older patients require longer, not shorter, hospital stays. Hence we see hospitals around the developed world expanding their facilities while leaders talk about the need for reductions.

THE POLITICAL RESPONSE

Governments have responded to the triple squeeze of rising costs, rising expectations and limited resources in surprisingly similar ways.

First, under WHO (and EU) leadership, they have renewed their commitment to health promotion and preventative medicine, often trying to influence the lifestyle of citizens in 'healthy' directions. Most countries now have their own health strategies following the principles of Health For All enshrined in the Alma Ata declaration of WHO.

In terms of delivery of clinical services, governments have moved to separate the issues of planning and commissioning health care from those of provision. Commissioning, in most countries, is seen as being a matter either for insurance companies regulated by government, or for government itself. Provision is, in most countries, left to the independent sector.

HEALTH SERVICE REORGANIZATION IN THE UK

The National Health Service (NHS) has been going through a succession of reorganizations since 1974. The general direction has been to reduce the number of statutory bodies and increase local autonomy in the running of the business. These are offset by tighter accountability structures.

This process entered its most radical phase in 1989, with the publication of a series of papers under the title *Working for patients*.[1] These introduced the concept of an internal market in secondary and tertiary health care, bringing Britain into line with policies agreed by both the WHO and the EU – that the commissioning of health care should be separated from the management of provision. Nevertheless, in Britain the Trusts responsible for provision remain within the NHS.

What has not changed
It is useful to remember that three central features of the British National Health Service remain intact: it is family doctor based, it is free at the point of need, and it is funded predominantly from taxation. A deep-seated commitment to equity of access has remained constant.

THE PROFESSIONAL AGENDA
Institutional turbulence affects every librarian working in health care to a greater or lesser extent. From the mid-1970s to 1990, the strategy of librarians in the UK was based around the concept of library services providing comprehensive multidisciplinary services to all staff in a health district.[2] They were to be coordinated by regions to provide professional leadership and resource sharing. National coordination was organized by the NHS Regional Librarians Group. Since 1990, both districts and regions have, in effect, disappeared.

Unimpeded access to the knowledge base for all concerned in health care remains a key principle for the development of library services. One of the professional challenges for librarians over the next decade will be to maintain this principle in the face of structural change and a competitive environment.

Equally important will be the need to meet two new challenges, each of which, in its own way, appears to offer the profession extreme options – to put itself at the very centre of health care priorities for the millennium, or to be relegated to the margins. These challenges arise from evidence based practice, and from the growth of medical informatics, and were expressed in some detail in the two Cumberlege seminars.[3, 4]

The challenge of evidence based practice
In responding to external and internal pressures for change, the effective application of research based knowledge has become the fundamental and central concern of all health care professions, and indeed underpins the process of change itself. This applies equally in developing the role of the commissioners of health care, in the direct application of clinical knowledge, in the empowerment of consumers and in the development of meaningful strategies for the health of the nation.

Evidence based practice encompasses all of these applications, but more challengingly it questions the validity of a great deal of what passes for knowledge in the medical world. It is claimed that much current practice is based more on custom than on research, that large parts of the research literature itself have been inadequately scrutinized, and that even review articles – a favourite resource of medical librarians – are rarely systematic and frequently biased.

These concerns have led to the creation of new types of literature. Systematic reviews, as sponsored by the Cochrane Collaboration, are among the most useful of these, each review being based on an exhaustive literature search and a detailed analysis of each contribution. These are published in electronic format to facilitate frequent updating and revision. Equally important is the development of clinical protocols outlining best current practice as defined by a variety of bodies, from Royal Colleges to insurance companies, and the growth of 'outcome studies' and effectiveness assessments, often with a substantial economic dimension.

Health care librarians are having to learn to deal with this burgeoning grey literature, much of it directly disseminated to the core users, and much of it in electronic form.

Equally, librarians need to develop a new role as a quality filter for their users in dealing with the more traditional forms of literature, which continue to grow apace. Not that librarians will replace the judgement of the professionals on the validity of what they read, but there is a real and expressed demand for help in selecting the likeliest sources of reliable answers as well as good quality information. To this end, librarians are just beginning to acquire the elementary skills of critical appraisal in relation to the scientific literature of health care.

At the same time, librarians may find themselves increasingly having to protect the interests of the user of information. There will always remain a need for open systems which enable the user to study the unorthodox as well as the officially approved view.

The challenge of new technology
Librarians have long been active in the use of information technology to solve library management and information retrieval problems. In the present decade it has become essential to go beyond this to explore the potential of electronically stored and organized information as a resource in its own right.

At its simplest level, this will mean librarians becoming expert in the use of network resources, not just of the Internet but also of private networks such as the developing NHS-wide network and other 'superhighways'. With an appropriate blend of traditional and newly acquired skills, librarians expert in navigating the network will be in a powerful position to support their users, either as intermediary searchers or as advisers.

To truly flourish in the new information age, however, librarians will need to come to grips with the new science of health informatics and its products, such as decision support systems, image browsers and interactive worksta-tions encompassing the patient record. Librarians have much to offer, not only in helping health professionals to use these, but also in helping with the design and implementation of user-friendly tools and in the pragmatic integration of systems. The risk is that both system developers and librarians themselves will fail to see and seize the opportunities now arising.

A starting point for this development of the profession can be in the collec-tion, organization and critiquing of the multimedia and interactive educational products now coming onto the market. The concern of librarians for the qual-ity of the literature can become the basis for a helpful role in relation to the information content and presentation of new media.

AN IDEAL OF SERVICE

If librarians will rise to the opportunities and challenges of the present decade, then we shall certainly enter the next millennium well placed to achieve the ideal of service put before us a century ago by George Gould:[5]

> I look forward to such an organization of the literary records of medicine that a puzzled worker in any part of the civilized world shall in an hour be able to gain a knowledge pertaining to a subject of the experience of every other man in the world.

Technically we have the capability to achieve this visionary standard. Health care workers can be provided with access within the hour to just the right amount of information, up-to-date, in usable form and quality controlled.

If this book helps those working in health library services, or preparing to do so, to move a little way towards the ideal, it will have achieved its purpose.

REFERENCES

1   Department of Health, *Working for patients*, London, HMSO, 1989.
2   *Providing a district library service*, King's Fund Centre, 1985.
3   *Health care information in the UK*, 1st Cumberlege Seminar, July 1992, British Library R&D Report 6089.
4   *Managing the knowledge base of health care*, 2nd Cumberlege Seminar, October 1993, British Library R&D Report 6133.
5   Gould, G. M., quoted in Colaianni, L. A., 'That vision thing', *Bulletin of the Medical Library Association*, **80** (1), January 1991, 1–8.

2   The medical and dental professions

❖   *Penny Cockerill*

Public librarians are not expected to know their users. The public library user could be seeking knowledge of any kind in the library. Those of us who provide information to doctors are expected to know not only that the senior registrar (SR) will require a different level of information on a given topic from that required by a senior house officer (SHO), but also what an SHO is. This chapter will attempt to name and describe the constituent parts of the medical and dental professions, because this knowledge of our users will make us much more effective information providers.

The administrative framework for health care is changing rapidly. Why should this concern us, if the practical work of healing is still the main task of the doctor? It is because even if the procedures remain the same, new aspects of medical work and new requirements of doctors dictate that their information needs are changing just as rapidly. The political and legal changes in the system of delivery of health care are described elsewhere in this book, but an understanding of current practice is vital, not only to our main task of information service, but as an aid to good communication with our users.

An example of the need to be aware of current practice is the growth in medical, or clinical, audit. Throughout the 1980s, North American doctors became increasingly involved in costly litigation to make them accountable to their patients. This individual responsibility sprang from the private fee-paying system. In the United Kingdom, doctors, or the National Health Service (NHS) as a body, have held a kind of collective responsibility for their work, closing ranks to support each other when medical expertise was questioned. The growth of consumerism and the influence of the media have put pressure on the medical profession to be more accountable to their patients, and as a consequence doctors began to work on a system of peer review and medical audit. Within the last five years, medical audit has become an accepted part of measuring quality and outcome in every conceivable field. Once the concept had been generally accepted, procedures had to be put in place that would enable measurement to be carried out. Not only did libraries have to support this activity, but many were able to bid for funding to do so. New journals and a whole new literature on the subject have appeared.

EDUCATION

Education, training, career structure and specialization follow similar patterns in the medical and dental professions. Undergraduate education for both careers in this country normally takes five or six years, with universities setting standards and awarding qualifications. Postgraduate vocational training is a feature of both professions, with specialization available in hospital, community or general practice. The option of teaching or undertaking research is open to doctors and dentists.

After qualifying, a doctor may specialize in either medicine or surgery. For both professions education is a life-long process. Formal education and training last from six to 12 or 13 years and may be followed by another 30 or more years of learning through practice, refresher courses and continuing education until retirement.

Undergraduate education

A degree in medicine and surgery or in dentistry is a prerequisite for qualification as a doctor or dentist. The content and structure of medical undergraduate education is continually evolving in response to General Medical Council (GMC) recommendations (published at intervals of about ten years), government requirements for doctors, and pressure from other interested bodies, such as the Royal Colleges. The organizational changes within the NHS as a result of the 1989 legislation,[1] and other reviews such as the Tomlinson report[2] and the Calman report,[3] have generated a debate in the literature covering all aspects of medical education, from undergraduate curricula, through junior doctors' hours to specialist postgraduate training. With regard to undergraduate education, the trend appears to be away from the acquisition of factual knowledge towards a greater reliance on mainstream clinical medicine (general medicine, accident and emergency medicine, general practice, psychiatry, and gynaecology and obstetrics) and a more problem-orientated approach, with emphasis on measuring educational outcome and the assessment of doctoring skills by means other than the traditional examination.[4]

The dental school syllabus still largely follows the traditional pattern and provides instruction, in the first year, of anatomy, physiology, biochemistry and dental anatomy, and in subsequent years, of conservative dentistry, periodontology, paediatric dentistry, orthodontics, anaesthesia, dental radiology, oral surgery, pathology and prosthetics. Medical courses lead to the award of a degree which may be, for example, BM (Bachelor of Medicine), MB BS or MB BCh (Bachelor of Medicine and Bachelor of Surgery). The degree holder is then a doctor, but has to continue training in a hospital post for a pre-registration year, spending six months as a house physician and six months as a house surgeon, until registered by the GMC as a medical practitioner licensed to practice in the UK. In dentistry the degrees awarded are either BDS (Bachelor of Dental Surgery) or LDS (License in Dental Surgery). A qualified dentist with one of these degrees is eligible to be included in the Dental Register and is allowed to practice.

Postgraduate education

The period of postgraduate education for doctors in hospitals lasts for between 10 and 15 years, until sufficient qualifications and experience have been obtained to ensure promotion to consultant. It follows a general pattern, whatever the specialty, of a period of general professional training in the post of Senior House Officer (SHO), followed by specialist postgraduate training in the posts of registrar and Senior Registrar (SR). Up to this level all doctors are known as junior hospital doctors and their local training, education and study-leave facilities are coordinated by clinical tutors. In Scotland, the Scottish Council for Postgraduate Medical Education coordinates the structure and organization of postgraduate medical education, while in England the Regional Postgraduate Deans are now budget-holders and training coordinators. Many other formal and informal organizations influence postgraduate medical and dental education (PMDE), including the British Postgraduate Medical Federation (BPMF) for the Thames Regions and the Standing Committee for Postgraduate Medical Education (SCOPME), but membership or fellowship of the appropriate Royal College is still essential for doctors wishing to progress within their chosen specialty.

Advanced qualifications, career structure and specialist training

Once doctors have completed the pre-registration year and been registered by the GMC, they must decide upon the branch of medicine in which they wish to work. Table 2.1 lists the specialties in medicine and surgery. The usual career posts in different fields are professor or senior lecturer, consultant, general practitioner principal and community physician. A doctor usually takes the necessary examinations at the earliest opportunity, but theoretically there are no age limits. Most Colleges provide a service designed to assist candidates to pass the relevant examinations.

The first hospital appointment after full registration is as an SHO. Promotion to registrar follows after a minimum of one year and more often three, depending on the qualifications being studied for and the number of registrar posts available in a particular specialty. The examinations are usually taken during appointment as registrar. This stage may be reached after a minimum of one year as a registrar, but is more commonly reached after two to six years in one or more posts. Senior registrars play a vital role in the NHS. A doctor will normally hold one or more senior registrar posts over a period of four years. The duties may involve working in several hospital departments (such as chest and general medicine) and almost certainly in more than one hospital. Senior registrars have clinical, learning, teaching and research functions.

Table 2.1 The specialties and sub-specialties in medicine and surgery

General practice	Thoracic surgery
Accident and emergency medicine	Urology
Medical specialities	**Anaesthetics**
General medicine	Anaesthetics
Cardiovascular disease	Intensive care
Clinical pharmacology and therapeutics	
Communicable diseases	**Obstetrics**
Dermatology	
Endocrinology and diabetes	**Gynaecology**
Gastroenterology	
Geriatrics	**Pathology**
Medical genetics	Haematology
Neurology	Blood transfusion
Occupational health	Chemical pathology
Paediatrics	Immunology
Palliative care	Medical microbiology
Respiratory medicine	Bacteriology
Rheumatology	Histopathology
Sexually transmitted diseases	Neuropathology
Tropical medicine	Forensic medicine
Public health	**Radiology**
	Diagnostic radiology
Surgical specialties	Radiotherapy and nuclear medicine
General surgery	
Neurosurgery	**Psychiatry**
Oncology	Adult psychiatry
Ophthalmology	Child and family psychiatry
Orthopaedics	Forensic psychiatry
Otolaryngology	Learning disabilities
Paediatric surgery	Psychogeriatrics
Plastic surgery	Psychotherapy

The Calman report[3] suggests that the period of training, including general professional training, should not exceed seven years after full registration for most specialties, and that the registrar and senior registrar grades should be combined.

General practice

General practitioners (GPs) have been in the forefront of change in the NHS, having been given extra responsibilities under their new contract which came into force in April 1991. They can now apply to become fund-holders, by which means they receive an annual budget with which to buy a defined range of services for their patients. The profession has been divided over the principle of fund-holding and the debate continues at the time of writing. In theory, GPs can now control more care for their patients, including certain services previously available at hospital outpatient departments, and refer fewer cases to hospital; where referral is necessary, the GP can choose where the treatment will be carried out. The primary health care team is growing, with more specialized clinics offered in health centres and general practices.

Education for general practice follows the pattern of undergraduate teaching by university departments of general practice, vocational training organized by regional postgraduate organizations, and continuing education coordinated by clinical and general practice tutors and regional advisers. The implications for future GPs of the changes in the NHS have yet to be translated into revised education programmes.[5]

Accident and emergency medicine

Any person can expect treatment at a casualty department. Therefore doctors working in this department, whether as a registrar specializing in trauma medicine or an SHO doing six months' rotation, can expect to be faced with any medical, surgical or psychiatric problem. Consultants in this specialty require a wide general understanding of medicine and surgery and normally possess the qualification FRCS, MRCP, FCA or MRCGP (see Table 2.2).

Medical specialties

In general medicine the doctor concentrates on internal disorders and is qualified as a physician. There are general physicians in medical units in all teaching hospitals and large district general hospitals.

Cardiovascular disease involves the heart and blood vessels, and physicians who specialize in this discipline are known as cardiologists.

Clinical pharmacology and therapeutics is concerned with drug actions and interactions, and drug therapy.

Communicable diseases are those in which infectious disease affects all age groups.

Dermatology is the diagnosis and treatment of disorders affecting the skin. Apart from primary skin disease, generalized disorders may be present in the skin or be complicated by cutaneous manifestations, so that there is an appreciable overlap with internal medicine.

Endocrinology is medicine applied to the endocrine glands, which include the pituitary, thyroid, parathyroid and adrenal glands. Defects of the pituitary gland cause diabetes, amongst other conditions.

Gastroenterology is the medical/surgical specialty concerned with the stomach and intestines.

Geriatrics is the medical care of old people, and is a developing specialty, no longer the forgotten branch of medicine. Gerontology is the scientific study of the ageing process.

Medical genetics deals with the medical aspects of heredity. Paediatricians, psychiatrists and physicians working with patients with learning disabilities all need information on this subject.

Neurology is the study of the brain and the nervous system.

Occupational health is concerned with diagnosis and treatment of work-related disease, which includes psychological problems.

Paediatrics is the medical and surgical treatment of children. It is one of the major divisions of medicine, and doctors work in hospitals and in the community for the purpose of prevention, early diagnosis of reversible disease and early detection of handicap.

Palliative care is the name for the specialty arising from treatment pioneered in the hospice movement for terminally ill patients. The treatment given suppresses symptoms rather than curing the underlying disease and the major focus of the specialty is cancer.

Respiratory medicine deals with the breathing function, the chest and lungs, as well as being closely connected with cardiology, thoracic surgery and anaesthetics.

Rheumatology is the medicine of connective tissue diseases, particularly arthritis and rheumatism, and the medical disorders of the locomotor system.

The treatment of sexually transmitted diseases is a specialty involving genito-urinary medicine and includes health education, preventive medicine and counselling.

Tropical medicine is concerned with the detection, diagnosis and treatment of infectious diseases prevalent in tropical countries.

Public health
Core functions of public health medicine are health promotion, assessing health care needs, planning future health care, monitoring the environment, and communicable disease control. Public health departments collect informa-

tion, disseminate statistics and carry out research.

Surgical specialties

The general surgeon, like the general physician, may remain a generalist or may specialize in one of many branches, such as orthopaedic surgery. The practice of surgery is defined as the treatment of injuries and diseases by manual operations.

Neurosurgery treats disorders and injuries of the central and peripheral nervous system. It is usually concentrated in specialist centres to which patients are transferred from general hospitals.

Oncology is the study of tumours, which may be treated medically or surgically, or usually by a combination of both.

Ophthalmology is a surgical specialty dealing with the eye and related physiology.

Orthopaedic surgery treats bone diseases and injuries. Many orthopaedic surgeons specialize in particular patient groups, such as children, or particular bones, such as the hand or hip.

Otolaryngology is the study of the ear and larynx, often extended to otorhinolaryngology to include the nose, when it is commonly known as ear, nose and throat (ENT). Specialists may be physicians or surgeons.

Paediatric surgery may be carried out mainly by general surgeons who have specialized in treating children, although there are some surgical units devoted only to children.

Plastic surgery deals with the surgical reconstruction of parts of the body, including skin grafting and microsurgery. This is another specialty where treatment tends to be in regional centres, because burns patients, needing special treatment, form a large proportion of cases.

Thoracic surgery concerns the chest and includes, therefore, the lungs, the oesophagus and the heart. Work is usually carried out in regional centres.

Urologists treat disorders of the urinary system. Common problems include prostate disorders, cancer and stones. Conservative renal surgery, reconstructive and plastic surgery of the urethra and the treatment of male infertility are also part of a urologist's work. Kidney transplantation is a growing aspect of the specialty.

Anaesthetics and intensive care

The anaesthetist (known in North America as the anesthesiologist) is responsible for the safe production of analgesia (pain relief) and anaesthesia (unconsciousness) for the performance of all types of surgical operations and diagnostic procedures. Responsibility extends to the pre-operative evaluation and preparation, and the immediate post-operative management, of the patient, and anaesthetists also deal with analgesia for childbirth, intensive care units, pain clinics, resuscitation, the management of casualty departments and clinical measurement departments. Anaesthetics is the largest single hospital specialty in the NHS.

Intensive therapy units (ITUs) provide care for critically ill patients. especially those requiring special support systems. ITUs may be general units, or specialized units caring for patients following specific procedures such as heart surgery, when they may be called coronary care units (CCUs).

Obstetrics and gynaecology
Obstetrics is the management of childbirth; gynaecology is the care of disorders of the female reproductive system. Early professional training in both specialties is combined, but practitioners later specialize in one branch.

Pathology and laboratory medicine
Pathology is the study of diseases or abnormalities, and the specialty is divided into six or seven major sub-specialties, for each of which a training in general pathology is the first stage.

Haematologists are concerned with blood disorders and diseases. They undertake the laboratory investigation of patients and may be responsible for the care of patients with specific disorders such as leukaemia and haemophilia. Consultant haematologists in hospital spend a part of their time administering the hospital blood bank, although the National Blood Transfusion Service has a centre in every region.

Chemical pathology is the study of chemical changes in disease. Clinical chemistry is concerned with laboratory investigations on patients and their interpretation. In the department of a large hospital there is often a top-grade biochemist (a scientist of consultant status) as well as the medical consultant.

Immunology is the study of the immune system and overlaps with several medical and paramedical disciplines.

Medical microbiology is the identification of bacteria, viruses and fungi, and their relationship to microbial diseases, to antibiotic treatments, and to public health and epidemiology issues. The Public Health Laboratory Service is a national network of medical microbiology departments based mainly in district general hospitals.

Histopathology is the study of disease processes and their diagnosis in man, and specifically the structural changes in tissues in disease. The histopathologist may also carry out autopsies.

Neuropathology is the study of abnormalities and disease of the nervous system.

Forensic medicine is a science that deals with the relation and application of medical facts to legal problems, and is also known as legal medicine.

Radiology
Radiology is the application in medicine of radiation (not to be confused with radiography, which is the use of radiation to photograph the interior of the human body). The diagnostic radiology department supports all clinical disciplines in hospitals. Facilities range from X-ray interpretation on fractures and chest problems to the performance of technical procedures such as ultrasonography, angiography (blood vessel X-ray), computerized tomography and magnetic resonance imaging.

In radiotherapy, ionizing radiations are applied to patients with malignant disease. The cost and complexity of radiotherapy usually means that it is concentrated in specialist centres.

The use of radio-isotopes taken internally requires the specialist supervision of a consultant in nuclear medicine.

Psychiatry
Psychiatry is concerned with mental health (as distinct from psychology, the scientific study of mental processes). Doctors begin to specialize in psychiatry at SHO or registrar level. They may sub-specialize when they have obtained Membership of the Royal College of Psychiatrists or an equivalent university diploma. Most psychiatrists in this country deal with general adult psychiatry in hospital and the community, including both acute and chronic mental illness. These include functional psychoses such as schizophrenia and the affective disorders, mental illnesses associated with damage to the brain, and the neuroses connected with anxiety, depression and hysteria. Consultants also advise GPs, who treat a great many mental and psychosomatic disorders.

Child and adolescent psychiatry deals with the intellectual, emotional and behavioural problems of children and their families. Specialists work in child guidance clinics, special schools, community and remand homes, as well as hospitals.

Forensic psychiatry is concerned with overlap or interaction between psychiatry and the law. Forensic psychiatrists assist the courts with such problems as criminal responsibility and fitness to plead, as well as treating offenders.

Other major branches of psychiatry are concerned with learning disabilities (mental handicap), the elderly (psychogeriatrics) and psychotherapy. Clinical psychologists treat emotional and social problems.

Dentistry
Any dentist may set up an independent or group practice, treating private or

NHS patients or both. A newly qualified dentist usually enters dental general practice by becoming a salaried assistant or associate in an established practice, with a view to becoming a partner after a specified period of satisfactory service. This period may be developed into formal vocational training.

The most important qualification for hospital dental work is FDS (Fellow in Dental Surgery) from one of the Royal Colleges of Surgeons; this ranks with the FRCS for general surgeons. Other higher qualifications in dentistry are the MGDSRCS (Member in General Dental Surgery of the Royal Colleges of Surgeons), the Diploma in Orthodontics, the Diploma in Dental Orthopaedics and the Diploma in Public Dentistry. A degree of Master of Dental Surgery is the usual postgraduate qualification for an academic career. Some universities also offer a Doctorate in Dental Surgery (DDS) or Dental Science (DDSc).

The community dental service is run by the local health authority or community NHS Trust. Operations are carried out in central clinics, and other work includes regular school dental inspections for each child and provision of the necessary treatment. The community dentist is responsible for education in dental hygiene.

The Royal Colleges

The Colleges usually offer facilities such as meeting and reception rooms, functions, a library, and residential accommodation for members at their headquarters, most of which are in London. Courses, seminars and other educational activities may be held regularly. Each College publishes at least one major journal, together with occasional publications and reports on specific topics which act as a focus for communication between members scattered throughout the UK and all over the world. All Colleges maintain a strict examination schedule, principal examinations taking place twice each year as a general rule, and are financed mainly by entrance fees and membership subscriptions. Table 2.2 sets out the Royal Colleges with their date of foundation and qualifications awarded.

Medical societies

The British Medical Association (BMA) and the British Dental Association (BDA) are national associations representing the medical and dental professions. They act both as trade unions and as powerful pressure groups. They are also learned societies in their own right. Both have substantial libraries. The BMA publishes the *BMJ* and other major journals such as the *British journal of ophthalmology*, and the BDA publishes the *British dental journal*. The Royal Society of Medicine (RSM) is another important learned society in medicine, again with an impressive library, and publishes original papers and meetings

Table 2.2 Dates of foundation and qualifications awarded by the Royal Colleges and their Faculties

College	Date founded	Qualifications awarded
Royal College of Anaesthetists	1992	FCA
Royal College of General Practitioners	1952	MRCGP, FRCGP
Royal College of Obstetricians and Gynaecologists	1929	DRCOG, MRCOG, FRCOG
Royal College of Pathologists	1962	DRCPath, MRCPath, FRCPath
Royal College of Physicians	1518	MRCP, FRCP
Royal Colleges of Physicians of the UK Faculty of Public Health Medicine	1972	MFPHM, FFPHM
Royal College of Psychiatrists	1971	MRCPsych, FRCPsych
Royal College of Radiologists	1939	FRCR
Royal College of Surgeons of England	1800	MRCS Eng, FRCS Eng
Royal College of Physicians of Edinburgh	1681	LRCP Ed, MRCP Ed, FRCP Ed
Royal College of Surgeons of Edinburgh	1778	LRCS Ed, FRCS Ed
Royal College of Physicians and Surgeons of Glasgow	1599	MRCP Glas, FRCP Glas, LRCPS Glas, FRCS Glas
Royal College of Physicians of Ireland	1654	MRCPI, FRCPI
Royal College of Surgeons in Ireland	1784	LRCSI, FRCSI

Initials denote Diploma (D), Membership (M), Licenciateship (L) or Fellowship (F) Surgeons are entitled to be addressed as Mr, Mrs or Miss once they have obtained Fellowship of the Royal College of Surgeons.

reports in *Journal of the RSM*. Almost every specialty and sub-specialty has its own society and group, many of which publish journals.

CONCLUSION

At the time of writing, the medical profession is in turmoil as a result of the introduction of the 'internal market' in 1991, and many changes are projected which will take at least the rest of this decade to implement. Therefore, whilst the information in this chapter will form a basis for the understanding of the medical and dental professions, it should also indicate to librarians that we should ensure that we are up to date with developments in the world of our users by reading widely, communicating with each other and, especially, communicating with our users.

REFERENCES

1   Department of Health, *Working for patients (Cmnd 555)*, London, HMSO, 1989.
2   Tomlinson, B., *Report of the inquiry into London's health service, medical education and research*, London, HMSO, 1992.
3   Department of Health, *Hospital doctors: training for the future. The report of the working group on specialist medical training*, London, DoH, 1993. (Calman Report).
4   Bewley, B., 'Reorganizing medical education', *British journal of hospital medicine*, **47** (1), 1992, 40–3.
5   Irvine, D., 'Educating general practitioners', *BMJ*, **307** (6906), 1993, 696–7.

3 Nursing, midwifery and health visiting

❖ Jean Yeoh

Nurses, midwives and health visitors constitute the largest group of health care professionals and provide almost half the workforce in the National Health Service.[1] They practise in a variety of fields and nurses can specialize in areas such as mental health, general, paediatric or learning disability nursing. Within these broad areas there may be further specialization into specific areas such as intensive care or oncology nursing. The largest proportion of nurses and midwives provide hospital based care. Some staff specialize in community care including health visitors, district nurses and community psychiatric nurses. Midwives can also be community or hospital based, although the majority are located in hospitals. Other employers of nurses include large organizations with occupational health nurses, the armed forces, private hospitals and nursing homes for the elderly. Midwives and health visitors regard themselves as belonging to professions that are quite distinct from nursing. For example, midwives distinguish themselves from nurses by arguing that pregnant mothers are not ill and that by and large midwives are dealing with healthy individuals rather than people suffering from ill-health. Among the three professions, nurses comprise by far the largest numerical group. However, for reasons of simplicity the term nurse will often be used inclusively in this chapter to describe midwives, health visitors and nurses.

Although the largest proportion of nursing staff still work in hospitals in the acute care sector, there is a move towards community based care, and the balance of numbers between hospital staff is shifting in the 1990s. However, the overall proportion of staff working in community areas is still comparatively small. Currently almost 90% of nursing staff are hospital based and 10% community based, with this latter figure including district nurses and health visitors.[1] Trends in the provision of health care suggest that the shift is permanent and likely to be confirmed throughout the decade.

There are a variety of reasons for a stronger emphasis on community care: hospital based care is expensive, care within their own community is regarded as more appropriate for patients and, in any case, new techniques have made day surgery and shorter lengths of stay in hospitals more likely. The approach to care has changed, based on targets for improving health initiated by the World Health Organization (WHO),[2] with a greater emphasis on health promotion, rather than treating illness. The WHO emphasized the need for primary health care, meeting basic health needs in the community in which people live. This initiative was followed by the British government's development of a health strategy that concentrated on specific targets and on the prevention of illness.[3] Nursing staff make a considerable contribution to health promotion in acute and community care.

WHAT IS NURSING CARE?

Traditionally, much of the work undertaken by nurses has arisen out of medical procedures and is based on the diagnosis and medical treatment of diseases. However, the nursing profession continues to attempt to move towards partnership with medicine rather than acting as 'handmaidens' to doctors. The development of a theory of nursing care based on research is part of the process of establishing an independent body of knowledge. Virginia Henderson's[4] definition of nursing is still widely used: 'The unique function of the nurse is to assist the individual, sick or well, in the performance of those activities contributing to health or its recovery (or to peaceful death) that he would perform unaided if he had the necessary strength or knowledge'.

Nurses work more closely with patients than any other health care staff and uniquely supply a 24 hour service. They provide intimate services for patients and generally coordinate the activities of a patient's day. The work of a nurse devolves around four main areas of operation. Firstly, nursing involves clinical care and doing things patients are unable to do for themselves, such as assisting with mobility, giving correct medication and measuring physiological conditions such as temperature or blood sugar levels. In acute hospitals, nurses may be involved in tests and clinical interventions which were previously only undertaken by medical staff.[5] Secondly, there is the management of care, which includes coordinating care and managing resources. Thirdly, nurses increasingly see their role as educative and as promoting health. This involves giving information to clients in order to maintain health or to prevent a recurrence of a recent illness, and giving patients the help they need in adapting mentally, socially and physically to their conditions. Nurses believe that attention to a patient's psychological and emotional needs is as important as physical care. Finally, the supervision of students gaining clinical experience is regarded as a key activity, and this extends the educational role of the nurse to the assessment of students' practical experience. Clinical areas receiving student nurses are expected to ensure that nursing care is soundly based in research. Many of the skills required for the delivery of nursing care draw on a number of disciplines including psychology, sociology, physiology and ethics.

The way in which nursing care is delivered and organized is changing to provide more integrated and patient focused care. Previously, care has been organized around tasks or activities and patients have not been able to relate to a particular nurse. This new mode of care is known as primary nursing and a designated nurse assumes responsibility for particular patients throughout their hospital stay. That nurse is the 'named nurse' for the duration of care. Another important development has been the increase in the number of nurses with specialist expert knowledge, known as clinical nurse specialists or advanced practitioners. They are highly qualified and responsible for developing innovations in nursing care and may operate in acute hospitals or in the community.

Community nursing

Most nursing activity in the community is carried out by registered health visitors (RHV) and district nurses (DN Cert). Other community nursing staff include practice nurses employed by GPs, who hold clinics, and provide health education and preventative screening. Specialist nurses, such as Macmillan nurses, deal with cancer care. School nurses are attached to schools and are involved in health surveillance and the health education of school children. Community psychiatric nurses deliver care for those with mental health problems. District nursing has its origins in the 19th century and the nursing at home of sick people living in poverty. Currently, district nursing enables patients who have nursing needs to remain within the community rather than receiving care in a hospital. The workload of the district nurse has increased as a result of community care policies in areas such as care for the terminally ill, early discharge from hospital and increases in day surgery.[6]

Health visitors have a preventive role rather than the provision of clinical care. The health visiting profession also has its origins in the 19th century, with efforts to improve public health following cholera outbreaks. Although health visitors have a remit for general community issues, in practice they have tended to concentrate on children from birth to five years old. A key component of their role is health promotion. The health visitor makes a contribution to 'at risk' families and may make referrals to social services or voluntary agencies. The distinction between different qualifications is likely to disappear with the introduction of the new discipline of Community Health Nursing. Current pre-registration nurse education provides students with substantial input on community settings to enable newly qualified nurses to work in either hospital or community. Legislation has been introduced to allow both district nurses and health visitors to prescribe a limited number of medicines and dressings. Previously only doctors have been able to write prescriptions.

The role of the community psychiatric nurse (CPN) had its beginnings in the

1950s and CPNs act as therapists to clients and their relatives. They are mainly based in community mental health centres and they work in multidisciplinary teams with psychiatrists and psychologists. CPNs often specialize by working with particular client groups such as the elderly, children and adolescents or people with long-term mental illness.

Midwifery

Midwifery staff comprise a relatively small group and form less than 10% of all nursing and midwifery staff. Until recently most midwives originally trained as nurses. However, there are now a number of direct entry courses for midwifery education, dispensing with the necessity of possessing a nursing qualification. Midwives are largely hospital based, although a proportion work as community midwives. There are also a small number of independent midwives working in private practice. In the UK most births take place in hospital and midwives are involved in the antenatal care of women, support and supervision of labour and post-partum care, including the transfer of mothers home from hospital. Midwives have an important role in areas such as family planning, genetic counselling, antenatal care and education. Community midwives work with hospital maternity units and attend mothers in their own homes until the care of mother and baby is transferred to health visitors.

STRUCTURE OF THE PROFESSIONS

Nurses are personally accountable for their practice and have a Code of Conduct to which they must conform for the maintenance of professional standards.[7] Midwives have a similar code called Midwives Rules.[8]

The United Kingdom Central Council for Nursing, Midwifery and Health Visiting, normally referred to as the UKCC, is the body which deals with standards of training and practice for those aiming to register as qualified practitioners, and further training for those already qualified. All nurses must register with this body. A key function of the UKCC is to protect the public interest by investigating and dealing with allegations of professional misconduct. This can include the removal of names from the register of qualified practitioners if allegations are proved.

In addition to the UKCC, there are four National Boards for Nursing, Midwifery and Health Visiting covering England, Northern Ireland, Scotland and Wales. The Boards are responsible for the approval of educational courses and institutions. Course approval is usually carried out conjointly with university partners.[9] The Royal College of Nursing (RCN), the Royal College of Midwives (RCM) and the Health Visitors Association (HVA) act as professional associations for their members. The RCN also functions as a trade union in negotiations with employers. These professional organizations also provide information and library services for their members.

Some care previously provided by nurses is now given by care assistants.[10] Care assistants are not trained as nurses but assist in the provision of nursing care. This is seen by many as part of a process of deskilling nurses where more tasks are given to care assistants because the numbers of nursing staff have been reduced. Diploma in Nursing students are no longer an integral part of the workforce and some of the work of student nurses has been taken over by care assistants. However, many in the nursing profession believe that care assistants do not always have the knowledge base to perform these activities. Care assistants receive training either through the National Vocational Qualification (NVQ) scheme or through the Scottish Vocational Qualification (SVQ) system and will have information needs arising from this. Conversely, nurses are also extending their role and undertaking activities previously performed by medical staff.

RESEARCH

Nursing research dates back to the early years of the National Health Service but it still suffers from comparatively small levels of funding. It does not have the substantial tradition of medical research and there is a considerable amount of small-scale research which does not produce generalizable findings. There is also evidence of poor dissemination of nursing research. Nevertheless, there are considerable efforts to develop a research based approach to care and to encourage the development of trained and experienced researchers with a nursing background.

The Department of Health[11] has said that: 'Basic research literacy is an essential prerequisite of knowledge-led practice. Nurses, health visitors and midwives need an understanding of the research process, the ability to retrieve and critically assess research findings and literature'. Most nursing research is carried out by academics in the university sector. However, other research initiatives are likely to arise from the work of clinical nurse specialists, whose role is to advance practice and provide staff development and support, and from Nursing Development Units which have been established to provide examples of best practice.

INTERNATIONAL NURSING

Nursing systems in North America and the UK are broadly similar, although there are differences in the way health care is organized. In general, the UK developments in nurse education and nursing practice follow those in the USA.[12] Specialist advanced nursing posts which allow greater autonomy in practice are increasing in the USA, and there has been an extensive training programme for these posts funded by the government. Primary nursing, in which patients are assigned designated nurses, is provided in a quarter of acute hospitals in the United States. In the USA there is an increase in the proportion of patients who are acutely ill. This is due to a combination of factors, including the impact of technological developments, new medical procedures and reduced lengths of stay in hospital as a result of the payment systems. Patients are more liable to require care in specialist critical care units which demand that nurses have in-depth technical and clinical knowledge.

These factors have had a similar impact on the provision of nursing care in Australia. Overall, there are a higher proportion of nurses in the USA and Canada, relative to the size of the population, than there are in the UK. This can be attributed in some part to the shorter length of stay in acute hospitals, leading to a need for more intensive nursing care. North America also has a considerably higher proportion of community nurses than the UK.

In Europe as a whole there is a tendency towards a north/south divide, with less evidence of district nurse or health visitor roles in southern Europe. Midwifery practice varies from country to country and has been illegal in a number of places. Some states in the USA still do not allow midwives to practise and midwifery was only legalized in Canada in the early 1990s. Where midwives do practise there are variations in role because some European countries have a higher proportion of home births than the UK.

The apprenticeship model of nursing care, which only began to change in the UK in the late 1980s, was eliminated in the USA after the Second World War along with hospital based schools of nursing. A much larger proportion of nurses in the United States are graduates and have qualifications at Masters level or above. Until the mid-1980s Australia also followed the Nightingale hospital based training system founded in the UK. The process of transferring basic nurse education into higher education was completed in 1993. Degree level nursing courses were introduced in 1992. Within the European Union (EU) there is mutual recognition of nursing and midwifery qualifications, allowing citizens of member states to practise in other countries. Nurse education programmes in all EU countries have to conform to specific European requirements.

LIBRARY AND INFORMATION NEEDS OF TRAINED STAFF

Trained nurses have long been regarded as poor users of libraries and they have tended to have a preference for books rather than journal literature.[13] This was largely because nursing was seen as a practical subject with little need for theoretical underpinning knowledge. However, even nurses who updated their knowledge frequently experienced difficulty in changing practice. Medical staff and managers rejected new ideas even when nurses were able to point to reliable research in the area concerned. The appointment of clinical nurse specialists in specific areas of practice is helping to develop medical and managerial recognition of the nurse's autonomy in decision making. It remains to be seen how much impact the new educational programmes for nurses will affect library and information use on qualification.

Trained staff information needs relate to a variety of clinical activities and service delivery. Primarily they focus on support for patient care and health education, but much of their library use will be generated by clinical teaching activities. Nurses will also have personal professional development needs. It is possible that competition from newly qualified nurses with Diplomas in Nursing will force nurses with the traditional Registered General Nurse (RGN) and Registered Mental Nurse (RMN) qualifications to undertake degree courses to maintain parity. Many nurses are already undertaking Masters level courses and above on a part-time basis and demand library support at their workplace. The widespread acceptance of the need for research based practice and the information requirements arising from this should mean a growing demand for library resources. Coincidentally, many of these developments are taking place at a time when trained nurses may find access to libraries increasingly difficult. Most libraries used by nursing staff have traditionally been based on hospital sites because nurse education has been established there. The trend towards university based nurse education will affect the library access of qualified staff, particularly where multidisciplinary health sciences libraries are inadequately developed.

Nurses are frequently unable to leave the clinical area during working hours and this factor needs to be taken into account when planning user education and training sessions, which should be timed to coincide with nursing shift patterns and changeover periods. Many nurses will be undertaking study while working and coping with family and other commitments. Some may well be using annual leave allowances to undertake open learning courses. These nurses will place a heavy demand on library services. The effect of the UKCC's Post-registration education and practice (PREP) proposals for mandatory updating can only be estimated but they are likely to unleash a large number of nurses who have not used libraries for many years and for whom libraries may initially seem intimidating. Sympathetic training in information skills handling will be required for this group, particularly that involving the use of information technology. Lack of experience in the use of information technology and some 'computer phobia' may mean that libraries will be providing training in basic computer literacy skills in addition to library skills, although this is likely to be a decreasing problem in the future.

In any case, the increasing number of community based staff will find hospital based provision irrelevant. New ways of providing services will have to be considered and these are likely to involve the development of links between the computer networks of information services and the nurse's workplace, which is becoming increasingly computerized. The future emphasis may well be on access to resources rather than close proximity to a physical collection. Growing numbers of staff working in the private sector may have problems accessing professionally run library services, apart from small bench collections, unless they are members of professional organizations such as the RCN, RCM and the HVA which provide information services.

EDUCATION AND TRAINING FOR NURSING

The end of the 1980s saw a fundamental change in nurse education, and until that time the majority of nurses were trained at two levels. Enrolled Nurses (EN) received a two year training and RGNs or RMNs received a three year training in schools of nursing on hospital sites. This is often referred to as the 'Nightingale' system of training. The students spent most of their courses in the clinical area, were regarded as part of the workforce and were treated as employees rather than students. Most training was done 'on the job' in the clinical area. Assessment was by end-of-course examination rather than continuously assessed course work throughout training. Little time was spent in the lecture room and therefore courses made limited demands on library services. For a small number of students, an alternative route to this method of gaining a qualification was by undertaking a university degree course which combined both academic and professional qualifications.

The implementation of Project 2000[14] saw the introduction of a Higher Education Diploma in Nursing that incorporates a professional qualification. This Diploma course consists of a Common Foundation programme of 18 months followed by one of four branching programmes in adult nursing, children's nursing, mental health or learning disabilities. Students are no longer part of the workforce and when undertaking clinical placements are supernumerary to the clinical staff. They receive a bursary during the course of study. Considerably more time is spent on theoretical learning and the acquisition of a better knowledge base. Overall, the course emphasizes health promotion and community based care with a larger proportion of placements being community rather than acute hospital based.

Pre-registration Diploma courses are only part of educational provision in nursing. Nursing degree courses are available at postgraduate and undergraduate level, and the English National Board (ENB) has introduced the Higher Award which is a flexible modular higher education programme. Post-registration education represents a considerable area of activity where nurses are undertaking qualifications which will enable them to work in specialist areas of nursing practice. There are also numerous short courses and, as the PREP proposals by the UKCC are implemented in full, then the whole nursing workforce will be required to undertake regular mandatory updating.[15] Much post-registration education, including traditional academic courses and numerous in-service training courses, has been provided by Colleges of Nursing. Current trends suggest that more in-service post-registration education will be provided by training departments within hospital trusts, and that academic post-registration courses will be provided by higher education institutions and universities.

Training for midwifery, health visiting and district nursing qualifications has tended to follow a pre-registration nursing course, although there are direct entry course for midwives at diploma level.

As a result of the Project 2000 reforms, the majority of nurses qualified at enrolled nurse level are undertaking conversion courses to obtain RGN or RMN qualifications, and it is likely that these courses will be offered until the late 1990s. To meet the heavy demand from this group, various flexible distance learning schemes have been put into place.

More flexible forms of educational delivery are becoming commonplace with the use of open learning methods. Alternative methods of delivering education for nurses have been implemented in response to the large numbers of students undertaking particular education programmes. Trained nurses are also experiencing difficulty in obtaining study leave for courses. Open learning is regarded as benefiting both employer and student in that time is not lost by the workplace and the employee is able to study around personal and other commitments. A variety of nursing courses are offered through the open learning route. These include post-registration courses and conversion courses. Open learning modules are sometimes incorporated into traditionally delivered pre-registration courses. There are also a number of standalone distance learning health sciences courses such as those offered by the Open University, Open College and the South Bank University Distance Learning Centre. A number of other open learning producers have targeted health care professionals. Flexible courses will have implications for libraries in terms of support materials required, funding and user education.

Those undertaking distance learning courses are likely to utilize the nearest available resources at their workplace or at local public libraries. There are a number of national distance learning schemes which are linked to specific educational institutions, although students are more likely to turn to their workplace libraries if resources are available there.

Traditionally, Colleges of Nursing have been based on hospital sites but the late 1980s saw the development of links with higher education institutions. The overall number of colleges or departments of nursing has reduced considerably, and the late 1980s and early 1990s saw a number of amalgamations prior to higher education integration. The trend is towards wholesale integration into higher education. The main library provision for student nurses is likely to move away from libraries based on hospital sites to university based provision. In some cases, university libraries have needed to establish nursing collections from scratch, but they are able to offer nursing students a wide range of subject disciplines. However, Trust libraries will need to consider the needs of students on clinical placements.

LIBRARY NEEDS OF STUDENTS
Pre-registration nursing students require a wide range of literature from the very early stages of their courses, drawing on a variety of subject disciplines. Student nurses make immediate and intensive use of journal literature and therefore require access to CD-ROM and other electronic databases to undertake literature searches in nursing and applied social sciences. As pre-registration courses progress, more time is spent on clinical placements in acute and community areas, and less time in the classroom. While students are on clinical placements they still require access to library resources to complete assignments, although the emphasis will be on more clinically based literature rather than the applied social sciences.

Library use by students is usually related to curriculum design and implementation, and nursing has adopted an adult self-directed approach to learning which is heavily resource based. Students require sophisticated information handling skills to support this educational ethos. Self-directed learning also makes particular demands on library space and its organization. Areas for students to work cooperatively on projects are required in addition to standard spaces for quiet individual study. The provision of seminar rooms for group work and discussion will be necessary. Librarians need access to teaching space to provide information handling skills teaching. As much user education is based upon the use of computer equipment it is essential to have rooms with dedicated training equipment.

EDUCATIONAL STAFF
Students are currently taught nursing by lecturers who mainly have nursing qualifications combined with teaching qualifications. In other subjects, such as the biological sciences or psychology, students are taught by lecturers who are not necessarily trained nurses. Lecturers in nursing are expected to maintain contacts with the clinical area and keep clinical skills up to date. Many are qualified to Masters degree level and gradually they are gaining doctorates to bring them up to the level of academic colleagues in higher education. As with other higher education staff, nursing lecturers are expected to maintain a research and publications profile. Nurse teachers are exponents of resource based learning and use a variety of teaching methods. It is not clear whether

this imaginative approach to teaching will continue as nursing becomes more firmly based in higher education. Larger student groups may necessitate a reversion to lecturing methods.

Educational staff have greater expectations of library services than hitherto as result of undertaking higher degrees and research in university institutions. Knowledge of higher education library provision has widened horizons in this respect. Their information needs are likely to be similar to those of other teachers in higher education.

CONCLUSION

The nursing profession is undergoing a period of great change, reflecting wider upheavals in health care provision in Britain. There are a number of key issues, and those having responsibility for library provision for nurses, midwives and health visitors will have to address these over the next few years. As a result of the transfer of nurse education into higher education institutions nursing will be one of many disciplines striving to obtain its share of the library budget. Higher education libraries are already facing growing student numbers. The move into higher education may not result in the automatic access to enhanced resources that was anticipated.

Library services for nursing staff in hospital trusts and in the community will have to be seriously considered in the light of the vacuum left by transferring educational provision to the university sector. A growing number of nurses are working in the private sector, often in small nursing homes and hospitals, without library services. A fundamental re-examination of library services for trained staff will be necessary as nurses seek to develop an autonomous nursing discipline and become more academically qualified.

REFERENCES

1 Department of Health, *Health and personal social services statistics for England 1993*, London, HMSO, 1991.
2 Board of the Faculty of Community Medicine, *Health for all by the year 2000: charter for action*, London, Board of the Faculty of Community Medicine, 1986.
3 Department of Health, *The health of the nation: a strategy for health in England*, London, HMSO, 1992.
4 Henderson, V., *The nature of nursing: a definition and its implications for practice, research and education*, London, Collier Macmillan, 1966, 15.
5 Audit Commission, *The virtue of patients: making the best of ward nursing resources*, London, HMSO, 1991.
6 Lightfoot, J. et al., *Nursing by numbers: setting staffing levels for district nursing and health visiting services*, York: Social Policy Research Unit and Centre for Health Economics, 1992.
7 UKCC, *Code of professional conduct*, 3rd edn, London, UKCC, 1992.

8   UKCC, *Midwives rules*, London, UKCC, 1993.

9   Pyne, R. H., *Professional discipline in nursing, midwifery and health visiting*, 2nd edn, Oxford, Blackwell Scientific, 1992.

10   UKCC, *The scope of professional practice*, London, UKCC, 1992.

11   Department of Health, *Report of the taskforce on the strategy for research in nursing, midwifery and health visiting*, London, Department of Health, 1992, 12.

12   Levine, E. *et al.*, *Nursing practice in the UK and North America*, London, Chapman and Hall, 1993.

13   Wakeham, M. *et al.*, The information needs and information seeking behaviour of nurses, Boston Spa, British Library (BL Research and Development Report 6078), 1992.

14   United Kingdom Central Council for Nursing, Midwifery and Health Visiting, *Project 2000: a new preparation for practice*, London, UKCC, 1986.

15   United Kingdom Central Council for Nursing, Midwifery and Health Visiting, *The report of the post-registration education and practice project*, London, UKCC, 1990.

4 The paramedical professions

❖ *Graham Walton*

Paramedical workers, allied health professionals, professions supplementary to medicine, remedial therapists, professions allied to medicine: to the person new to health sciences librarianship, trying to establish who is served by these terms must appear daunting. The position is complicated through there being no consensus at either national or international level as to who does, and who does not, fall into the category of paramedical professions. Brandon and Hill[1] have described the confusing situation concerning definition in the United States. They give an indication that over 200 professions and occupations could fall into the category of 'allied health'.

The definition of the paramedical worker in *Mosby's medical, nursing and allied health dictionary*[2] indicates that paramedical professions are health workers other than physicians, dentists, podiatrists and nurses.

For purposes of simplification, this chapter will restrict coverage to what are termed 'professions allied to medicine' (PAMs) in the UK National Health Service (NHS). Table 4.1 shows the relevant professions and their professional bodies with the dates of foundation and numbers of registered members. The 1960 Professions Supplementary to Medicine Act[3] brought into being the Council for Professions Supplementary to Medicine (CPSM).

There is a separate Board for each of the seven professions within the CPSM. These legally autonomous Boards take responsibility for approving courses and training institutions, registering those who have acquired the appropriate qualifications, and enforcing standards and discipline. The legal, administrative and financial framework for these Boards is provided by the CPSM. The supervision and coordination of the Boards is also the obligation of the CPSM. Pickis[4] describes the issues with which the CPSM is currently involved.

The professional bodies mentioned in Table 4.1 have broader functions. They are concerned with the professions' extended interests in society and overseeing the economic aspects. They also have a commitment and involvement in their practitioners' body of knowledge and skill levels.

Table 4.1 Professions supplementary to medicine

Profession	Professional body	Date formed	Number of members*
Physiotherapy	Chartered Society of Physiotherapists	1984	23,757
Occupational therapy	British Association of Occupational Therapists	1974	13,702
Radiography	Society of Radiographers	1920	16,846
Dietetics	British Dietetic Association	1936	3,472
Chiropody	Society of Chiropodists	1945	7,111
Orthoptics	British Orthoptic Society	1937	1,092
Medical laboratory science	Institute of Medical Laboratory Sciences	1942	20,830

*Council for Professions Supplementary to Medicine *Annual report 1992–1993*, London, CPSM, 1993.

The work of the CPSM, the Boards and the professional associations is becoming ever more crucial in health care. Richardson[5] has identified the underlying issues to be faced. With the needs of the patient being the focus, the PAMs are being drawn closer together. There is some demand for the 'multiskilled worker', with concern being voiced about the 'over-professionalized Health Service'. Questions are being raised about the appropriateness of some of the treatment involving the PAMs. This means it is important that the role of PAMs in the multidisciplinary team is identified. The factors that make each PAM unique in health care delivery also have to be made clear and explicit. Unless this is achieved by the interested parties there will be a struggle to survive the rigours of the market place.

WORK OF PROFESSIONS ALLIED TO MEDICINE
The various professions do not make up a very large percentage of the NHS workforce. In England alone there are 850,653 NHS employees[6] but there are 86,810 PAMs registered with the CPSM.[7] Those registered with the CPSM are not necessarily employed in the NHS and also may be working worldwide. Despite not having a high profile in terms of manpower in UK health care, they perform a wide range of important and varied activities.

Physiotherapist
Physiotherapy (physical therapy in North America) has been used in some form since ancient times in Greece and China. The underpinning rationale

behind the physiotherapists' work is the need to help patients achieve as active a life as possible after illness or accident.

Williams[8] argues that three components – massage, medical gymnastics and medical electricity – are central in the treatment methods adopted by physiotherapists. Patients such as stroke victims, or those with special needs, depend on long-term treatment from the physiotherapist. Conversely, those suffering from sports injuries or accidents may only need short term assistance.

Practising physiotherapists draw upon the following core areas in their work: anatomy, physiology, neurology, orthopaedics and cardiopulmonary medicine. They are also becoming increasingly aware of other topics, such as communication and research skills.

Most physiotherapists are based in hospitals but there has been a gradual movement to employing more in the community. In the range of PAMs, the physiotherapist is the most likely to find work in the private sector. They are also very often the lead health professional in sports related injuries.

Occupational therapist

Occupational therapists aim to help people gain independence in their day-to-day living, such as dressing, feeding and bathing. The occupational therapist works with the patient in selecting activities which will help in achieving this independence. Physical exercises to improve coordination and balance, strengthen muscles and enhance movement are selected. Equally important for the occupational therapist is the psychological focus of their treatment. This will relate to the patients' self-confidence, anxiety and ability to live a full life.

The occupational therapist does not need such a detailed knowledge of anatomy and physiology as the physiotherapist. A deeper awareness and insight into psychosocial areas is necessary, as is a more complete awareness of the range and purposes of the aids and equipment available.

Occupational therapists work in hospitals, the community, special schools, the voluntary sector and social services.

Radiographer

The diagnostic radiographer's concerns are the production of images to help diagnose illness or injury. There have been major changes and developments in the technology available to the diagnostic radiographer in the past 20 years. These include nuclear medical resonances, angiography, and high frequency sound waves (ultrasound) and associated Doppler techniques, as well as computerized tomography. Images are essential for the modern diagnosis and treatment of illness.

Therapeutic radiographer

More contact with the patient occurs with the therapeutic radiographer. They are responsible for the planning and use of X-ray beams or radioactive substances in treating diseases. Most often these will be cancer related. The strength of radiation and location to which it will be applied are decided by the radiologist. The therapeutic radiographer takes responsibility for the accurate administration of the dosage and the care of the patient throughout treatment.

Again, an understanding of anatomy and physiology is essential for radiographers. They also need an in-depth knowledge of medical physics and the nature of the diseases they work with. Most radiographers are employed within the hospital setting.

Orthoptist

The diagnosis and treatment of disorders associated with binocular vision is the remit of orthoptists. They work in teams comprising ophthalmic opticians, nurses, doctors and ophthalmologists. Most of their work is concerned with screening the elderly and very young, who make up much of their clientele. This necessitates working in both the hospital and the community. Orthoptists draw heavily on the ophthalmology knowledge base.

Dietitian

Within the health care setting, dietitians are primarily educationalists. They work at many levels, from individual patients to fellow health professionals and the general public. Included in their diverse activities are advising women on nutritional standards in the antenatal or postnatal periods, establishing special diets for people suffering from different conditions and becoming involved with diet related health promotion campaigns.

The core element of their work is nutrition/dietetics and the relationship with diseases, pregnancy and the health of the elderly and young. The NHS is the largest employer of dietitians in the UK, and they work in both the hospital and the community.

Medical laboratory scientific officers

The investigation of body fluids and tissues is the primary function of the medical laboratory scientific officer (MLSO). MLSOs can specialize in seven areas. These are blood transfusion, cellular pathology, clinical chemistry, haematology, immunology, medical microbiology and virology. Although specialty dictates which subject area, a broader knowledge linking specialties is now required in all disciplines. Development of the 'newer' area of immunology has been promoted by feedback from all the established disciplines.

Chiropodist

Chiropodists are expert on conditions of the feet. Their main aim is to prevent immobility caused by disease or injury in the foot. This can involve undertaking minor surgery and analysing walking patterns. Like physiotherapists, chiropodists frequently find employment by becoming private practitioners.

Relevant subjects include orthotics, biomechanics, surgery and the foot. Chiropodists work in a variety of environments including hospitals, residential homes and health centres and clinics.

Other paramedical professions

It would be wrong to assume that the paramedical professions include only those under the CPSM umbrella.

Speech and language therapists were not grouped with the others in the Professions Supplementary to Medicine Act, 1960[9] as their work was deemed to be as much within education as medicine. Their role is to help people overcome problems of communication. They diagnose, assess and treat communication disorders including those of articulation, language, voice and fluency.

Clinical psychologists are employed in the NHS and are another profession often labelled paramedical. This profession developed in the mental health services but has now expanded to include a wide range of clients.

The following professions, among many others, could also be considered as being paramedical: psychotherapists, emergency medical technicians, audiologists, drama therapists, art therapists and chiropractitioners.

There are health professionals who apply a range of alternative or complementary therapies. Maher[10] defines these therapies as dealing with the sick person as a whole and not dependent upon chemical drugs. He identifies 45 different therapists including homeopaths, osteopaths, iridologists, reflexologists and acupuncturists.

New practitioners evolve to meet the changing demands in health care delivery. For example, the role of transplant clinicians' assistant (TCA) only came into existence in this decade.[11] The health sciences librarian will need to become acquainted with the diverse range of possible users and not be too dismayed by the problems of categorization!

EDUCATION

Until the early 1990s, most PAMs training took place in small monosubject schools, usually in health services accommodation. This facilitated the development of close links with the clinical environment, but Williams[12] has identified various drawbacks. The main role of teaching staffs was organizing students to provide student support for the clinical departments. Owing to their non-graduate status, the relationship developed with medical staff was that of a subordinate rather than a colleague. The curriculum reflected the medical model where PAMs merely apply the treatment prescribed by doctors. Research was limited and when it occurred the PAM was normally involved only with data collection. The analysis and evaluation was then completed by medical staff.

The need to move on from this position was identified by the Boards who initiated the movement to graduate courses. It proved possible for degree courses to be the same length as the previous three year diploma courses. This was achieved by the recognition that clinical practice is not just the acquisition of skills but contributes towards the students' academic growth. The clinical placement has become an integral part of the PAMs students' development. These changes have been achieved by gradually transferring the education and training of PAMs into higher education.

The rationale behind these changes is that the graduate PAMs will become effectively equipped to participate in the provision of multidisciplinary patient care. They will be able to demonstrate the information technology, problem solving and evaluation skills that are necessary.

Dietetics has been at degree level since 1985. MLSOs have traditionally gained professional qualifications through part-time study in higher education. The first orthoptist graduate entered the profession in 1994. In 1991, diploma courses in occupational therapy and radiography were still recruiting students. The focus of the degree courses will be to educationally develop the students rather than to deepen their professional knowledge. Students will be encouraged to develop reflection and self-awareness as well as a wide perspective of their profession. It is likely that they will study psychosocial areas, information technology and research skills.

Apart from the assimilation of PAMs education and training into higher education, courses are becoming modularized and credit, accumulation and transfer (CAT) rated. A degree course will be composed of various units each with a CAT level (diploma/degree/honours degree/postgraduate) and a number of points. PAMs students complete the requisite core modules and then make up the remainder of their degree through modules they choose. This development will increase the opportunities for students to learn with others from different disciplines. There will also be increased flexibility and choice for the student. Opportunities to move from one university to another will be created.

Existing diplomates will understandably feel some pressure to upgrade their qualification to degree level. This will be easier to achieve through modularization and CAT. Experienced PAMs will be able to produce a portfolio for which they will be given academic credit for their experiential learning. They will be able to choose the units at the appropriate level and offering the points they need for the qualification they are seeking. Open learning/distance learning will also be an option for the continuing education needs of PAMs.

Higher education is still grappling with the modularization of its teaching programmes, including those for the PAMs. It necessitates a radical reorganization with substantial lateral thinking if the changes are to be achieved successfully. It is fair to say that some of the issues to be addressed have not been identified yet. It will take some time before the procedures, techniques and principles are in place.

RESEARCH

The PAMs professional literature has underlined the importance of becoming both a consumer of research findings and a research practitioner.[13-15] There have also been indications that this commitment to research is often lacking.[16-18] There are two factors which may reverse this position: the need for research based practice, and the graduate PAMs.

In the introduction to this chapter the pressures resulting from market forces driving health care delivery were alluded to. PAMs have to be able to show the value of their work and provide evidence for the consumer and fellow health professionals. They have to be able to defend their practice and show that they have the abilities and aspirations to be vital members of the multidisciplinary team. This will be achieved by providing research based care and by undertaking investigations into the treatments for which they are responsible.

Williams[19] has produced a comprehensive overview of research issues for PAMs. The potential for future PAMs research resulting from the creation of 'new' universities from the former polytechnics is identified. This will allow freer competition for research funding and, coupled with PAMs training moving into higher education, should increase opportunities. Of all the PAMS, dietietics has been in the higher education sector the longest. This has resulted in staff working on a national and international basis, regularly publishing and also creating research student posts. Both Williams[20] and Schiller[21] recognize that PAMs academics new to higher education will not necessarily have the requisite skills. Both also identify continuing education programmes for the PAMs educator as a possible solution.

LIBRARY PROVISION FOR PROFESSIONS ALLIED TO MEDICINE

When the training of PAMs was based in small individual health service schools, libraries were underdeveloped. Students were taught using methods which placed little reliance on enquiry or project work. They were not expected to take responsibility for their own learning. Some of the larger schools did develop significant libraries for the students they served but these were the minority. There also exist some specialist libraries serving specific professions. The PAMs professional bodies have not seen the provision of a library and information service to their members as one of their major functions. The Chartered Society of Physiotherapists and the College of Occupational Therapists have created information officer posts, but they supply limited services.

A study day on the library needs of PAMs found that standards of service were variable and access often difficult.[22] At this study day it was outlined that PAMs often have recourse only to libraries intended primarily for other professions.

An independent organization Information Focus for Allied Health (InFAH), was established in 1993 to represent the needs and interests of librarians serving PAMs. A further significant development was the production of a book on the paramedical literature.[23]

There are also difficulties in supplying a library and information service because of the comparatively small numbers in one PAMs discipline in a single trust or hospital. In an evaluation of a regional library and information service,[24] only 4% of use was from PAMs. This pattern of use may change as the graduate PAM, accustomed to using library and information services, commences practice. A survey of first year occupational therapy degree students indicated that 33% used the library on a daily basis.[25]

The need for equality of access to library and information services for the PAMs as well as doctors as nurses has been stressed in the 1985 King's Fund Centre publication.[26] A further problem is the diversity of the literature relevant to the PAMs. They need a wider range of information from the sociology and psychology disciplines.[27] Brandon and Hill[28] point out that the position is compounded by the lack of distinct literature for some of the professions. They also argue strongly for the need for collection development in the area of allied health.

There are two roles that the librarian serving the PAMs will need to develop and expand: user instruction and promotion of electronic information sources. With PAMs undertaking research and further study they do not always have the information skills needed to succeed. PAMs are also having to demonstrate these skills in their work. The librarian therefore has to become a teacher in imparting the skills of information retrieval, analysis and synthesis. Various programmes, especially in occupational therapy, have been devised.[29-31]

Opportunities provided by electronic information are mentioned elsewhere in this book, and will add a further dimension to the ways in which the librarian can help the PAMs.

REFERENCES

1   Brandon, A. N. and Hill, D. R., 'Selected list of books and journals in allied health

sciences', *Bulletin of the Medical Library Association*, **78**, 1990, 233–47.

2   Anderson, K. N. (ed.), *Mosby's medical, nursing, and allied health dictionary*, 4th edn, St. Louis, Mosby, 1994.

3   Professions Supplementary to Medicine Act, London, HMSO, 1960.

4   Pickis, R., 'Standard practice', *Therapy weekly*, **19**, 3 June, 1993, 4.

5   Richardson, B., 'Practice, research and education – what is the link?, *Physiotherapy*, **79**, 1993, 317–22.

6   Department of Health, *Health and personal social services statistics: 1993 edition*, London, HMSO, 1993.

7   Council for Professions Supplementary to Medicine, *Annual report 1992–1993*, London, CPSM, 1993.

8   Williams, J. I., 'Physiotherapy is handling', *Physiotherapy*, **72**, 1986, 66–70.

9   Professions Supplementary to Medicine Act, op. cit.

10 Maher, G., *Starting a career in complementary medicine: a manual/directory of courses in alternative and complementary medicine*, 2nd edn, Harrow, Tackmart Publishing, 1992.

11 Caine, N., 'Heart to heart', *Health service journal*, **103**, 16 September 1993, 22–4.

12 Williams, C. S., 'The research challenge for the professions allied to medicine', *Journal of the Royal Society of Health*, **113**, 1993, 81–6.

13 Richardson, B., op. cit.

14 Ellis, M., 'Why bother to research?', *British journal of occupational therapy*, **44**, 1981, 115–6.

15 Atkinson, H. W., 'Heads in the clouds, feet on the ground', *Physiotherapy*, **75**, 1988, 542–7.

16 Rothstein, J. M., 'Clinical literature', *Physical therapy*, **69**, 1989, 895–6.

17 Grabois, M. and Fuhrer, M. J., 'Physiatrists' views on research', *American journal of physical medicine and rehabilitation*, **67**, 1988, 171–4.

18 Williams, C. S., op. cit.

19 Williams, C. S., op. cit.

20 Williams, C. S., op. cit.

21 Schiller, M. S. et al., 'Research skill needs and research environment of allied health faculty: implications for continuing education', *Journal of continuing education in the health professions*, **9**, 1989, 183–92.

22 Clark, K., 'Library needs of paramedical professions', *NISG newsletter*, (4), Spring 1984, 5–6.

23 Hewlett, J. (ed.), *Keyguide to information sources in paramedical sciences*, London, Mansell, 1990.

24 Bond, S., Bailey, P. and Walton, J. G., 'Evaluation of a regional service for nurses and paramedics in the Northern Region', *Nursing times* (Occassional Paper), **78**, 1982, 85–8.

25 Walton, G.,Bissessur, R. and Cooper, R., 'Survey of library and information use by health care students', *Health libraries review*, **10**, 1993, 57–74.

26 King's Fund Centre, *Providing a district library service: proposals arising from a series of workshops held in 1983*, London, King's Fund Centre, 1985.

27 Carmel, M., 'Users of biomedical libraries', *Health libraries review*, 3, 1986, 28–34.

28 Brandon, A. N. and Hill, D. R., op. cit.

29 Griffin, N. L. and Schumm, R. W., 'Instructing occupational therapy students in information retrieval', *American journal of occupational therapy*, 46, 1992, 158–61.

30 Mularski, C. A., Nystrom, E. and Grant, H. K., 'Developing information-seeking skills in occupational therapy students', *American journal of occupational therapy*, 43, 1989, 110–14.

31 Lyne, S. and Walton, G., 'Integrating information skills into a Diploma in Occupational Therapy course', *British journal of occupational therapy*, 53, 1990, 92–4.

5 Planning for health: the intelligence function

❖ Andrew Booth

In many countries, health care systems are facing increasing difficulties, both in matching supply of services to demand and in matching costs to the resources that they receive. Some causes are common to a large number of countries, as in the escalating costs of interventions as a result of scientific and technological progress. Other causes are health care system specific and depend on the political, social and economic environment within which health care is being delivered.[1] Common problems have led to convergence in a common form of health care system; that of the 'internal market'.[2] However, as Sheaff[3] points out, the specific type of internal market varies from country to country. Many health systems (The Netherlands, Russia, Poland, Sweden, France and, with local variants, the United Kingdom) have developed hybrids from the eight or more types that Sheaff identifies. Similar reforms have been debated in Germany, Italy, the USA and many developing countries.[4]

The concept of the internal market involves what is known as 'managed competition' and recognizes that whilst competition is a powerful stimulus for efficiency, it is woefully inadequate in terms of equity.[5] The market, therefore, has to be regulated, either directly through a 'managing structure'[2] (such as the British National Health Service Executive) or indirectly, such as through contract mechanisms administered by purchasing agencies. The hypothesis, that a 'state-regulated, but also competitive and commercialized, health care market (or "quasi market") will extract more health services from health care budgets'[3] was the driving force for an ultimately unsuccessful policy initiative from the Clinton Administration in the USA. It was also the impetus for health care reforms in western European countries such as the Netherlands and the United Kingdom.

Within the specific context of health planning, the regulated management of competition may be seen as a response to the limitations of its precursors of the 1970s and early 1980s: the conflicting philosophies of 'rational planning' and 'incrementalism'.[6] The former seeks a comprehensive and corporate approach to handling broad social problems and in doing so incurs a huge information overhead. The latter, through partisan mutual adjustment, tends to thwart the need to tackle high level problems, particularly those where radical change is required. Managed competition, however, seeks to address areas for health gain through the setting of desired goals or targets. These targets may either be global, such as those of the World Health Organization's *Health for all by the year 2000*,[7] or national, such as those in the United Kingdom's *Health of the nation* document.[8] The next stage is to encourage those commissioning or delivering health care to reach these goals through a programme of incentives or controls. Within the limits imposed by such a framework, healthcare organizations should be free to innovate or to achieve cost improvement, as local circumstances allow.

The popularity of the internal market in all its many variants needs to be seen within the context of the many trends, and indeed tensions, which have characterized health planning and management during the late 1980s and early 1990s. A seminal conference held by the World Health Organization in 1986 identified these as follows: centralization *versus* decentralization; strategic planning *versus* the operation of market forces; resource allocation; multisectoral collaboration; the split between purchasers and providers; and the trend towards planning for 'health' rather than planning for 'health services'.[9] The response of the Government of the United Kingdom, following the promptings of leading American health policy analyst Enthoven,[10] was to embark on a series of reforms which were not only to reshape health care delivery but also to redefine the landscape of information provision for health care planning.

PURCHASING FOR HEALTH

In England, the movement towards an internal market was signalled by the appearance, in 1989, of the Conservative Government's proposal document, the White Paper *Working for patients*.[11] The reforms contained therein were revolutionary enough to excite considerable interest amongst the international health care community.[12] However, the United Kingdom was by no means unique in differentiating between those who plan and purchase health care services on behalf of their populations – the purchasers – and those who deliver the services – the providers. The Conservative Government was pursuing a cost-cutting imperative driven by increasingly expensive interventions, economic recession and the demographic trend towards an ageing population. The irony was, however, that an oft-cited *raison d'être* was demand for improved efficiency: this in a health care system that spent 6% on administration compared with 22% in the market-driven United States.[12]

National priorities such as *Health of the nation*[8] and the *Patient's charter*[13] are set centrally by the Department of Health and the National Health Service Executive. In each of eight regional offices these priorities are then interpreted in the light of the health characteristics of the regional populations. A framework is thus provided within which those purchasing health care services operate.

Working for patients heralded a new role for health authorities (HAs) who had previously been responsible both for the planning of health care services and for the management of acute and community units within their geographical areas. Decision making about operational matters was to be delegated from HAs to hospitals and their associated management units. The idea was that HAs could then

> concentrate on ensuring that the health needs of the population for which they are responsible are met; that there are effective services for the prevention and control of diseases and the promotion of health; that their population has access to a comprehensive range of high quality, value for money services; and on setting targets for and monitoring the performance of those management units for which they continue to have responsibility.[11]

These stages, comprising needs assessment, service planning and specification, contracting, purchasing and monitoring, are all part of what is now known as the 'commissioning process'.

Commissioning was also a task for the new family health services authorities (FHSAs) (formerly the Family Practitioner Committees) who held responsibility for general practitioners (GPs) within their boundaries. The common of purpose for HAs and FHSAs coupled with a need to increase their purchasing power led, in many cases, to formal mergers. Elsewhere, organizations were involved in the sharing of support functions (such as information processing and epidemiology), contract processes (such as contract negotiations and review) or collaboration with other bodies (such as local authorities).

A further group emerged under the provisions of the White Paper to plan for the health of their population. Those general practices that met a list size threshold were permitted to become general practice fund-holders (GPFHs) and given new powers to purchase some secondary and community services. During the mid-1990s the Government sought to encourage a greater uptake of GP fund-holding. The ultimate target was 100% fund-holding and to this end the list size threshold was reduced, together with experimentation with 'total fundholding' (where selected fund-holders could also purchase acute and emergency services). The idea was that GP fund-holders, with their more detailed knowledge of their own 'patch', would become more involved in assessing the health needs of their populations.[14]

The stimulus given to locally sensitive service provision by the GP fund-holding initiatives undeniably brought some improvements in access to, and delivery of, health services. It also led to concern being expressed over equity, with the phrase 'a two-tiered system'[2] receiving much prominence. Within the information domain there has also been a variant of 'a two-tier' system. It is only at the health authority or commissioning agency level that purchasing power has been sufficiently large to allow investment in the provision of dedicated information services to those planning for health. The next section will therefore focus on the business management activities of those working in larger purchasing organizations.

MANAGING THE BUSINESS OF HEALTH COMMISSIONING

In many ways the commissioning process is typical of the 'management process'[15] in general, and corresponds with its various stages: assessing the internal and external environment, formulating change, implementing change and supervising routine operations. Therefore one approach to defining the user characteristics of those who plan for health is to focus on the various stages of the commissioning process. It will also be useful to examine some of the information needs associated with each stage.

Needs assessment

Health care planning has been based on the twin factors of supply (what is provided) and demand (what is asked for). The rationale for a change in role for those planning services was in acknowledgement of a third component, a prerequisite to these considerations, namely need (what people could benefit from). The sphere of planning for health thus includes all interventions that impinge on the health of a population regardless of where resources have previously been allocated. Joint commissioning, where 'seamless' packages of care are delivered across the traditional health care and social care divide, is intended to address many of these wider issues.

Needs assessment, the investigation of the population's ability to benefit from health care, combines three approaches:[16]

- epidemiological assessments of the ability to benefit from health care
- comparative assessments of health and health service locally, regionally and nationally
- a 'corporate' view of health care needs, taking account of the views of all the stakeholders including local residents, GPs, voluntary organizations, community health councils, etc.

Information implications

A rich variety of sources is required for needs assessment. The epidemiological approach requires demographic information together with prevalence, morbidity and mortality data. This information has to be matched with knowledge about the relative effectiveness, outcomes and costs of appropriate services. As a blueprint for this process, the project team, charged with the task of preparing HAs for their new purchasing role, commissioned a series of research reviews.[17] Each research review synthesized epidemiological information on a common health condition, e.g. coronary heart disease, family planning and mental illness.

Health services had been weak in providing information on effectiveness and outcomes. The pioneering work of Ian Chalmers[18] in the area of pregnancy and childbirth provided a useful model to follow. Such a lead was followed by the University of Leeds, who produced a series of 'Effective health care bulletins'[19, 20] on topics such as glue ear and infertility. The Nuffield Institute for Health's UK Clearing House for Information on the Assessment of Health Outcomes[21] has improved coverage of a contiguous area with its database of outcome projects and regular outcomes briefings. The Department of Health has also directly contributed to the field with the development of population health outcome indicators.[22]

The comparative approach is founded on three requirements: data for health and health services both locally and elsewhere, a comparable basis for analysis, and 'intelligence' on other factors to be taken into account. The centrally produced 'Health service indicators'[23] package and the centrally commissioned *Public health common data set*[24] address the first two of these factors. However, they lack sensitivity for more sophisticated multivariate analyses. Facilities that use such resources, such as the Cambridge Needs Assessment Workstation, are constrained by the necessity to gloss or define data. At a local level, data on costs, available through routine financial returns and supplemented by detailed costing of particular services, are used as a basis for options' appraisal.

The corporate view, though initially the least developed of the three approaches, has subsequently been stimulated by developments connected with *The patient's charter*. A number of guides to obtaining the views of users of health services[25] have been produced whilst projects such as Local Voices[26] have addressed such issues.

Service planning and specification
Once the process of needs assessment is complete, attention turns to the pattern of resources required to deliver packages of care. Considerations of appropriate technologies, staff levels and skill-mix, and acceptability of service delivery help to shape the planning process.

Information implications
Publications and reports of the Royal Colleges, clinical consensus documents and guidelines on care are of paramount importance in formulating a service

specification.[27] A problem lies in their ad hoc nature – some conditions are covered by multiple reports whilst others are barely acknowledged at all. Increasing use is being made of systematic reviews, meta-analyses and reports from randomized controlled trials, and this has led to the development of resources such as the Cochrane Centre in Oxford.[28] The NHS Research and Development Programme is seen by many as a way of ensuring a more even coverage of health technology assessment. In this connection, the Reviews and Dissemination Centre, based at the University of York, is attempting to identify areas previously under-represented by systematic review.

The emphasis of research and development in the NHS can be seen to have shifted from original health services research towards the systematic review of scientifically conducted trials. Information workers, grounded on principles of literature searching and information retrieval, are becoming alert to opportunities that this shift presents. Health care library professionals in the United Kingdom are not as advanced in the areas of meta-analysis and evaluation as their counterparts in North America.[29,30] The participation of local health librarians in the Critical Appraisal Skills for Purchasers (CASP) project in Oxford Region demonstrates the contribution that trained information professionals can make to these multidisciplinary techniques.

Contracting and purchasing

Once purchasers have determined appropriate patterns of care, they fix these within the context of anticipated activity levels. A number of options are available to the manager formulating a contract. Routine, comparatively low cost procedures exhibiting little fluctuation in demand may be handled through a 'block contract'. More volatile or high cost activities may be purchased at a minimum level, with additional payments on a per case basis (so-called "cost and volume contracts'). Very high cost activities may be handled on a purely cost per case basis. Common procedures might be shared amongst a number of providers, whereas specialist interventions might require referral to a regional specialty unit. Because of the inadequate levels of information for extrapolating demand, a number of purchasers reserve sums of money for extra-contractual referrals (ECRs). Other procedures, ranging from *in vitro* fertilization to tattoo removal, are often either explicitly or discreetly removed from the purchasers' contract coverage.

The purchasing process requires not just the setting of contracts but also associated activities such as market assessment (deciding which providers can provide what services to what standard) and negotiation.

Information implications

Information underpins all facets of the contracting process. NHS contracts contain five major sections: contract, volume, price, quality and information. A knowledge of the provider organization, its internal politics, theatre utilization, skill mix and activity levels will all inform the contract decision. Financial information on specialist inflation levels, wage costs and overheads will determine strategic planning. These are just typical examples; the 'rainbow pack'[31] supplies practical case studies of the information required for contracting.

Monitoring and evaluation

In many ways, the monitoring and evaluation phase corresponds to that for needs assessment and forms the 'closing of the loop'. Needs assessment combines investigation of specific health needs with an overall strategy based on the health of the resident population. Evaluation likewise has two foci: evaluation of individual contracts and evaluation of the purchasing strategy. Feedback on the success of individual contracts comes from a number of sources. Users of services, or GPs as their agents, provide critical comment on whether their needs have been met. Outcomes of the service are compared with anticipated benefits. Explicit standards included in the contract are compared with actual practice. Data on contract activity can be a specified 'deliverable' that, together with 'market intelligence', informs the revision of specifications and renegotiation of contracts. At its broadest level, the purchasing strategy will be evaluated against the national agenda and local priorities to assess its continuing relevance.

Information implications

Several sources mentioned earlier are also used to support the monitoring phase. *Health service indicators* provide national comparative data against which to measure local performance. Consumer feedback on actual services, as opposed to projected ones, will inform the purchaser's evaluation and will need to be collected and stored in a systematic way. Local newspapers, council minutes and other ephemeral materials reflect community perceptions of services. Purchasers require materials on market research, questionnaire design and statistical techniques such as sampling. Collections of guidelines and protocols must constantly be updated so that quality assurance mechanisms retain their relevance.

INFORMATION MANAGEMENT IN PLANNING FOR HEALTH

A definition of intelligence

In order to fulfil their new roles, purchasers are required to devise practical arrangements to:

a. assemble, analyse and interpret a wide range of information and knowledge about health and health services to support health care needs assessment and service evaluation; and

b. secure the views of local people, local practitioners and experts about health and health services.[32]

Historical data on finance and activity levels (traditional information strengths in the National Health Service) were no longer to be enough in planning future services. They were to be augmented by a wide range of qualitative information: expert assessments, local opinions, research and material on effectiveness and outcomes. Additional quantitative information, demographic and epidemiological, was also to be used so that an iterative pattern of 'more of the same' would be avoided. A project team, set up by the National Health Service Management Executive in October 1989 to support the HAs (project 26), attempted to convey adequately the extent of this new information requirement by adopting the word 'intelligence'. This term, with its origins in the military and commercial domains, was chosen to signify 'the full range of knowledge (text and numbers) and to distinguish it from the term information conventionally used to describe routine health service data systems'.[32] In addition, the term was used 'to emphasize the value of 'soft' data as much as 'hard', to emphasize that the body of intelligence required was a mix of local as well as information from other sources and to imply that knowledge must be used in the context of decision making'.[32] 'Intelligence' was portrayed as a three-dimensional cube comprising numerical and textual, routine and ad hoc, and local and national information.

Sheaff and Peel[33] identified further key distinctions between 'intelligence' and typical NHS 'information' provision.

Intelligence:-
- is concerned less with the past and present and more with the future
- involves the exercise of judgement from senior experience
- is highly dependent on context.

They went on to state that this requires not a 'traditional library model' but rather a 'business model' of information management. A dual threat to this model lies both in an outdated view of libraries and librarians held by some health managers, and in the temptation for information professionals to fall into the all-too-common trap:

Perhaps the biggest challenge is to get away from the traditional image of a concern for assembling stocks of books to one where the real task is as a knowledge broker using networks and various sources to support the creation of local intelligence.[34]

This was made explicit in the *Purchasing intelligence* document:

> While a basic core of readily accessible material may be required, the main aim should be to create a flexible resource capable of using the wide range of networks and knowledge to assemble appropriate intelligence.[32]

Adoption of a business paradigm acknowledges the heterogeneity of information whereby some types require central control whilst others can be decentralized. It also allows access for NHS organizations to techniques with a long pedigree in the corporate business world. A foremost example of this is the information needs analysis, the so-called 'information audit'.[35]

Information audit

New organizations, or existing organizations realigning to new objectives, need to arrive at a definition of their information requirements.[36] Just as the process of health planning starts with needs assessment, information planning has as its prerequisite the information needs analysis. For perhaps the first time, a centrally produced government publication[32] identified the first two steps of a local action plan as:

> a. conduct an audit of existing local information and library facilities to identify those which could form part of a future service . . .
> b. focus this audit on the local priorities and health needs assessment objectives . . . .

The information audit, which matches information requirements to the business of an organization, is therefore a valuable first stage tool in the creation of an intelligence function.

DEVELOPING AN INTELLIGENCE FUNCTION

The development of an intelligence function involves four complementary elements:

- skills
- alliances
- rules
- facilities and technology.

It will perhaps be helpful to deal with each of these elements in turn.

Skills

Staff in purchasing intelligence units need a range of skills and knowledge which has been identified as follows:[37]

(i)   sources of all kinds of information
(ii)   techniques for identification of information needs
(iii)   organization of text and numeric data, in particular, knowledge of database software for text retrieval and of relational database management and statistical handling software
(iv)   information system development, especially the ability to devise logical specifications
(v)   search skills, text and numeric
(vi)   evaluation and critical appraisal of data and its pro-active dissemination
(vii)   advice on intelligence gathering
(viii) liaison with information technology (IT) personnel, together with support skills such as numeracy and computer literacy.

This list, compiled by the programme director of one of the leading health information management courses, makes no claim to comprehensiveness and might usefully be supplemented by two additions. For an understanding of the health planning process, it is helpful for information staff also to have an awareness of project management methodologies such as PRINCE,[38] and of geographical mapping tools such as those employed by the WISPUR[39] purchasing project.

Skills required by purchasing intelligence staff are not exclusively technical. If they are to encourage and elicit the necessary information they will require, in addition:[40] persuasion/influencing; facilitation; networking; lateral thinking; consultation; negotiation; and focusing. As all the necessary skills are unlikely to be found in any one individual, a multidisciplinary team approach will usually be required. Whether skills deficits are addressed on a unit basis, as at well established and well resourced facilities such as that of the Cambridge Health Authority, or, more commonly, through individual development, it is clear that it is not desirable for health care librarians or information officers merely to take refuge in traditional areas of expertise.

Support for the continuing professional development of those seeking to define the new role of purchasing 'intelligence officer' is found, to varying degrees, from three associations: IFM Healthcare (Information for the Management of Healthcare), the NHS Management Librarians' Group and a much broader-based professional group, ASSIST (the Association of Information Management and Technology Staff in the NHS). IFM Healthcare, founded as a subgroup of the Medical, Health and Welfare Libraries Group, is a natural focal point for staff of the new intelligence facilities and, indeed, for information staff from non-librarianship backgrounds. Such support comes through an active programme of workshops, study days, publications and information exchange, the principal instrument being the quarterly *IFM Healthcare newsletter*. In contrast, the NHS Management Librarians' Group, true to its origins as a closed support and self-help group, has increasingly seen library-trained purchasing intelligence officers assume its vacant positions. ASSIST was formed following the release of the Information Management and Technology (IM&T) Strategy in December 1992. This association does not have its own professional journal, but the interests of its members are covered through the pages of the *British journal of healthcare computing and information management* (monthly).

Alliances

The concept of 'alliances' is rooted in the recognition that no agency can hope to acquire the requisite skills and resources to the depth that the commissioning process demands. The world of health librarianship has always acknowledged that locally held information resources must be finite. Regional networks and cooperatives have attempted to address local deficiencies. In addition, local alliances have been formed between postgraduate medical librarians, school of nursing librarians and drug information officers. With the development of a new area of information need – that for purchasing intelligence – a new pattern of alliances has had to be woven: census data have traditionally been held within the public library sector; epidemiological data are usually housed with the local department of public health medicine; and community studies have been the domain of local university and college departments. Meanwhile, the hospital library holds national and professional reports, the information department covers the range of finance, personnel and activity data, and the CHCs hold surveys of service use and customer satisfaction. Add to the picture the diversity of information held in the various departments of the district, metropolitan or county councils – housing, social services, environment, education, leisure services, transport and police – and one gets a clear idea of the task facing the information professional.

To attempt to provide a national infrastructure upon which local links could be developed, the three major health care planning information providers at the Department of Health, King's Fund Centre and the Nuffield Institute established a Healthcare Management Information Consortium.[41] Areas for coordination and strategic development include the exchange of bibliographic records, the construction of a core thesaurus, and a joint collection development policy. One of the strengths of the consortium was that the partners administer the three most significant databases for health planning in the UK: the Department of Health's *DHSS-Data*, the Nuffield Institute's *HELMIS* and the King's Fund's collection management system.

The need for those planning for health to share information and benefit from shared learning has been recognized not only in the development of 'learning sets' but also through an enhanced variant of the networking model, a 'Purchasing innovations network'.[42] This collaborative venture between the King's Fund College and King's Fund Centre provides a learning network and information exchange supported by a textual database and a 'purchasing innovations' bulletin.

Rules

Rules relate both to access to the information and to its subsequent use. In a market-based health care system information can be commercially sensitive, particularly where it relates to contracts, and yet the empirical nature of purchasing, whilst still in its infancy, requires reliable comparative data. Essentially what is required is an arms-length exchange of data where individual identities are subsumed in the interests of comprehensive coverage. This was the basis for an abortive NAHAT (National Association of Health Authorities and Trusts) contracts database[43] as well as for the Audit Commission's work on comparative performance indicators.[44]

Rules also attempt to ensure that information is only used for the purposes for which it has been collected and that these purposes are placed within the context of explicit data definitions. Anecdotal evidence indicates that, initially at least, some purchasers were using research publications produced by provider units as 'intelligence' to inform their purchasing decisions. With the subsequent development of rules the prospect of such an occurrence has receded.

In a traditional information context, rules can also be applied to the means by which access is provided to the intellectual content (as opposed to the physical form) of the information. Cataloguing, classification and indexing of purchasing intelligence resources have tended to follow local (or regional) practice rather than meeting common standards that might permit more widespread exchange between similar facilities. The complexity of the situation is compounded by the national picture, where the IM&T Strategy is based around the Clinical Terms project[45] and Read Coding and Classification system,[46] whilst the NHS Research and Development Strategy takes the United States' National Library of Medicine Medical Subject Headings (MeSH) as its guide. The *DHSS-Data* thesaurus remains the most widely accepted tool amongst the NHS management library community, although the King's Fund Centre's Information Resources Department has made purchasing intelligence a particular focus in its own in-house thesaurus.

Facilities and technology

Broadly speaking, facilities for planning for health within the NHS have evolved locally at a purchaser or commissioning agency level. There are therefore few examples of national significance outside the traditional academic and service development sectors. Examples of the former, all university based, are the Health Services Research Unit at Brunel, the Centre for Health Economics at York, the Health Services Management Unit at Manchester, and the Health Care Evaluation Unit at Bristol, whilst Aberdeen is home to the Health Economics Research Unit. The Nuffield Institute for Health (University of Leeds), mentioned above in connection with the Outcomes Clearing House, also houses a *Community care database*. Foremost in the latter category is the King's Fund Centre with its Services for Health and Race Exchange (SHARE). An isolated example of a facility that has grown up outside these sectors is the Public Health Research and Resource Centre, formed by collaboration between North Western Regional Health Authority and four constituent HAs, and based in Salford. A network based, rather than site-specific model, is South and West Region's grey literature database (*FERRIT*).[47]

Technology, for supporting the planning process, has been based around two major initiatives: the Developing Information Systems for Purchasers (DISP) project[48] and the Cambridge Needs Assessment and Planning Workstation.[49] The former consists of a number of modules designed to address information needs for the various stages of the contracting process. The latter is a multipurpose workstation that brings together 'hard' statistical and census data with 'soft' information. In addition, it permits 'what if' modelling as part of its executive information system capability, and is supported by a tool box of word processor, spreadsheet and geographical mapping facilities. Finally, the workstation can be used for accessing online and CD-ROM based external databases. Although experimental, in the sense that uptake has been confined to a few select sites, the Needs Assessment and Planning Workstation gives perhaps the clearest and most concise indication that the range of resources required for planning for health is at least as complex as those required for any large scale corporate planning activity.

INFORMATION LABOUR FORCE REQUIREMENTS

Much attention has been focused in the literature[37, 50-53] on the personnel requirements for information functions within the new NHS. Clearly, there is a continuing need to develop an 'amphibious breed' of information professionals, equally at home in statistical and textual environments, as well as to increase the uptake of basic information handling skills amongst managers in general. It is to this end that the University of Wales at Aberystwyth worked with the NHS Training Directorate (NHSTD) to offer a Masters and a Diploma in Health Information Management. An initial three-to-one predominance in applications from NHS information managers and information officers over librarians has subsequently approached parity. Similar, but by no means identical, courses sponsored by the NHSTD are now offered in health information management by the Universities at Manchester and Loughborough, with other related courses at Warwick, Keele, Sheffield, Glasgow and City University, London.[53]

The NHSTD, recognizing that the market is not able to meet the need for information skills within the NHS, commissioned a Training Needs in Information Staff project as part of the national IM&T Strategy. This project drew up learning specifications to assist in local planning and provision of IM&T. At the same time, the NHSTD continues to address information skills for managers in general through a number of complementary training packages aimed at raising awareness of IM&T and at promoting an information culture in the NHS.[54]

CONCLUSION

Sir Duncan Nichol, then Chief Executive of the NHS Management Executive, emphasized the essential part played by information in the following comment:

> If purchasing is the engine for improving NHS performance, then information must be the fuel that drives the engine.[55]

In recognition of this, the early 1990s were characterized by the spotlight being focused on the information requirements of the new NHS, with two national seminars, chaired by Baroness Cumberlege, on 'Health care information in the UK' (1992) and 'Managing the knowledge base of healthcare' (1993), and the subsequent appointment of an NHS Libraries Adviser. The challenge for health care information workers now, as then, is to ensure that they play an active and central part in the health planning process. They cannot afford to continue as spectators, and to view such a core NHS activity from the sidelines.

REFERENCES

1 Borgonovi, E. and Brovetto, P. R., 'Management challenges and markets', *International journal of health planning and management*, 9 (1), 1994, 25–38.

2 Sheaff, R., 'What kind of healthcare "internal market"? A cross-Europe view of the options', *International journal of health planning and management*, 9 (1), 1994, 5–24.

3 Sheaff, W. R., 'The international scene', in Sheaff, W. R. and Peel, V. J., *Best practice in health care commissioning*, Harlow, Longman, 1993, Section 1.4.

4 World Health Organization, *Evaluation of recent changes in the financing of health ser-*

vices, Geneva, WHO Study Group, 1993.

5   Battistella, R., 'Health services reforms: political and managerial aims – an international perspective', *International journal of health planning and management*, **8** (3), 1994, 265–74.

6   Lee, K., 'Competition versus planning in health care: implications for corporate and individual incentives, efficiency and control', *Australian health review*, **14** (1), 1991, 9–34.

7   World Health Organization, *Health for all by the year 2000*, Geneva, WHO, 1986.

8   Department of Health, *Health of the nation: a strategy for health in England*, London, HMSO, 1992.

9   World Health Organization, *Planning and management for health: report of a European conference*, Euro Reports and Studies No. 102, Geneva, WHO, 1986.

10 Enthoven, A. C., *Reflections on the management of the National Health Service*, London, Nuffield Provincial Hospitals Trust, 1985.

11 Department of Health and Social Security, *Working for patients*, London, HMSO, 1989.

12 Organization for Economic Cooperation and Development, *The reform of health care: a comparative analysis of seven OECD countries*, Paris, OECD, 1992.

13 Department of Health, *The patient's charter: raising the standard*, London, DoH, 1991.

14 Wilson, B., 'How to do health needs assessment', *Fundholding*, **20** (9), 1993, 12–14.

15 Latimer, B. and Mason, A., *Information for action*, London, Institute of Health Services Management, 1992.

16 National Health Service Management Executive, *Assessing health care needs: a DHA project discussion paper*, London, NHSME, 1991.

17 Stevens, A. and Raftery, J. (eds.), *Needs assessment: an epidemiologically-based approach*, Oxford, Radcliffe Medical Press, 1992.

18 Chalmers, I., Enkin, M. and Keirse, M.J.N.C., *Effective care in pregnancy and childbirth*, Oxford, OUP, 1989.

19 Long, A. F. and Sheldon, T. A., 'Enhancing effective and acceptable purchaser and provider decisions: overview and methods', *Quality in health care*, **1** (1), 1991, 74–6.

20 Ibbotson, S. L. *et al.*, 'An initial evaluation of effective health care bulletins as instruments of effective dissemination', *Journal of management in medicine*, **7** (2), 1993, 48–57.

21 Long, A. F., Bate, L. and Sheldon, T. A., 'Establishment of a UK Clearing House for Assessing Health Services Outcomes', *Quality in health care*, **1** (2), 1992, 131–3.

22 Department of Health, *Population health outcome indicators for the NHS 1993, England: a consultation document*, London, Department of Health, 1993.

23 Davidge, M. and Harley, M., 'Purchasing by numbers', *Health direct*, (24), 1992, 6–7.

24 University of Surrey, Institute of Public Health, *Public health common data set 1994*, London, DoH, 1994.

25 McIver, S., *An introduction to obtaining the views of users of health services*, London,

King's Fund Centre, 1991.

26 National Health Service Management Executive, *Local voices: the views of local people in purchasing for health*, London, NHSME, 1992.

27 Webster, D., 'How to . . . produce a service specification', *BMJ*, **302** (6790), 1991, 1450–1.

28 Chalmers, I., Dickersin, K. and Chalmers, T. C., 'Getting to grips with Archie Cochrane's agenda', *BMJ*, **305**, 1992, 786–8.

29 Schell, C. L., 'Meta-analysis: a tool for medical and scientific discoveries', *Bulletin of the Medical Library Association*, **80** (3), 1992, 219–22.

30 Smith, J. T., 'Decision points in the integrative research review process: a flow-chart approach', *Medical reference services quarterly*, **10** (2), 1991, 47–72.

31 Five Regions in conjunction with Greenhalgh Limited, *Using information in contracting*, Macclesfield, Greenhalgh Limited, 1993.

32 National Health Service Management Executive, *Purchasing intelligence*, October 1991, London, NHSME, 1991.

33 Sheaff, W. R. and Peel, V. J., *Best practice in health care commissioning*, Harlow, Longman, 1993.

34 Dunning, M., 'Editorial – purchasing intelligence', *Health libraries review*, **9** (3), 1992, 95–6.

35 Orna, E., *Practical information policies: how to manage the information flow in organizations*, Aldershot, Gower, 1990.

36 Booth, A. and Haines, M., 'Information audit: whose line is it anyway?', *Health libraries review*, **10** (4),1993, 224–32.

37 Hepworth, J. B., 'Staffing intelligence services: a survivor's guide', *Health libraries review*, **9** (3), 1992, 52–61.

38 National Health Service Management Executive, Information Management Group, *Project management training news* (journal).

39 Wain, R., 'Mapping the health of the nation', *British journal of healthcare computing*, **9** (6), 1992, 20–3.

40 Peel, V., *Sharing the same kettle: developing health intelligence for purchasing health authorities*, Manchester, Health Services Management Unit, 1992.

41 Haines, M. P. J., 'Developing HMIC', *Library management*, **14** (3), 1993, 22–7.

42 Booth, A., 'Purchasing Innovations database: supporting a learning network', *IFM Healthcare newsletter*, **4** (3), 1993, 19–20.

43 Maheswaran, S. and Appleby, J., 'Building quality standards into contracts', *Health direct*, (22), 1992, 6–7.

44 'Audit Commission: the health service', *NAHA briefing*, 27 April 1990, 1–4.

45 Brown, P., 'Talking the same language', *British journal of healthcare computing and information management*, **10** (9), 1993, 26–7.

46 Swayne, J., 'A common language of care?', *Journal of interprofessional care*, **7** (1), 1993, 29–35.

47 Prior, P., A needs assessment grey literature database, in Booth, A. (ed.), *Purchasing intelligence: proceedings of an IFM healthcare study day*, London, IFM Healthcare, 1992, 33–7.

48   'Appendix', in National Health Service Management Executive, *Purchasing intelligence*, London, NHSME, 1991.

49   'Appendix 2. Needs assessment and planning workstation', in Peel, V., *Sharing the same kettle: developing health intelligence for purchasing health authorities*, Manchester, Health Services Management Unit, 1992.

50   Brittain, J. M., 'The emerging market for information professionals in the UK National Health Service', *International journal of information management*, **12** (4), 1992, 261–71.

51   Brittain, J. M., 'New opportunities for NHS librarians and information scientists', *Health libraries review*, **10** (1), 1993, 10–19.

52   Brittain, M., 'Jobs go begging in the new model NHS', *Library Association record*, **94** (6), 1992, 382–3.

53   Hepworth, J., 'Through the training maze', *Health service journal*, **101** (5282), 1991, 33–4.

54   Brittain, M. and Maggs, J., 'Ships in the night', *British journal of healthcare computing and information management*, **10** (7), 1992, 20–2.

55   National Health Service Management Executive, Information Management Group, *Information for effective purchasing*, London, DoH, 1993.

6 Consumer health information: information for the public, patients and carers

❖ *Robert Gann*

Writing in the previous edition of this book in 1981, Roy Tabor predicted that the next major advances in the health of people will be determined by what individuals are able to do for themselves and for society at large. Looking back over the past decade, this trend has proved to be more marked than even Roy could have predicted, with far-reaching implications for the information professions.

During the 1980s and 1990s, increasing attention has been given to the provision of information on health care issues to patients, relatives, carers and the wider public. Over this period, medical libraries have had an increasing inclination and ability to provide information to patients. At the same time, there has been a blossoming in new consumer health information services, which aim to combine the subject expertise of the medical library with the accessibility of the public library. And there has been an unprecedented expansion in the amount of published literature on health topics for lay people.

A NEW TERMINOLOGY

Librarians and other information workers providing these kinds of services often use the term 'consumer health information' (CHI) to describe this area of health information work. Having information is the first step to every healthy choice we make: weighing up the risks and benefits of treatment, choosing a healthier lifestyle, using the health service, joining a self-help group, claiming welfare benefits. The term 'health care consumer' can be used to include all members of the public who use (consume) health services. Health services might be provided by family doctors, hospitals, community care and the private sector. But equally they include the informal care provided by self-help groups, families and friends, and the self-care which we provide for ourselves. For this reason the term 'health care consumer' is often preferred to the term 'patient'. Most people only regard themselves as patients when they are actually receiving professional health care. On the other hand, we are users or consumers of health care almost every day of our lives.

To be strictly accurate, even the term 'consumer' is a misnomer in the health care context. We produce just as much health care (self-care and mutual support) as we consume from professional services. For this reason, some commentators are beginning to reject the rather passive concept of consumer as recipient in favour of the notion of the 'coproducer'.[1] Furthermore, there is a growing awareness that ordinary people need information not only to make individual *consumer* choices but also to act as empowered and assertive *citizens* acting as *communities* to influence service planning.[2] Consumer, coproducer, citizen, community – the abbreviation CHI encompasses them all.

SOCIAL AND POLITICAL CHANGE

There are a number of reasons for the development of consumer health information services. One is undoubtedly an increasing consumerism in society generally, which is reflected in our behaviour as patients. People are no longer content to be told what's good for them; they want access to information which enables them to weigh up risks and benefits, and to make informed choices between options in health care.

NHS reforms

This new health consumerism has been encouraged by government health policies which emphasize consumer choice. Roy Tabor identified the 1976 government report *Prevention and health: everybody's business*[3] as an early manifestation of this approach. During the 1980s these priorities became more and more explicit. The NHS White Paper *Working for patients*[4] urged health authorities to provide to patients 'clear information about the facilities available . . . and clear and thoughtful explanations of what is happening – on practical matters such as where to go and who to see, and on clinical matters such as the nature of the illness and its proposed treatment'. The subsequent NHS and Community Care Act 1990 aimed to introduce a 'reformed' NHS in which 'provider units' (NHS Trusts) attract patients through quality health care provision, which involves a greater level of patient information and education provision than ever before. GPs are being encouraged to 'shop around' for treatment where waiting times are shortest, leading to a demand for opening up previously closed areas of information on waiting lists. In turn, the intention is that GPs will attract patients to their practices with practice information brochures, health promotion clinics and easier ways of changing doctor. The NHS reforms may be politically unpopular but there is no doubt that they have produced a fertile climate for the development of better information for patients.

There now seems to be a political consensus on the need for more consumer health information. The 1990 Labour Party policy document *A fresh start for health*[5] supported the development of a patient population which is 'more self confident, more assertive and more knowledgable'. Labour's Charter for Patients would provide for 'the right of patients to gain more information about courses of treatment. Patients who are better informed about alternative forms of treatment, and who participate in the management of their case are more likely to cooperate in beneficial changes in their lifestyle and may contribute to better prospect of a successful outcome'. This is in sharp contrast to the prevailing attitude as recently as the 1970s, which could be summed up as 'a little knowledge is a dangerous thing'. Informed health care consumerism is now the orthodoxy.

Information and patient's rights
This new orthodoxy is most clearly expressed in *The Patient's Charter*[6] launched by the government in 1991. The Charter lists ten rights to health care which patients have within the NHS. The first seven are established patient rights and then there are three new rights which came into effect in April 1992. The Patient's Charter Rights are

1 to receive health care on the basis of clinical need, regardless of ability to pay
2 to be registered with a GP
3 to receive emergency medical care at any time
4 to be referred to a consultant acceptable to you, when your GP thinks it necessary, and to be referred for a second opinion if you and your GP agree this is desirable
5 to be given a clear explanation of any treatment proposed, including any risks or alternatives, before you decide whether you will agree to treatment
6 to have access to your health records
7 to choose whether or not you wish to take part in medical research or training
8 to be given detailed information on local health services, including quality standards and maximum waiting times
9 to be guaranteed admission for treatment within two years from being placed on the waiting list
10 to have any complaint investigated and to receive a full and prompt written reply.

The Patient's Charter depends crucially for its success on information. The right to be registered with a GP depends on the availability of information about local GP services (which practices have a female partner, which offer complementary therapies, where ethnic minority languages are spoken, etc.). The right to a second opinion depends on information being available about

consultant special interests and centres of excellence. The right to an explanation of treatment and the right to access to health records are concerned
entirely with information.

The right to information on health services available locally, quality standards, how to complain and waiting times for treatment is new. The guarantee of treatment within two years (now 18 months) has created a demand for
information on comparative waiting times for treatment to allow patients and
their GPs the opportunity of identifying shorter waiting times for treatment if
the operation cannot be carried out locally within the guaranteed time.

Recognizing this need for health information for the public, the government
required all regional health authorities (RHAs) to set up consumer health
information services from April 1992. The Department of Health issued Health
Service Guidelines HSG(92)21 providing a detailed specification of the services
to be provided. RHAs were instructed to set up a local call rate helpline (subsequently changed to a freephone service) to provide the public with information on local NHS services, waiting times, complaints procedures, Patient's
Charter standards, coping with illness and treatment, and maintaining good
health.

Information and personal health

The new health consumerism may in part be politically inspired, but a growing body of research evidence demonstrates that providing information to
patients has significant benefits. Giving patients information leads to more
truly informed consent, increased patient understanding and satisfaction,
increased compliance with treatment, and quicker and less stressful recovery
from illness and surgery. A comprehensive overview of the topic, which analyses over 300 studies, is *Communicating with patients* by Philip Ley.[7]

Information and public health policy

A further factor in the increased availability of health information for lay people has been a growing realization of the limitations of high-tech medicine in
producing further real advances in the health status of the population. This has
been recognized in a series of statements from the World Health Organization
(WHO) supporting the goal of 'health for all' by the year 2000. WHO's *Targets
for health for all*[8] sets 38 measurable targets for member states, covering not only
medical concerns (reducing disease and disability) but also the promotion of
healthy environments and healthy personal lifestyles. 'Health for all will be
achieved by people themselves. A well informed, well motivated and actively
participating community is a key element for attainment of the common goal.'

The 'health for all' approach was adopted in the UK public health strategy
The health of the nation[9] which set targets for improving health in five key areas:

coronary heart disease and stroke; cancer; mental illness; sexual health; and accidents. *The health of the nation* White Paper once again emphasized the vital role which an informed public has to play in achieving a healthier nation.

Achievement of a strategy for health for all means:
- ensuring everybody has the best possible information to understand influences on health
- the necessary support to improve health
- involving people more in decisions about options and priorities in health care.

A good deal of the rapid growth in awareness of the limitations of medical science and the importance of informed lay people can be attributed to the global AIDS pandemic, an issue which even Roy Tabor could not have predicted. Doctors and scientists have been largely powerless in the face of a grave threat to the health of the population. The most effective weapon we have in the fight against HIV infection and AIDS is information – ensuring that ordinary people are informed accurately about risks to their health, and that they adopt healthy and responsible lifestyles. The increasing importance of health information for the public was underlined most dramatically in 1987 by the delivery to every home in the UK of a government leaflet entitled *AIDS: don't die of ignorance*.

DEVELOPMENTS IN INFORMATION SERVICES

American models
The first information services on health issues for consumers began in the United States. An illuminating article by Harris[10] has traced the early chronology. More detailed analysis of the US consumer health information scene would require a separate publication (and several have been written). The most notable contributions are from Alan Rees in his comprehensive reviews of American consumer health information materials[11] and the development and management of consumer health information services in the USA.[12] The latter book also contains summaries of CHI services in Britain, Canada, Australia and New Zealand.

The first UK consumer health information services
The late 1970s saw UK library services increasingly concerned with the provision of information relevant to people's everyday lives. Public libraries began to develop community information services, many with guidance from the British Library/Library Association research project on community informa-

tion.[13] Health information was recognized as being a key element of community information but, while public librarians have always been mindful of their responsibility to the public, they were not always confident in handling medical information. For their part, medical librarians had the subject knowledge but very few were both ready and willing to open up their resources to the public. However, there were the beginnings of an enthusiasm to develop CHI services in the UK which would combine the best of both public and medical library worlds.

Lister Health Information Service
The first library service for patients to be established in the UK was the Health Information Service (HIS) based at the Lister Hospital, Stevenage.[14] During the 1980s the HIS extended its innovative work into the development of patient information collections in general practice.[15] The Lister HIS is based on an extensive collection of some 3000 subject files made up largely of cuttings from medical and popular journals. It was the subject of a detailed British Library/College of Health evaluation in 1987.[16] This study reviewed the UK and US literature on consumer health information services, and went on to evaluate the service provided by HIS. Perhaps the most interesting aspect of the report is the extensive quotation from a series of group discussions held with patients, members of voluntary groups and health professionals. The discussions revealed widespread dissatisfaction with information giving and evidence of poor communication when information is given verbally, without written back-up. Following the group discussions, use made of HIS was monitored for a month, and a comparison made with use of Help for Health in Wessex over a similar period. The report concluded that the services were becoming more similar with time, and between them they offered an appropriate model for development of CHI services in the UK.

Help for health
Closely following the Lister service, the Wessex Help for Health information service was established following a 1979 research project funded by the British Library (newly established when Roy Tabor compiled his chapter but destined to have a major effect on the development of health information services for consumers). The project drew attention to the wealth of support available to patients and the lack of an effective mechanism for communicating this information.[17] In 1991 the service became an independent charity, The Help for Health Trust, and now provides a range of CHI services to health authorities and other agencies on a contract basis.[18] Later the same year, the Help for Health model was adopted by the then Secretary of State for Health, William Waldegrave, as a basis for the national network of Regional Health

Information Services established under the Patient's Charter.

In 1988, Help for Health had received funding from the Department of Health to establish Wessex Waiting Line, a phone-in service for general practitioners and patients on waiting times for treatment throughout the Wessex Region. A database was developed which presents information on every consultant in the Region, with their waiting list for treatment ranked in order, allowing GPs to 'shop around' for treatment where the waiting list is shortest.[19] Wessex Waiting Line operates largely on a phone-in basis, but a pilot group of GPs has also been supplied with the system on a computer disk, updated quarterly. The database is also available on Family Health Services Authorities wide-area networks and on County Council networks (Hantsnet in Hampshire, and Access in Wiltshire). There is considerable potential for tying waiting list information more closely to other consumer health information, ensuring that patients waiting for treatment have access to information about support groups, patient information literature, etc., which could make their wait more bearable.[20]

The new wave of consumer health information services
For almost ten years the HIS and Help for Health were alone in the UK in providing library and information services dedicated wholly to the needs of health care consumers. Over the last few years a new wave of CHI services has developed. The reasons for this sudden flowering are various (political emphasis on consumer friendly health services, new funding sources, and availability of CHI databases such as Help for Health's Helpbox).[21] The government requirement to establish health information centres in the 14 former regions has obviously had a major impact. It is encouraging that these services are happening in a variety of settings with different client groups, making imaginative use of different funding sources and management structures.

Non-library sources of consumer health information
Libraries are by no means the only, or even the most important, source of consumer health information.[22-23]

Responsibility for providing information on health issues to the general public also rests with a variety of statutory and voluntary agencies. Community Health Councils were set up in 1974 as 'patients' watchdogs'. Based in every district health authority (HA) in the UK (200 in all), they provide information on local health services and patients' rights and handle complaints.[24] Local health education or health promotion departments have a responsibility for promotion of good health and prevention of illness in the local community. Health promotion departments adopt a variety of approaches, including sophisticated marketing techniques and 'community development' work with local self-help groups. This range of approaches is leading to recognition of an equally wide range of information needs.[25]

Outside the NHS and within the specific field of disability there has developed a network of over 100 DIAL (Disablement Information and Advice Lines) groups. These independent advice services are run by disabled people for disabled people.[26] DIALs are based on the Citizens' Advice Bureau (CAB) model. These generalist advice services usually have a paid coordinator and a number of volunteers, and are to be found in almost every town in the UK. First set up during World War Two, there are now 900 CABs, utilizing 23,000 volunteers and answering two million enquiries a year. The most common enquiries relate to social welfare, consumer issues, debt and housing.[27]

Some of the most exciting activity in the area of information provision has come from self-help groups for specific health problems. The UK has a rich heritage of voluntary activity in the sphere of health and welfare, and since the 1960s this philanthropic tradition has been complemented by a boom in the number of mutual aid groups formed by people with a common problem.[28] Growth has been particularly strong in the areas of disability, women's health and, more recently, HIV/AIDS.

New developments and current trends
After a decade of rapid development of CHI services it is worth considering where CHI services are heading. A number of clear trends can be identified, which are characteristic of the growing maturity of the specialism. These have been analysed in review articles from the British and American perspectives.[29,30] They include:

- increasing concern with the establishment of CHI networks for shared development of quality standards and training;
- development of CHI databases in a range of formats;
- extension of CHI services into new areas of quality of care and effectiveness of treatments.

Networks for quality
Consumer health information services are beginning to make an important contribution to quality and consumer choice in health care. At the same time they are also developing ethical standards[31] and applying the principles of quality assurance to their own services.[32] By 1990 it was recognized that there were now sufficient numbers of CHI services to merit closer networking to maintain current awareness, develop standards and benefit from local good practice. It was no longer good enough that CHI services were provided at all, they had to be done well. As a result an independent network organization, the

Consumer Health Information Consortium (CHIC) was launched in 1991 with a conference at Loughborough University.[33] CHIC has been instrumental in developing core standards for CHI services covering issues such as confidentiality, access, speed of response and accuracy of information.

Another contribution to the development of quality services has been the increase in training opportunities for CHI staff. A review of education and training in information management in health care published in 1992[34] included a chapter on consumer health information, describing training initiatives in areas including communication skills, information sources, disability and ethnic awareness, and stress management. Training in these areas is increasingly being provided by professional bodies, library schools and non-library agencies including National Association of Citizen's Advice Bureaux and the National Disability Information Project.

Indexes and databases

Popular medical index, edited by Sally Knight of the Health Information Service in Stevenage, was identified as the unique UK index to consumer health information by Roy Tabor in 1981. Over ten years later it remains so. Issued quarterly, with an annual cumulation, it indexes popular medical books, selected professional journals (*BMJ*, *Lancet*, *Nursing times*, *Scientific American*, etc.), and popular periodicals including women's magazines. The US equivalent is *Consumer health and nutrition index* (Oryx Press), edited by Alan Rees. This also covers specialized and general sources of consumer health information. The quarterly journal *Health libraries review* (Blackwell) includes a regular column entitled 'Consumer health information' (formerly 'Patient information'). The column provides updates on consumer health information activities in the UK and abroad, and reviews new publications.

Alan Rees's *Consumer health information source book*[11] is also available on CD-ROM as part of the *Health reference center* (Information Access). The *Health reference center* may point the way forward for easy access to consumer health information. One disk contains a shelf of consumer health reference books (a medical dictionary, a home medical encyclopedia, a book of medical tests, and a pharmacopoeia), an index to several hundred popular health and professional journals, many of them in full text, and a directory of support groups and information services. At the moment the high cost and almost exclusively American coverage makes the *Health reference center* of limited interest to British consumer health information providers. But as CD-ROM technology becomes cheaper so the potential for swift access to comprehensive information for the public grows.

Even more interesting is the development of interactive videodisc systems which involve patients in shared decision making.[35] First developed in the USA, these are now being piloted in the UK by the King's Fund Centre. The aim is to review the published research on the outcomes of different treatment options and to present this information in a way which is tailored to the individual patient's history and priorities. By providing information about the risks and benefits of different treatment options, patient's are actively involved in decisions about their own care.

Quality of care and effectiveness of treatments

Over the past ten years we have become accustomed to the increased availability of information for patients, carers and the wider public. This has been stimulated by growing expectations on the part of an increasingly consumerist public, a new political consensus on information for citizens characterized by the Patient's Charter, and considerable shifts in the attitudes of professional groups.

Yet much of the information that we supply to health consumers remains general and superficial. It does not answer the fundamental questions that we all have when making decisions about treatment and care. Patient's Charter 'league tables' illustrate this well. From June 1994, health authorities will be required to publish information for the public on the performance of hospitals. These 'league tables', published in newspapers and available in health service premises, libraries, etc., will for the first time give information about how successful hospitals are in meeting Patient's Charter targets on, for example, waiting times for treatment, assessment in accident emergency departments, cancellation of operations, and waits in outpatients etc.

The publication of these tables has been criticized as being superficial and misleading. If this information is collected and available it should of course be in the public domain. A greater concern should be: does it answer the questions the public want to know? We tell patients how long they will have to wait and what the environment will be like, but very little about whether the treatment will be any good when they do get to see the doctor. As an article in the *New England journal of medicine* observed in 1988,[36] 'Patients are forced to judge medical care on quality of amenities because they rarely have suitable information to base it on anything else'.

Patients are led to believe that the NHS provides a consistent quality of service. This is clearly not the case. Research shows significant variations in outcome of surgery depending on the choice of surgeon.[37] Furthermore, many treatments which have been carried out for years have been shown to be of questionable benefit. The new emphasis on scientific reviews of the outcome and effectiveness of treatments, being carried out by the Cochrane Centre in Oxford and elsewhere, has recently led to the value of interventions being challenged, including surgery for glue ear,[38] dilatation and curettage,[39] and cholesterol screening.[40] Yet patients are still being asked to consent to treatments (and the public to fund health care initiatives) without accurate information on their effectiveness.

In 1988 the US Congress published a report on providing information to the public on quality of medical care.[41] The report stated that providing information to consumers on quality of care

- enables people to avoid poor quality providers
- educates the public on concepts of quality
- injects competition into the medical marketplace
- stimulates clinicians to improve practice.

To enable this US consumers should have information on

- hospital mortality rates
- adverse effects of treatments, including hospital acquired infections
- disciplinary actions against doctors
- patient satisfaction with care provided.

We have come a long way in the last ten years in providing the public with information on the health services available to them, on self-help organizations, and on everyday self-care. If we are to realize the full potential of health information services for consumers we must now grasp the nettle of providing information about quality and outcomes of treatment. It will not be easy to present this information in an understandable way, but that is our challenge as information providers.

REFERENCES
1 Tudor-Hart, J., 'Two paths for medical practice', *Lancet*, **340**, 1992, 772–5
2 Coote, A., 'Public participation in decisions about health care', *Critical public health*, **4** (1), 1993, 36–49
3 *Prevention and health: everybody's business*, London, HMSO, 1976.
4 Department of Health, *Working for patients*, Cm 555, London, HMSO, 1989.
5 Labour Party, *A fresh start for health*, London, 1990.
6 Department of Health, *The Patient's Charter*, London, HMSO, 1991.
7 Ley, P., *Communicating with patients*, London, Croom Helm, 1988.
8 World Health Organization, *Targets for health for all*, Copenhagen, 1985.
9 Department of Health, *The health of the nation*, London, HMSO, 1990.
10 Harris, C. L., 'Hospital based patient education programs and the role of the hospital librarian', *Bulletin of the Medical Library Association*, **66** (2), 1978, 210–17.
11 Rees, A. M. and Hoffman, C., *Consumer health information source book*, Phoenix, Oryx Press, 1990.

12   Rees, A. M., *Managing consumer health information services*, Phoenix, Oryx Press, 1990.

13   *Community information: what libraries can do: a consultative document*, London, Library Association, 1980.

14   Knight, S., 'Letting the genie out of the bottle', *Health education journal*, **46** (3), 1987, 134–5.

15   Collings, L. and Knight, S., 'Patient information collections in general practice', *Health libraries review*, **7** (3), 1990, 166–8.

16   Kempson, E., *Informing health consumers*, London, British Library/College of Health, 1987.

17   Gann, R., *Help for health: the needs of health care practitioners for information about organisations in support of health care*, BLR&D Report 5613, London, British Library, 1981.

18   Gann, R., 'Health information in the new NHS', *Health libraries review*, **7** (4), 1990.

19   Laurance, J., 'Hospital waiting lists rise again', *Sunday Times*, 13 November 1988, 1–2.

20   Gann, R., 'Ways of keeping patients waiting in comfort', *Guardian*, 31 October 1990.

21   'Health information services: submission to LISC by the Library Association Medical health and Welfare Libraries Group', *Health libraries review*, **6** (2), 1989, 83–8.

22   Gann, R., *The health information handbook*, Aldershot, Gower, 1986.

23   Gann, R., *The health care consumer guide*, London, Faber, 1991.

24   *Representing the consumer: Community Health Councils fifteen years on*, London, Association of Community Health Councils, 1989.

25   Gann, R., 'Information services and health promotion: what libraries can do', *Health education journal*, **45** (2), 1986, 112–5.

26   Burgess, P., 'Keeping the lines open', *Community care*, 8 August 1985, 16–18.

27   Citron, J., *Citizens advice bureaux: for the community, by the community*, London, Pluto Press, 1989.

28   Wolfenden, J., *The future of voluntary organisations: report of the Wolfenden Committee*, London: Croom Helm, 1978.

29   Gann, R., 'Consumer health information: the growth of an information specialism', *Journal of documentation*, **47** (3), 1991, 284–308.

30   Rees, A., 'Communication in the physician-patient relationship', *Bulletin of the Medical Library Association*, **81** (1), 1993, 1–9.

31   Rothstein, J. A., 'Ethics and the role of the medical librarian: health care information and the consumer', *Bulletin of the Medical Library Association*, **81** (3), 1993, 253–8.

32   Gann, R., 'Assuring the quality of consumer health information', in Taylor, M. H. and Wilson, T., *Performance measurement: the quality assurance approach*, Library Association/Canadian Library Association, 1990.

33   Gann, R. and Needham, G., *Promoting choice: consumer health information in the 1990s*, Winchester, Consumer Health Information Consortium, 1992.

34 Gann, R., 'Consumer health information services', in Brittain, J. M. and Abbott, W., *Information management and technology in health care: a guide to education and training*, London, Taylor Graham, 1992.

35 Kasper, J. F., Mulley, A. G. & Wennberg, J. E., 'Developing shared decision-making programs to improve quality of health care', *QRB*, June 1992, 183–90.

36 Elwood, P. M., 'Outcomes management: a technology of patient experience', *New England journal of medicine*, **318** (23), 1988, 1197–1202.

37 McArdle, C. S., 'Impact of variability among surgeons on postoperative morbidity and mortality and ultimate survival', *British medical journal*, **302**, 1991, 1501–5.

38 'The treatment of glue ear in children', *Effective health care*, No 4, November 1992.

39 Coulter, A., 'Diagnostic dilatation and curettage: is it used appropriately?', *British medical journal*, **306**, 1993, 236–9.

40 Sheldon, T., 'Big screen ending', *Health service journal*, **103** (5356), 1993, 32–3.

41 US Congress Office of Technology Assessment, *The quality of medical care: information for consumers*, Washington, DC, 1988.

7 Planning and presenting the library

❖ *Anne M. K. Collins*

The way in which the library is to be presented begins at the planning stage. The planning and design of a new library is an exercise in librarianship. The technical details are best left to the experts on architecture, building, lighting, ventilation, information technology (IT) and so on, but the librarian must contribute professional knowledge and experience if the end result is to be an efficient and pleasant library. It is essential that the librarian be involved from the earliest stages of planning because only the librarian, among all the experts, is in a position to identify the requirements of a successful library.

PREPARATION

For most librarians, planning a new library, or even remodelling an old one, is a rare experience. It provides the opportunity to re-examine the mission, objectives, collection policy, staffing and service provision of the library. It may be that none of those involved has planned a library before. In the excitement of planning one's 'own' new library, it is important not to neglect the value of a second professional opinion. Never be the only librarian involved in planning a library. Not only are two heads better than one, especially in tackling problems, errors and omissions, but two voices are stronger than one in the event of disagreements with architects or authorities such as library committee chairs, clinical tutors or college principals.

In choosing a colleague for consultation or membership of the planning team, look out for someone with experience of planning a library and living with the consequences. NHS regional librarians are a good source of planning experience covering a wide range of circumstances and equally good as a source of contacts with other colleagues.

It is also very useful to look at other libraries and to collect ideas about arrangements that have worked well, or not so well. There are also other ideas to be gleaned from other buildings such as banks, shops and hotels, all of which are designed to provide a service. The Library Brief must provide the design team with all the details of the library's requirements. Even the most obvious (to the librarian) should be written down. The Department of Health

Design Briefing System, published in notebook form to accompany its Health Briefing Notes provides a useful *aide-mémoire* for this part of the process.[1a, 1b]

Some time should be spent reading about library planning. Metcalf[2] is an important source of reference and includes useful appendices containing data, a glossary and an annotated bibliography. Thompson[3] is a useful source and Doran[4] provides an up-to-date review of the literature.

Whether planning a new library or remodelling an existing one, many of the considerations are the same. Since the design of the library should be based upon its objectives, it is necessary to consider what the library must provide. Certain features are common to all libraries whether they be in teaching hospitals, postgraduate medical centres or colleges of health, varying only in scale. There must be places for readers to sit, with surfaces upon which they can work, a catalogue must be available and there must be a service desk where readers' questions can be dealt with and where the issue and return of loans can be recorded. There must be somewhere for the library staff to work and for the accommodation of a stock of books and the display of current periodicals. There should also be facilities for photocopying, using audiovisual materials, displays and exhibitions. IT now has a place in every type of library for information retrieval, public access catalogues, the use of networks to link buildings, housekeeping and office functions.

There are four aspects to be considered - the people to be served, the services that are to be provided, the materials that are to be housed, and the relationships between them.

PLANNING FOR READERS

Space requirements
The number of potential readers will determine the size of the library. The authority responsible for financing the library building may have a minimum standard allocation of space based upon the number of readers. For example the University Grants Committee allowed 2.3 m² per reader seat or 1.25 m² for each full time equivalent (FTE) student,[5] while the Department of Health guidelines[1a, 1b] refer to Thompson[3] for the calculation of areas but provide some useful ratios on which to base the calculations. The Library Association's recommended standard for libraries in hospitals in 1972[6] was that 2 m², including a table and chair, should be allowed for each reader. The shift to student centred learning makes the ratios of potential users to number of reading places suggested in these 1980s documents unreliable for any library used by students. The growth of IT in libraries, both for housekeeping tasks and for readers, has made a radical rethink of space allocation essential.

The pattern of use of the reader population will also affect planning decisions; for example, if a large proportion of the users are students with a timetable of lectures, there will inevitably be a marked fluctuation in use, with many students entering and leaving at the beginning or end of lecture periods. The entrances and the service desk must be designed to cope with this maximum flow of readers under these conditions.

Location

The location of the library is important and a very strong case should be put for the selection of a suitable site. It should be as near to its users as possible but it should not be so located that it becomes a thoroughfare.

The library should be on one level, but if this is not possible there must be lifts between the floors so that loaded book trolleys can be moved around easily. For small changes of level there must be ramps that can be negotiated with a book trolley.

Another aspect of the location of the library is its relation to other facilities. The creature comforts of the readers must be catered for and, unless they are available close by, toilet and cloakroom facilities should be provided. The provision of a snack bar is not a library function but it is useful to have an eating place within walking distance for those who must spend several hours studying.

A different, but nevertheless important, feature of the location of a library is the use made of the floors above, where a library forms part of a larger building. The danger of water damage to the books if laboratories are located above the library is not inconsiderable for, as Fry[7] pessimistically states 'every laboratory sink runs over once every eight years'. The same danger is present wherever water is being used, for example toilets, canteens or bar facilities. Flat roofed buildings are notorious for their less-than-perfect water repellent features, so a free-standing building should, if possible, have a pitched roof.

There is often demand for round-the-clock access to the library for clinical staff and, if this facility is to be made available then the library must be sited in an area which is open throughout the 24 hours and has lighted access corridors. If the requirement is really for a place to work rather than for access to the whole library collection it is worth creating, at the planning stage, a room that can be made available when the rest of the library is locked. If this can be achieved and will satisfy the demand, the library stock will be much better protected.

PRESENTING THE SERVICE

The arrangements of the different functions within the library should be designed for the maximum convenience of the users and the most efficient use of the facilities.

Public areas
In the public areas of the library, those categories of materials and functions which are most heavily used should be located nearest to the entrance. It is important that readers should have an immediate picture, upon entering the library, of the basic services they are likely to require. The main features of the library – the service desk, the catalogue, the book stock, the periodicals and the reading places – should either be clearly visible or be clearly signposted or located on a plan.

Service desk
This area is the nerve centre of the library and as such it must be exceptionally well planned. The service desk has to perform numerous and vital functions in the library. Not only must it have plentiful and well planned space for the issue and return of loans, dictated by the type of loan system in use, but its staff may deal with interlibrary loan requests, perform a readers' advisory function, or control short loan or reference collections. There should be ample space close by for the storage of books, not only returned books awaiting shelving but also reserved books and, if one exists, the reference or short loan collection. Small libraries operating a system of self-service loans should have an appropriately equipped place for this which should include instructions in the working of the system. There must be space for book trolleys to be manoeuvred within the area and also easy passage for them to other parts of the library.

The type of issue system in use will have the major influence on the design of the issue desk. If it is manual, it is important to ask, at the planning stage, will it be automated in the future? The height of the counter should be comfortable for both the staff and the users, but will depend largely upon whether the staff will be sitting at normal desk height or standing or sitting at 'bar stool' height. The latter arrangement requires a height of about 900 mm, but if they staff sitting at desk height then about 660 mm is appropriate, and this will require a raised ledge at the front for readers, set at about 900 mm. A study in 1983 by Grey and Wilson[8] found that a flat surface at the higher height was the best solution, with staff sitting on high stools with firm footrests. The stools should have adjustable back supports and variable seat heights. The top surface of the counter, if computer terminals are in use, should be about 1500 mm × 800 mm for each terminal.[9] Books, and especially heavy bound journals, need to be passed backwards and forwards to have barcodes read and date labels stamped, so a uniform flat surface is best. If money changes hands there should be a secure drawer or a till. Tailor-made drawers and pigeon-holes designed to organize and facilitate the use of counter stationery and records will all improve the efficiency of this part of the library.

The service area should be designed to give enough length so that staff can provide an efficient service at peak times, taking account of the number of simultaneous transactions that are likely to take place, but it must also be possible to operate it efficiently with a reduced staff at slack times. A telephone must be conveniently positioned so that it is accessible to the member of staff on duty and, if the library covers a large enough area to warrant it, a warning bell to indicate impending closure is useful. A Tannoy system is better still as this gives scope for relaying other messages to users, for example paging. A box for returned loans is valuable in unmanned libraries. This should be designed so that books deposited in it can only be removed by the librarian, thus ensuring that loan records can be cancelled before the book is borrowed again. Such a box can be useful for out-of-hours returns even if the library is only open when staffed. In this case it should be movable so that it can be placed outside when the library is closed.

Entrance and exit checks
If an electronic security system is to be installed, this should be considered when the issue counter is being designed. The interaction between automated systems and exit check devices has long been a cause of concern. The solution of separating exit checks and issue desks by a considerable distance minimizes the risk of interference but increases the difficulty for staff, since it is necessary for them to be close to the exit check if it is activated. Screening of the equipment can reduce the distance by which they have to be separated.

Display areas
The smallest of libraries should have a notice-board which may be used to display notices of professional interest to the users or to publicize aspects of the library service, recent accessions, etc. If more space is available, a set of screens and a glass-topped display cabinet allow more scope for exhibitions or displays relating to the library. They must be located where they will attract the attention of the users as they enter or leave the library, because they are unlikely to be coming to the library solely to look at a display. Another type of display is the dispenser for library leaflets, hospital or campus map etc. This too should be located where it will be seen by anyone entering the library.

Catalogue
If there is only one copy of the catalogue it will be used by both readers and staff, so it must be sited where it is possible for the readers to progress from it to the shelves while the staff should have easy access to it when cataloguing and also when they are performing reference functions for readers. The practice of placing catalogues in large open areas is not always easy with computer catalogues because of access to power and communications, and positioning

close to walls or columns is more suitable. The space required for a computer catalogue terminal includes, as a minimum, space for the equipment itself and space for the reader to use a notebook. A table-top surface of about 700 × 1000 mm is recommended as sufficient for this.[1b] Extra space will be needed if a printer is also provided. Tables for computer catalogue terminals can be at a height either for sitting (650–690 mm) or for standing (900 mm). The theory is that if they have to stand readers will move on and free the terminal as soon as possible, but this is not proven at this stage of computer catalogue development. At least one terminal at sitting height should be available for extensive catalogue consultation or for disabled readers.

Current periodicals
Current periodicals are a vital aspect of the library service and the way in which they are displayed should reflect this. Readers often like to browse among the current periodicals and it is a good idea to provide easy chairs in this area of the library.

Meetings and library instruction
If it is planned to hold meetings or to provide any kind of formal instruction in the library a room should be designated for this purpose. It should be furnished in such a way that it can be used for meetings or, by simple rearrangement, for lectures. Stacking chairs will provide this flexibility. To allow for the use of teaching aids, such as overhead projectors and computer facilities, the room must be equipped with the necessary power points, computer network connections, black-outs and lighting controls. The danger of trailing cables should be borne in mind when planning outlets for power and network connections. If separate space is not available for this purpose, it may be feasible to use a room set aside to house the library's historical collection or the audio-visual room as a seminar room. This combination of functions is practicable because none of them will make constant demands upon the accommodation. Libraries in postgraduate centres and colleges of health may be able to use the facilities of the centre or the college for meetings or lectures.

Group work areas
In libraries serving students, fundamental changes in the methods of teaching and learning have created changes in the ways the library is used. Project based learning has brought groups of students, working together, into the library. This deviates from the traditional quiet study atmosphere of the library and can cause friction between the two types of user. If a separate room cannot be provided, an area designated for group work, screened if possible from other parts of the library, will help to defuse the situation.

Audiovisual facilities
Audiovisual facilities should be in a location where their use will not disturb the users of more conventional library material while remaining pleasant for those watching or listening. This may be either a room dedicated to this use or the area set aside for group work. if one exists. The use of headphones will minimize the disturbance. Users of the equipment may need supervision or instruction, so facilities should not be located too far from library staff. Security is another consideration to be taken into account when selecting the location.

Paging
One requirement peculiar to the library serving health service personnel is the possibility that some of the users may need to be paged or summoned to the telephone. Doctors on call often spend some of their time in the library. If their hospital 'bleep' system is within range, their only requirement will be to have access to a telephone. If doctors cannot be contacted in this way it puts a strain on library staff time if they have to call people themselves. Internal paging systems are available and in a large library this is worth consideration. It is preferable to have the wiring for this carried out during the construction of the library. Alternative, less costly, methods may be to designate a specific area where anyone on call can work, or to install a notice-board where names can be written up if there is a message.

Photocopying
Photocopying machines require supervision and servicing by library staff. They generate a considerable amount of noise, heat and waste paper, and these aspects should all be taken into consideration when locating them. In a large library a separate room is necessary with adequate ventilation, work surfaces where papers can be sorted, guillotined and stapled, adequate storage space for paper supplies and for the disposal of waste paper. Readers will not wish to carry materials long distances from the shelves to copy them and library staff will be in demand to replenish paper supplies and clear the occasional paper jams, so the siting of a photocopying room requires careful thought.

Staff working areas
If the library is to function efficiently, the staff workroom areas must have adequate space for all the preparatory activities to be carried out. Even in a small hospital library, where limited room is available, space must be set aside for the librarian to prepare material for the shelves. Proportionately more space may need to be allocated to this in a small library than in a larger one. Space should be provided for plenty of shelves, adequate storage , ample work tops for binding preparation, packing and unpacking, and book processing and

repair, as well as desk space for the staff. A logical flow of materials from one process to another in the staff workroom area should be considered when the location of accommodation is being planned. Conveniently situated sinks and toilets, as well as the provision of secure personal lockers for the staff, will also contribute to efficiency.

PRESENTING MATERIALS
The library provides space for books, journals, and other materials. There must be adequate space for the existing stock but also room for at least ten years' growth.

Books and bound journals
Medical books and journals require more space than most, and the average number of medical books which will fill a standard shelf is 15.[10] Stacks 2200 mm high with seven shelves, each 255 mm in depth, will make full use of the available space. The shelves must, of course, be adjustable. Loaded stacks are very heavy, and if compact shelving is used this loading increases even more. The recommended practice[11] is to construct all library floors so that they are strong enough to carry a live load of up to 150 lb/ft² (7.324 kN/m²). To allow for future rearrangements, the whole floor should meet this specification.

Current periodicals
Current periodicals should be displayed in a fashion that will encourage browsing and the most satisfactory way of achieving this is to place them on flat sloping shelves. It is usually convenient to store unbound parts of the same volume close by and many manufacturers supply units for this purpose. The slope is hinged and the shelf can be lifted to provide access to a storage shelf underneath. These have the disadvantages of being rather bulky and also that lifting the hinged shelf disturbs other periodicals displayed there and other readers who may be using issues on the same slope. A more compact method is sloping shelves alternating with flat shelves on normal uprights. The flat shelves can then be used to store piles of unbound issues immediately below the current copy of each title.

Abstracting and indexing publications
These publications are a less significant part of the collection than they were, having been ousted to some extent by electronic materials such as CD-ROM. They are nevertheless an important part of any collection, and require different treatment because they will be used in a different way. This material grows faster than other parts of the collection so there must be plenty of space for expansion. For example *Cumulated index medicus* for 1992 occupies 125 mm of

shelf space as compared with 75 mm in 1982.

Readers will consult many volumes at the shelves so it is necessary to provide suitable accommodation. One method is to attach desk plates to the shelves at around 1100 mm, and provide stools of the correct height. Alternatively, it has been found to be satisfactory to house the materials in low shelf units with wooden tops at a comfortable height for use as a consultation shelf by a standing reader.

Non-book materials
Audiovisual materials need special storage units because their shape does not lend itself to storage on conventional shelves, and magnetic tapes or discs should not be stored on metal shelves because this can interfere with the quality of the recordings. Specially designed storage equipment is available in wood or plastic for housing slide collections, audiotapes, videotapes, compact discs, and similar material. The selection may be influenced by the policy of the library, depending on whether readers have free access to the materials or whether they are issued by library staff.

Rare books, archives or special collections
If the library includes a rare book or other special collection, then provision will have to be made for this material to provide both security and the necessary environmental conditions for the preservation of the paper and bindings. Locked, glass-fronted cases provide protection for the stock while at the same time leaving the often attractive bindings visible. If the collection is to be housed in a separate room it should be possible to control temperature, humidity and exposure to sunlight in order to preserve the material. Doran[12] describes a well planned archive and special collection.

Information technology
Computers are used by both readers and staff for information retrieval from CD-ROMs and videodiscs, as well as through networked links to remote sources of information; use of personal computers (PCs) is increasing, and there has been a growth in computer assisted learning using expert systems and other interactive software. This increases the need for flexibility. There must be access to power and telecommunications and this is best discussed with local IT or computer staff. Completely flexible provision is impractical and plans will have to arrive at compromises. It is possible to obtain 'wire management' furniture with built-in trunking for power and data cables, but this is expensive and some other form of trunking may have to suffice. An excellent document on the topic was produced by the SCONUL Advisory Committee on Buildings,[13] which also contains a useful bibliography.

LAYOUT

Having defined the space required for the stock, the readers, the equipment and the services, and also having set out the specific requirements of each, the detailed layout of the library can be planned.

The keynote of this part of the exercise is flexibility. The stock may grow more rapidly in one area than another because of unexpected developments, the emphasis on different aspects of service may change and unforeseen demands may be made upon the space available. It will be necessary to have a clear plan for the present but this should not preclude changes in the future.

After fixing the entrance and the location of the service desk, areas should be designated for shelving and seating. The siting of staff work areas and other special functions can all be defined on the plan, taking into account their relation to one another and their special requirements.

Having identified the number of seats and the length of shelving required, they must be fitted into the space available. The positioning of windows and doors and of supporting pillars will have a direct bearing upon the final arrangements. Within these constraints, it is wise to lay out the stacks to fit in as many as possible, while they are still comfortable to use for readers and staff.

Shelving

Aisles between stacks must be wide enough for the bottom shelf to be adequately lit and for a reader to bend to see the book labels on that shelf. The use of the collection influences the size of aisle needed. Another local consideration is whether it is deemed necessary to get a book trolley down the aisle for shelving or whether the ranges are short enough to allow shelving from the end or from a central aisle. The depth of shelves being used and the space available will also influence the decision; Metcalf[4] says that an aisle width of 838–864 mm is adequate but that if the needs of wheelchair users are taken into account an aisle width of 1067 mm is required. Taking the smaller figure and with ranges 500 mm deep a width of 1370 mm on centres is necessary. (Metcalf[5] defines 'on centres' as 'the distance between the centres of two pieces of similar equipment or construction placed parallel to each other. Generally used in connection with stack ranges, carrels in a reading area, tables in a reading room . . . '.)

Long ranges are best avoided, particularly in heavily used areas, and a run of six shelves (6 m) is probably the longest that should be adopted without a central aisle in a large library, while a run of four shelves may be too much in the smallest library.

Compact or mobile shelving, while seemingly an attractive way of maximizing storage space, is expensive and is unsuitable for open access areas on the grounds of inconvenience to readers and staff, who will have to wait to gain access to a set of shelves while another reader occupies a different aisle.

The book stacks should be stable and it may be necessary to brace the whole area because, if shelves are loaded unevenly there is a danger of one stack tipping and producing a domino effect.

Shelves for current periodicals should be further apart, say 1070 mm–1500 mm, particularly if sloping shelves are used for display, because readers will need to be able to stand back to look at what is available. In a small library it is often better to have a single row of display shelves, perhaps arranged on three sides around easy-chair seating.

Seating

Seating should be distributed around the library so that readers need not walk far with the material they have taken from the shelves. A variety of seating types should be provided to cater for the different needs and tastes of users. This should range from a limited number of easy chairs and perhaps a few low tables in the browsing area close to the current periodicals, to carrels. Easy chairs and low tables provide a relaxed atmosphere for scanning journals, while carrels, which consist of desks with visual barriers and include a book-shelf above the desk, are designed for readers who need seclusion for their work. Conventional desks or tables are preferred by some readers for all types of work in the library. If space is available, a small number of lockable study-rooms may be provided, but open carrels usually give enough privacy for those who want it and take up less floor-space.

Flexibility is again important when planning seating layouts. One method of achieving this is to build up the different types of accommodation from two or three basic units. Tables big enough for one reader can be arranged in a variety of combinations to provide accommodation for, say, six readers. They can also be combined with similar tables fitted with a back plate to produce semi-private workplaces. More secluded working places can be created by the same size tables fitted with back and half-side panels. If these units are combined, a fairly large number of readers can work in relative privacy in a small area. Units for use in this way should have a working surface of at least 900 mm × 570 mm. Carrels should be rather larger and should provide at least 1.2 m² of working surface. A bookshelf should be incorporated into the screen round the desk-top but care must be taken that its size and position do not cut off the light to the working surface. As a rough guide, a shelf 200 mm deep and 250 mm above the working surface is satisfactory.

The height of the screens around any of these types of working places should be adequate to cut off vision for the user when seated but it need not be so high that it creates a claustrophobic impression. Screens 470 mm above the table-top have been found to be adequate.

Public access technology
Readers using IT equipment will require greater space. A rule of thumb is that an increase of at least 50% will be required for desk-top surfaces providing IT facilities, but this may be a conservative figure. Only a percentage of study spaces will need to be of the necessary size and suitably equipped for IT use. The proportion will vary depending on the institution. If study spaces are located in open areas the most appropriate furniture for IT equipment is an open carrel of about 700 × 1250 mm with surrounds of sufficient height to deaden keyboard sounds and equipped with ducting for cables.

Variety
Readers like to study in different types of environment and it has been found that all the variations possible using basic table units are favoured by different readers. Some readers habitually work in the same place while others have different preferences according to what they are doing at any particular time. Clearly, a small library will be unable to accommodate many reading places, but even so, variety should be provided. Even three seats should be made as different as possible with, for example, one in a corner, one in the open and an easy chair.

Some examples of plans of libraries of very different sizes are shown in Figures 7.1 and 7.2 to demonstrate how the basic principles of layout apply whatever the size.

LIGHTING
The provision of adequate lighting is complex and should be left to the architect. The librarian can, however, insist upon certain minimum requirements. These have increased over the years and the most recent recommendation is a standard of 300–500 lux for study areas.[16] The same level of illumination is recommended for the use of visual display units (VDUs)[17] so that it should be possible to use IT equipment in the same study area. It is essential that the spine lettering on books on the bottom shelves can be read and the needs of library staff, many of whom will be working with computer equipment, must also be remembered. A guarantee of adequate illumination should be obtained before any lighting scheme is agreed.

Although a certain amount of natural lighting may be available, this will have to be supplemented on dull days and in the evening and can be discounted in calculations. To make the best use of the available natural light, reading places should be near the windows. Stacks should be at right angles to the source of light to reduce the blocking effect.

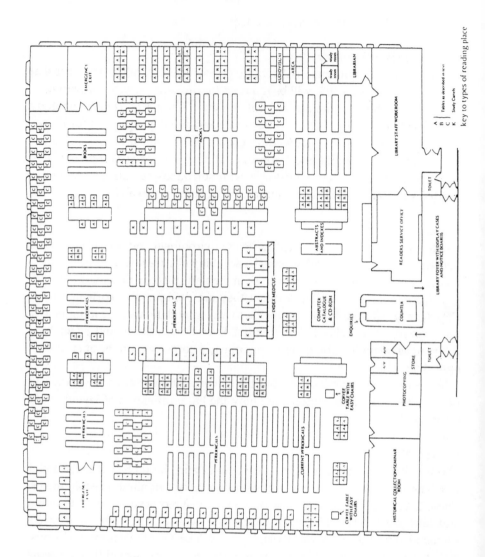

Fig. 7.1   Plan based on the Medical and Dental Library, University of Leeds

Lighting over stack areas should run at right angles to the stacks or else must be carefully aligned with the aisles in order to provide adequate illumination for all the shelves. The latter method could be a danger to future flexibility as the existing aisles must be maintained. If the shelving is to be fitted with canopies, this will affect the lighting and must be taken into account in the planning.

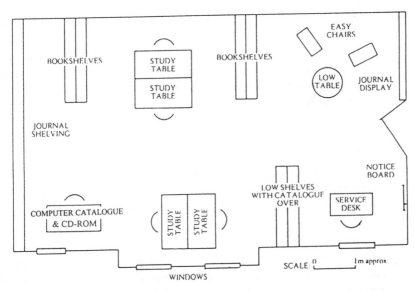

Fig. 7.2 A small library where, in spite of limited space, a variety of working places has been provided

Over notice-boards and in special display areas it is useful to have special lighting, such as adjustable spot-lights, that can be used to enhance the display.

The switches for all the lights should be together on one panel so that they can be easily switched on or off from a central point, but at least one light should be controlled from a switch near the door that is used by staff, so that opening or closing the library can be accomplished without difficulty.

OTHER EQUIPMENT

In addition to the shelving, seating, staff desks and workstations for IT equipment, the planning should also make provision for many smaller items of equipment. Book trolleys, light alloy steps, Kicksteps, notice-boards, display cabinets, and ample storage space for stationery, files and equipment should all be included in the list of necessary equipment. It is much easier to obtain these items during the planning and equipping of a new library than later on, so it is advisable to allow a generous margin for future developments in the initial estimates. A large library with many metres of shelving requires a surprisingly large number of book trolleys and Kicksteps. The number of trolleys required is largely governed by the number of books likely to be returned on one day – a trolley will only take 30 volumes comfortably on the top shelves – and the staff available to carry out reshelving.

A variety of book trolleys is available and different styles are convenient for different purposes, so it is advisable to have some with flat shelves and some with a central division to use for books standing upright. All trolleys should have wheels with a diameter of at least 180 mm for ease of movement, particularly if the floor is to be carpeted. The wheels should be positioned to provide the maximum stability and one pair should be pivoted so that the trolley can be easily steered. Trolley sizes should be selected in relation to the size of aisles where they are to be used and the types of material to be transported, and should not be so large that, when loaded, they are heavy to push.

SIGNPOSTING

The guiding of a library plays a very important part in its effective use. This begins outside the library, with adequate signposting to bring the readers there and to provide information about opening hours. Once inside the library, the signs should give readers a feeling of security by showing clearly and simply where to find things.

Signs and guides fall into two categories – directional and instructional. Directional signs may be designed to guide readers to the right area or to help them locate specific items. A plan of the library, prominently displayed close to the entrance, helps readers to orientate themselves and to gain a picture of the spatial relationships, while signs with directional arrows either suspended from the ceiling or mounted on walls or pillars allow them to find their way about. Many readers seem reluctant to admit to not knowing their way around, but find signs helpful and welcome.

Detailed labelling on the ends of stacks may be limited to the inclusive titles of the journals or the classmarks of the books shelved in that range, or may list everything to be found there. Flags attached at right angles to the shelves can be read from a distance if large lettering is used. Plates attached to the ends of the stacks allow more detailed information to be provided but usually have to be read at close quarters.

The functions of rooms should be clearly indicated on the doors and other features, such as catalogues, an enquiry desk and the issue desk, should also be conspicuously labelled. It should be possible to read these signs from some distance and from as wide an angle as possible, and this can often be achieved most effectively by suspending signs from the ceiling.

Instructional signs must also be clearly legible, but generally from a closer range. These will include information about how to use the catalogue and various items of equipment such as audiovisual equipment and photocopiers.

All notices and signs in the library should be well made and professional looking. The best effect is produced if they can be standardized so that the same typeface is used throughout and there is a clear sense of continuity. Negative instructions, the 'do not' notices, should be kept to a minimum, but if they are necessary they can sometimes be rephrased, for example, 'Thank you for not smoking'.

FINISHING TOUCHES
The colour scheme and the finishes of the furniture can add immeasurably to the overall impression of the library and to the comfort of those who work in it. Architects tend to have very strong ideas about colours and it is important to ensure that they have taken into account the material that is to be housed in the library and the functions it is to fulfil. Readers do not want to be distracted by extremes of colour but nor do they want to be surrounded by a dull, lifeless room.

Carpet on the floors not only gives a feeling of comfort but provides effective noise reduction and is easy to maintain and clean. Carpet should always be antistatic. The colour of flooring has a substantial impact on overall light levels.

The materials and colours selected for shelving, reading tables and chairs and the issue counter should all contribute to the overall picture and give an impression of a well planned whole. Metal shelves are available in a wide range of colours and should be carefully chosen since they form such a major part of the library. If seats are to be upholstered a washable fabric should be chosen. Table-tops should be easy to work on so the surface should be smooth and non-reflective. A dark coloured table-top is often held to be more restful, but if the room tends to be gloomy a light coloured wood such as beech might be preferable.

PUBLICITY
When a new library has been created, or when a new look is taken at an existing one, there is scope for presenting the library by publicizing the services it can offer and by the use of instruction leaflets, library newsletters, posters and even electronic information through networked information systems.

The widespread availability of word processing, desk-top publishing and laser printers has brought professional looking publications within the reach of most libraries. Well thought out and nicely produced guides to different aspects of the library service, using a standard format to give continuity, can be used to enhance the profile of the library.

Computer based 'point of information' library orientation and guidance systems can be developed using commercially available authoring software, and will provide both an introduction to the library for new users and also locational and factual information for other users.[18]

If the library is part of an institution that has a networked information system, the library can use this to publicize itself with details such as opening hours and news about exhibitions or other special events.

CONCLUSION

When a new library has been created or an existing one has been remodelled, the planning process is not over. Presenting a library is a continuous process made necessary by the frequent changes and developments that take place throughout the life of a library. Whenever alterations are made it is important to return to the first principles in order to keep the overall picture right.

REFERENCES

1a Great Britain, Department of Health, *Accommodation for education and training,* Health Building Note 42, London, HMSO, 1989.

1b Great Britain, Department of Health, *Accommodation for education and training,* Design Briefing System Notebook 42, London, HMSO, 1989.

2   Metcalf, K. D., *Planning academic and research library buildings,* 2nd edn, by P. D. Leighton and D. C. Weber, Chicago, American Library Association, 1986.

3   Thompson, G., *Planning and design of library buildings,* 3rd edn, London, Butterworth-Architecture, 1989.

4   Doran, B. M., 'Planning a new medical library: a personal perspective and review of the literature', *Health libraries review,* **6** (2), 1989, 63–75.

5   Atkinson, R. (Chairman), *Capital provision for university libraries: report of a working party,* London, HMSO, 1976.

6   The Library Association, *Hospital libraries: recommended standards for libraries in hospitals,* London, Library Association, 1972.

7   Fry, A., 'Library planning, furniture, and equipment', in Annan, G. L. and Felter, J. W. (eds.), *Handbook of medical library practice,* 3rd edn, Chicago, Medical Library Association, 1970, 291.

8   Grey, S. M. and Wilson, J. R., *Ergonomics of library issue desks,* Final Report, (BLR&D Report 5849), London, British Library, 1983.

9   SCONUL Advisory Committee on Buildings, *Information technology and library buildings,* SCONUL Doc 89/52R, London, SCONUL, 1989.

10 Metcalf, K. D., *op. cit.,* 559.

11 Metcalf, K. D., *op. cit.,* 327.

12 Doran, B. M., *op. cit.,* 72–3.

13 SCONUL, *op. cit.*

14 Metcalf, K. D., *op. cit.,* 138.

15 Metcalf, K. D., *op. cit.,* 579.

16 Chartered Institute of Building Services, Lighting Division, *CIBS lighting guide: libraries,* London, CIBS, 1982.

17 Chartered Institute of Building Services, *CIBS technical memorandum on lighting for visual display units,* London, CIBS, 1981.

18 Biddiscombe, R. and Watson, M., 'How Tommy the Tome is treading on some toes: a multimedia approach to helping library users', *Library Association record,* **95** (9), Technology Supplement, 1993, 11–13.

8   Computerized literature searching

❖   *Susan Gilbert*

Computer searching dates from the 1960s and the so-called information explosion of that time. Computers were first employed in the abstracting and indexing industry to speed the production process of hard copy products such as *Chemical abstracts* and *Index medicus*. This resulted in computer files of bibliographic data which could also be searched.

Early searches were not interactive. They were performed in batch mode at specialist centres. No modifications could be made to the search during the search process, and the user might have to wait several weeks to receive the printout.

The next major step was the introduction of interactive or online searching. The searcher could now interrogate the database directly and receive a report on each search query immediately. Searches could be adapted and modified as they progressed in the light of the reports. The databases were mounted on large mainframe computers by hosts such as Lockheed (later DIALOG). They were usually accessed using a dumb terminal. This terminal would be connected to the telecommunications network using a telephone and acoustic coupler to convert the signals. The cost of these searches was relatively high and it was only the larger libraries that introduced this service in the 1970s.

In the 1970s and 1980s, the story mirrors that of the computing world in general: more sophisticated equipment, faster communications and processing speeds, more reliable telecommunications networks, and rapidly falling search costs. In the 1980s, small medical and health science libraries could afford to introduce online services.

Charging for online searching was related to the length of time spent online. Speed of searching was therefore an important factor in keeping down search costs. The search interfaces were command driven so a knowledge of the interface was essential for searching. This is still the case, but competition from other sources is challenging database hosts to look at and revise their interfaces and charging mechanisms. However, in the 1980s it was very much accepted that online searching required the services of a skilled intermediary, usually the librarian. The introduction of CD-ROM (compact disc – read only memory) databases in the late 1980s was to revolutionize the established pattern of computer searching.

CD-ROM allowed large databases, previously requiring mainframe computer storage, to be compressed on to a small number of optical discs. These discs could be made available to libraries or individuals on a subscription basis, rather as the printed versions of the indexes were marketed. Once the discs and equipment required for searching have been purchased there are no additional search costs. Fast searching is no longer essential. The search interface provided with these CD products is menu rather than command driven. Expert searching is no longer essential. CD-ROM is a product designed with the end user rather than the search intermediary in mind. The move from mediated to end user searching has been rapid. CD-ROM products have become hugely popular with health sciences staff and students. The spread of CD-ROM through health science libraries has been the main change in computer searching in the early 1990s.

EQUIPMENT FOR COMPUTER SEARCHING
The basic equipment requirements for accessing remote databases online are a personal computer and communications software. If the searching is to be carried out using the telephone to connect to the telecommunications network, a modem will also be required. Users with access to the Joint Academic Network (JANET), which offers gateways to the telecommunications network and direct access to some remote hosts, will just need a connection locally to JANET. As with all computer systems, the advice is to purchase the most computing power you can afford. Today's new machine is going to look old fashioned in two to three years' time. Check all the specifications from database hosts and telecommunications networks, and make these available to the equipment supplier. Ask for a demonstration of the equipment accessing the required remote service before purchasing.

There are many communications packages on the market, PROCOMM Plus, Crosstalk, PC Anywhere and Headline being a few examples in use in the health sciences. This type of software allows the personal computer (PC) to emulate a terminal so that it can access the remote host. As well as performing this function, several other features are also desirable. The software should allow for the storage and automatic execution of complex log on procedures, and re-execute them if they fail first time. It should allow for searches to be entered before logging on to the host. It should also be possible to transmit the search line by line. It should be possible to log searches and search results to disk.

The equipment required for CD-ROM searching is a PC and one or more CD-ROM players. These latter come supplied with CD-ROM interface cards and the software, such as Microsoft Extensions, required to allow the PC to access the compact disc. Check the specifications of the machine required to run the CD-ROM databases carefully. CD systems are becoming more and more demanding on computing power and memory, particularly with the popularity of and the move towards Windows interfaces. CD-ROM suppliers will advise on equipment requirements for their databases.

When purchasing CD-ROM drives, consider the following. How many drives are required? A multidisc database such as *MEDLINE* can be infuriating to search year by year. Would it be better to buy a version that allows searching over a number of years? These will require three or four CD drives to operate. Can the chosen CD players operate together in this way? Would a CD tower holding eight or more discs be more appropriate? Is it better to have an internal or external CD drive? The former are neater, the latter more flexible if drives have to be swapped between machines for any reason. Are they mainly to be used by end users and are the users going to need to change the discs? If so, how robust are the drives, particularly the disc loading parts? Do the discs stay protected in caddies throughout the search? Can they be sealed in the caddies in some way (if only with Sellotape) to discourage users from investigating further? At least the advent of 3½ in floppy disks has rescued the librarian from the regular chore of extracting compact discs from the old 5¼ in floppy drives.

DATABASE HOSTS

Database hosts offering access to a variety of biomedical databases are Data-Star DIALOG (Europe), the result of a recent merger, BRS, DIMDI and BLAISE-LINK. The databases available are mostly bibliographic. Full text databases are far more common in the legal and financial fields. Searching these databases is normally via a command language, although hosts are now introducing end user menus. The command language varies from host to host. Charges are made for online time and for each reference printed, and there is usually a royalty charge for the database producer. Because of competition from other sources, there have been moves to reduce the online time charges to encourage browsing, and not to penalize the less expert searcher. To balance this, charges for references printed have usually been increased. It is important to realize that charges vary greatly from database to database, although they may be accessed via the same host. *MEDLINE* and all the other National Library of Medicine databases are considered to be in the public domain and are thus relatively cheap to search, while searches on *BIOSIS* or *Psychinfo* will run up significantly higher charges, as will the management databases.

A major problem with online searching via remote hosts is its open ended demand on the library budget. This has led to the questionable practice of recharging searches to the readers in many libraries. CD-ROM subscriptions and equipment might be expensive but they are fixed costs and, as such, can more easily be included in a budget proposal. The obvious competitive move would seem to be for database hosts to start offering fixed rate access to their databases. Few moves seem to have been made in this direction as yet.

In the academic community, the Combined Higher Education Software Team (CHEST) has negotiated fixed cost access to several databases of interest to the health sciences. They have done this in two ways: firstly, by arranging for databases to be mounted at Bath University by Bath Information and Data Services (BIDS), searchable through an interface developed in-house; and secondly, by negotiating access to the Online Computer Library Centre (OCLC) First Search service via JANET and the Internet. BIDS have so far loaded the ISI family of citation indexes (science, social sciences, and arts and humanities), Excerpta Medica's *EMBASE*, and the British Library's new *Inside information* database. This last is a journals' content information service. Academic institutions may subscribe to these databases at a fixed annual cost. For this they receive unlimited online time, and there is no additional charge for printing references. The service is menu driven and designed for end users. The service also incorporates a document ordering service in conjunction with the British Library Document Supply Centre (BLDSC). Passwords can be made available to any member of the subscribing institution. Access to JANET is usually essential. Problems can arise in medical schools where staff with medical school contracts can be given access to the service while those on NHS contracts cannot. Separate NHS contracts to access *EMBASE* can be negotiated. This option has not aroused much interest so far, partly because of cost, but also because NHS personnel do not often have access to JANET. However, negotiations are at present underway to extend JANET access to the NHS.

The CHEST deal with OCLC First Search is rather different. OCLC mounts a large number of databases to be searched by their own software. The deal allows institutions to select from several subscription options. Each option offers a selection of databases, including *MEDLINE*. The fixed subscription allows access to all the databases in that option. The search interface is designed for the end user and access is allowed to all members of the subscribing institution.

CD-ROM SUPPLIERS

CD-ROM databases are purchased from suppliers on a subscription basis. They are marketed under licence and the terms of the agreement should be scrupulously adhered to. The more popular databases may be available from more than one supplier; for example, there are several versions of *MEDLINE*. Other databases may only have one supplier so there may be no choice of search interface. Suppliers are usually willing to arrange free trials of databases in libraries so that database content and search interfaces can be evaluated. It can be very helpful to obtain the reactions of end users to new interfaces. These are often very different from those of the experienced online searcher.

Initially, CD-ROM databases were purchased for and loaded on standalone workstations. If the queues grew too long, a second copy of the CD and workstation needed to be purchased. Networking has changed all this. CD-ROM products can be networked over local- and wide-area networks. Considerations on networking might take the following into account. Is there an existing reliable network? Would administration of a new network fall on library staff or is there computer unit support? Will the CD perform well over the network? Response times on CD systems can slow considerably when there are several users accessing the system. On the positive side, networking makes access to workstations within the library more flexible and, if networked across the organization, it makes the databases available at the user's office or laboratory. This is extremely popular with end users.

Medical schools in particular have been exploring another option, that of transferring the database on to hard disk in their computer units and networking from there. Eight to ten gigabytes of hard disk space is required for *MEDLINE*. Response times from the hard disk are much faster so the problems of performance degradation with simultaneous users is virtually eliminated. The British Medical Association has recently introduced this type of networked *MEDLINE*, with the added feature of dial up access. The service can therefore be made available to members nationwide. Networked CD-ROM systems are usually charged per simultaneous user. The number of permitted users is specified in the licence. There may also be a network license fee to pay. Pricing for networked systems has not really settled into a pattern yet.

Possibilities for access to bibliographic databases are changing rapidly. The variety is likely to increase with the growth in networks and links to JANET and the Internet. A fully networked NHS would offer enormous possibilities for database sharing and access.

DATABASES FOR THE HEALTH SCIENCES

There are a large number of databases available that are relevant to the health sciences. There are general databases covering the whole of medicine or nursing, and specialist databases covering subject areas such as cancer, AIDS and toxicology. There are databases which overlap with health sciences and contain much useful information, for example in psychology and the social services. Physics, chemistry or management databases might also be required at times to answer queries. One concern about the trend towards using CD-ROM, rather than accessing remote hosts, is that it tends to limit searches to the databases on site, rather than the most appropriate database available. It would be impossible to list all the available databases here. Detailed lists can be found in Lyon[1] and Norris[2] and the latest *CDROM Directory*.[3] Catalogues of database hosts and CD-ROM suppliers can also be useful. The following is just an outline of a few of the major ones.

MEDLINE

This is probably the most widely used database in the health sciences field. Produced by the National Library of Medicine, it is the computer version of *Index medicus*. It covers the fields of medicine and medical research. The online version includes the separately published *International nursing index* and *Index to dental research*. Subject areas related to medicine are included: biochemistry, pharmacology, clinical psychology, etc. It is available from 1966 onwards from most online sources. It is usually updated weekly on remote hosts and monthly on CD-ROM. A total of 3500 journals are indexed, some selectively. The coverage is international. Some journals from the allied health professions are included, but coverage of such areas as physiotherapy and occupational therapy is by no means exhaustive.

EMBASE

Produced by Excerpta Medica this is the other major medical database. It also indexes about 3500 journals, with worldwide coverage. Surprisingly, the overlap with *MEDLINE* is as small as about 35%. The particular strength of this database is drug information and related areas. If a drug information search is not finding much information, a search on *EMBASE* often yields additional information. Its coverage of European literature is stronger than that of *MEDLINE*. The fields of clinical medicine, medical and medical related research are well covered. Areas such as nursing are not included. The database is updated weekly online and monthly on CD-ROM. It is also marketed in subject sections, e.g. cardiology, anaesthesiology, neurosciences, which are updated quarterly. The database is also available from BIDS.

CINAHL

The *Cumulative index to nursing and allied health literature* covers nursing literature and that of the professions allied to medicine. It is available from 1983 onwards. Around 330 core journals are indexed, together with selective input from 3000 others. Books and university nursing dissertations are also indexed. Coverage of professional issues in nursing, nursing theory and education is excellent. Specialist nurses looking for articles in clinical areas might need to supplement their searches with a trawl of a medical database as well. A particular problem with this database is that many of the American journals indexed are not readily available in colleges of nursing in this country. It is updated bimonthly on CD-ROM and monthly online.

Psychinfo/Psychlit
Psychinfo, the computer version of *Psychological abstracts*, is available via remote hosts from 1967. *Psychlit*, on CD-ROM, is available from 1974. It overlaps with *MEDLINE* in the areas of psychology and clinical psychiatry. It is very useful in the areas of general psychology, counselling, child development, child abuse, family therapy and psychoanalysis. It is updated monthly online and quarterly on CD-ROM.

ASSIA
Applied social sciences indexes and abstracts is a database designed to provide information for people working in the social/caring services. Its core subject area is applied social sciences, but it also includes sociology, psychology, law and politics, as they relate to social services. The database is British, although journals from other countries are also included. The British coverage makes this database important because for many searches on the social aspects of medicine, references retrieved from American databases are of limited relevance. The database is available from 1987 and is updated every two months.

DHSS-Data
There is no CD-ROM version of this database. It is the database of the Departments of Health and Social Services Library. It combines the contents of *Health services abstracts* and *Social services abstracts*. It covers such areas as health services and health service administration. The coverage includes journal articles, books, pamphlets, government publications and NHS circulars. It is a useful source for NHS management enquiries. Available from 1983, it is updated weekly.

Science citation index/Social science citation index
The citation searching facilities on these databases make them a useful additional resource when literature searching. Using these databases it is possible to locate papers that have cited a paper of relevance to a search. This approach can provide a very useful addition to subject searching, and can be a very effective way of broadening a search. The databases are both available via remote hosts and BIDS. There is also a CD-ROM version of *Science citation index*.

SEARCH PREPARATION
It is a very rare user that presents the librarian or search intermediary with a totally clear, unambiguous search request. Requests for information are usu-

ally couched in general terms such as 'Can you do a search on TB?'. The reference interview is therefore a vital part of the search preparation. If possible, time should be spent discussing the reader's requirements. What aspect of the topic do they want to focus on? Is the information for a research project or do they just need a couple of articles for a teaching session that afternoon? Do they just need current information or is older material important? Unfortunately, in busy libraries it is not always possible for searcher and reader to meet to discuss the search topic. In these circumstances, a well designed search request form is required. The form should encourage the reader to describe the topic in sentences rather than just listing keywords. It should also ask for basic limiting factors such as language restrictions, whether human or animal research is of interest, the age and/or sex of subjects required, and the number of years to be searched.

Opinion varies as to whether the reader should sit in on the search session. It certainly provides the searcher with immediate feedback which should improve search quality. However, it can also slow down the search process, as readers carefully read individual titles trying to decide what is relevant. This can increase online search charges enormously, particularly if the database being accessed is not one of the cheaper ones such as *MEDLINE*. CD-ROM is very useful in this respect. Indeed, when the searcher is satisfied that the search strategy has been successful, readers can be shown how to browse, select and print, and left to make their own choices. This might even encourage readers to try their own hand at searching next time.

The approach to searching tends to vary depending on whether a remote host or CD-ROM is the source of the data. Search preparation is vital when online time is being charged. Thinking needs to be done beforehand so that the search can be executed speedily and efficiently. There is less pressure on time for CD-ROM searches so even the expert searcher might well adopt a more relaxed approach, spending more time exploring different options, developing the search strategy while searching, browsing through the results and following up the index terms of relevant papers.

The principles and methods of computer searching tend to be common to most bibliographic databases, regardless of format or host. There will be variations as to how the features are implemented between database hosts and CD-ROM interfaces. The searcher needs to have a knowledge of the database to be searched and an understanding of the search interface. The preparation of a search involves analysing the search request and breaking it down into its component parts. The concepts are then translated into the controlled language of the database using a thesaurus. Boolean operators (AND, OR, NOT) are then employed to represent the desired relationships between the concepts. The search can now be input into the computer and, in theory, relevant references are retrieved. In practice, computer searching is an inexact science, and online modifications might well be needed before the desired results are obtained. There is always going to be a compromise between precision and recall. Should the search be broad, missing little but retrieving large numbers of references for the reader to sift? Should it pinpoint key reference, resulting in a short, highly relevant printout but possibly missing other useful references? There is no right answer. Different readers will have different requirements. The pre-search interview or form should help the searcher to decide whether to err on the side of precision or recall.

There are many other features available to the searcher that can be used in conjunction with, or instead of, thesaurus terms and Boolean operators. Free text searching allows for words to be retrieved from titles, abstracts or other fields, bypassing the controlled language of the thesaurus. This can be a very useful facility if the thesaurus does not contain a term that adequately describes the required concept. There is no subject heading for National Health Service in the *MEDLINE* thesaurus, for example. Care is needed when using free text searching, unless the search interface offers some facility for matching up English and American spelling. If this facility is not available, a free text search for BEHAVIOUR in an American database would miss the available references containing BEHAVIOR. Synonyms can be a problem with free text searching as can words having several different meanings. A free text search for HEART ATTACK is not going to retrieve articles using the term MYOCARDIAL INFARCTION. A free text search for the speech defect CLUTTERING is also likely to retrieve articles on the problems of cluttered computer disks, and bats having problems with sonar. Plurals and tenses can also cause problems. Most databases offer a truncation feature to help with this. CATALY$ (the truncation symbol varies from host to host) will retrieve CATALYST, CATALYTIC, CATALYSIS, CATALYSING. Again, this useful feature has a negative aspect. DIET$ will certainly retrieve required articles on DIET, DIETS, DIETARY and DIETING; however, in a medical database it will also retrieve a huge number of records containing information about chemicals containing the stem DIETHYL. Many databases also offer a 'wild card' option for use within a word. WOM?N will retrieve WOMAN and WOMEN. Adjacency and proximity operators allow the searcher to specify that certain words must occur next to one another or within a certain number of words within the text. This can help tighten up a free text search. Provided the searcher is aware of the pitfalls free text searching can be an extremely useful additional search tool.

Different databases offer different additional features to the searcher. International databases that cover many languages will usually offer the option of limiting the search results to specific languages. Databases covering human and animal studies will usually offer the choice of excluding either of those categories. It may be possible to limit searches to males or females, to particular age groups, or to a particular publication type such as a literature review.

Different databases may well require different search styles. There is often a marked difference in the type of searching required to search medical and social science databases. The former has a formal 'hard' terminology which is usually well expressed by the thesaurus. Searches can often be constructed economically using a few thesaurus terms. The 'soft' terminology of the social sciences often requires many more synonyms and related terms to be input for a topic to be covered adequately. When there is a rigid thesaurus it is important for the searcher to be aware of how this thesaurus is applied by the indexers. The thesaurus for *MEDLINE* is MeSH (Medical Subject Headings), that for *EMBASE* is EMtree, and *CINAHL* has a similar thesaurus. Each of these has a system of preferred terms, arranged hierarchically. Permitted qualifiers or subheadings can be added to these terms. Using MeSH, a search for the surgical treatment of lung cancer would be expressed as LUNG NEOPLASMS/surgery not LUNG NEOPLASMS AND SURGERY. Familiarity with these qualifiers and their strengths and weaknesses is important for effective searching. Using an appropriate qualifier can help to focus a search more closely. Overuse can narrow a search too much, as useful general articles are excluded.

The hierarchical structure of the three mentioned thesauri is important. In each case the indexing policy is to use the most specific term available. A search for the term EYE will not therefore retrieve articles on IRIS or RETINA. The very useful 'explode' feature allows whole hierarchies of terms to be searched.

Tightly controlled search strategies using thesaurus terms will be appropriate for some searches. For others, a broader approach using free text searching might yield better results. One topic might be an obvious candidate for a particular database, another might need to be searched in two or more databases to get satisfactory coverage. Searchers need to be flexible in their approach to searching, and to be prepared to modify their approach, possibly more than once, if a search is proving particularly difficult.

SEARCH OUTPUT AND FEEDBACK

There is now more than one way of supplying search results to readers, although a printout on continuous stationery remains a popular option. The results look more impressive if they are incorporated into a word-processed document, headed by the requesters name and search topic. Personal computers are everywhere these days. Requesters might prefer to have the results supplied on a floppy disk so that they can store them on their own machines.

Perhaps the results can be e-mailed to the requester over a local-area network (LAN). When supplying results in electronic format the searcher will need to know how the requester is planning to store them. If they are to be incorporated into a personal database using personal bibliographic software, a different output format might be required.

Personal bibliographic software has become very popular in the past few years. It enables users to set up databases to store their references with the minimum of work. The software comes with preset formats for different publication types. More importantly, the systems can import records directly from CD-ROM and remote host databases, without the user having to rekey references. They are searchable offering many of the search features of online systems. They can output references in a number of journal formats, enabling easy preparation of reference lists for publications. Reference Manager, Pro Cite, End Note and Papyrus are examples of popular packages.

However the search results are supplied, the covering letter, note or proforma should at the very least give the name and telephone number of the searcher, and should invite the requester to call if not satisfied with the results. The databases searched should also be noted, together with the time span covered. In a small library, obtaining feedback on searches might not be a problem. The searcher might also be the person who deals with the resulting interlibrary loan requests. In a larger library, it is often difficult to find out how satisfied readers are with their searches. In these circumstances a user satisfaction survey ought to be carried out at intervals. Nothing elaborate is required; the survey form need only ask a few questions such as: how many references are relevant?, how many references will you read?, has the search answered your question? Of course, only a proportion of the forms will be returned but this will at least give the searcher an indication of the readers' opinions of the service. This is not necessarily an indication of the quality. Literature searching should be part of the library's quality management programme. Searchers should be encouraged to attend courses to keep up to date. Peer review sessions can also be a good way of improving search skills.

END USER SEARCHING

End user searching arrived with a bang with the introduction of CD-ROM systems. User friendly interfaces, together with the removal of the time and money constraints on searching, have brought about a complete revolution in literature searching. This revolution aroused much concern in the library world. How could end users perform searches of similar quality to those of experienced searcher? What could or should librarians be doing to ensure some level of competence in end user searching? Should end users be allowed to use CD-ROM at all? Most libraries introducing CD-ROM instituted a training programme for end users. Some made attendance at these courses compulsory before access to the CD-ROM was permitted. Some even arranged formal tests of competence.

This was all fairly easy to control with one or two workstations and databases. These days, the CDs are often accessed over a LAN. The end users do not even need to come to the library to use the systems. Even in libraries, the level of demand for services has made formal control of access more difficult. Should librarians worry about this? There was never much discussion about whether readers should be allowed access to *Index medicus* or *Psychological abstracts* without training.

End user searching is different from trained intermediary searching. Speed may not be of the essence. End users may not have another five searches waiting to be done. They may wish to browse the search results carefully before deciding on relevant articles. During this browsing, they might come across interesting articles on other aspects of the topic which they may also decide to follow up. There may also be many occasions when an exhaustive search of the literature is not required, and a few relevant references will suffice. If the search strategies employed by end users, however inefficient they appear to the trained searcher, get to this point reasonably quickly, then they have achieved their aim. 'Good enough' searching may well be all that is required.

This is not to say that librarians should reject all responsibility for end user searches. There are causes for concern. Plutchak[4] particularly identified the problem of the satisfied but inept user: the person who searches the database inefficiently and ineffectively but is quite happy with the results. All librarians who work with CD-ROM can describe the inadequacy of the approach of some end users. Some readers input one term and then prepare to sit for hours browsing hundreds or even thousands of records, including foreign language references that they would not be able to read. Some students type in essay titles and give up on retrieving zero references. Others make totally wrong assumptions about the thesaurus terms and the way they are used, leading to very poor search results.

What can librarians do about this if we accept that end user searching is here to stay? The new role of the librarian is probably to act as trainer and adviser. If staffing permits, training should be offered to all potential end users, and an adviser/troubleshooter should be available close to CD-ROM workstations in the library. Experience suggests that if a librarian goes to help one reader, this usually results in several more 'while you're here' queries from readers at adjacent workstations. Prompt cards and brief guides available at the workstations can also help, but it can be time consuming to keep these up to date. Librarians should also feed back their experiences of end user searching to the CD-ROM suppliers in order to influence the development of the interfaces.

On the whole, end user computer searching is a cause for celebration. Readers are enthusiastic about the CD-ROM databases and are keen to learn how to use them. Volumes of printed indexes or mysterious mediated searches never generated this interest. A development that encourages health sciences personnel to take a more active interest in their professional literature can only be a good thing.

THE FUTURE

Computerized literature searching in the health sciences is changing rapidly. The increasing availability of networked information, including access to the Internet, will bring further changes. Discussion lists, electronic colleges and journals may radically alter the pattern of health sciences publishing, which will have major implications for literature searching. In five years time the picture may look very different from the one outlined here.

REFERENCES

1   Lyon, E., *Online medical databases*, London, Aslib, 1988.
2   Norris, C., 'Online and CD-ROM sources of information retrieval', in Morton, L. T. and Godbolt, S. (eds.), *Information sources in the medical sciences*, London, Bowker Saur, 1992, 87–108.
3   Finlay, M. (ed.), *The CDROM directory: 1993*, 11th edn, London, TFPL Publishing, 1993.
4   Plutchak, T. S., 'On the satisfied and inept user', *Medical reference services quarterly*, 8 (1), 1989, 45–8.

9 Current awareness services

❖ *Lorraine Bate*

The aim of a library is to provide access to literature based knowledge. That knowledge base exists far beyond the boundaries of the library itself and is expanding rapidly. Current awareness services are the means by which the library filters the continuous flow of information on behalf of the user. Updating services may go beyond published matter, for example in alerting users to conference events, but the core of the service will be literature based.

The current awareness service is a useful promotional tool. When services are continually subject to the need to justify their existence, a visible information service actively seeking to meet the current awareness needs of its users – ideally to be one step ahead of them – is effective promotion for the library and information service. The successful current awareness service is timely, accurate, relevant and appropriate. Achieving this is dependent upon the needs of the users and the human and technical resources available to maintain the service.

A current awareness service may be provided to alert users to new book or journal material received in the library, or to the recent literature in a given subject area. The mode of service delivery will range from a recent acquisitions list, through to customized updates delivered electronically from externally produced sources. The purpose of the service – to update on material received or to update in the subject literature – will also determine the need to call upon external sources. The nature of the current awareness services offered will also be shaped by the audience for which the service is intended.

PRINCIPLES OF CURRENT AWARENESS SERVICES
A number of factors bear upon the delivery of current awareness services.

Users
Library and information service users have differing needs for current awareness services. Researchers require updating in the subject areas of their work or interests. Managers need information from a range of disciplines which bear upon issues of service delivery. A survey of health service managers' informa-

tion needs by the Health Management Information Service (HELMIS) in 1989 indicated a high need for current information on quality control and perfor- mance assessment, but a lower need to be updated on hospital administration and the management of support services.[1]

Users' requirements can be determined by a questionnaire administered to any new staff in the organization and on a regular basis to existing employees to ascertain any change in information needs. Remember also to establish any areas the user wishes to be excluded from the service. In using external sources this may, for example, mean the exclusion of foreign language material. Medical researchers may wish to see all original research matter; others may wish to be alerted to review articles only. Whitehall[2] advocates interviews with users to determine fully their specific needs. Attendance at project meetings will also increase the relevant subject knowledge of the information profes- sional and encourage closer working relationships with the user. The success of a current awareness service will depend to a great extent on the information professional's own awareness of developments and on actively seeking to meet the needs of the user. Users who, unprompted, approach a library enquiring about the availability of a customized current awareness service are in the minority; it is the responsibility of the information professional to actively promote the service.

Coverage

Is the service aiming to update users on the recent subject literature or to alert them to material received on-site? A current awareness service alerting users to material received may include brief details of journal articles in addition to monographs. Where this is the case it is important that the user is aware of the source journals included, and therefore what is not included, in the informa- tion service. This can be met by providing a brief title index of sources scanned for each issue. The nature of current awareness services based on on-site resources will largely be determined by the library's collection development policy.

A current awareness service aiming to update the user in given subject areas should ensure coverage of the core journals in which material of relevance will appear. In the majority of cases, a subject based service will require the inclu- sion of information from external sources; the volume of publishing and tight- ening budgets mean fewer libraries are able to rely on in-house resources for acceptable subject coverage. Information from secondary sources will there- fore be required to supplement the in-house service. The inclusion of the core journals will not ensure comprehensive coverage of the relevant literature, but as the volume of literature means comprehensive coverage is no longer possi- ble in many areas of medical and health literature, limiting the current awareness service to core subject journals may be acceptable to the user. It should also ensure the inclusion of the major primary sources in which the most relevant material is likely to appear.

Timeliness

How important is the currency of the service? Is a monthly service sufficient or is a weekly, or daily service required? For researchers requiring comprehensive coverage a monthly service may suffice. For the health service manager who needs to be kept updated with developments, a more frequent service is required. In the 1989 HELMIS survey of health managers[1] all areas of information rated as of high value by respondents scored more for news/current information than for retrospective material.

The sources used in the current awareness service will also affect currency. Reliance on external sources can mean a delay of several months between publication of new material and its appearance in a secondary source. The currency of a service based on in-house resources depends on the speed with which the information staff can disseminate it to their users. (This will in turn depend on the means of information dissemination adopted).

Relevance

Is the material selected for inclusion in the service relevant to the user? Even for a general current awareness service, aimed at updating a majority of users with a generic bulletin, there must be an element of selection to ensure appropriateness. Through either the selection of external sources for the service or the inclusion of on-site sources we are choosing the most appropriate material for the task. The degree of selectivity will depend on the level of service. If a service based on selective dissemination of information (SDI) is offered, material will be selected for alerting to the individual users according to their specific subject interests and expressed information needs. Relevance will also require different responses from the information professional according to the needs of the user. Material of specific subject relevance is easier to identify and to retrieve through keyword search on an in-house database or external electronic source. Material of relevance to the general practitioner or health service manager, spanning a range of disciplines and highlighting issues impinging on present and future service delivery, is not easily located through automatic search of keyterms. The provision of current awareness services to these audiences will require greater attention to selection criteria if maximum relevance is to be achieved.

Content

How informative is the current awareness service? If it is in the form of a list of bibliographic references, does it include an abstract? Unless provided as a rapid alerting service, as with the dissemination of journal contents pages, lists of references containing only author and title are of limited use. Blick and Magrill[3] found that in 92% of the citations in a titles-only pharmaceutical research bulletin, users found the titles sufficiently indicative of coverage. In many medical and scientific areas this will be the case, the precise nature of the subjects being reflected in the titles of the corresponding literature. In other areas of the health sciences, for example nursing, health service management and public health, titles will be less indicative of content.

Ease of use

The means of service delivery should be accessible to the user, requiring the minimum amount of effort to benefit from its content. If delivery is by list of references or bulletin, is it easy to read – is the print clear and the arrangement obvious to those who wish to refer to a specific section? If the service is by disk or bulletin board, are the instructions for use included and the screen arrangement helpful? Whatever the mode of delivery, a listing should contain a maximum of 50 abstracts per monthly issue. More than this will begin to add to the information overload the service is intended to circumvent. In the 1970s Bloomfield[4] and Lovelace[5] advocated limits of 20 references for SDI and 40 references for generic bulletins. Clearly this will depend on the frequency of the service and the subjects being covered. The prolific literature production of the 1990s compared with earlier decades also means potentially longer current awareness listings, requiring the application of tighter relevance criteria in order to limit the listing to a manageable length. User needs will also determine the size of update. A researcher's needs for high recall will render a longer listing acceptable. The manager or busy clinician is less likely to spend time reading through 50 abstracts. Achieving maximum relevance with the minimum number of references is again the result of carefully determined selection criteria.

A current awareness service should provide a document delivery service for items to which the user has been alerted. Some authors on the subject deem it an essential part of the service.[6,7] Where staffing resources permit, document supply is clearly an important part of a current awareness service. In practice, however, resources may not stretch to document supply. The user should be informed of the situation in either case. Again, it should be clear whether the source document is available on-site, particularly where the references have been taken from external sources. If a document request service is available, the ability to request by a document number rather than by bibliographic details adds to the accessibility of the service.

Cost

At any given point, the information professional should be able to demonstrate the cost effectiveness of a service. A number of elements must be considered here. The costs of staff time involved in an in-house service should be weighed against the direct costs of a bought-in service in the context of the benefits and drawbacks of each, as outlined above. Blick[8] provides a useful grid for the assessment of the appropriateness of forms of current awareness services, which should also help in determining their cost effectiveness.

Altogether more difficult to determine is the cost of an information service in relation to the value placed on it by the users. One method is to assign a value in terms of the hours saved by using an information service. In 1976 The Oncology Information Service (later Leeds Medical Information) reported users' estimates that the service saved between 6000 and 12,000 hours per year.[9] Whitehall[10] described two studies, at Trent Polytechnic and UKAEA, Harwell, in 1986, which attempted to address such issues and which also highlighted the problems of doing so, for example in asking users to assign a cash value to the information received. Nevertheless, information professionals need to be aware of such arguments if at any point they are required to illustrate the cost benefits of the service.

Feedback

The current awareness service should be continually monitored by the service provider. The relevance of the information to the user, both in subject coverage and the nature of the material included (e.g. primary research report, review article), should be ascertained. A brief evaluation questionnaire should be attached to the bulletin or SDI listing at regular intervals. Frequency should be quarterly to six-monthly; a questionnaire administered more frequently than this is less likely to be completed by the user.

METHODS OF CURRENT AWARENESS DELIVERY

The last ten years have seen developments in information technology which have contributed greatly to the provision of information services, including current awareness. The processing of material for computer entry can delay the delivery of current awareness services, however. Basic manual techniques can sometimes alert users more quickly to recently received in-house material. The circulation of journal contents pages, or the journal itself, are both well used methods for the notification of new periodical material. The pros and cons of each method are explored by Whitehall:[11] the advantage of immediate circulation by contents page, with a limited indication of content, must be assessed against the disadvantage of full issue circulation in the loss of currency for users further down the list. Whitehall also describes techniques of journal circulation to help minimize problems associated with journal issues being away from the library for a period of time.

As Rowley[12] points out in an update to her 1985 review of bibliographic current awareness services, manual in-house updating services are continuing to fulfil a role because of the importance attached to timeliness. The need for this role is perhaps more important now than in the mid 1980s when information technology was seen as the answer to the information professional's increasing workloads. Computer packages have radically changed the production of current awareness services, but a manual service alerting individuals to significant journal articles or reports will disseminate information faster than a generic monthly current awareness service generated electronically. Services offered will be determined by staffing resources available. An ongoing alerting service is more demanding of staff time than a monthly SDI service produced automatically by running individual computer loaded profiles against each database update. A generic monthly current awareness bulletin is in turn less time consuming to produce than individual SDI.

Much has been written about the use of information technology in the production of current awareness services and it is not intended to rehearse this here. Rowley's 1985 review provides a summary of computer software facilities and is a useful checklist for the acquisition of packages for current awareness services. Microcomputer packages now have many of the facilities previously available only on main-frame versions. Systems which permit the arrangement of references by broad subject headings, as well as by the indexing keyterms used ordinarily for subject searching, are a prerequisite for current awareness bulletins; those which have a storage facility for search profiles are a requirement for SDI.

Computer printed output has been improved greatly by modifications to retrieval software and the availability of high quality printers. Where required, references can be downloaded to a personal computer (PC) package and the contents combined with additional text from non-database produced current awareness (as may be the case in newspaper scanning) or of in-house produced references where the bulletin is produced from both external and internal sources. Desk-top publishing can add greatly to the presentation of a printed bulletin. Besson describes the development of a package to reformat references from *Current contents on diskette* and *MEDLINE* at the Medical College of St Bartholomew's Hospital.[13]

Where external sources are used in the production of SDI, many database hosts provide an automatic searching service alerting the user in print or machine readable format. The basic 'save-search' facility available on most database hosts will store SDI profiles to be executed at regular intervals. Here the onus is on the user to run the search.

Current awareness journals produced by external commercial sources can be purchased and circulated to users. The delay in the publication of the source material and its appearance in a printed bibliographic source varies widely and should be determined prior to purchase. The *Current contents* series of compilations of current journal contents is very current, this secondary source frequently appearing in the library before the arrival of the primary journals.

As with the provision of in-house current awareness services, the value of an externally produced current awareness product is increased by a supporting full-text document delivery service. Some publishers will offer this as part of a total service. Others will provide document delivery where the source document cannot be obtained through local libraries.

Access to the source document is a factor in the selection and purchase of secondary sources. A current awareness service, however speedy and relevant, will lose impact if the user cannot access the source material. It is clearly of benefit to the library if such material is obtainable from the current awareness product supplier if not readily available locally.

NON-PRINT CURRENT AWARENESS

The development of bulletin board and electronic mail technology enables the more rapid delivery of current awareness services than postal service will allow. The results of an SDI search may be delivered online to be scanned onscreen by the user or for import to a user's personal bibliographic database. The practicalities, and technological, staffing and copyright issues involved in the delivery of an electronic current awareness service are described in reports of services recently established at the Royal Free Hospital School of Medicine and at Portsmouth Polytechnic.[14] It is interesting to note that where networking has permitted the online delivery of search results, the majority of users have opted to receive the updates on disk.

The launch of contents page journals on disk in 1990 (*Current contents; Reference update*) has added to the potential of electronic current awareness services. While still taking the form of a compilation of current journal contents pages, the disk versions are searchable, greatly adding to their value as a current awareness tool by the inclusion of an SDI production facility.

In the United States, developments in online alerting services have included the loading of *Current contents* information onto an integrated information environment at the Yale School of Medicine.[15] The Oregon based US Healthlink is similarly an approach to updating which includes recent literature and news on, for example, drug interactions. An online clipping service provides for the SDI needs of the user.[16]

HEALTH CARE CURRENT AWARENESS SOURCES

Externally produced current awareness sources are variously available in print, on disk and online. The medical and health sector is the most prolific producer of literature and this is reflected in the range and number of secondary sources available. The following cannot aim to be a comprehensive review of sources; it is therefore intended as an overview of widely available sources. It is worth investigating local medical and health libraries and research institutes to determine current awareness products and services which may be available to external users.

Electronic contents page services

Current contents on diskette (CCOD) and *Reference update* have been discussed in their capacity as tools for innovative dissemination of information in the technological context. CCOD, from the Institute of Scientific Information, is the disk version of the *Current contents* series of printed journal contents page compilations. A significant development has been the inclusion of abstracts in the disk version. Three of the six titles – *Life sciences, Clinical medicine* and *Social and behavioural sciences* – cover medical and health literature. *Reference update* was developed by Research Information Services (USA) for use with Reference Manager personal database software. A third product, *Medical science weekly*, is produced by Elsevier. All are published in weekly updates. A comparative study of the currency of CCOD, *Reference update* and *Medical science weekly* is reported in a 1991 article by Grainger and Lyon.[17] This has the advantage of being a UK based study reflecting issues of European coverage. Bakker explores in-depth the subject strengths and weaknesses of the three in a 1992 study.[18] An excellent overall comparison of CCOD and *Reference update* is provided by Hanson and Cox.[19] As the authors report, the products (now both owned by the Institute of Scientific Information) are continually undergoing modification and development. CCOD, *Reference update* and *Medical science weekly* are all available in standard and 'de-luxe' versions which cover a larger number of journals and include abstracts.

Parallel developments in current awareness services based on the scanning of journal contents pages include the British Library's *Inside information*. This provides information on the Library's 10,000 most used journals and is available online and on CD-ROM. Even with the facility to purchase sections of the whole database, however, this service is going to be too expensive for all but the larger medical libraries. A viable alternative is to purchase and network the service on a consortium basis, giving each member library remote access to the database. *Contents first*, from the Online Computer Library Centre (OCLC), is a further source of contents page information available online, with document delivery back-up. SWETS and Blackwell's Subscription Services similarly offer document delivery of full-text articles as a complement to their *SWETScan* and *Uncover* contents page services.

Subject based sources
Medicine

The two major medical bibliographic database sources are MEDLINE and EMBASE. Both are updated weekly, MEDLINE at a rate of 5000 references and EMBASE with 8000 references per week. The need for targeted SDI is evident. With this in mind the most recent month's additions to MEDLINE are made available online in a separate *SDILINE* file. MEDLINE includes coverage of the nursing and dental literature. EMBASE does not cover these areas but is stronger on pharmacological and environmental health subjects. EMBASE also has greater coverage of European journals. The currency of MEDLINE online through various hosts and on the CD-ROM version is explored by Grainger and Lyon.[20] US online hosts were found to load MEDLINE files quicker than European hosts, the delay between the appearance of the primary journals and the inclusion of their contents on MEDLINE being 15 weeks. The delay between database availability online and on CD-ROM was found to be a further five weeks.

Since cost is a possible factor against the use of online sources for current awareness, one alternative is the MEDLINE *updates* service from the British Library Medical Information Centre, produced monthly on disk. The 33 titles include updates on alcoholism, cystic fibrosis, hearing and women's health. A wide range of titles is available from the Sheffield University Biomedical Information Service (SUBIS) produced from a core list of journals scanned in-house.

The National Library of Medicine itself produces *Current bibliographies in medicine*, a series of yearly updates on specific topics. The contents of EMBASE are published in a number of abstract journals available in hard copy and on disk. *Excerpta medica* titles currently number 44; the frequency of publication varies according to title. Other major online sources in the medical field include Chemical CA-Search and BIOSIS. *Chemical abstracts* is also published weekly and includes information on patents, conference proceedings and books, in addition to journal articles. From the same source, *CASelects* is a bimonthly alerting service on selected medical/chemical topics. *Biological abstracts* is published bimonthly and covers genetics, biochemistry, immunology and nutrition.

Other subject specific sources include coverage of recent HIV and AIDS literature in the *HIV bulletin* from the library of the Public Health Laboratory Service, relating specifically to microbiological aspects of diagnosis and transmission, and *Current AIDS literature* from the Bureau of Hygiene and Tropical

Disease in London. *AIDS abstracts* (formerly *AIDS information*) is produced monthly by Leeds Medical Information (formerly known as the Oncology Information Service) based at the University of Leeds. Further AIDS news and current literature information sources are described in Roberts *et al.*'s excellent 1987 review of AIDS literature.[21]

In the broader field of cancer, a number of printed current awareness sources are available, including *Cancergrams* from the US National Cancer Institute and *Current clinical cancer* from Leeds Medical Information. These and other sources are listed in the 1992 edition of *Information sources in the medical sciences* published by Bowker-Saur.[22]

Public health literature is as diverse as the definitions of the discipline itself. From the Bureau of Hygiene and Tropical Diseases *Public health news* is a monthly updating newsletter reporting from the newspaper and journal literature. *Abstracts on hygiene and communicable diseases* is the journal literature only version. Coverage includes environmental health, community health and diseases and their control. The Public Health Laboratory Service weekly *Library bulletin* contains references to the recent literature on the diagnosis and control of communicable diseases. In an article published in 1986, Price and Burley review current awareness sources on occupational diseases.[23] Sources reviewed include *MEDLINE*, two of the hard copy bulletins produced from *Excerpta medica* (*Section 17 – Public health; Section 35 - Occupational Health and Industrial Medicine*) and *CIS abstracts*.

Current clinical information

A range of publications exists to update clinicians on reviews of recent developments and research. The Royal Society of Medicine copublishes *Current medical literature*, a series of quarterly subject specific listings of selected significant literature with editorial comment. Other titles publish the review papers themselves; these include the Churchill Livingston *Recent advances* series and the Current Science *Current opinion* series.

An ongoing issue in the field of medical research information has been the length of time between the author submitting an article and its appearance in the journal. The time taken in peer review and the technologies of paper publication have meant delays in the publication of an original article of up to 12 months. For the information professional using secondary sources to supply a researcher on published medical research, a further three to six months can be added to the total time delay.

The desire to reduce this overall delay has received particular attention in the field of clinical trials information. One attempt to overcome this in the cancer field has been *Physician Data Query* (PDQ), an online database containing information on current clinical trials and consensus information. However, for protocol information it is still dependent on the literature published in peer-reviewed journals. More recently the launch of the *Online journal of current clinical trials (OJCCT)* has sought to cut down the delay between acceptance and appearance of a peer-reviewed article to 48 hours.[24, 25] Aimed at the end-user, the database has an automatic search facility responding to search terms entered online by the user, who will then be alerted to the appearance in *OJCCT* of items of relevance by the chosen method of delivery, by post or fax. To date, take-up has been poor, however. It appears the end-user has yet to be converted to this new mode of journal content dissemination.

Information on clinical alerts recently issued by the US National Institutes of Health have been made available in the *MEDLARS* online news message, as well as being made available in full-text online on the National Library of Medicine's (NLM) *HSTAT* (Health services/technology assessment text) database. Within *MEDLINE*, protocol and guideline information is now easier to retrieve through NLM's recently added publication type categories of 'guideline' (general conduct and administration of health care activities) and 'practice guideline' (statements, directions, principles for specific clinical circumstances).

Drug information
Pharmacy and pharmacology are particularly well served by information sources. *MIMS (Monthly index of medical specialities)* is the major source of updated drug information. Health service Regional Drug Information Services may also provide local alerting services in addition to drug enquiry services. A range of databases cover drug information including *EMBASE, TOXLINE,* and *International pharmaceutical abstracts. Excerpta medica* produces the *Drug literature index. CASelects* include titles relating to drug dosage and interactions.

Nursing and allied health
The three major secondary sources for nursing literature information are the *International nursing index (INI), CINAHL (Cumulative index to nursing and allied health literature)* produced in the United States, and *Nursing bibliography* from the Royal College of Nursing (RCN) in the UK. At the time of writing, the RCN is exploring the production of the Bibliography on CD-ROM. *CINAHL* and *INI* are available on CD-ROM and on a number of online hosts, *INI* as an integral part of the *MEDLINE* database. For the provision of updating services on nursing literature neither is currently an effective source. *Nursing bibliography* is more useful for retrospective searching and *CINAHL* and *INI* (together with a heavy bias toward US literature) are subject to the problems previously mentioned of using external sources for current awareness service provision. The British Library Medical Information Centre produces five nursing literature titles (*Core British nursing; Core literature in geriatric, paediatric, psychiatric, surgi-*

cal nursing) in the *MEDLINE* *updates* series.

A number of topic-specific current awareness titles will be of interest to health professionals. The Institute for the Study of Drug Dependence (ISDD) produces *Drug abuse current awareness bulletin*, a monthly title listing of material received in the ISDD Library. *Drug abstracts monthly* is a selected listing of more important items with abstracts. From the Centre for Policy on Ageing, *New literature on old age* is useful for both researchers and practitioners and is published six times a year. *Ethnic minorities health* is a current awareness bulletin produced by Bradford Community Health NHS Trust. Two current awareness publications from the Health Education Authority (HEA) provide a useful overview of these areas plus others relevant to the field of health education and promotion. The titles-only *Journal articles of interest to health educators* and the *Current awareness bulletin* with abstracts to selected articles are available through subscription to the HEA journal *Health lines*.

The Library of the Royal College of Midwives produces *Current awareness service: a list of recent literature on midwifery*. This is a monthly listing of references without abstracts on a range of topics relevant to the field. The Midwives Information and Resource Service (MIDIRS) seeks to update the midwife through the quarterly issue of packs containing full-text copies of recent articles of note. The Health Visitors Association produces the quarterly *HVA current awareness bulletin*.

Allied health
The literature of the paramedical fields is covered only in part by the major online sources. Recognizing this gap, the *Current Awareness Topics Services* (*CATS*) developed by the British Library Medical Information Centre produces monthly literature indexes in complementary medicine, physiotherapy, occupational therapy, rehabilitation and terminal care, which are available on disk. A number of other current awareness listings are produced by national institutes and professional associations. These are comprehensively described in *Keyguide to information sources in paramedical sciences*.[26]

Health care management
The literature of health care management cannot be as clearly defined as that of medicine and allied health. Increasingly, the attention paid to the outcome of health care delivery is blurring the distinction between the clinical and non-clinical literature. This is illustrated by the US Health Planning and Administration Database, a joint production of the National Library of Medicine and American Hospital Association, which incorporates some material from *MEDLINE*. *Health management update*, issued ten times a year, and the bimonthly *Community care update* are two current awareness bulletins produced from the

database of HELMIS at the University of Leeds. *Health service abstracts* is produced from *DHSS-Data*, the database of the library of the UK Departments of Health and Social Security.

A FINAL NOTE

The nature and extent of current awareness services that a library and information service is able to offer depend on the human, technical and financial resources available. The success of the service depends upon the information professional's commitment to maintaining a high quality service. At its best, a current awareness service is an effective promotional tool and an asset to the organization; at its worst the service will do little more than add to information overload leading to a devaluing of the service. Left unattended this may lead to hostility towards the service which may then be judged expendable. A successful service will reflect the awareness of the information professional's needs and aims of the organization and will confirm their place as an important part of it.

REFERENCES

1   Health Management Information Service, *HELMIS marketing: final report* (unpublished), Leeds, University of Leeds, Nuffield Institute for Health, 1990.
2   Whitehall, T., 'Cost, value and effectiveness of current awareness services', in Whitehall, T. (ed.), *Practical current awareness services from libraries*, Aldershot, Gower, 1986, 91–103.
3   Blick, A. and Magrill, D., 'The value of a weekly in-house current awareness bulletin serving pharmaceutical research scientists', *Information scientist*, **9** (1), 1975, 19–28.
4   Bloomfield, M., 'Current awareness publications; an evaluation', *Special libraries*, *60*, October 1969, 514–20.
5   Lovelace, E., 'Analysis of a current awareness service in a hospital library', *Australian library journal*, 27 (14), 1978, 215–20.
6   Rowley, J. E., 'Current awareness or competitive intelligence: a review of the options', *Aslib proceedings*, 44 (11/12), 1992, 367–72.
7   Richards, D., 'Dissemination of information', in Dossett, P. (ed), *Handbook of special librarianship and information work*, 6th edn, London, Aslib, 1992, 318–49.
8   Blick, A., 'The choice is yours! Choosing the best method for current awareness provision', in Whitehall, T. (ed.), op. cit., 15–23.
9   Collins, A. M. K. and Lever, R., *Oncology Information Service, interim report*, Leeds, University of Leeds Medical Library, 1976 *cited in* Carmel, M. (ed.), *Medical librarianship*, Library Association, 1981, 205.
10 Whitehall, T., 'Cost, value and effectiveness of current awareness services', in Whitehall, T. (ed.), op. cit., 91–103
11 Whitehall, T., 'Alternatives for current awareness service (CAS), in Whitehall, T. (ed.), op. cit., 1–14.

12 Rowley, J. E., 'Bibliographic current awareness services – a review', *Aslib proceedings*, **37** (9), 1985, 345-53.

13 Besson, A., 'Text reformatting and current awareness services in a medical library using Reform', *Library micromation news*, **34**, 1991, 12–14.

14 Cox, J and Hanson, T., 'Setting up an electronic current awareness service', *Online*, **16** (4), 1992, 34–43.

15 Paton, J. A. *et al.*, 'Online bibliographic information: integration into an emerging IAIMS environment', in *Proceedings of the Annual Symposium of Applications in Medical Care*, 1992, 605–9.

16 Yasnoff, W. A., 'US HealthLink: a national information resource for health care professionals', *Journal of medical systems*, **16** (2/3), 1992, 95–100.

17 Grainger, F. and Lyon, E., 'A comparison of the currency of secondary information sources in the biomedical literature. I. Weekly current awareness services', *Health libraries review*, **8** (3) 1991, 150–6.

18 Bakker, S., 'Subject strengths and weaknesses of four current awareness services on diskette', *Health libraries review*, **9** (4), 1992, 131–43.

19 Hanson, T. and Cox, J., 'A comparative review of two diskette-based current awareness services: Current Contents on Diskette and Reference Update', *Database*, **16** (3), 1993, 73–81.

20 Grainger, F. and Lyon, E., 'A comparison of the currency of secondary information sources in the biochemical literature. II. MEDLINE online and on CD-ROM', *Health libraries review*, **9** (4), 1992, 138–43.

21 Roberts, S., Shepherd, L. and Wade, J., 'The scientific and clinical literature of AIDS: development, bibliographic control and retrieval', *Health libraries review*, **4** (4), 1987, 197–218.

22 Morton, L. and Godbolt, S. (eds.), *Information sources in the medical sciences*, 4th edn, London, Bowker-Saur, 1992.

23 Price, C. and Burley, R. A., 'An evaluation of information sources for current awareness on occupational diseases', *Journal of information science*, **12** (5), 1986, 247–55.

24 Keyani, A., 'The Online Journal of Current Clinical Trials: an innovation in electronic journal publishing', *Database*, **16** (1), 1993, 14–23.

25 Seago, B. L., 'Online Journal of Current Clinical Trials: issues for the 1990s and beyond', *Medical reference services quarterly*, **12** (1), 1993, 1–6.

26 Hewlett, J. F. (ed.), *Keyguide to information sources in paramedical sciences*, London, Mansell, 1990.

SOURCES

Abstracts on hygiene and communicable diseases, Current AIDS literature and *Public health news*, CAB International, Wallingford, Oxfordshire OX10 8DE.

AIDS abstracts and *Current clinical cancer*, Leeds Medical Information, University of Leeds, Leeds LS2 9JT. Published by Carfax Publishing Company, PO Box 25, Abingdon, Oxfordshire OX14 3UE.

Biological abstracts, BIOSIS, 2100 Arch Street, Philadelphia, PA 19103–1399, USA.

European Help-Desk: Vital Information Ltd, 30 Hockliffe Street, Leighton Buzzard, Bedfordshire LU7 8HP.

Cancergrams, US National Cancer Institute, International Cancer Information Centre, Bethesda, MD 20892, USA.

Chemical abstracts and *CASelects*, Chemical Abstracts Service, 2540 Olentangy River Road, PO Box 3012, Columbus, OH 43210, USA.

CIS abstracts, International Occupational Safety and Health Information Centre, International Labour Office, CH-1211 Geneva 22, Switzerland.

Current awareness service: a list of recent literature on midwifery, The Library, Royal College of Midwives, 15 Mansfield Street, London W1M OBE.

Current awareness topics services (CATS) and *MEDLINE updates*, British Library Medical Information Centre, Boston Spa, Wetherby, West Yorkshire, LS22 7BQ.

Current contents on diskette and *Reference update*, Institute of Scientific Information, 3501 Market Street, Philadelphia, PA 19104, USA. European branch: Brunel Science Park, Brunel University, Uxbridge UB8 3PH.

Current medical literature, Royal Society of Medicine, in association with Current Medical Literature Ltd, 1 Wimpole Street, London W1M 8AE.

Drug abstracts monthly and *Drug abuse current awareness bulletin*, Institute for the Study of Drug Dependence, Waterbridge, 32–36 Lowman Street, London SE1 OEE.

Ethnic minorities health, Bradford Community Health Trust, c/o Medical Library, Field House Teaching Centre, Bradford Royal Infirmary, Bradford, West Yorkshire, BD9 6RJ.

Health management update and *Community care update*, HELMIS (Health Management Information Service), Nuffield Institute for Health, University of Leeds, 71–75 Clarendon Road, Leeds LS2 9PL.

Health Service Abstracts, Library and Information Service, Department of Health, Room 5C07, Quarry House, Leeds LS2 7UE

HIV bulletin and *Library bulletin*, Public Health Laboratory Service, 61 Colindale Avenue, London NW9 5DF.

Journal articles of interest to health educators and *Current awareness bulletin*, Information Centre, Health Education Authority, Hamilton House, London WC1H 9TX.

Medical science weekly, *Excerpta medica* (printed sections), and *Drug literature index*, Excepta Medica Publishing Group, Elsevier, PO Box 1527, 1000 BM Amsterdam, The Netherlands.

MIDIRS, Midwives Information and Resource Service, 9 Elmdale Road, Clifton, Bristol, BS8 1SL.

New literature on old age, Centre for Policy on Ageing, 25–31 Ironmonger Row, London EC1V 3QP.

Nursing bibliography, RCN Library, Royal College of Nursing, 20 Cavendish Square, London W1M 0AB.

Online journal of current clinical trials, Electronic Publishing, OCLC Online Computer Library Centre, 6565 Frantz Road, Dublin, OH 43017-3395, USA.

SUBIS, Sheffield University Biomedical Information Service, 1 Northumberland Road, Sheffield S10 2TT.

10   Serials in the health sciences

❖   *Felicity Grainger*

Serials are published in instalments regularly or irregularly and carry an International Standard Serial Number (ISSN). They include newspapers, periodicals and journals. This chapter will concentrate on scientific and medical journals, and its aims are to outline general principles of journal librarianship, concentrating on aspects specific to biomedicine, and to attempt to predict future developments.

For detailed information on all aspects of the subject an Aslib publication *Serials management:a practical handbook* edited by Margaret Graham and Fiona Buettel is invaluable.[1] Tony Stankus has given an interesting personal perspective and immense subject detail on journals in the life sciences.[2]

Enormous changes are taking place in journal publication at the moment. Editors are looking closely at the role and quality of the journals, particularly of the general medical titles. They are aware, as are librarians, that journal articles are failing to provide for the needs of clinicians, and are starting to address the problems. Another change has resulted from rising prices of journal subscriptions which have caused a cycle where cancellations have in turn led to further increases in subscription costs. Provision of selected articles by alternative methods has led to a completely different way of looking at journal material – thinking in terms of individual articles rather than of subscribing to a journal. This is a trend away from holdings and towards access – the virtual library.

We librarians need to remain very much aware of the trends so that we can assess them and utilize those developments which are appropriate for the library service which we are providing. Meanwhile, we still have to deliver a service based on established practice while gradually introducing new methods and educating our users to new ways of thinking. Our responsibility is to provide the information required by our users by utilizing new developments in such a way as to maximize the information accessed within available resources. The users can describe their needs, but our expertise helps us to identify the best way in which to obtain the material they need. We are accustomed to doing this in other areas of library and information work, for instance indexes and bibliographic databases, but now it is extending to journal provision, which had been relatively stable since journals were first established in the 17th century.

We will look at the origin and types of journals and how journal material is used by people working in medical practice and research in the biomedical field. Selection mechanisms for a holdings list – in these times this more often involves a process of deselection – will be compared and a brief introduction given to procedures for managing the collection. Finally an attempt will be made to predict future changes so that we can plan to incorporate those appropriate for our own library services.

GUIDES

Ulrich's international periodicals directory: a classified guide to current periodicals, contains detailed bibliographic information on periodicals on all subjects worldwide. The National Library of Medicine (USA) produces the annual *List of journals indexed in Index medicus* which includes 3200 biomedical, dental and nursing titles and gives country of origin and standard abbreviation in Vancouver format.

FUNCTION AND IMPORTANCE

As it is in journals that descriptions of new observations and research results are first published, they remain the most important published format for both authors and readers. From the point of view of the author, publication in a refereed journal is a major measure of research activity. The drive to publish is, however, eroding the primary role of journals as that of communicating scientific discovery.[3, 4] This is borne out by the few times papers are cited. The Institute of Scientific Information indexes (ISI) about 10% of journals published worldwide and, of these, 46.4% in medicine and 41.3% in biological sciences remained uncited in the four years following publication.[5] As ISI indexes mainstream journals, the figures for uncited papers are likely to be even higher in the 90% of journals not included.

From the point of view of the reader, journal articles are the most up-to-date published format and only here is the original material to be found in its full and 'accurate' version.

Emphasis on journal material as a source of information is being heightened by the ease of retrieving references to specific subjects using available and user-friendly bibliographic databases: in the biomedical field *MEDLINE* is particularly important.

The resulting demand for journal articles and the discovery that they do not answer the questions being asked (for which they were never written), has recently led to a critical examination of the role of medical journals and the degree to which they fulfil it. Papers and subsequent discussions have been written up as a conference report[6] and as series of articles in the *Journal of internal medicine.*[7] Some of the problems identified and attempts proposed to address the short-comings, will be discussed in the section on journal use.

TYPES OF JOURNALS

The first scientific journals were multidisciplinary, carrying articles on all subjects. Although many of these continue, and include such highly prestigious titles as *Proceedings of the Royal Society* and *Nature,* journals have become increasingly specialized. Only in the early 19th century did high quality medical journals appear, and in this century journals devoted to medical specialties were launched. Increasing specialization still continues.

Primary journals

It is in primary journals that the first reports of new research results and observations appear. In some areas, and for a major discovery, there is enormous competition to publish first, and there are journals which specialize in quick reporting. These include prestigious titles such as *Nature* and *Science,* and journals such as *Biochemical biophysical research communications,* whose short reports will later be followed by a full article published elsewhere. The other primary journals vary in their content, some being more 'archival' in the sense that their articles are more lasting and are cited in the literature for many years.

Scientific journals

Science journals play an important part in the medical library of an organization where research is being carried out. In 1993 more than £300 million was spent by the National Health Service on research, and this was not restricted to medical research institutes and university teaching hospitals.

The journals which contain relevant material include the traditional preclinical subjects (also known as the basic medical sciences): anatomy, biochemistry, physiology and pharmacology. Cell and molecular biology have emerged as fundamental to advances in medical research which also draws on disciplines as diverse as psychology and physics. Tony Stankus' book[8] is useful in describing the subject disciplines in life sciences and medicine and gives details of important journals in the subject areas.

General medical journals

Editors of general medical journals see the role of their publications as being to improve patient care by means of raising awareness of issues. They do this by recording developments in clinical medicine in the form of research findings, results of clinical trials and case reports, and by carrying editorials on general issues.[9] Review articles are increasing in both numbers and the value accorded to them.

Specialist journals

In the latter half of the 19th century specialty societies were founded and by 1991 there were 23 separate medical specialties, some of which have subspecialties and even sub-subspecialties.[10] Lock discerns five or even six tiers of specialization.[11]

This further division of clinical medical specialties is paralleled in research, which has seen titles devoted to more and more narrow topics, finally concentrating on single organs (*Brain, Pancreas*) and then organelles (*Mitochondria*). A problem for the librarian is that it is unlikely that many people in any but a very large institution will be working on such a narrow field and a choice must usually be made between providing general material for many or specialized material for a few.

Trends

In addition to the trend towards specialization in content, there have been other changes. Important among these are review journals and electronic delivery.

Review journals

Because of the enormous increase in the number of papers being published, scientists and clinicians have difficulty enough in keeping abreast of their own particular subject. Reading primary articles in order to maintain a picture of peripheral subjects and of developments in science and technology in general has become impossible.

Reviews provide syntheses of knowledge on a subject gleaned from primary articles. Their popularity is increasing, not only because of the problems associated with primary literature (too much and too detailed for any but those working in the field), but also because they can be located by bibliographic databases and are published more quickly than books.

The past few years have seen the addition of new titles to existing series, e.g. W. B. Saunders *Seminars* series and the launch of an important new series of review journals, the *Current opinion* series produced by Current Biology Ltd. The format is structured and ranks papers in order of importance.

A further stage in the organization of reviews has been developed at the Cochrane Centre in Oxford, where systematic reviews have been commissioned in the area of perinatal care. These are distributed as the *Oxford database of perinatal trials* on diskettes accompanied by a newsletter drawing attention to some of the most important new data. This is a radical attempt to ensure that any literature search includes a synthesis of the most recent findings in the subject and the Cochrane Centre, together with collaborating centres in other countries, is extending the work to other specialties.

Electronic journals

This is a subject over which more ink has been spilled than has yet been saved. In concept they are identical to traditionally published journals but the material is retained in electronic form and not printed on hard copy. Articles are written, submitted for publication, refereed and distributed over a network.[12] The first peer-reviewed scientific journal distributed electronically and not available in hard copy was the *Online journal of current clinical trials*, launched in 1992 as a collaborative venture between the Online Computer Library Centre (OCLC) and The American Association for the Advancement of Science (AAAS). It has not been as successful as hoped, for reasons which include slowness of printing and an apparent initial reluctance on the part of contributors,[13] but the medium remains a valid one for publishing and a discussion on its future appears in the last section of this chapter. Some titles are produced in parallel on hard copy and electronically, e.g. *New England journal of medicine*.

It is important to remember that journals originally published in hard copy which are later archived into electronic format are not strictly electronic journals.

USE

If it were possible to describe concisely the use made of journals by clinicians and research workers in the biomedical field, the work of librarians would be a great deal simpler, but certainly less interesting.

As with libraries in general, journals are used in a complete spectrum of ways because of the range of material, and the needs and types of users. Published material ranges from anecdotal clinical case notes to detailed results of laboratory based research, and users' needs vary from previous observations to chemical data. Furthermore, users are heterogeneous in the ways in which they approach libraries and librarians, and the information they provide.

One feature peculiar to medical libraries, particularly in hospitals, is the element of urgency of some requests when information is needed to assist with treatment.

CATEGORIES OF USERS

Research scientists

Of the three major groups of users of biomedical literature – scientists, clinicians and students – journals are best suited to research workers.[14] The strengths of journal articles – their currency, detail and descriptions of methodology – provide a basis for scientists to build on. These characteristics are less suited to clinicians and students who, although they want up-to-date information, often find that primary articles are not only too narrow but too numerous to read.

Clinicians

Studies[15, 16] have shown that clinicians spend, on average, less than two hours each week in reading the medical literature. For their needs – those of being alerted to advances in health care and of obtaining access to the most accurate information on specific problems – they turn to journals,[17, 18] despite the fact that these have been found so wanting.[19–21] It is not clear whether the poor use subsequently made of journal material for clinical practice[22] or further research[23] is because of the imperfect way in which the available literature is searched[24] or whether it stems from the inadequacy of the material.[25]

Awareness of the flaws in the literature are recognized by editors as well as users[26, 27] and attempts to address these are discussed below, in the section on the future of journals.

Students

With the changes in the curriculum of science education and of medical and nursing training, more emphasis is being placed on individual study than in the previous intensive teaching programmes. The implications of this for libraries are enormous[28, 29] and will inevitably lead to a greater reliance on journal material at undergraduate level.

The unsuitability of primary articles, which by their nature are narrow and detailed and frequently concerned with methodology, is leading libraries to increase their holdings of review journals.

REQUIREMENTS OF JOURNALS

Journals are used in two distinct ways. They may be read when published or may be used as an archive of articles for subsequent referral. This distinction has been used in the cost-cutting exercises made necessary by increasing journal costs in times of decreased funding. The difference in use has enabled a split in the methods in which journal material is delivered by libraries: *holding* versus *access*. The former refers to the traditional collection of journals by subscribing to the hard copy and the latter to provision of articles on demand by using some method of document delivery service.

Journals as current awareness

There is in each subject discipline a core of titles that forms essential reading for anyone who wishes to keep abreast not only of newly reported observations and results, but also of news and current opinion through editorials and letters.

Reading these core titles is sometimes combined with scanning contents pages of additional titles. This 'browsing' is used by many as their sole method of surveying the literature. There is a danger in over-reliance on core medical titles because of the scatter of topics in the literature. Weiner and his colleagues, for example, found that only 15% of original work on the risk of breast cancer from oral contraceptives appeared in obstetrics and gynaecology journals.[30]

Journals as archive

References to both newly published and older articles can be located as a result of current awareness services, literature searches, communication from colleagues and citations in other articles.

Literature searching using bibliographic databases will be discussed elsewhere, but a brief account of the ways in which journal articles are located is appropriate here, as often more than one method is employed and these have implications for selection of titles for hard copy subscription.

Selecting the required articles

Some clinicians have used *MEDLINE* online for years, but its transfer to CD-ROM, along with the production of current awareness weekly diskettes and other commercially produced databases and datasets, and the availability of databases through the Bath Information and Data Services (BIDS) over the Joint Academic Network (JANET), have brought the possibility of searching to most hospitals, research institutes, universities and colleges and to more individuals. Many use a combination of browsing the hard copy and database searching to identify articles of interest. The opposite end of the spectrum from those who read only a few core titles is represented by those who rely for literature searches on intermediaries.

How, then do we maximize the chances of our readers finding and reading the material they need? The retrieval of references and obtaining the full text of articles not held by their own libraries is discussed in other chapters (Computerized literature searching and Managing document delivery services). For now, the question to be addressed here concerns the selection of the journals collection by the holding library.

SELECTION OF JOURNALS COLLECTION

Few librarians come to a new site enabling a fresh look to be taken at the journals required. Most inherit not only a holdings list but also a mechanism for selection, often consisting of a library committee composed of users of the service.

Selection of titles required is relatively simple if the organization is dedicated to a focused subject area. The real problem arises when a collection is attempting to cover the breadth of health care and its scientific foundations. Furthermore, the smaller the budget the greater is the problem. Even in universities and medical schools, as a result of increases in subscription costs way beyond inflation, few budgets are adequate for a comprehensive collection of titles in all major specialties.

The Blackwells agency inflation figures show that the average price for a medical periodical increased from £95.16 to £185.75 between 1985 and 1993. This does not represent a steady incremental increase, as factors such as exchange rates influence the price of imported titles.

There is rarely any problem in compiling a list of journals required; the difficulty is in cancelling titles from a holdings list. Yet the continual increase in subscription prices and the need to take at least some new titles make this an exercise that few librarians can avoid.

Selection criteria that the librarian can use (other than the strident voices of assertive consultants) include surveys of usage, core lists, coverage by indexing and abstracting services, citation data, and cost effectiveness. Another factor is the availability of the material from other sources, including rapid document delivery services.

It is usual for a combination of these factors to be considered when drawing up a list of journals to be retained.[31-33]

Use surveys

Most surveys are library based, relying on some method of recording usage of journals in the library and often depending upon participation of the users. Reshelving by library staff can reduce the subjectivity of this approach.[34] User based surveys can be flawed by users failing to record their use, or genuinely not recognising that a casual inspection of the journal constitutes 'use'. The system can also be abused by people, anxious to retain a title, assigning an artificially high usage rate. These surveys are inadequate to measure actual need as they ignore journals which are used elsewhere (personal copies, other libraries) and those which would be used if they were available.

They do, however, reveal use patterns which show a consistency in that a small proportion of journals are used frequently. Surveys almost invariably show that most titles are used very infrequently or not at all, and Warren[35] points out that they negate the idea that libraries should be comprehensive. Beyond a small core of titles, it requires large increases in holdings to improve significantly the percentage of satisfied requests.

Core lists

Since 1965 the *Bulletin of the Medical Library Association* has published every two years a list of books and journals categorized by subject as a selection guide for a small or medium sized medical library.[36] Because of the list's emphasis on North American texts, the British Medical Information Working Party produced *Core collection of medical books and journals 1992*, which includes British and international book and journal titles suitable for sites in the United Kingdom.[37] The intention is that this list should also be updated every two years.

The emphasis of both lists is on books: but they are also useful in identifying essential journal titles.

Coverage by indexing sources

Appearance of journal titles in indexes and databases indicates that they are mainstream titles, and also that their articles will be retrieved through literature searches. Paradoxically, in a very specialist institution this may militate against holding the titles in hard copy because these articles can be retrieved by other means when required: to concentrate on buying titles which are not indexed actually increases the information content of the library. Despite this, most libraries still seem to want to restrict their holdings to major titles.

Citation data

Bibliometric methods are being used (and many would say abused) for evaluating research, research institutions, research workers and journals.

Citation data are produced by ISI and published annually in *Journal citation reports*. The most commonly used figure for assessing journals is 'impact factor'. This is a measure of the frequency with which articles in that journal are cited, which supposedly reflects the importance of the articles and therefore the journals in which these are published. The variation in the number of articles published in different journals is allowed for.

Citation data, in combination with other factors, have also been used in deselection of journal subscriptions in libraries.[38, 39]

Cost effectiveness

It is impossible to measure the value of information in the area of clinical medicine. There is sometimes a need for instant access to published information, and decisions to cancel titles which might in the future be needed urgently are difficult. But as it is impossible to subscribe to all titles, these decisions have to be taken. Assessing cost-effectiveness of journals involves monitoring the amount they are used and calculating the cost of obtaining papers from other sources. Where few articles are consulted in expensive journals there can be a strong case for cancelling the subscription, even though these may be journals previously thought to be 'core' titles.[40]

SERIALS MANAGEMENT

Since the previous edition of this book in 1981 there have been improvements in services provided by subscription agents which have improved the ordering, recording and management procedures to support the journal holdings of even small libraries.

An Aslib publication edited by Margaret E. Graham and Fiona Buettel, *Serials management: a practical handbook*,[41] provides information on these aspects and many more. The *Newsletter on serials pricing issues* is a free periodical and its subject coverage is broader than its title suggests. *Serials* is a publication of the UK Serials Group, and is free to members.

These publications deal with journal management in general. A few aspects of the topic are particularly relevant to medical libraries.

Subscription agents

A small library will probably order all its titles from a single agent although a large academic library may have more than one. A comprehensive list of agents is given in the Aslib book.[42]

A major criterion for choice of subscription agent will be the type and level of support offered. Most now provide online access for ordering, checking publication dates of issues, and claiming for non-arrivals. The PC-based packages provided also have a recording facility and produce financial reports which allow for fund accounting. The efficiency and ease of use of the software will be important for making a decision.

Other factors to consider are approachability of staff at the agency, whether a named person is available to be contacted directly, for instance.

Claiming for issues which fail to arrive on time is a task fraught with problems and the systems provided by agents should be investigated. It is important to know the quality of their reporting information about the progress of claimed issues.

An agent should be prepared to provide estimates of inflation for the following year for budgeting purposes. The great problem of budgeting is that to ensure continuity of delivery the orders must be placed and paid for by October, before the actual price for the following year's subscriptions is known. The larger agents have an advantage in being in regular contact with publishers at a high enough level to have access to any pricing information that is available.

Agents are in competition for accounts and are therefore prepared to make efforts to explain their services, even to librarians with a small subscription list.

In addition to obtaining literature describing services, librarians should ask for demonstrations and even a visit. Useful information can be gleaned from the experience of colleagues; an agent is rarely going to tell you about the bugs in the system and personality problems of support staff. But bear in mind that some colleagues may be unwilling to admit mistakes. Furthermore, the tendency to listen to anecdote and take the known path can lead to choices being made and products being purchased long after they are outdated and have been replaced by better and cheaper options.

Automation

In order to justify funding for automation of journals control there should be clearly stated service benefits or cost savings. Library automation is a fast-moving area and selection of a system will depend on which one fulfils essential criteria. The automated systems provided by the agents (see above) are discounted if tied to their supply of the journals. Most large libraries automate their serials management using an integrated system which may run in parallel with the agents' system. Anyone who is considering an integrated system should be aware of the need for electronic data interchange (EDI) between the library's and the agents' systems so that the library system can access, for example, invoicing information.

Access and loans policy

Despite the wide use of photocopying, some readers still wish to borrow journals, particularly recent issues. A circulation list provides for this by sending to named people newly arrived issues before they are put on display in the library. However, the delays incurred by the time journals spend on desks and in briefcases make this less popular with junior staff who are low down or not on the circulation list. By the time the 'current' issue arrives in the library it is no longer current at all.

A short loan arrangement is safer than a strict reference-only rule in any but the most secure library; if an item is borrowed illegally it is difficult to return. I know of no literature on the subject, but it is often claimed by medical librarians that clinicians are the worst offenders for illegal borrowing and for failing to record their loans.

Growth and storage

The increase in size of a collection for storage needs to be taken into account. New titles continue to appear, with a doubling in the total number of new titles every 10–15 years.[43] Although not all survive and some older ones cease, the survivors also contain more pages each year, taking up more shelf space.

Binding

One of the first targets for cost cutting has been binding. Although it protects journals, makes storage easier and reduces loss, it is expensive and unpopular with readers. It reduces ease of photocopying and quality of copies, and makes the journals unobtainable while at the binders. There used to be a decrease in use of journal articles between six months and two years after publication, corresponding to the time after the initial period when the volume was read and before the articles began to be cited in the literature. With the increased use of bibliographic databases, articles are retrieved more constantly and there is no convenient lull in demand during which the volume can be bound. The absence of journals 'at binding' is a real problem in medical libraries, where they are often needed urgently.

Archiving

Alternative methods of storing back-runs are worth considering. Microform is the cheapest but is becoming dated, and the quality of indexing and retrieval cannot compete with electronic forms. These include disc storage – CD-ROM (compact disc read only memory) and WORM (write once read many times) – and online electronic storage where journal articles are stored on remote computers and distributed over wide-area networks.

These methods of storage and transmission are expensive at present, but as they become more widely used it is likely that prices will fall. Factors such as reduction in prices of hardware, sharing of hardware with other functions and access to networks will bring electronic archiving within the range of more libraries (see also the section on The future of journals).

Retention and weeding

Electronic or microform storage will help to contain the rapid expansion of a collection, but this remains a serious problem in many libraries. Although the frequency with which the material is used drops with its age, medical journal literature is still required for many years and needs to be kept for as long as possible. If disposal becomes necessary, some of the criteria used for inital selection can be applied, particularly those of frequency of use and of availability in libraries close by. It is always a good idea to offer sets of journals to other libraries in the UK and abroad, before discarding. Some African and eastern European countries may have large gaps even in their major national resource libraries.

Missing issues and duplicates

Claims for non-arrivals should be made to the agent within a specified time to ensure that free issues are sent. For help with replacing missing issues, a duplicates exchange scheme exists in the UK for medical journals. It is at present administered by Mr Donald Orrock, Medical School Librarian, Ninewells Medical Library, Ninewells Hospital and Medical School, Dundee DD1 9SY.

THE FUTURE OF JOURNALS

It is interesting to speculate on whether the trends which we have already touched on – growth in volume of material published, greater generalization of general journals and specialization of specialty titles, and a continued increase in emphasis on review journals – will continue and whether there will be new developments as yet unsuspected. But probably the biggest question is the extent to which the electronic medium will play a significant role in archiving, and eventually in publishing, what has until now been a stable hard-copy medium.

Such speculation is not just idle curiosity. We need to attempt to predict future developments in publishing in order to plan for our libraries, even if the relevance of the changes to our own situations is not yet obvious.

Growth

The number of journals follows the quantity of research material being produced and published, which in turn follows the number of scientists working in the field.[44, 45] This pattern may be complicated in the future by the influence that information technology (IT) has had on research productivity,[46] which allows more results to be produced by the same number of research workers. Lock gloomily forecasts 50,000 biomedical titles in 50 years time (estimating between 15,000[47] and 25,000[48] now).

Content

In the concluding talks at the 1991 Conference on the Future of Medical Journals, the present editor of the *BMJ* envisaged general medical journals becoming more general and taking a more active role in addressing issues such as better health care and education.[49]

Review journals

Review journals have become more important and clearly fill a need for provision of a synthesis of the primary literature. With increasing subject specialization, review articles on interdisciplinary subjects, on subjects peripheral to the main interests and on subjects and techniques which underpin research, are likely to be even more significant.

The emphasis placed on standards of reviews at the recent Cumberlege seminar[50] is likely to raise the level of interest in reviews, and the Cochrane Centre in Oxford may well become the focus. The situation where almost two years after publication 72% of obstetrics units in England did not have access to the *Oxford database of perinatal trials* and 14% of consultants in a survey had not heard of it[51] may come under scrutiny.

Electronic publishing
It is clear that personal preference alone will not decide whether research results and medical information will be delivered electronically; the future medium will be determined largely by cost. Franklin believes that because so much new information produced is manageable only by computer, interrogation of data in electronic form, including the full text of journals and research results, will become the norm.[52]

Electronic journals
One of the obstacles to the movement towards communicating electronically rather than in printed journals has been the lack of formal acknowledgment of work not published in refereed journals. The recommendation in the Follett Report,[53] that refereed articles published electronically be accepted in the next University Research Assessment Exercise, should remove this obstacle, in the UK at least.

Developments over the past few years may lead, if not to a solution, at least to an admission that things cannot continue as they are. These factors include advances in technology and recognition of the anomaly in which the public sector pays twice for its own intellectual property, in subscribing to journals that publish the results which the public sector funded initially. The Follett Report recommends funding a series of projects to elevate both the status and acceptability of electronic journals; if this were to be achieved, electronic publishing might enable authors to take over distribution of their own research results, the intellectual property remaining with the funding bodies and host institutions.

Despite the medical field being a leader in the adoption of CD-ROM, fewer titles are appearing electronically in medicine than in science. The reason may lie in the absence of wide-area networking in the health service. When the NHS Information Management and Technology strategy is implemented, and when users access the Internet, the market for distributed data is likely to improve. Smith predicts that general medical journals will continue in hard copy and that it is the high-tech specialist titles which will be distributed electronically.[54]

Archiving
Production of documents as word-processed files makes possible their storage and character-stream transmission. It is likely that this will be the storage and transmission medium, rather than printing onto hard copy for later image

transfer to microform, image transmission by Fax, or digitization by optical character recognition (OCR).

We have already seen the appearance of parallel versions of journals – for instance, *New England journal of medicine* is available in hard copy, CD-ROM and on BRS *Core collection of medical literature* online – and the number of such titles may increase. Electronic storage may be used in preference to binding the hard copy in order to save space, to avoid volumes being removed for binding, and to remove the problems of missing and damaged issues.

The large-scale cutting of journal subscriptions resulting from rising costs has forced librarians to look at alternative methods of providing articles. Now that users have had to accept these alternative methods for some journals, the possibility is being explored of replacing a larger proportionof subscriptions, or even all, with efficient systems of current awareness services and individual article supply (CASIAS). This has already been implemented in some libraries; for example, Aston University has subscribed to ADONIS, which stores around 500 biomedical titles on CD-ROM. The library at the Royal College of Physicians and Surgeons in Glasgow has cancelled most subscriptions in favour of document delivery. It will be interesting to learn of the impact of these pioneering initiatives.

Management of electronic data

Funding for the storage and maintenance of electronic data, and for its management for later distribution, presents a huge challenge.[55] If ownership is to be retained by the producers, standards and means of control will have to be established at the outset.

REFERENCES

1   Graham, M. E. and Buettel, F. (eds,), *Serials management: a practical handbook*, London, Aslib, 1990.

2   Stankus, T., *Making sense of journals in the life sciences: from specialty origins to contemporary assortment*, New York, Haworth Press, 1992.

3   Lock, S. (ed.), *The future of medical journals*, London, British Medical Journal, 1991, 1–8.

4   Böttiger, L. E., 'Medical journals in transition – from author to reader', *Journal of internal medicine*, 232, 1992, 195–7.

5   Hamilton, D. P., 'Research papers: who's uncited now?', *Science*, **251**, 1991, 25.

6   Lock, S. (ed.), 'The future of medical journals', London, *British medical journal*, 1991.

7   Minisymposium, 'Medical journals – today and tomorrow', *Journal of internal medicine*, **232**, 1992, 195–228.

8   Stankus, T., *Making sense of journals in the life sciences: from specialty origins to contemporary assortment*, New York, Haworth Press, 1992.

9   Lock, S. (ed.), 'The future of medical journals', London, *British medical journal,* 1991, 1–8.

10   Fletcher, S. W. and Fletcher, R. H., 'Responsibilities of medical journals to readers', *Journal of internal medicine,* **232,** 1992, 223–8.

11   Lock, S., 'Perspective from the editor of the British Medical Journal', *Bulletin of the Medical Library Association,* **80,** 1992, 107–9.

12   McKnight, C., 'Electronic journals – past, present and future?', *Aslib proceedings,* **45,** 1993, 7–10.

13   Brahmi, F. A. and Kaneshiro, K., 'The Online Journal of Current Clinical Trials (OJCCT): a closer look', *Medical reference services quarterly,* **12,** 1993, 29–43.

14   Weiner, J. M., Shirley, S., Gilman, N. J., Stowe, S. M. and Wolf, R. M., 'Access to data and the information explosion: oral contraceptives and risk of cancer', *Contraception,* **24,** 1981, 301–13.

15   Currie, B. F., 'The importance of medical periodicals for the continuing education of physicians', *Association of Hospital Medical Education,* **7,** 1975, 1–2.

16   Stinson, E. R. and Mueller, D. A., 'Survey of health professionals' information habits and needs conducted through personal interviews', *JAMA,* **243,** 1980, 140–3.

17   Harris, J. J., 'Survey of medical communication sources available for continuing physician education', *Journal of medical education,* **41,** 1966, 737–55.

18   Stinson, E. R. and Mueller, D. A., 'Survey of health professionals' information and habits and needs conducted through personal interviews', *JAMA,* **243,** 1980, 140–3.

19   Warren, K. S. and Goffman, W., 'The ecology of medical literatures', *American journal of the medical sciences,* **263,** 1972, 263–73.

20   Lock, S., 'Perspective from the editor of the British Medical Journal', *Bulletin of the Medical Library Association,* **80,** 1992, 107–9.

21   Haynes, R. B., 'How journals could serve clinician readers better', in Lock, S. (ed.), *The future of medical journals,* London, British Medical Journals, 1991, 116–26.

22   Williamson, J. W., German, P. S., Weiss, R., Skinner, E. A. and Bowes, F. III., 'Health science information management and continuing education of physicians', *Annals of internal medicine,* **110,** 1989, 153–60.

23   Altman, D. D., 'The scandal of poor medical research', *BMJ,* **308,** 1994, 283–4.

24   Jones, R., Grainger, F., Evans, S., Scouller, J., Lachland, M. and Torrance, N., 'Sloppy use of literature often to blame', (letter) *BMJ,* **308,** 1994, 591.

25   Lock, S., ' Perspective from the editor of the British Medical Journal', *Bulletin of the Medical Library Association,* **80,** 1992, 107–9.

26   Lock, S. (ed.), 'The future of medical journals', London, *British medical journal,* 1991.

27   Minisymposium, 'Medical Journals – today and tomorrow', *Journal of internal medicine,* **232,** 1992, 195–228.

28   Rankin, J. A., 'Problem-based medical education: effect on library use', *Bulletin of the Medical Library Association,* **80,** 1993, 36–43.

29   Capital Planning Information, *Library and information services to support Project*

2000, NURLIS Phase I: a report to The Royal College of Nursing and the British Library, British Library R&D Report 6088, Stamford, Capital Planning Information, 1992.

30 Weiner, J. M., Shirley, S., Gilman, N. J., Stowe, S. M. and Wolf, R. M., 'Access to data and the information explosion: oral contraceptives and risk of cancer', *Contraception*, 1981, 301–13.

31 Hunt, R. K., 'Journal deselection in a biomedical research library: a mediated mathematical approach', *Bulletin of the Medical Library Association*, 78, 1990, 45–8.

32 Deurenberg, R., 'Journal deselection in a medical university library by ranking periodicals based on multiple factors', *Bulletin of the Medical Library Association*, 81, 1993, 316–9.

33 Bourne, C. P., 'Planning serials cancellations and cooperative collection developments in the health sciences: methodology and background information', *Bulletin of the Medical Library Association*, 73, 1985, 387–9.

34 Hunt, R. K., 'Journal deselection in a biomedical research library: a mediated mathematical approach', *Bulletin of the Medical Library Association*, 78, 1990, 45–8.

35 Warren, K. S., 'From papyrus to pixels: information technology and the future of biomedical publishing', in Smith, S. (ed.), 'The future of medical journals', London, *British medical journal*, 1991, 149–71.

36 Brandon, A. N. and Hill, D. R., 'Selected list of books and journals for the small medical library', *Bulletin of the Medical Library Association*, 81, 1993, 141–68.

37 Hague, H., Jackson, M., *Core collection of medical books and journals*, London, Medical Information Working Party, 1992.

38 Smith, T. E., 'The Journal Citation Reports as a deselection tool', *Bulletin of the Medical Library Association*, 73, 1985, 387–9.

39 Deurenberg, R., 'Journal deselection in a medical university library by ranking periodicals based on multiple factors', *Bulletin of the Medical Library Association*, 81, 1993, 316–9.

40 McSeán, T., 'Managing periodicals subscriptions: improving cost-effectiveness', *Serials*, 4, 1991, 53–7.

41 Graham, M. E. and Buettel, F. (eds.), *Serials management: a practical handbook*, London, Aslib, 1991.

42 Graham, M. E. and Buettel, F. (eds.), *Serials management: a practical handbook*, London, Aslib, 1991.

43 Lock, S., 'Journalology: evolution of medical journals and some current problems', *Journal of internal medicine*, 232, 1992, 199–205.

44 Lock, S., 'Perspective of the editor of the British Medical Journal', *Bulletin of the Medical Library Association*, 80, 1992, 107–9.

45 Huth, E. J., 'The information explosion', *Bulletin of the New York Academy of Sciences*, 65, 1989, 647–61.

46 Meadows, A. J., 'Communicating research – past, present and future', *Serials*, 4, 1991, 49–52.

47 Lock, S., 'Journalology: evolution of medical journals and some current problems', *Journal of internal medicine*, 232, 1992, 199–205.

48   Lock, S., 'Perspective of the editor of the British Medical Journal', *Bulletin of the Medical Library Association*, **80**, 1992, 107–9.

49   Smith, R., 'Through the crystal ball darkly: medical journals and the future', in Lock, S. (ed.), 'The future of medical journals', London, *British medical journal*, 1991, 187–210.

50   British Library, *Managing the knowledge base of health care*, British Library R and D Report, 6133, 1994.

51   Paterson-Brown, S., Wyatt, J. C. and Fisk, N. M. 'Are clinicians interested in up to date reviews of effective care?', *BMJ*, 1993, **307**, 1464.

52   Franklin, J., 'The position of paper in the emerging world of bioinformatics – could the journal be threatened?', in Lock, S. (ed.), 'The future of medical journals', London, *British medical journal*, 1991, 172–83.

53   Follett, B. (ed.), Joint Funding Council's Libraries Review Group, *A report for HECFE, SHEFC, HEFCW and DENI*, Bristol, Higher Education Funding Council for England, 1993.

54   Smith, R., 'Through the crystal ball darkly: medical journals and the future', in Lock, S. (ed.), 'The future of medical journals', London, *British medical journal*, 1991, 187–210.

55   Law, D., 'Beyond CD-ROM: wider horizons in the provision of electronic information', *Health libraries review*, **11** (1), March 1994, 52–6.

FURTHER READING

Graham, M. E., Buettel, F. (eds.), *Serials management: a practical handbook*, London, Aslib, 1990.

Lock, S., (ed.), 'The future of medical journals', London, *British medical journal*, 1991.

Stankus, T., *Making sense of journals in the life sciences: from specialty origins to contemporary assortment*, New York, Haworth Press, 1992.

11   Books in the health sciences

❖   *Shane Godbolt*

The growth of scientific literature that has taken place this century is well documented. Emphasis has been placed on the increase in periodical literature, but books too form part of the 'information explosion'. Book output in Britain remains very much higher than in the US, with 1992 figures recorded as: R. R. Bowker (US) 49,276, and Whitakers (UK) 78,835.

Medical science in the UK, as defined by Dewey classification, accounted for 3438 titles in 1993 (2596 of which were new titles). In total output medicine lay third, being outstripped only by fiction and children's literature.[1]

Books assist in the dissemination of information by providing a convenient means of access to recorded knowledge. It is true that a medical book is out-of-date when it is published, but this does not invalidate its use as a digest of available knowledge in a physically handy form. Depending on their purpose and intended audience, books perform the functions of:

- presenting information in a pre-digested form
- collecting scattered information
- providing orientation in a subject
- providing access to established facts
- summarizing available knowledge
- evaluating current trends and conflicting views.

They require no special equipment, and between their covers they contain their own list of contents and an index to allow the user to look up any specific information required. Rising costs have affected every area of library provision but considering the amount of information most books contain they remain remarkably cheap. Many titles are within personal as well as library budgets. Scanning the reviews of the more specialized texts, however, reveals an unhappy trend, as these are invariably designated 'now affordable only by your library'.

The primary literature of medicine consists of theses, research reports and original work reported in the periodical literature or read as papers at congresses. Access to it is by means of the secondary literature, which is composed of review articles, abstracts, indexes, catalogues and books of all types. As periodicals are the main source of primary information so books are the main source of secondary information and should form an important part of any collection, particularly one serving student populations. The balance between books, periodicals and other resources is a matter for the individual librarian to decide, based on the needs of the particular institution.

Searching for information from books requires a different approach from searching for relevant articles from the periodical literature. The techniques appropriate to searching the periodical literature are often off-putting to all but the specialist or the enquirer motivated by a specific need for the latest information. Many users are happy to satisfy their information needs by using the library catalogue or browsing on the shelves to select an appropriate book. They may go on from this to update and deepen their knowledge by using the periodical literature, but no advanced information need can exist until the user has acquired familiarity with the subject of interest via the use of books. Another factor in the use of books as information sources is the practical aspect that most libraries lend books but do not lend periodicals, and other resources require special equipment to use.

The 20th century has seen increasing specialization in the medical sciences, which has led to problems in communication between disciplines. At the same time, barriers between the sciences no longer exist in the formal way they used to. Each discipline contributes to the others and this bridging between subjects is reflected in an increasing emphasis on integration in the medical curriculum. Subjects are no longer taught in isolation. Clinicians, basic medical scientists and other health care professionals share curriculum development, and research teams are multidisciplinary. Books have an important role in the integration of knowledge in the medical and allied sciences. An example may be cited in the field of cellular and molecular biology, where discoveries in recent years have had important implications for almost every other discipline. This has resulted in numerous books being written to relate these discoveries to existing knowledge in traditional disciplines. New disciplines are being created in the vortex of change and the book literature reflects these growth areas in, for example, increasing numbers of titles in the neurosciences, consumer health information and on health care reform.

Some sections of the health care community rely heavily on books for their information needs – medical undergraduates and student nurses are examples – but in a health care library today, potential users are not likely to be only those commencing their careers. In a climate of continuing change in the nature and delivery of health care, the importance of ongoing professional education has become increasingly recognized and valued in the professions. The concepts of lifelong learning and continuing professional development are exemplified by the cultural shift to evidence based health care and pro-grammes such as the post-registration education in practice scheme of the United Kingdom Central Council for Nursing, Midwifery and Health Visiting (UKCC). It is therefore vital for all users that the library maintains a collection of up-to-date books and the interest of readers will be maintained if a constant flow of new books passes into stock, however modest the quantities in which they are added.

The days have passed when serious educational books were superficially unattractive. Modern book production, with its eye-catching covers and imag-inatively laid out contents, appeals to readers accustomed to glossy modern packaging.

The librarian should recognize the place books occupy in information trans-fer and dissemination and do everything possible to exploit this.

TYPES OF BOOK

A UNESCO conference in 1950 defined a book as a 'non-periodical literature publication containing 49 or more pages not counting the covers'. This prosaic definition conceals the scope and variety of material. Fifty-seven types, includ-ing non-print formats, are identified in an exhaustive list published in *Doody's annual*.[2] The main categories are described below.

Quick reference books

These include dictionaries, directories, pharmacopoeias and data books. They are authoritative works giving access to established facts and they are essential items in every collection. With the advent of CD-ROM as an increasingly acceptable distribution medium, many reference-type works are also available in this format.

Examples include:

- *Directory of medical and health care libraries in the United Kingdom and Republic of Ireland*, 9th edn, London, Library Association Publishing, 1994
- Reynolds, J. E. F. (ed.), *Martindale: the extra pharmacopoeia*, 30th edn, London, The Pharmaceutical Press, 1993 (also available on CR-ROM)
- *Medical directory* – annual (also available on CD-ROM)
- *Hospital and Health Services Yearbook* – annual
- *Mosby's medical, nursing and allied health dictionary*, 4th edn, St Louis, Mosby, 1994 (a well known, authoritative, illustrated work).

Standard works of reference

All major areas of medicine and surgery are covered by one or more titles which are known by reputation and use as standard. They provide access to knowledge in depth in subjects at an advanced level. Almost without exception they are large, multi-author works, expensive even by library standards, but they are extremely valuable as they cite references to original literature sources in support of facts and statements, thus providing the evidence from the knowledge base. They are usually too detailed to serve as textbook guides to their subject.

Examples include:

- Brocklehurst, J. C., Tallis, R. C. and Fillet, H. M., *Textbook of geriatric medicine and gerontology*, 4th edn, Edinburgh, Churchill Livingstone, 1992
- Cameron, S. *et al.* (eds.), *Oxford textbook of clinical nephrology*, 3 vols., Oxford, OUP, 1992
- Goodman and Gilman, *The pharmacological basis of therapeutics*, 8th edn, New York, Pergamon Press, 1990.

Postgraduate textbooks

In no other profession is the need to specialize so paramount and the number of courses leading to further qualifications so numerous as in medicine.

This ensures a good market for textbooks at the postgraduate level on all aspects of medicine, surgery, nursing and professions allied to medicine.

Textbooks are open to criticism for presenting current expert opinion rather than the evidence upon which the opinions are based. However, despite these limitations, both general and specialty textbooks are a good starting point for subject orientation or a quick refresher before a more intensive search. Being normally amongst the most heavily used material in the library, textbooks may be kept separately or loaned for shorter periods, according to local library policies.

Examples include:

- Churchill Livingstone's *Recent advances* series is a well established source and covers a wide range of topics in medicine
- Blackwell Science publishes an important series entitled *Advanced nursing*
- Mann, C. V. and Russell, R. C. G (eds.), *Bailey and Love's short practice of surgery*, 21st edn, London, Chapman and Hall, 1992, is standard and frequently revised
- *Conn's current therapy* and *Harrison's textbook of internal medicine* are published in new editions frequently
- *Scientific American medicine* is published under a continuous revision arrangement whereby different sections are updated at intervals

Texts for basic study

Production of books for undergraduate use flourishes in the medical sciences, some at an introductory and some at a more advanced level. Major publishers have produced a series of introductory textbooks aimed at the undergraduate market in recent years. Blackwell Science offers a range of titles in the *Lecture notes* series which is well produced in paperback, written by British authors of impeccable credentials and is popular and well used by medical students. In recent years the Wolfe Publishing Company, whose series of medical atlases has filled a gap, has become well established publishing in paper and hardback to cater for students and libraries. There is virtually no topic in the undergraduate medical curriculum which is not suitably covered by this type of material.

The nursing literature forms a separate entity which is well catered for. The huge changes in nurse education, as it moves into higher education, and in the profession at large, operating increasingly from a community base, are well reflected in the scope and range of new course textbooks published recently.

Examples include:

- Churchill Livingstone's *Skills for caring* series
- the *Integrated studies series* from Campion Press, which is produced for students undertaking Project 2000 courses and covers areas such as basic theory, life sciences and research methodologies.

Monographs

A monograph consists of a treatise on a single subject. It may be written by a single author or by several, but it is always an advanced level work. A well documented monograph with a comprehensive bibliography acts as an extended review article and has the same advantage in that the literature has been searched exhaustively and the evidence has been found and evaluated up to a particular point in time and may only need updating by the user.

Publishers in the field include Academic and Pergamon Press, who publish works of an advanced nature geared to a multidisciplinary audience. Monographs may also appear in series, examples being *Monographs of the Physiological Society* and the *CIBA Foundation symposia*.

Theses and dissertations

Most of the smaller medical libraries do not hold this type of material and larger ones will only hold those originating from their own institutions. Larger medical libraries may subscribe to *Index to theses* published by Aslib. This covers all theses accepted for higher degrees by UK universities and also indicates which have been deposited with the British Library Document Supply Centre. It is available on CD-ROM.

Pamphlets and other ephemera

Pamphlets are short, topical and written with a particular object in view. They may quickly lose their currency and they raise problems of storage and retrieval. Pamphlets may be ordered and treated as books, though for series such as those published by the Office of Health Economics (OHE) it may be practical to place a standing order and record the item in the periodicals index before cataloguing. Many useful and attractive pamphlets are available free from drug companies, though some feature advertising prominently or are written to extol the virtues of a specific product. The *Update Postgraduate Centre* series contains well produced pamphlets on clinical topics, usually free on application by postgraduate centre libraries and reasonably priced for others. Many very useful pamphlets are produced by the statutory bodies for nursing. The UKCC has published important documents on, for example, *Confidentiality, Code of professional conduct, Midwives rules* and *Administration of medicines*. The Royal College of Nursing (RCN) produces regular very valuable documents, for example, *The standards of care* series. These publications are available to libraries on subscription at very reasonable cost, via the RCN documentation service.

Reports

A report is a work written by a task force or particular group specifically commissioned to study a particular issue or problem. The contents may have wide implications. They present cataloguing problems and may be difficult to trace. Examples are:

- Tomlinson, B., *Report of the enquiry into London's health service, medical education and research. Presented to the Secretaries of State for Health and Education,* London, HMSO, 1992
- Calman, K., *Hospital doctors' training for the future. Report of the Working Group on Specialist Medical Training,* London, Department of Health, 1993

These examples are generally known by the name of the chairperson. Reports may also emanate from important bodies in the profession such as the Royal Colleges (including the RCN) or the Standing Conference on Postgraduate Medical Education (SCOPME).

Research reports in, for example, the pharmaceutical industry may be confidential, creating special problems in storage and administration.

The annual report of a research or teaching institution will almost certainly contain a list of its staff and other important information concerning its development and work. Good examples of this type are the Medical Research Council's annual report and the biennial report of the Wellcome Foundation. Many such reports are available free on application to the institution.

Government departments generate a great deal of report literature. Two annual reports from the Department of Health contain valuable statistical and other data: the *Annual report* and *On the state of the public health* report of the Chief Medical Officer are both published by HMSO. This type of report may be received on standing order and kept in sequence with other government publications, with other reports, with serials, or by subject, as the practice of each library dictates. They present few problems compared with other types of report.

Many reports on social and medical subjects are published by governmental bodies and by charitable organizations. They vary from substantial documents to pamphlets, and become known by a variety of names. Important reports are often mentioned in the press on the day of publication.

Perhaps the most difficult reports of all are those generated within the National Health Service (NHS). These are not commercially published and are therefore unavailable through conventional indexes, but are normally identified via *DHSS-Data* or *Health service abstracts* from the Departments of Health and Social Security Library. The DHSS Library is a deposit and indexing centre for all internal NHS reports. A useful comprehensive source is produced by Chadwyck-Healey on CD-ROM covering all government, including non-HMSO, publications. This literature is extensively covered in the next chapter.

Conference proceedings, symposia etc.

This grey area consists of multi-author works generated by a gathering of experts. The published work is often catalogued and shelved with the book collection, although the contents are usually no more than a collection of papers with a common theme. The quality varies enormously, from carefully edited accounts of important meetings, to mere photolithography of the authors' typescripts with little editing and no index.

This type of publication has grown enormously and its importance is reflected in attempts at bibliographical control such as the *Index to conference proceedings* produced by the British Library in both hard copy and on CD-ROM.

THE COLLECTION DEVELOPMENT PROCESS

Acquisition of suitable materials is the foundation of all the library's services. It is an exciting activity in which the librarian has a vital role, particularly in maintaining the overall balance of the collection. There should be mechanisms for involving library users in the process, but some may be over-enthusiastic for their own subjects and must be treated diplomatically. It is therefore important that the final decision rests with the librarian. Acquisition covers selection, ordering, accessioning and payment.

Selection policy

To formulate a policy, it is vital for the librarian to have a clear understanding of the work and aims of the library's parent organization. Some libraries have written policies. The formulation of this is a valuable exercise, crystallizing the role of the library and setting out the goals to be aimed at in building the library's collection. It is an internal standard that the library aims to reach. It is also a valuable document for use within the parent organization to press for adequate financial support. The policy must be realistic, but it deals with principles in defining what the library should get rather than reporting what it does get. It may be used as an instrument to further library development over a number of years.

Major factors that should be considered are:

- the purpose of the institution of which the library is part – is it involved in teaching, research, patient care or a mixture?
- the educational courses, if any, for which the institution is responsible
- groups within the institution for whom services will be provided; it may be appropriate to carry out an analysis of user needs particularly at a time of rapid change
- collection development policies of any network of which the Library is a part, for facilitating resource sharing.

Depending on the type of library, the groups for whom provision is made may include: students (medical, nursing and others); research workers; medical staff; trained nurses; teaching staff in all health care professions; paramedical staff (social workers, speech therapists, dietitians, physiotherapists, occupational therapists, radiographers, etc.); managers and administrative staff; and general practitioners and other community based workers.

The librarian must promote and encourage the use of the library and ensure that proper provision is made for all who need it. A library committee consisting entirely of medical users may overlook the needs of others and assume that the library is solely for the use of medically qualified staff, so it is important to include representatives of all groups and to stress the cost effectiveness of a multidisciplinary library to which all professions have access on equal terms. A collection development policy should define the subjects to be included and the appropriate level of coverage. Four levels may be distinguished:

(1) *exhaustive* – a complete collection of materials in a given subject, normally only appropriate for a very specialized institution or for an institution's own publications
(2) *comprehensive* – books and other materials sufficient to provide users with ready access to current information

(3) *reference* – one standard reference book and appropriate texts for students in each subject

(4) *skeletal* – one standard text, suitable for subjects outside the coverage of a normal health sciences collection, for example, chemistry and physics.

Priorities should be subject to re-evaluation to take account of new developments, in the work or functions of the institution. New departments may be established, new research be initiated, educational curricula may change, new partnerships and collaboration be established, all of which influence the library's collection development policy. Increasingly, as prices rise and electronic sources become easily and readily available, local policy, particularly in the small library, will be to provide access to information. The skill of the librarian will lie in the selection of core documents which are carefully targeted to meet user needs and to act more in the role of an information consultant or broker.

Sources of information for selection are of two types: those that describe publications already in existence, usually known as 'core lists', and those that list new and forthcoming items. Core lists are vital for the creation of a basic stock on any topic, and are also useful for revising an existing collection. Their use is controversial and there is a useful discussion of some of the issues involved in a recent World Health Organization (WHO) Newsletter.[3] A key resource is: Hague, H. (comp.), *Core collection of medical books and journals 1994/5*, London, Medical Information Working Party, 1995. Covering almost 1000 titles, this comprehensive list provides a selection of standard works for medical and health care libraries at varying prices and levels, and includes sections on complementary medicine and health administration. Nursing material is covered in some excellent lists produced by Haigh and Hochland Ltd including: Martin, J. (ed.), *Advanced professional education for post registration nursing*, Manchester, Haigh & Hochland, 1993. The editor is Head of Research and Curriculum at Lancashire College of Nursing and Health Studies and the publication, which is interdisciplinary in scope, covers a wide range of subjects, including ethics, management, and health care reform as well as nursing practice and research.

A brief but good list has been produced by Paul Moorbath, 'Books used on Project 2000 courses', *Nursing standard*, 7 (39), 16 June, 25–8. This discusses the results of a survey of 'essential' or 'background' titles on reading lists from a survey of Project 2000 colleges, and weights some 40 titles. Other lists of core standard works are: British Council, *Core list of library materials: medicine*, Libraries, Books and Information Division, Medlock Street, Manchester M15 4PR; and for those concerned with libraries in developing countries: World Health Organization, Regional Office for the Eastern Mediterranean

(Alexandria), *List of basic sources in English for a medical faculty library*, 6th edn, 1992 (WHO-EM-HLT-006-E-L).

Specialist lists have been produced by two Royal Colleges: Royal College of General Practitioners, Information Resources Centre, *Books for general practice and primary health care, 1991*, London, RCGP, 1992. This lists 140 publications with full details and annotations, under broad subject headings.The Royal College of Psychiatrists produces lists which are regularly revised and updated: *Lists of books suitable for a psychiatric library 1988–1993*, and *Key books for a psychiatric library*, which is a short list of about 40 titles at a purchase price deliberately set at around £1000 for the small medical library.

In addition, the American list by A. N. Brandon and D. R. Hill may be mentioned. Published first in 1965 this has been regularly revised and updated. The most recent appeared in *Bulletin of the Medical Library Association*, **81**, 1993, 141–68, and included 606 books and 143 journals covering all branches of medicine, surgery and the specialties. Predecessors of the list have been intended as a selection guide for a small or medium-sized medical library, but it is recognized that, owing to rapidly rising prices, the primary use of the list may be to provide a basic collection for a consortium of hospital libraries or a network sharing library resources. Two hundred items suggested for initial purchase by smaller libraries are indicated by an asterisk. Although the bias is to American literature, some other English language material is included and the list forms a useful supplement to the *Core collection*. One useful feature is a costing of the entire list at 1993 prices – approximately £58,000 – and for the 200 asterisked items and journals only, approximately £22,000. A minimal core list of 85 books identified for the first time in 1993 would cost £8000. A companion version by the same authors covers allied health: 'Selected list of books and journals in allied health', *Bulletin of the Medical Library Association*, **82** (3), July 1994, 247–64. This is the sixth edition and suggests 415 books and 76 periodical titles in allied health subjects, largely American and Canadian; 177 books and 32 periodicals are identified for core purchase. Finally, reflecting the changing emphasis in health care, S. Virtue's 'Recommended list of business/management books for the hospital library', *Bibliotheca medica Canadiana*, **15** (3), 1994, 156–62 may be consulted.

It is important to be aware of new publications relevant to the library's collection. Various useful sources may be identified. Specialist booksellers' lists, usually produced weekly, are invaluable. Examples are the Cambridge based company Cambridge Medical Books, Haigh and Hochland of Manchester and the medical lists of Dillons Bookshop, London. *The Bookseller* (Whitakers, weekly) is useful for general professional awareness of trends in the publishing and book trade as well as for its weekly listing of all newly published English Language titles, which covers medicine, nursing, psychiatry, psychology and other broad subject areas of relevance to the health care library. Publishers circulars are voluminous and untidy but important sources. Advertising leaflets can be used as part of the current awareness service and passed directly to specialist staff. Most publishers also produce an annual catalogue, and collections of these relevant to the library's interests should be built up.

Book reviews in journals may be checked. Of particular value are those in the *British medical journal* and *The Lancet*, where the major medical publishers also advertise. Regular books review supplements also appear in journals such as *British journal of hospital medicine, Nature* and *New scientist*. For nursing books *Nursing times*, which appears weekly, publishes a regular section of reviews, while *Journal of advanced nursing* is useful for reviews of higher level texts.

Innovative services are provided by a newly launched American company, Doody's Publishing Inc., set up in 1993. The publications have been endorsed by the Medical Library Association and are offered at a reduced rate to members. The key publication is *Doody's journal: health sciences book reviewing*, a bimonthly journal evaluating about 250 titles in each issue. Reviews are structured, independent and speedy, and have been welcomed by US librarians. A British version is under discussion. Recently there have been useful reviews of CD-ROMs in health sciences libraries[4] and of online sources of health sciences book reviews.[5]

The process of selection starts with routine checking of the library's usual sources for new editions, monographs, standard texts, government publications, reports and new books of interest. The aim is to ensure that all relevant subjects, core to the library's users, are kept up to date and enlarged if necessary. Recommendations from users (particularly teaching staff) should be encouraged, and suggestions should be considered in the light of legitimate needs and the overall balance of the collection. Users should always be notified whether or not a book they suggest is purchased by the library. Interlibrary loan requests should be monitored periodically to ascertain which individual items warrant purchasing and whether any specific subject areas need attention.

Evaluation and the decision to purchase

In most medical libraries a large proportion of annual expenditure is permanently allocated to periodicals and new editions, therefore great care must be taken with the allocation for individual publications. It may be advisable to divide funds on a monthly or quarterly basis, so that it will be possible to purchase important publications appearing late in the financial year.

Not all publications that appear relevant need to be purchased. If the quality of the work or standard of presentation is inferior, or if the information is already available in other titles in the library's stock, the book need not be considered. An experienced health care librarian should be able to evaluate many new books by using appropriate criteria:

1. standing of the book evidenced by the number of previous editions
2. credentials and standing of the author in the field
3. reputation of the publisher for producing works of a high standard in the subject.
4. endorsement, e.g. a foreword written by an acknowledged expert or on behalf of a professional body
5. comparison of dates of reference with the date of publication
6. clarity of layout and quality of diagrams and illustrations
7. quality and adequacy of index
8. is its physical make-up and binding such that it will stand up to heavy use?

The librarian may need to liaise, formally or informally, with subject experts which is helpful in building links between the library and its users and also in disseminating information about newly published work. The final decision on purchase should rest with the librarian, and depends on whether it usefully complements other works already in the collection and who will find it useful; books with a very restricted audience may be better borrowed for interested readers than bought for the library. More should be selected than can be afforded so that there is the possibility of choice amongst different titles. The librarian must aim above all to keep the collection balanced. A balanced library does not mean equal coverage in all subjects. It is important to provide better coverage for fields in which there is enthusiastic work going on and lesser coverage in areas that evince little interest.

Multiple copies
Ideally multiple copies of works in constant demand should be provided, but financial constraints may make this difficult. When funds are limited, the librarian needs to consider whether it is better to have more than one copy of a heavily used work or to extend the range of the collection by acquiring items that may be in less demand.

Ordering
Orders should be placed with an experienced medical bookseller who will often be able to supply books directly from stock. Services offered should include delivering books on approval and making up special subject lists or other regular lists to aid selection. They may also include a variety of technical processes, such as labelling or covering, and this should be considered. The

time of today's librarians and information specialists needs to be focused on service development and support to users, not on processes which it may well be cost effective to outsource.

Wherever possible, the librarian should deal directly with the bookseller. Within the NHS, it is necessary to develop good relationships with supplies departments unfamiliar with the idiosyncracies of the book market, or suitable booksellers and ordering policies. Multiple copy order forms, which may be computerized, are helpful for even the smallest library. In some regional library systems and in most provincial university library systems, order slips have been standardized. The multiple copies of order forms can perform a variety of functions according to the system preferred by individual librarians. Uses which may be considered are: copy in library order file; copy to bookseller; copy in catalogue or separate 'items on order file' in the library; copy to notify a recommender of purchase.

Most large medical library systems are computerized and acquisitions is one of the modules within an integrated package. Many smaller libraries run personal computer (PC) software and can move records simply through the processes of requesting, ordering, receiving, accessioning and cataloguing. Wherever possible, processes should be done cooperatively to aid resource sharing and coordination within any network that the library is part of.

Payment

Every library, however small, should maintain its own records of expenditure on books and other items. The contents of packages should be carefully checked on arrival and compared with invoices or delivery notes against the order file. Errors or omissions must be promptly followed up and invoices either dealt with or passed to the central accounts department for attention.

Gifts

It is good policy always to accept gifts courteously while reserving the library's right to dispose of material. Gifts should be graciously acknowledged and, where appropriate, a bookplate recording the name of the donor and date of the gift should be inserted in the volume.

Stock revision

The acquisition of new material must be linked with a policy for discarding old and outdated stock if an effective library service is to be maintained. Medical information becomes out-of-date quickly but unevenly. Many standard texts appear regularly in new editions. Depending on how rapid development has been, a new edition may be held for reference only and the previous edition loaned. It is unsatisfactory to have out of date material mingling with new books on the shelves. Ideally there should be an annual review of all items over ten years old, and some may need discarding earlier.

Liaison with subject experts will be necessary and a policy should be worked out to suit the library and its users. It may be worth offering conference proceedings or specialized monographs to the British Library before destroying them. A few very large or specialized libraries have an archival function and must therefore be very cautious about discarding.

Book prices

To maintain a policy of adequate growth in the book collection, it may be necessary to estimate the funds required. The *Index to academic book prices*, published semi-annually by the Library Management Research Unit of Loughborough University, includes medicine. *The Bookseller* also publishes a half-yearly average prices summary across all fiction and non-fiction, which is useful for comparison.

CATALOGUING AND CLASSIFICATION

The growth of all branches of medical literature and the natural desire of readers to be able to help themselves necessitate arranging the stock in a logical and comprehensible manner. All guides to the contents of the collection should be clear and easily understood. Cataloguing and classification are complementary. Together they provide the key to material contained in the library, reveal its contents, link related subjects and guide readers to actual material on the shelf.

The impact of new technology

Today in most medical libraries the card catalogue has been replaced by the catalogue on computer, or online catalogue. The cataloguing software used in medical libraries varies depending on the size of the library. Large scale integrated library systems with cataloguing, acquisitions, circulation and online publication cataloguing modules are found in the academic libraries. These packages usually structure and index the catalogue record according to standard MARC (machine readable cataloguing) format, in Britain's case UK MARC. Smaller medical libraries often choose text retrieval software that will run on a standalone or networked PC. These packages may or may not include housekeeping modules. Text retrieval packages offer increased flexibility when structuring and indexing the catalogue compared with MARC records, but compatibility with MARC should be a consideration when selecting software.

Shared cataloguing systems

Shared cataloguing systems have potential benefits to librarians in saving time and producing cataloguing information of a uniformly high quality. They have been developed in some NHS regional library networks and by larger libraries where a medical library is part of a larger system, for example, most of the provincial universities with medical schools have shared cataloguing schemes such as BLCMP (Birmingham Libraries Cooperative Mechanization Project) or OCLC (Online Computer Library Centre). The time and cost savings experienced by larger libraries participating in shared cataloguing schemes are considerable.

One of the advantages of regional library systems in the NHS has been the opportunity to involve small library units in cooperative cataloguing schemes. Wessex Regional Library and Information Service (WRLIS) was the first to set up cataloguing as a central service for the libraries in the region. Each library in the system catalogues the acquisition if it was the first to generate an order within WRLIS. The union catalogue has been in existence since 1970 and the central database holds 55,000 records. Output has, until now, been on microfiche, but WRLIS is prototyping a CD-ROM and dial-up OPAC.

In both South East and South West Thames Regions, a centralized service has been built up. The services are similar to that in Wessex, whereby the first library in the region to order is responsible for producing catalogue data. The time taken to process new titles is reduced and the records themselves are of uniformly high quality. All three cooperative systems provide extensive training and guidance on cataloguing. There are also procedures in place to check the quality of records submitted to the union catalogues.

Conventional cataloguing

The librarian in a small library should not spend a great deal of time on cataloguing but rather should be providing reference and user support services. If the catalogue is compiled according to simple rules, compatible with the *Anglo-American cataloguing rules*, it will serve its purpose well. Most medical libraries are small, working collections and any system must be judged functionally. When it is considered that the average time taken to catalogue a book has been calculated as 20 minutes, it is clear that not all material may be worth the time and effort involved in cataloguing. Pamphlets, reprints and other ephemera may be stamped with the date of arrival and displayed or shelved in a box with associated subject material. A simple system should operate so that these items may be ruthlessly discarded when no longer current.

Catalogue entries for the author or corporate bodies responsible for their publication are essential. Entries should be included for joint authors, editors and series. For reports it is wise to include an entry for the chairperson, the title, or any colloquialism by which readers may search for the report. Cataloguing in publication (CIP) data may be useful in giving guidance on the choice of entries.

Subject indexing

Subject indexing is crucial to retrieval. Headings should be chosen from an accepted standard list of terms. Medical Subject Headings (MeSH) is published annually as Part 2 of the January issue of *Index medicus* and is widely adopted by medical libraries. It is compiled by experts at the National Library of Medicine (NLM) and it may be regarded as authoritative. The terms are compiled to index periodical articles, making it a very comprehensive list, suitable for all but the most specialized medical library. Medicine changes rapidly and classification schemes quickly fall behind as medical knowledge advances whereas MeSH is updated annually. If readers are familiar with MeSH headings it is easier to consult their own library's catalogue if it uses MeSH terms. Conversely, a MeSH based subject catalogue will introduce new readers to standard headings before they make acquaintance with *Index medicus* or *MEDLINE*. The use of MeSH is widespread in British medical libraries and contributes to uniformity and standardization in subject cataloguing.

Problems will be encountered in using the MeSH list owing to its American origin. Spelling will need to be anglicized; for example, 'esophagus' to 'oesophagus'; 'pediatrics' to 'paediatrics'. Usage also differs between the UK and the USA: the American term 'neoplasms' is used in preference to 'cancer'; 'adrenaline' is referred to as 'epinephrine'. There is no heading for National Health Service and index terms are inadequate to describe British health care, particularly in a period of intense change. Several of the regional library services have produced their own thesauri to address this problem. South West Thames Regional Library Service publishes the *Subject cataloguing guide* (4th edn, 1994) to supplement MeSH, and additional headings have been adopted from other thesauri. The Departments of Health and Social Security Library Services have compiled a comprehensive health care thesaurus, *DH/DSS-Data Thesaurus* (2nd edn, 1993).

Generally, the headings chosen should be as specific as possible. For example, a book on diseases of the middle ear should not be indexed under 'Head' or 'Ear' but 'Ear diseases'. Similarly Emery's standard short textbook *Introduction to medical genetics* should not be indexed under 'Genetics' but under 'Genetics, medical'. Subheadings should also be used. A textbook of physiology of the heart will be indexed under 'Heart, physiology'. Headings should be chosen that describe the main subjects of the book; while most catalogue records only have two or three subject headings assigned to them, cataloguing software does offer the possibility of increasing the number of subject headings.

Enriched cataloguing

It has been stated that ' . . . in times of declining resources for libraries, addition of content revealing information might help optimize use of a book collection and aid in more effective resource sharing . . .'.[6] The US MARC Advisory Committee is seriously considering changes to the MARC format to accommodate detailed table of contents information.[7] These are issues that need to be taken seriously in the light of research, which shows that users of online catalogues are often less than satisfied with the results of a search. Moving beyond the standard bibliographic catalogue by enriching catalogue records is one answer to users' dissatisfaction. Book catalogues can be enriched in a number of ways, e.g. by including abstracts, contents and author affiliations. The number of subject headings can be dramatically increased, or terms taken from the index of the book itself can be used as subject headings. These enhancements have been tested in a number of studies with positive results.[8, 9]

One of the brakes on the widespread introduction of enriched cataloguing has been the costs involved. For example, in most medical libraries, keyboarding contents is not a viable option. The use of scanning technology is restricted by copyright law at present. One option is to incorporate enriched data that is already available in electronic format into the catalogue. Book Data produce *BookFind* a CD-ROM of approximately two million bibliographic records, half of which are enriched. Researchers at City University in London and North West Thames Regional Library Service have been experimenting with using *BookFind* records which can be downloaded into a catalogue without breaching copyright law.

Enriched catalogues present many challenges for software, particularly in the design of public access catalogues and the ability of the software to cope with the natural language found in abstracts and contents. The large number of records that can be retrieved when searching an enriched catalogue, and the capacity of software to weight search terms or rank the retrieved records, are areas for development.

The commercially available databases for medical journals have been enriched for many years now, and services that provide journals contents pages, such as *Inside information* from the British Library and *CARL Uncover* from Blackwells, are becoming standard bibliographic tools. Equal access to medical books can be achieved with enriched cataloguing.

Classification

There has been a great variation amongst medical libraries in Britain on the choice of schemes. With the adoption of MeSH there has been a major shift to use NLM classification. A sample of 300 libraries, taken from *The directory of medical and healthcare libraries in the United Kingdom and the Republic of Ireland 1994-5* (9th edn, London, Library Association Publishing, 1994) provides the following figures on classification:

National Library of Medicine	135
Dewey decimal	57
Library of Congress	17
Universal decimal	14
BLISS	7
Own scheme	70

General classification schemes such as Dewey, University Decimal Classification (UDC) and Library of Congress (LC) are not recommended for a small medical library, but may be used in medical libraries that are part of larger systems, for example in use in a higher education institution. In medicine, updating is also vitally important. Barnard, for example, was last revised in 1955 and has been replaced by NLM in most libraries.

National Library of Medicine scheme
The National Library of Medicine system is the major published classification specifically intended for a health care collection. *National Library of Medicine classification* appeared in its 4th edition in 1978 and a new edition is expected in 1995. It has the advantage of fitting into the Library of Congress classification scheme, which has schedules outside the field of medicine and its related subjects. It allows for specific entry, bringing together in one place all aspects of a topic. It is the most widely used classification scheme for health care libraries throughout the English speaking world, thereby making cooperative schemes easier and offering uniformity for users and library staff alike.

Some modifications to the NLM scheme are required for its use in the UK. The cataloguing cooperatives in Wessex and elsewhere, with their multidisciplinary libraries, have experienced some problems, and modifications have been agreed within the cooperatives. Wessex, for example, produces its own classification *Wessex classification scheme* (2nd edn, 1994), which has been expanded in the areas of health services management and nursing.

Guiding the reader
Depending on the type of shelving used, various methods of shelf guiding may be appropriate. Shelves and end panels of bays should be clearly labelled with classmarks and subjects to enable readers to browse. Some readers are 'catalogue resistant'. The enterprising librarian can use ideas such as a simple flow chart to put across information and encourage users to help themselves (see Figure 11.1). Whether guides and labels are produced in the library or with the aid of an outside department, such as a medical illustration department, they should be neat and professional.

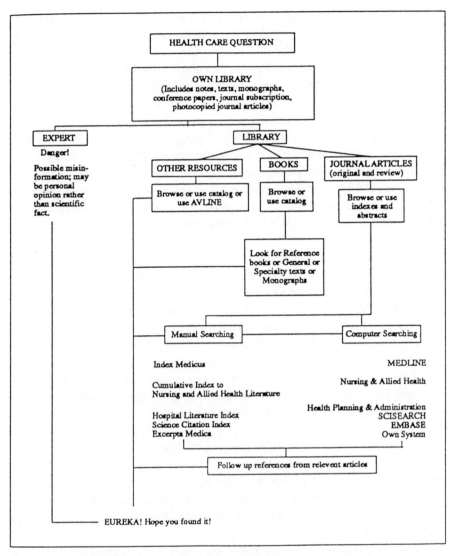

Fig. 11.1 Flowchart for guiding library users (reproduced with permission from Williams, R. M., Baker, L. M. and Marshall, J. G., *Information searching in healthcare*, New Jersey, Slack Inc., 1992; distributed by McGraw-Hill)

Whither the book?

Questions and challenges face the librarian and traditional publisher in a context in which: enabling technology is becoming more sophisticated; hardware prices are falling; and developments in computer networks and supernetworks continue to affect all aspects of information provision, access and application. Doody[2] predicts that available technology will contribute to the efficiency of book publishing by decreasing the time between delivery of copy and appearance of the published product. However, prices for books will continue to rise. Traditional publishers will continue to dabble in electronic media but health sciences publishing may be in for major upheavals as new information technology driven companies enter the information-hungry health care professional and student markets.

An example of a traditional publisher taking new opportunities is Mosby, which has launched a range of medical interactive CD products, many based on their parent texts but containing full colour images, video sequences, animated three-dimensional simulations and interactive self-tests. Springer-Verlag has produced a standard work *The comprehensive classification of fractures: long bones* on CD-ROM. The program provides a radiographic example for the classification, enables the user to examine the fracture in an original X-ray, and indicates the proposed treatment for the fracture from Springer's companion work *Manual for internal fixation*. The technology allows flexibility and contributes to the integration of knowledge and new ideas, for example, a database feature to store patients' data is included on the CD-ROM package.

In a useful report and discussion of the key issues relating to digital books, Akeroyd indicates a role for on-demand publishing services in keeping books in print, by being able to print single copies at reasonable cost.[10] An excellent and highly relevant overview of current key issues is given by Feldman,[11] a strategic consultant in electronic publishing. In a paper commissioned to review the impact of electronic book technologies and media on the UK higher education sector, he highlights McGraw-Hills' Primis project as an exemplar for the future. Launched in 1989, the project allows course teachers to select sections of materials held by McGraw-Hill on a large, digitized database of course textbooks and supplemental publications, add their own sections of locally originated course material and have their personally anthologized book printed, bound and delivered in any quantity from one copy upwards, all within a matter of days.

Electronic publishing will not mean the death of the printed book but will expand horizons and offer new possibilities. We shall see the emergence of new multimedia information products, many interactive, along with new flexible and effective ways of publishing traditional printed material focused to meet customer requirements.

There have been collections of medical books in Britain and Europe since the early Middle Ages. The rise of the journal as the principal vehicle for disseminating new knowledge challenged their supremacy, but the 'information explosion' established books as the most important sources for accessing information. Their role has changed over the years but their usefulness remains.

ACKNOWLEDGMENTS

I am greatly indebted to Louise Jones, who has rewritten and revised the sections on Cataloguing and Classification, and to many others for information and ideas, particularly Howard Hague, John Hewlett, Leonard Malcolm, Gill Terry and Jane Williamson.

REFERENCES

1 *The Bookseller*, London, Whitaker, 18 February 1994, 64–72.

2 *Doody's health sciences book review annual 1993*, Oak Park, IL, USA, Doody Publishing Inc., 1994.

3 *Liaison (Newsletter of the WHO Office of Library and Health Literature Services)*, 4 (2), August 1993.

4 Chiang, D., 'CD-ROMs in health sciences libraries', *Medical reference services quarterly*, **12** (2), Summer 1993, 67–81. This list is largely derived from the annual Meekler publication *CD-ROMs in print*. It covers *MEDLINE* versions, full-text journals and books, specialty databases and miscellaneous material.

5 Goddard, C. F., 'Online sources of health sciences book reviews', *Medical reference services quarterly*, **12** (4), Winter 1993, 23–6.

6 Weintraut, T. S. and Shiniogucki, W., 'Catalog record content enhancement', *Library resources and technical services*, **37** (2), 1993, 167–80.

7 Wittenback, S. A., 'Building a better mousetrap: enhanced cataloguing and access for the online catalog', in Ra, M. (ed.), *Advances in online public access catalogs*, vol. 1, 1992, 74–92.

8 Van Ordern, R., 'Content-enriched access to electronic information: summaries of selected research', *Library hi tech*, **8** (3), 1990, 27–32.

9 Beatty, S., 'Subject enrichment using contents or index terms: The Australian Defence Force Academy experience', in Ra, M. (ed.), *Advances in online public access catalogs*, Vol. 1, 1992, 93–104.

10 Akeroyd, J., 'Digital books?', *On-demand printing and publishing*, London, Library and Information Technology Centre, 1994.

11 Feldman, T., 'Electronic books', in *Libraries and IT. Working papers of the information technology sub-committee of the HEFCs' libraries review*, Bath, UKOLN, The Office for Library and Information Networking, 1993.

12   Grey literature in health care

❖   *Sheila Padden*

The aim of this chapter is to provide a practical guide to the location and acquisition of grey literature, both used and produced within the NHS, to highlight its attendant problems and to suggest that librarians themselves have an important role to play in improving the bibliographic control of grey literature.

Andrew Smith[1] has given a detailed discussion of grey literature in general, and provides a list of recommended readings. This chapter will concentrate on the extreme end of the spectrum, on the 'dark grey' literature.

Most writers agree that the major defining characteristics of grey literature are its unavailability through normal book selling channels, its invisibility in bibliographies and the subsequent difficulties faced in tracking it down. Most librarians, especially those working in special libraries, are familiar with the sometimes frustrating features of grey literature. Documents are often flimsy, undated, lacking conventional bibliographic information, produced in small numbers and may be free or prohibitively expensive. Librarians may be offended by their inconsistent titles, their lack of index or date, inadequate references and seemingly ephemeral nature.

Despite its elusive nature, its failure to conform and its many shades of grey, this literature is worth pursuing for the sake of its intrinsic value – its content and its currency. In any discipline it is at the cutting edge. It is highly specialized in content and audience. Its currency reflects political and public opinion, current practice and research. Its dynamic 'here and now' nature makes it an essential element of information services supporting a rapidly changing health care system.

LIBRARIANS' SKILLS

The successful pursuit and control of grey literature depends initially on the development of special skills and the application of unconventional methods.

In the first place, librarians must acquire a working knowledge of their own organizations: decision-making processes, committees and working groups, and the documents they produce. They must be conversant with the role of the organization, its relationships with the environment and the effect on the organization of fiscal and legal changes.

Like Autolycus, the good librarian is 'a snapper-up of unconsidered trifles', sending for reading lists and following up incomplete references, scanning journals and newspapers for reviews, recording items of potential interest and developing a network of personal contacts.

Membership of national and local groups is an excellent method of widening this network, of gaining access to library acquisition lists and subject bibliographies and generally keeping up-to-date in a complex environment. Networking is particularly valuable for the small or single-handed unit, as many successful grey literature queries depend on personal contact, or on access to documents intended for local readership.

THE IMPORTANCE OF GREY LITERATURE IN HEALTH CARE

All disciplines produce and use grey literature, but recent changes in health care have affected the volume and range of medical grey literature. For clinicians and managers, paramedical staff and professions allied to medicine, access to current information is vital. Developments in computer technology mean that 'invisible colleges' can now communicate by e-mail and bulletin-boards, encouraging the growth of non-published documents. An increasing number of bulletin-boards and electronic journals on clinical topics are now available on Internet.

Changes in the NHS during the last decade – the *Griffiths report*,[2] *Working for patients*,[3] *Caring for people*,[4] *The health of the nation*,[5] and the recent review of regional functions – have all played a significant part in the growth of grey literature. Each reorganization results in working papers, guidance, policy statements and working party reports. The voluntary and independent sector respond with their views, attempting to influence agendas and evaluate policy.

As well as increasing the volume of literature, these changes affect the information needs of health staff at all levels and in all disciplines. The pressure of the market increase the need for business and management information. Medical and management staff undertaking continuing professional education need access to library services, and as a result produce a body of highly topical grey literature. The potential value of this knowledge has been highlighted by Hepworth.[6]

The following discussion of the various types of grey literature includes information for clinicians and managers, purchasers and providers. The common denominators are its elusiveness and its poor exploitation.

TYPES OF GREY LITERATURE
Government information
Non-HMSO grey literature

It has been estimated that the 'grey' titles issued each year by government departments outnumber the titles published or distributed by HMSO. A valuable supplement to HMSO's regular publication lists is the *Catalogue of British official publications not published by HMSO*, published quarterly and annually by Chadwyck-Healey. This catalogue lists documents from over 500 government funded or supported agencies which are not available from HMSO. It includes journals and audiovisual materials, and provides addresses. The publishers can supply microfiche copies of most documents. It is possible to subscribe to a specific subject collection such as 'health and medicine'.

Health care librarians will find this publication useful to gain access to documents from agencies such as

- NHS Executive Directorates
- Management Executive for Wales and Scotland
- Department of Health and Social Services Inspectorate, Regional Offices
- Medical Research Council.

Two examples are (1) the statistical series from the Statistics and Research Division of the Department of Health, a unit that produces statistics on hospital activity, general practice, personal social services and pharmaceutical services, and (2) profiles of local authority social services. Chadwyck-Healey also produces *UKOP*, a quarterly CD-ROM database which includes official HMSO publications as well as those 'not published' by HMSO. Details are available from Chadwyck-Healey, Cambridge Place, Cambridge CB2 1NR.

NHS Executive documents

NHS Executive documents often relate to initiatives established in *Working for patients*.[3] Topics include case-mix, medical audit, day surgery, management information systems and needs assessment. The majority of these are the result of specific projects such as 'Local voices', the epidemiological reports resulting from the DHA Project and the Research and Development Strategy. These projects are often supported by an accompanying newsletter or bulletin which provides information on progress and new documentation. Publications are listed in *NHS Executive news*, a monthly newsletter available from NHS Publishing Services, Skipton House, 80 London Road, London SE1. A second source of information is the NHS Executive Communications Unit at Quarry House, Quarry Bank, Leeds LS2 7UE.

Department of Health Circulars

This is a generic term embracing a wide range of numbered series. Circulars are distributed daily to NHS managers at all levels on a 'need to know' basis. They relate to current policy and initiatives, and may both provide and request information. Each circular has a unique serial number which aids filing. In some regions, databases of circulars have been established allowing access by subject as well as serial number. Circulars are not published by HMSO and in the first instance should be sought within the hospital or health authority. In the final resort, *Health service guidelines* (HSG series) can be obtained from the Department of Health Leaflets Unit, No. 2 Store, Manchester Road, Heywood, Oldham OL10 2PZ. *Executive letters* (the EL series) can be obtained from: The Public Enquiry Office, Department of Health, Room 444, Richmond House, 79 Whitehall, London SW1A 2NS.

Lists of circulars issued by the Department of Health are published monthly in *Health service abstracts,* and are listed in the journals *Health services management* and *IFM Healthcare newsletter.* They are also available online from *DHSS-Data* via Data-Star/DIALOG.

Apart from these examples, there are many thousands of 'grey' documents produced each year by national statutory and non-statutory bodies, academic research units and the voluntary sector. Both purchasers and providers require access to this literature and to the various printed and computerized reference tools discussed below.

An accessible source which should not be overlooked is the press. Reports and research findings which may be controversial or newsworthy are often featured in the quality newspapers, as well as in the *BMJ, Health service journal* and *Nursing times.*

Health authority literature

The various levels of health authorities – purchasing authorities, community health councils and the newly established NHS executive regional offices – produce their own literature, much of it in response to national initiatives and management changes. The following selective list gives some indication of the size and scope of this:

- minutes and agenda papers
- annual reports
- public health reports
- strategic plans
- working party papers
- statistical series and bulletins
- medical audit plans

- policy documents
- research and surveys
- health needs assessment surveys
- public opinion surveys
- financial statements

Most of these documents are intended for local use and some may be restricted by their confidential nature. Even within the issuing authority they may be difficult to locate, and the location of older documents may depend on the personal memory of a member of staff. Retention and recording of regional health authority (RHA) documents has usually been the task of libraries or registries, and these are often the best places to commence enquiries. Regional offices with well developed professionally managed libraries are more likely to deposit copies of regional documents in the library, so that they are retained, recorded and disseminated by means of regular acquisition lists.

The remaining authorities have less well developed information services, particularly for textual information. The establishment of purchasing intelligence units (referred to elsewhere in this book) will ultimately improve access to health service grey literature at the purchasing level. The creation of a network of personal contacts and membership of local support groups is the most effective way of gaining access to this body of information.

With the exception of one or two regional health authority libraries, very few attempts have been made to solve the problem of locating and disseminating local health authority documents. The best documented is a database of locally produced and unpublished documents established within South Western RHA in conjunction with the University of Bristol.[7] This database could well serve as a model for other NHS regions. The South West Thames Region has a system based on the network of medical libraries, each of which is obliged, under its funding contract, to seek out and collect locally produced grey literature and to index local items for a regional database of information resources. The three regions which have established cooperative catalogues report between 10% and 30% of unpublished items. These systems all depend upon librarians themselves contributing documents for inclusion, and provide purchasers with access to a valuable corpus of academic and NHS information.

Purchaser needs

The changing role of health authorities, purchasing consortia and general practice fund-holders has provided an impetus to analyse their information needs. As purchasers of health care, their first task is the assessment of the health needs of their population. This requires access to textual and statistical information, standards and guidelines from Royal Colleges or other professional groups, survey methodology, census and related demographic information, and to both published and unpublished epidemiological studies. In addition, they require practical information on national and local priorities, contracting, marketing and outcome measures.

Their information needs go beyond conventional health service documentation. The increase in intersectoral cooperation leads to requests for publications from social services, the Home Office and the police service, the Departments of Transport and Employment for road accident and employment figures, voluntary organizations and community service groups. Information is needed on housing and pollution, local authority infrastructure, transport and sports facilities.

Provider needs
Providers are the NHS Trusts and general practices which provide direct patient treatment.

Medical staff have access to hospital or postgraduate medical centre libraries and have always made good use of the 'knowledge base' which supports medical and clinical practice. New perspectives and emphases have increased the need for speedy access to information on current good practice, innovation, clinical trials and outcome measures.

The medical audit cycle often uses 'semi-grey' literature on which to base its standards and guidelines, and the process itself produces a wealth of grey literature: clinical protocols, implementation plans, specialty reports and annual reports. These internally produced papers are intended largely for a local audience, but their value can be enhanced by dissemination through an audit group or newsletter. This is a real opportunity for librarians to extend their networks, prevent wasteful duplication, and in so doing raise the profile of their information service.

The Peckham Report[8] was the foundation of the NHS Research and Development Strategy (NHS R&D). It has been established to encourage the systematic culture of research within the NHS, and to record and disperse research results. The strategy includes the *NHS research and development project registers system*, a database of planned and current NHS research, to which projects are added at local level through a regional network of R&D coordinators. The intention of the project is to make its coverage and availability as broad as possible, and ultimately for it to be available to universities via the Joint Academic Network (JANET) and to the wider world through the Internet.

Statistical grey literature
Most government statistics concerning health services are published by the

Department of Health or the Office of Population, Censuses and Surveys (OPCS) and are available from HMSO. A published, but often ignored, source of current statistics worthy of mention here is *Hansard*, the daily account of parliamentary proceedings.

At local level, statistical information services are well developed, and the designated information officer can give advice on the range and availability of information.

A wealth of local public health, epidemiological and demographic statistics is contained in the annual public health reports produced by regional and district health authorities. Their annual financial reports, along with those from family health service authorities and community health councils are a good source of local financial information.

The purchasing function and the increased need for intersectoral cooperation have increased the need for access to local authority statistics. County and district councils produce a varied range of statistics; these should include ward profiles, welfare benefits, housing, unemployment, road accidents and pollution. Council environmental health departments provide morbidity statistics on notifiable diseases, cancers and dental health.

Community health statistics are held by local community health NHS trusts, and include patient activity, family planning and district nursing statistics.

AN INTERNATIONAL PERSPECTIVE

A concise account of the efforts and problems associated with national collections of grey literature can be found in Auger.[9] The following section draws on his discussion of attempts to acquire and disseminate literature in the USA and Canada, Japan and Europe, and this book and its references are recommended for readers wishing to investigate further.

In Britain, the richest collection of grey literature is held at the British Library Document Supply Centre (BLDSC) at Boston Spa. This collection consists of over three million reports in microform, as well as doctoral theses, conference proceedings, translations and local authority reports, a significant percentage relating to medicine and health care. Reports on medical and health care topics are included in BLDSC's *British reports, translations and theses* and *Translations index*.

Whilst specializing in the collection of British material, BLDSC also adds to its collection of foreign material with the aid of the American National Technical Information Services (NTIS), ERIC and other international bodies. Thus it is a valuable UK gateway to international documentation. Access to this collection is via Customer Services, BLDSC, Boston Spa, Wetherby, West Yorkshire LS23 7BQ.

The UK is the largest contributor to *SIGLE*, an acronym for *System for infor-*

mation on grey literature in Europe. This is a bibliographic database produced by the European Association of Grey Literature Exploitation (EAGLE). Coverage is from 1981, and the database holds contributions from eight European countries, for which it provides details of the national centre in the country of origin from which documents can be obtained. It includes, for example, documents from regional and district health authorities, city councils, housing corporations and the Royal Colleges. *SIGLE* is available both online via BLAISE-LINK and STN, and on CD-ROM. A useful summary of the development and operation of *SIGLE* can be found in Hasemann.[10]

Contact: European Association for Grey Literature Exploitation, Bureau Jupiter, Postbus 90407, DIL-2509 LK, The Hague, The Netherlands.

Librarians seeking German language grey literature in the medical and health care fields are well served by two publications. *FTN* (*Forschungsberichte aus Technik und Naturwissenschaften*) is a bibliography of projects sponsored by the German Federal Ministry for Research and Technology. It is available on STN, and is published quarterly by VCH Verlag in Weinheim. A second printed source is the *Bibliography of medicine* produced in 1993 as part of the GVB series published by K. G. Saur of Munich. This is a bibliography of 'German-language publications outside the book trade' and includes literature from Switzerland and Austria.

In France, an international bibliography with French emphasis covering science and medicine, is the PASCAL *Bibliographies internationales* produced by INIST, a technical information centre created by the Centre de Documentation Scientifique et Technique.

SECONDARY SOURCES OF GREY LITERATURE

A growing number of printed and computer based bibliographical services attempt to control grey literature. Their format and scope vary, and the librarian should take time to evaluate each one according to user needs. Many are based on the ideal of a central national information network, collecting records at local level, and making both the records and information for direct personal communication available to all interested parties.

The following annotated alphabetical list includes both international and British paper, online and CD-ROM sources. It is not exhaustive but does attempt to cover gateways to both clinical and non-clinical sources.

Bradford Community Health

For librarians requiring access to information on the health aspects of minority groups, *Ethnic minorities health* is invaluable. Produced quarterly in Bradford, it provides both reprints and a literature search facility. Although many of the records are from published sources, the bulletin covers conference proceedings, theses and much useful grey literature.

Contact: Medical Library, Field House Teaching Centre, Bradford Royal Infirmary, Bradford, West Yorkshire BD9 6RJ.

CINAHL

The *Cumulative index to nursing and allied health literature* (CINAHL) is an American publication available in printed, CD-ROM and online format via Data-Star/DIALOG. Despite its American bias, it is a useful source of dissertations, standards and conference proceedings. It should be available in most academic and College of Health libraries.

Departments of Health and Social Security

The library of each Department produces four separate abstracting journals, which combine to form *DHSS-Data*, an online bibliographic database available via Data-Star/DIALOG.

Health service abstracts is the most useful source of British non-clinical grey literature. It includes books, book chapters, NHS Executive publications, reports and periodical references. Published monthly, it includes a list of Health circulars received in the libraries. The subject and author index cumulates annually.

Contact: Department of Health Leaflets Unit, No. 2 Store, Manchester Road, Heywood, Oldham OL10 2PZ.

Its sister publication, *Social services abstracts*, is similar in format and coverage, but is published by HMSO. *Nursing research abstracts*, also available from the Department of Health Leaflets Unit, includes unpublished studies and current research. *Selected abstracts on occupational diseases*, available from the Department of Health Leaflets Unit, is published quarterly and covers occupational diseases and their causes, occupation related cancers and respiratory diseases. In addition to published research, the bulletin includes UK research projects.

Economic and Social Research Council

The *RAPID* database holds information on Economic and Social Research Council (ESRC) research awards and publications. Subjects covered include health and health studies, research methods and welfare services. 'Publications' in an all-embracing term which includes conference papers, non-refereed articles and audiovisual material. Access to the database is via JANET and the Internet.

Contact: ESRC *RAPID* Project, Computing Services, Main Library Building, University of Edinburgh, George Square, Edinburgh EH8 9JL.

European Commission: Medical Research Division

The *European Union biomedical and health research* newsletter has appeared three times a year since 1978, and concentrates on national research into medical or health problems in Europe. In addition to short features, it includes brief details of current projects with the aim of bringing together specialist expertise. Project details include the name and address of project leaders so that personal contact can be made.

Contact: European Commission, DG XII-E-4, Medical Research Division, Rue de la loi 200, B-1049 Brussels, Belgium.

Health Care Literature Information Network

HECLINET, the database of the Health Care Information Network, has been available in printed and online format since 1969, and covers the entire range of European literature, both grey and white, on hospitals and health care. It specifically aims to 'fill the gaps' left by North American databases like *MED-LINE*. *HECLINET* draws material from each national institute, concentrating on non-clinical aspects of health services and including conference reports, theses and company publications. *HECLINET* is available in printed version bimonthly, and online via DIMDI.

Contact: Institut für Krankenhausbau, Dokumentation Krankenhauswesen, Strasse des 17 Juni 135, D-14055 Berlin, Germany.

King's Fund Centre

The growing volume of grey literature resulting from medical audit has already been noted. The King's Fund Centre has established an information service specifically for those involved with the administration and practice of medical audit. Four databases provide access to audit contracts and bibliographic records of audit reports deposited with the King's Fund.

SHARE, also established at the King's Fund Centre, is a bibliographic database containing health and race information. Information officers for all databases can be contacted at the King's Fund Centre, 126 Albert Street, London NW1 7NF.

The Library Association

The Library Association Health Libraries Group (HLG) produces a quarterly newsletter for members. It includes short articles and references on a wealth of grey literature of interest to medical librarians in all fields. Its 'current literature' columns 'cover the most recent literature in medical, health and welfare librarianship and information services'. It includes journal articles, grey and conventional literature, and details of dissertations and theses received by the editor.

Contact: Health Libraries Group, c/o The Library Association, 7 Ridgmount Street, London WC1E 7AE.

The *IFM Healthcare newsletter* is a quarterly newsletter produced for members of IFM Healthcare, as subgroup of The Library Association. A regular bulletin-board alerts readers to new publications from the NHS Management Executive, and other Department of Health units, and is particularly valuable for non-HMSO material. It also includes a selective list of recent Health circulars.

Contact: IFM Healthcare, PO Box 19, Cheadle Hulme, Cheadle SK8 6DJ.

London Research Centre
ACOMPLINE is the database of the London Research Centre. It holds over 180,000 citations, published and unpublished, in the field of urban affairs and planning. Of interest to health care libraries, and especially to those providing information to purchasing agencies, are references to population and housing. *ACOMPLINE* is available online and on CD-ROM.

Contact: London Research Centre, Parliament House, 81 Black Prince Road, London SE1 7SZ.

Longman Cartermill: Current research in Britain
Current research in Britain (CRIB) has been available in printed and online format since 1981 and is produced in collaboration with the British Library. It is a national register of current academic research projects being carried out in the UK. The printed version is available in four volumes: biological sciences, physical sciences, social sciences and humanities. Project details provide the location and description of research and research personnel, information on sponsoring bodies and references to both published and unpublished papers.

Contact: Longman Cartermill Limited, Technology Centre, St Andrews, Fife KY16 9EA.

Nuffield Institute for Health
The *Community care innovative practices database* provides access to a wide range of literature of interest to those involved in managing or providing care in the community, both purchasers and providers. The database is the work of a national information network, and includes any material, published or unpublished, which has been produced as the result of a project or initiative. A broad range of topics includes hospital discharge arrangements, contracting, residential care and management development.

Contact: Community Care Information Manager, Nuffield Institute for Health, University of Leeds, 71–75 Clarendon Road, Leeds LS2 9PL.

A second valuable source of grey literature from the Nuffield Institute, and an element in the NHS R&D Project, is the UK Clearing House for Information on the Assessment of Health Outcomes. It aims to establish a collection of published and unpublished studies on the effectiveness of health service intervention, including topics such as quality assurance, validation measures, clinical trials and needs assessment. The project produces a newsletter and update bulletin, and access to the database is available on a subscription basis.

Contact: Information Manager, UK Clearing House for Information on the Assessment of Health Outcomes, Nuffield Institute for Health (address as above).

Royal College of Nursing
The *Royal College of nursing bibliography* is published monthly, and is available from the Royal College of Nursing Library. As well as books and articles, it includes theses.

Contact: Royal College of Nursing, 20 Cavendish Square, London W1M 0AB.

The Volunteer Centre UK
VOLNET is a database accessible online via JANET and the Internet, and on CD-ROM. It holds references to newspaper articles, books, journals and reports on a wide range of social subjects. Data are provided by leading social welfare organizations, including Barnardos and The Volunteer Centre UK. The database also includes a directory of social action research, a file of members of parliament, and overseas development information. Subjects covered include community care, elderly people, health and health services.

Contact: The Volunteer Centre UK, 29 Lower King's Road, Berkhamsted, Hertfordshire HP4 2AB.

The World Health Organization
The World Health Organization (WHO) is a prolific source of both published and grey literature. Whilst some of this is distributed through HMSO, the remainder is often difficult to locate. *WHODOC* lists all WHO publications including periodicals, technical and policy documents, as well as documents emanating from WHO funded programmes. *WHODOC* is published bimonthly and cumulates annually. References are given in English, French and Spanish where applicable, and the subject index is also trilingual. *WHO-LIS* is the organization's bibliographic database.

Contact: Office of Library and Health Literature Services (HLT), WHO, 1211 Geneva 27, Switzerland.

THE WHITENING OF GREY LITERATURE – THE LIBRARIAN'S ROLE

When discussing the problems associated with the location and acquisition of grey literature, it is easy to forget that users are unconcerned about its 'greyness' – they 'need to know what has been written, where it has been published and in what form'.[11] The librarian's task is to acquire and deliver it. Once grey literature is received in the library, its 'greyness' ceases to be an issue, and its value as a document rests on its currency and content.

The users who are unconcerned about the greyness of the literature they request are likely to be equally unconcerned, or unaware, that they are themselves producing grey literature. It is at this point that librarians can play an active role, and at the very least can ensure that documents produced by their own organizations carry basic bibliographic information. Librarians can be active on two levels, domestic and local.

At the domestic, or in-house level, the librarian can bring to the attention of staff the potential value of the literature they produce, and the need to regard this as publicity or public relations material. Any document that is either distributed or available to staff outside the organization should carry a date of publication, an author or issuing department, and a contact for further copies. Titles on the cover and title page should be consistent. If an organization is willing for a document to be printed in large enough numbers for it to be made available nationally, it should be priced and application should be made for an ISBN. This single act, which turns grey literature white, will ensure that deposit copies are requested, and the document will then be included in the national bibliography. At a stroke most acquisition problems disappear.

Locally, the librarian can play a successful role in collecting and disseminating locally produced grey literature. Information is costly to produce, and essential to corporate survival. The fact that it is grey does not lessen its value but does necessitate extra effort to make it available to others. A local or regional database, available to both medical and management staff, to purchasers and providers, to all NHS authorities and units may well prevent the reinvention of many wheels and ensure the optimum use of resources.

REFERENCES

1   Smith, A., 'Grey literature' in Bromley, D. W. and Allott, A. M., *British librarianship and information work 1986–1990, volume 2*, London, Library Association Publishing, 1993, 111–22.
2   NHS Management Enquiry Team, *NHS management inquiry*, London, Department of Health, 1983.
3   Department of Health, *Working for patients*, Cm 555, London, HMSO, 1989.
4   Department of Health, *Caring for people: community care in the next decade and beyond*, London, HMSO, 1989.

5 Department of Health, *The health of the nation: a consultative document for health in England*, Cm 1523, London, HMSO, 1991.
6 Hepworth, J. B., 'Work-place research: health information courses yield a growing resource', *IFM Healthcare newsletter*, 4 (4), 1993, 7–13.
7 Prior, P. and Faulkner, A., *A regionwide database of locally produced, unpublished documents in the South Western Region*, University of Bristol Health Care Evaluation Unit, 1992.
8 Department of Health, *Research for health – a research and development strategy for the NHS*, London, HMSO, 1991.
9 Auger, C. P., *Information sources in grey literature*, London, Bowker-Saur, 1994, 23–35.
10 Hasemann, C., 'SIGLE: access to grey literature in Europe', in *Inter-lending and document supply. Proceedings of the 2nd international conference held in London, November 1990*, Boston Spa, IFLA Office for International Lending, 1991, 71–3.
11 Vickers, S. and Wood, D. N., 'Improving the availability of grey literature', *Interlending review*, 10 (4), 1982, 125–30.

FURTHER RECOMMENDED READING

Allison, P., 'Stalking the elusive grey literature', *College and research library news*, 48 (5), 1987, 244–6.
Chillag, J. P., 'Grey literature: its supply and bibliographic access at the BLLD', *Catalogue and index*, 78, 79, 1985, 6–8.
Levin, M. A., 'The 'grey' ghetto: key issued related to public policy research literature', *Collection building*, 10 (1–2), 1989, 29–33.
van Loo, J., 'Medical and psychological effects of unemployment: a 'grey' literature search', *Health libraries review*, 2, 1985, 55–62.
Macdougall, J. and Brittain, J. M., *Use of information in the NHS*, Library and information research report 92, London, British Library, 1992.
Norton, T., 'Grey literature', *State librarian*, 31 (2), 1983, 16–17.
Posnett, N. W. and Baulkwill, W. J., 'Working with non-conventional literature', *Journal of information science*, 5, 1982, 121–30.
Smith, A., 'Grey literature in the social sciences: a BLDSC perspective', *Assignation*, 7 (2), 1990, 6–8.
Wood, D. N., 'The collection, bibliographic control and accessibility of grey literature', *IFLA journal*, 10 (3), 1984, 278–81.

13   Audiovisual information

❖   *Margaret C. Stewart*

Since earliest times medical education has relied heavily on illustrative teaching materials in addition to the printed or spoken word, utilizing the best and most sophisticated aids available.[1] They were always visual – from the earliest drawings[2] and models to Muybridge's zoopraxiscope, which projected photographs to demonstrate movement – and then incorporated sound, or audio, with the advent of wax cylinders, gramophone records, sound films, audiocassettes, video and compact discs.[3] As the extent of medical knowledge has grown, students and teachers have made increasing use of audiovisual materials to augment or even replace the work of the human instructor:

> Many studies carried out over the last two decades have established that audiovisual materials and videorecordings can be as effective in teaching a variety of skills and modifying attitudes as other, perhaps more traditional methods of teaching. Audiovisual teaching is often better and more meticulously prepared for recording and preservation than is traditional teaching, which is usually ephemeral.[4]

Because they are seen, like textbooks, to be essential teaching/learning materials, it is frequently the expectation that audiovisual programmes should form part of library stock, especially in institutions playing an educational role. For this reason it is not uncommon for librarians taking on responsibility for medical libraries to find that they incorporate non-book stock for which their training and experience may not have prepared them. Yet there is no reason why librarians should not be able to apply their subject and technical expertise to an audiovisual programme.

This chapter is intended to highlight the areas in which audiovisuals need special attention or where particular problems may arise.

AUDIOVISUAL OR NON-BOOK MATERIALS – WHAT ARE THEY?

'Audiovisual' is an umbrella term generally used to denote a range of formats frequently used for educational materials. What they have in common is that they cannot easily be termed 'books' – hence the alternative name 'non-book materials' – and that they cannot usually be used without some form of play-back equipment.

Although we are often told that the videotape[5-9] and interactive videodisc[10-15] have superseded all other forms of audiovisual, and although new titles are almost exclusively in these formats, medical students and teachers still demand programmes in the older audiovisual formats. In addition to video, 16 mm films, 35 mm slides[16] – some with accompanying audiotapes – and filmstrips are likely to remain in the stock of many medical libraries for the foreseeable future. Added to these are the less technological teaching aids: posters, models[17] and photographs. There will also be an increasing demand for compact discs, videodiscs and computer-aided learning programmes (including the phenomenon known as multimedia,[18] which may draw on a combination of any of the above formats, and also the recently developed liquid crystal display panel which can project information from a microcomputer screen for the benefit of a larger audience).[19] Holography[20] and hypermedia[21] have also been mooted as medical education tools. Different teaching situations may call for any of these formats depending on the teaching style of the instructor, the target group and the technology available. Definitions of the formats, their development and their most appropriate uses are given in Pinion[3] and elsewhere.[22-24] Each format also poses its own storage and retrieval problems which need to be overcome if it is to be made easily available to the user.

SELECTION AND ACQUISITION
The first stage in building up a collection is to find out what materials exist. For much of the time this initial identification of useful items is done by the library user requesting titles reviewed in specialist publications or recommended by colleagues. This relies heavily on serendipity, and librarians have become accustomed to filling gaps in their users' awareness and thence their collections by consulting a range of bibliographic aids. With regard to non-book materials, this process is far more complicated because of a lack of bibliographic control.[25] Some countries now include non-book materials in their major bibliographic tools: others provide specific guides, some even subject-based like the *National Library of Medicine audio visuals catalog.*[26] Despite a number of initiatives in the past (e.g. *British catalogue of audiovisual materials*)[27] and discussion between such interested bodies as The Library Association, the British Library and the British Universities Film and Video Council (BUFVC), Britain still lags sadly behind.[3] However, the British Library's *Strategic plan 1993–2000* promises that:

Acting within our leadership role in the maintenance of the national archive collection of British publications, and in conjunction with other media archives and appropriate bodies in the UK, the Library will continue to urge the Government to extend legal deposit provisions to cover electronic documents and audiovisual and multi-media materials.[28]

It is not possible to buy specialist audiovisuals casually; they are not included in the regular stock of either book or video shops. Traditionally the publishers or producers of audiovisuals have also been the distributors, dealing directly with the customer[29] who has to rely on their printed catalogues for information. Increasingly, however, both the small production company and the academic institution producing audiovisuals on a larger scale are finding it helpful to make their materials available through specialist distribution agencies which both sell and hire non-book materials on a commercial basis and which are used to dealing with individuals as much as with institutions. The most significant of these for health librarians are Oxford Educational Resources and Concord Video and Film Council.

Even so, the librarian who wishes to be as well informed as possible about new non-book materials still needs to consult a variety of sources. Jones[30] tried to cover all the most helpful sources; although now out of date, this publication is still a guide through the maze of catalogues and directories available.

Another useful starting point is the regularly updated BUFVC *Distributors*,[31] providing details of audiovisual suppliers for over 40 subjects. Some of the directories listed are guides to everything produced on a particular subject, e.g. the publications of the Mental Health Media Council. Others are simply the catalogues of individual producers or distributors such as the University of Southampton. Also included are the multidisciplinary suppliers such as Concord Video and Film Council. The Appendix to this chapter lists other directories which are invaluable in tracking down audiovisual materials and their producers or distributors.

The BUFVC maintains a database of educational audiovisuals, *AVANCE*,[32] from which it compiles lists of materials on specific topics. In addition, the Information Service holds an extensive collection of catalogues and reference works from which it can answer most enquiries. BUFVC also offers an off-air television recording back-up service to supply Educational Recordings Agency licence holders (see below) with video copies of television programmes broadcast within the last two months. Valuable BUFVC publications include the *Researcher's guide to British film and television collections*,[33] the *BUFVC handbook for film and television in education*[31] and a termly magazine *Viewfinder*. Its services are available to all members, and membership is held by most UK universities as well as being open to smaller academic institutions and related professional organizations, commercial bodies and researchers.[34]

The British Medical Association (BMA) Library also answers a range of enquiries, drawing on its unrivalled collection of medical films and videos.

For nursing subjects, the English Board for Nursing, Midwifery and Health Visiting offers the *Health care database*, which includes audiovisuals alongside information on research, organizations and career opportunities in nursing, midwifery and health visiting.

The major online service listing medical audiovisuals is the National Library of Medicine *AVLINE*,[35] available through MEDLARS or on microfiche as *Health sciences audiovisuals*, updated quarterly. However, its American origins are very clear in the materials selected for inclusion, which can limit its usefulness to British or European users needing to obtain materials quickly.

Another US online service which must be mentioned is *AV-ONLINE*, the largest of all audiovisual databases, holding details of over 400,000 programmes on a wide range of subjects including health-related topics. This is now available in the UK on CD-ROM, updated half-yearly.

Given the high cost of many audiovisuals, the question of whether purchase or hire is the more appropriate option is more significant than with books. Hire means that programmes are available for only a very short time, usually the date set for a specific showing and just one or two days each side. Passing all requests through to a purchasing agency, either internal or external to the organization, is not necessarily a practical option because of the time delays involved in passing the item from purchasing agency to library user and then having to return it within a matter of days.

Evaluation

Because of costs, but also because of the risk of damage or illicit copying, many programmes are not available on approval. Larger suppliers like Concord may make items available for paid preview, not unlike a short hire period. Others offer previews at their own premises or at venues across the country. Organizations such as the BUFVC, the International Visual Communications Association (IVCA) and the European Multimedia Centre also offer members the chance to preview materials at their London offices.

The Information Centre of the Wellcome Institute for the History of Medicine holds a reference collection of nearly 400 biomedical film and video titles suitable for use in university teaching and research, more than 100 popular science and medicine videocassettes and audiotapes, and viewing copies of medical–historical films and videos. The Centre is open to academic and professional users, students and the general public.[36]

Where it is not possible to obtain a programme for preview or to view it at a special centre, directories of reviews or of competition prize-winners are useful aids to selection.[37-41] For medical films, the best established award scheme is probably the annual BMA Film Competition. All past winners are described in the BMA Library catalogue:[42] reviews of winning titles also appear in the quarterly *Journal of audiovisual media in medicine*.

Guidance on setting up selection and evaluation procedures is offered in a number of publications, which the librarian, as much as the teacher, would find of interest.[4, 43-46] The Centre for Interactive Video in Education at Sheffield Hallam University maintains *Evaluating learning technology*, a free database, available on IBM-compatible diskette, of international research since 1985 on the application of interactive technology to education.

CATALOGUING

If the purpose of a conventional library catalogue is to present the complete library collection to the user, regardless of which items may be temporarily unavailable, then this purpose assumes even greater importance for a collection of audiovisuals. For this reason, the catalogue must be especially accessible and 'user-friendly' to encourage browsing.

It is difficult to assess from the exterior of a video or 16 mm film, for example, exactly what topics it covers, although some commercially supplied programmes carry the equivalent of a publisher's blurb. Thus the catalogue entry needs to carry not only the physical descriptive details but also a summary of the contents, both presented in terms that the casual user can understand without needing library staff to 'translate' jargon or abbreviations. Users must also be able to ascertain the sort of equipment required for any particular item, i.e. is it compatible with machinery available to them, and suitable for the planned audience?

There are so many more physical details to record for audiovisual materials than for books that people working in this field have found it necessary to use a number of guides in addition to the standard *Anglo-American cataloguing rules*.[47-51] The important thing for the librarian to establish before adopting any of these published standards is the level of detail which will be required by the library users – it is all too easy, where audiovisual formats are concerned, to concentrate on recording the medium rather than the message. If users need to know the content of a programme, slide by slide or frame by frame, so be it, but a briefer overview may suffice. Some materials will not be held permanently by the library and consideration must be given to the amount of cataloguing detail they will need if too much staff time is not to be devoted to something ephemeral, e.g. recordings made off-air from broadcast television, which may only be kept for a limited period.[52]

Allied to this is the question of whether audiovisuals belong in the main library catalogue or in a separate sequence. If the non-book materials are genuinely seen as a natural part of the library stock, it is hard to see why they should not be included in the main catalogue (although it may be helpful to maintain a separate section in addition, for stocktaking purposes). Although some users may come looking for an example of a particular format, e.g. a film, most will be hunting for teaching material on an individual subject and may be prepared to consider a variety of formats. It does not help if they have to search more than one catalogue; the chances are that where there are separate catalogues for different types of material, the audiovisual collection will be seen as marginal and remain under-used.[53]

STORAGE

Arguments for physical integration of the library collection itself are similar to those for integration of the catalogue. It is very helpful for the user, especially the 'browser', to have all the formats housed together by subject. This adds to the likelihood that users will find it as natural to select audiovisual media as books when they need teaching or learning materials on any subject.[54,55] The packaging of most videotapes makes it easy to store them on the shelf alongside books.[56] (For a different view, see Chapter 7.) Other formats may not fit so neatly without special attention: 16 mm film and filmstrips tend to some in metal cylinders, slides in rectangular plastic boxes or flimsy display sheets;[57] and audiotapes, computer disks and compact discs in small plastic cases. However, it is possible to repackage these in boxes or folders which will fit onto open bookshelves.[58] Only perhaps gramophone records (increasingly rare), videodiscs and large or bulky items such as posters and models (much used in health education) cannot be adapted in this way.

One of the drawbacks to a fully integrated collection may be the expense, in terms of both material and staff time, of the necessary repackaging.

Moreover, media such as films, tapes, etc., are sensitive to extreme fluctuations in temperature and humidity such as may occur in open-access libraries where heating/air-conditioning systems are turned off at night, weekends and public holidays.[59] For long-term storage they are better kept where the environmental conditions are relatively stable, and in containers chosen for their protective qualities rather than for their physical shape and appearance.[60]

Each librarian will have to determine where the balance of advantage lies.

USE OF THE AUDIOVISUAL COLLECTION

Since very few libraries will have built up an audiovisual collection without a prior demand from users (and are frequently likely to have inherited the core of the collection from some other department no longer willing or able to maintain it), the likely usage requirements are probably predetermined. Thus decisions on storage and loan *versus* reference will largely be governed by existing external factors. It is the librarian's task to adapt these into feasible practical arrangements which will meet established demands and encourage new types of use.

Use within the library

Facilities may have to be provided for staff and students to preview materials or indeed use them for individual or group work. This may mean individual study carrels, or even a separate room, with adequate sound-proofing and visual screening to prevent disturbance of other library users.[61, 62] Where special security measures are employed to protect bookstock, they should also be extended to cover the non-book materials if possible.[63]

Special equipment will be needed for each format, and will have to be maintained in good working order. In the first instance, the core collection may be accompanied by appropriate equipment purchased by another department. Sooner or later, however, the library will be in the position of needing to select and purchase additional equipment.[64] A useful starting point to selection is the series of user guides (*USPECs*)[65] published by the National Council for Educational Technology. The next stage will be to view and perhaps try equipment at the showroom of a large supplier. Suppliers can be identified from a number of helpful directories.[66-70] It may then be helpful to hire for a period to assess both the suitability of the chosen equipment and the volume of use. It is a good idea to take out service contracts, especially for the more expensive and complicated pieces of equipment, as they are liable to receive heavy and untutored use. Library staff need to know how to operate all the equipment but they would not generally expect to perform routine maintenance and emergency repairs.[71-73] There may be technicians (or service contracts) available from elsewhere in the institution so liaison with the appropriate departments is vital. Clear written instructions for users should always be available alongside each piece of equipment in addition to any personal instruction which library staff may be able to provide.

Equipment provision also poses security implications – video recorders and the like are very attractive to thieves. All pieces of equipment should be indelibly and clearly marked with the library name, perhaps even painted with a bright band of colour to make them difficult for thieves to sell without exciting attention. When not in use they should be locked away securely. Adequate all-risks insurance is vital.

Loans

It is most likely that users will need to be able to borrow audiovisual materials, especially medical staff who need to use materials with groups of students. There is no reason why the existing book loans system should not be applied to non-book materials, with the addition of one or two additional safeguards.

Since audiovisual materials are prone to accidental damage at the hands of inexperienced users, it should be standard practice for them to be checked after each loan. An immediate visual check can spot external damage or missing components: a rapid run-through at a later convenient time will indicate other faults. Users should be encouraged to report (without fear of blame) any faults that they notice or any operational difficulties which may be indicators of potential problems. If use is heavy, it may be worth investing in a rapid scan device to minimize staff checking time. Some repairs are straightforward and can be carried out by library staff; for others, the material may have to be sent away for expert treatment.

Some libraries ask users, before the first borrowing, to provide details of equipment that they intend to use. This alerts users to the importance of using the correct apparatus and checking compatibility of materials, but it may be considered as another level of bureaucracy, which can alienate users.

One way of ensuring that the correct equipment is used is to lend it with the audiovisual materials. This, in turn, incurs the extra expense of purchasing sufficient equipment and of maintaining it properly after totally unsupervized use in possibly unsuitable conditions. The risks of loss of expensive equipment are great and the above comments on security and insurance apply with even greater force.

Interlibrary loans
For reasons ranging from expense of materials to lack of bibliographic control and paucity of suitable collections, interlibrary loan of audiovisual materials is not well established.[74,75] However, regional networks have been set up and are increasingly active. To date, these operate outside the British Library umbrella, but it is to be hoped that gradually an efficient countrywide network will emerge. In the meantime, the willingness of librarians to lend to other institutions, even on a very local basis, can only help.

COPYRIGHT
Copyright, as it applies to audiovisual materials, is significantly different from copyright on printed matter in that the concept of 'fair dealing' does not apply, i.e. it is not permitted to copy even a small part of an audiovisual programme. However, the Copyright Designs and Patents Act 1988 made provision for 'licensed' copying and also licensed rental. This allowed organizations concerned in the production and distribution of audiovisuals to form agencies to permit some copying on specific terms or to restrict loans/rental.

The first such agency set up following the Act was the Educational Recordings Agency (ERA) which is concerned with recordings made off-air from broadcast television.[76] Television programmes are frequently of more than ephemeral interest and to other than the lay audiences for whom they may have been intended. In the past, obtaining legal copies of such programmes was not easy: now ERA license holders are in a position to view them at other than broadcast times and even to retain them for future use with different groups.

The circulation of computer software by libraries has caused much concern,[77] since some copying, e.g. to make working copies, is essential. Some manufacturers will not permit their software to be loaned by libraries because of the fear of illegal copying. As yet there are no licenses for rental rights for computer software in the UK. However, a project under way under the auspices of the British Library is constructing a model for monitoring usage of digital information and thus improving its copyright protection.[78]

Non-digital sound recordings, i.e. records, tapes and compact discs, are covered by an agreement between The Library Association and the British Phonographic Industry Ltd, governing loans by public and educational libraries for private, domestic or educational use.[79]

In 1944 the Design and Artists Copyright Society launched a slide library licensing scheme with the aim of enabling use by students, teachers, etc., and also allowing artists to derive financial benefit from the reproduction of their work. Licences have been available since the end of 1994[80] and details are available from the Society at Parchment House, 13 North Burgh Street, London EC1V 0AH.

To date, there are no licensing schemes relating to 16 mm films or videotapes.

USER EDUCATION

Users of audiovisuals within the medical library fall into two groups, which can be loosely terms 'the converted' and 'the unconverted'. 'Converted' users are already convinced of the value of audiovisuals and probably come to the library knowing exactly what they want, and convinced that they know how to use it. Guidance for these users needs to avoid alienating them. The 'unconverted' need to be convinced of the usefulness of audiovisual materials to their specific situation and shown how to use the most appropriate formats. In both cases, the aim is to increase the users' awareness of the materials available and their effective use, and to limit damage during use.

Probably the best means of demonstrating the effectiveness of audiovisuals as teaching media is for the library to use them. A good audiovisual programme introducing and illustrating all the library facilities will help with general library user education as well as showing the usefulness of this sort of teaching medium. Some institutions will have a technical unit which can produce such a programme to library specifications, or sometimes an appropriate ready-made programme can be bought in from outside. Some libraries produce their own teaching materials.[81] Expert guidance is offered by Cullen and Kirby,[82] Abel *et al.*[83] and Thompson.[84]

In addition to such a general library introduction, instructions need to be provided about use of specific media. The novice user may appreciate personal advice from a member of staff, but frequently time will not allow this degree of detailed service. A more universally applicable solution may be to have a series of short, instructional, audiovisual packages available on the optimum use of different formats and types of equipment, for personal study within our outside the library, backed up by basic instruction sheets included with each loan of programme or equipment. Costs of producing and duplicating such sheets, by whatever in-house method is available, should be offset against the potential cost of replacing misused media and equipment.

It cannot be stressed too strongly that the audiovisual collection must be included in any course of user instruction offered by the library so that it is seen as an integral part of the library facilities.

STAFF TRAINING

The days when libraries could afford to appoint a full-time member of staff to act exclusively as audiovisual librarian are largely gone, and we are back to the state where this responsibility is generally shouldered by someone who also plays a more general role in the library. It is not reasonable, therefore, to assume that the audiovisual librarian either has a background (or even a particular interest) in audiovisuals or will be available much of the time to provide specific assistance to users. Thus it is important that as many library staff as possible have some familiarity with the audiovisual collection and the appropriate use of the various media, and can use any equipment kept in the library; being 'no good with machines' is not an adequate excuse for not helping a user when other staff are not immediately available.

Firstly, the person with responsibility for audiovisual services must become familar with the different media and their uses, and with operating equipment in the library.[85] If background and previous training have not been adequate in this respect, short courses are available. Many are listed in the *International yearbook of educational and training technology*.[70] The BUFVC also offers courses in locating audiovisuals, which include some basic discussion. Alternatively there are self-instructional texts which can be used as the basis for in-house training.[24]

Among the journals that aim to keep the librarian up-to-date with new developments in the audiovisual world, and frequently mention or review new products, the most helpful are probably *Journal of audiovisual media in medicine* (Butterworth-Heinemann on behalf of the Institute of Medical Illustrators), *Audiovisual librarian* (audiovisual groups of The Library Association and Aslib), and *Viewfinder* (BUFVC).

Other staff should receive basic training from the audiovisual librarian as part of their induction training, or should be sent on external courses if more appropriate. Reputable suppliers of equipment are generally happy to provide basic instruction to staff groups when new equipment is purchased, and as many staff as possible should be encouraged to take advantage of this. Refresher training sessions, run whenever convenient by the audiovisual librarian, are a helpful way of making sure that all staff are confident about handling non-book materials.

CONCLUSION

There is still a tendency for audiovisuals to be seen by many librarians as something of an intrusion, and by some educators as an optional extra, despite research proving their value.[4, 15, 86] While it is true that if they are ignored for long enough they probably will go away – squeezed out of existence by other perceived priorities when budgets are restricted – the need for their teaching effectiveness will continue. Therefore the health care library that wishes to offer the best service to its users must continue to encompass non-book materials; in fact it should ignore format and concentrate on obtaining the most appropriate material, whether book or non-book, in every instance.

> Perhaps the portent that Educational Technology is coming of age will be when I find it as easy to locate teaching materials across all popular media as I can a book. I believe that our libraries alone can achieve this.[87]

REFERENCES

1   Donald, G., 'The history of medical illustration', *Journal of audiovisual media in medicine*, **9**, 1986, 44–9.
2   Archer, P., 'From the beginning: an historical view of medical art', *Journal of audiovisual media in medicine*, **12**, 1989, 51–62.
3   Pinion, C., 'Preserving our audiovisual heritage: a national and international challenge', *Audiovisual librarian*, **19** (3), 1993, 205–19.
4   Marshall, R. and Evans, R., 'Is your audiovisual teaching effective?', *Journal of audiovisual media in medicine*, **15**, 1992, 17–21.
5   Hargie, O. and Morrow, N., 'Analytical and practical considerations of illustrative model video-tapes', *Journal of audiovisual media in medicine*, **6**, 1986, 65–8.
6   Scroggie, I., 'Videorecording and high-definition television systems for the late 1980s: a review', *Journal of audiovisual media in medicine*, **6**, 1986, 91–4.
7   Pinnington, A., *Using video in education and training*, London, McGraw-Hill, 1992.
8   Mir, M. *et al.*, 'The use of videotapes in improving clinical performance in the final MB examination', *Journal of audiovisual media in medicine*, **10**, 1987, 131–6.

9   Van Reenen, J., 'Adult learning and video training in health care', *Journal of audiovisual media in medicine,* **13**, 1990, 143–5.

10 Bryce, C. and Stewart, A., 'How to use videodiscs in medical education Part 1', *Medical teacher,* **5**, 1983, 6–9.

11 Bryce, C. and Stewart, A., 'Videodiscs in medical education Part 2', *Medical teacher,* **5**, 1983, 57.

12 Grills, C., 'Training, researching and learning with videodisc', *Videodisc/teletext,* **1**, 1981, 14–17.

13 Holmes, R., 'Laser disc technology: the implications for medicine and medical information', *Audiovisual librarian,* **14**, 1988, 201–10.

14 Kwan, R. *et al.*, 'Use of interactive video in teaching history-taking to medical students: a pilot project', *Journal of audiovisual media in medicine,* **11**, 1988, 121–4.

15 Culbert, A. *et al.*, 'Interactive videodisc as an instructional tool in medical education', *Methods of information in medicine,* **28**, 1989, 357–9.

16 Cull, P., 'Making and using medical slides', *British journal of hospital medicine,* **47** (2), 1992, 132–5.

17 Smith, D. and Lucas, L., 'The human skeleton: an overlooked but effective visual aid'. *Journal of rheumatology,* **20** (6), 1993, 1088–9.

18 Ramaiah, C., 'Multimedia: a new instructional tool', *International information, communication and education,* **11** (2), 1992, 177–86.

19 Wong, K., 'The use of the liquid crystal display (LCD) panel as a teaching aid in medical lectures', *Medical teacher,* **14** (1), 1992, 33–6.

20 White, N., 'Holography – the clear plate syndrome', *Journal of audiovisual media in medicine,* **10**, 1987, 135–7.

21 Hutchings, G. *et al.*, 'Hypermedia in biomedical education: a case study', *Journal of audiovisual media in medicine,* **15**, 1992, 77–80.

22 Beard, L., 'Aids to medical education', *Media in education and development,* **15**, 1982, 28–30.

23 McArthur, J., 'Conventional and high-technology teaching methods for educating health professionals in developing nations', *Journal of audiovisual media in medicine,* **5**, 1982, 21–6.

24 Jones, M., *Non-book teaching materials in the health sciences,* Aldershot, Gower, 1987.

25 Miller, P., *Production and bibliographic control of nonbook materials in the UK,* London, Polytechnic of North London, 1985 (British Library R&DD Report 5869) (SOLIS research report no. 16).

26 National Library of Medicine, *National Library of Medicine audiovisuals catalog,* quarterly, with the fourth issue being the annual cumulation, Bethesda, National Library of Medicine.

27 British Library, *British catalogue of audiovisual materials,* 1st experimental edn, London, British Library Bibliographic Services Division, 1979. Also, 1st supplement, 1980; 2nd supplement, 1983.

28 British Library, *Strategic plan 1993–2000,* London, British Library, 1992, paragraph 62, quoted in Pinion, C. and Lorimer, C., 'Seen and heard', *Audiovisual librarian,* **19** (1), 1993, 15–16.

29   Pemberton, J., *Policies of audiovisual producers and distributors: a handbook for acquisition personnel*, 2nd revised edn, Metuchen, NJ, and London, Scarecrow, 1990.

30   Jones, M., *International guide to locating audio-visual materials in the health sciences*, Aldershot, Gower, 1986.

31   Grant, C. and Sarmiento, M. (eds.), *Distributors: the guide to video and film sources for education and training*, London, BUFVC, 1990. From 1994 onwards, *Distributors* is to be incorporated in *BUFVC handbook for film and television in education*, London, BUFVC, expected May 1994.

32   Terris, O., 'AVANCE: a multimedia database', *Audiovisual librarian*, **16**, 1990, 112–15.

33   Oliver, E. (ed.), *Researcher's guide to British film and television collections*, 4th edn, London, BUFVC, 1993.

34   Sarmiento, M., 'The British Universities Film and Video Council', *Health libraries review*, **10** (3), 1993, 147–9.

35   Suter, E. and Waddell, W., 'AVLINE: a data base and critical review system of audiovisual materials for the education of health professionals', *Journal of medical education*, **57**, 1982, 139–55.

36   Clark, M., 'The Wellcome Trust: science and the art of medicine', *Viewfinder*, (19), November 1993, 13–15.

37   Blake, V., 'The role of reviews and reviewing media in the selection process: an examination of the research record', *Collection management*, **11**, 1989, 1–40.

38   Stetler, S. (ed.), *Audio video review digest 1989*, Detroit, MI, Gale Research, 1990.

39   Truett, C., 'Evaluating software reviews: a review of the reviews', *Library software review*, **3**, 1984, 371–8.

40   Verny, R. and Heider, M., 'Selecting and using video programs', in Van Son, L. (ed.), *Journal of audiovisual media in medicine, 13, Video in health*, White Plains, New York, Knowledge Industry Publications, 1982, 97–124.

41   Provan, J. and Hunter, J. (eds.), *Health media review index: a guide to reviews and descriptions of commercially-available non-print material for the medical, mental, allied health, human service and related counselling professions*, Metuchen, NJ, Scarecrow, 1985.

42   British Medical Association, *Catalogue of films and videos in the British Medical Association library*, London, Library Association Publishing, 1993.

43   National Council for Educational Technology, *How to find and adapt materials and select media*, Coventry, NCET, 1985 (Open Learning Guide 8).

44   Romiszowski, A., *The selection and use of instructional media: a systems approach*, 2nd edn, London, Kogan Page, 1988.

45   Doll, C., *Evaluating educational software*, Chicago, IL, American Library Association, 1988.

46   Bearon, L. *et al.*, 'Video journal club: combining video evaluation and continuing education', *Gerontologist*, **33** (3), 1993, 415–18.

47   Urbanski, V. *et al.*, *Cataloguing unpublished nonprint materials: a manual of suggestions, comments and examples*, Lake Crystal, Minnesota, Soldier Creek Press, 1992.

Also see review of/commentary on this book: Turp, S., 'Sweat or magic?', *Audiovisual librarian*, **19** (2), 1993, 136–41.

48 Olson, N., *Cataloguing of audiovisual materials: a manual based on AACR2*, 3rd edn, Minnesota Scholarly Press, 1992.

49 Olson, N., *Cataloguing computer files*, Lake Crystal, Minnesota, Soldier Creek Press, 1992 (revised 3rd edn of *A manual of AACR2 examples for microcomputer software and video games*).

50 Yee, M., 'Integration of non-book materials in AACR2', *Cataloguing and classification quarterly*, **3** (4), 1988, 1–18.

51 Woakes, H., 'The cataloguing of audiovisual materials', *Audiovisual librarian*, **11**, 1985, 78–92.

52 Turp, S., 'Guidelines on cataloguing off-air videorecordings', *Audiovisual librarian*, **18** (2), 1992, 94–112.

53 Evans, T., 'Making media work', *AV user*, (25), 1990, 22–4.

54 Weihs, J., *The integrated library: encouraging access to multimedia materials*, Phoenix, AZ, Oryx Press, 1991.

55 Sutherland, P., *The management of integrated learning resources*, Brighton, Council of Polytechnic Librarians, 1992.

56 Hedges, M., 'Managing an integrated video collection', *Wilson library bulletin*, **67** (10), 1993, 32–5.

57 Sutcliffe, G., 'Management of slides by departments of medical illustration and medical libraries in university teaching hospitals', *Journal of audiovisual media in medicine*, **13**, 1990, 135–42.

58 Weihs, J., *Accessible storage of nonbook materials*, Phoenix, AZ, Oryx Press, 1984.

59 Thompson, A., Editorial, *Audiovisual librarian*, **18** (1), 1992, 2–3.

60 Thompson, A. (ed.), *Storage, handling and preservation of audiovisual materials*, The Hague, IFLA Round Table on AV Media, Nederlands Bibliotheck en Lektuur Centrum, 1983 (AV in action 3).

61 Thompson, A., 'Guidelines for the provision of video viewing facilities in libraries', *Audiovisual librarian*, **10** (4), 1984, 189–94.

62 Holland, G., 'A checklist for planning and designing audiovisual facilities in health services libraries', *Bulletin of the Medical Library Association*, **72** (4), 1984, 362–9.

63 Scherdin, M.-J., 'Security systems protect audiovisual materials', *Library and archival security*, **11** (1), 1991, 23–34.

64 Crowe, V., 'Choosing technologies for school library media centers: hardware selection', *Drexel library quarterly*, **20**, 1984, 51–63.

65 National Council for Educational Technology, *USPECS and USPEC information sheets*, Coventry, National Council for Educational Technology.

66 *Audiovisual directory*, Croydon, EMAP Vision, annual.

67 *AV market place*, Ann Arbor, MI, Bowker, 1993.

68 *Equipment directory of audio-visual, computer and video products*, Fairfax, VA, International Communications Industries Association, annual.

69 Henderson, J. and Humphreys, F. (eds.), *Audio-visual and microcomputer handbook*,

4th edn, London, Kogan Page, 1984.

70   Osborne, C. (ed.), *International yearbook of educational and training technology*, London, Kogan Page, annual.

71   Schroeder, D. and Lare, G., *Audiovisual equipment and materials: a basic repair and maintenance manual, vol. 1*, Metuchen, NJ, Scarecrow, 1979.

72   Schroeder, D. and Lare, G., *Audiovisual equipment and materials: a basic repair and maintenance manual, vol. 2*, Metuchen, NJ, Scarecrow, 1990.

73   Farrington, J., 'Preventive maintenance for audio discs and tapes', *Notes*, **48** (2), December 1991, 437–45.

74   Cornish, G., 'Interlending of audiovisual materials: a neglected national resource for medical and health libraries', *Health libraries review*, **4**, 1987, 164–71.

75   Cornish, G., 'Report: National Committee on Regional Library Cooperation', *Audiovisual librarian*, **15**, 1989, 103–6.

76   Wall, R., 'Copyright news', *Aslib information*, **19**, 1991, 250–3.

77   Norman, S., 'Guidelines on computer software', *Audiovisual librarian*, **19** (1), 1993, 42–4.

78   Keates, S., 'Copyright protection in the electronic AV environment: the CITED model', *Audiovisual librarian*, **19** (4), 1993, 287–9.

79   Pinion, C. and Lorimer, C., 'Seen and heard', *Audiovisual librarian*, **20** (1), 1994, 12–13.

80   Duffield, R., 'Proposals for a slide library licensing scheme', *Audiovisual librarian*, **19** (4), 1993, 285–6.

81   Malley, I., 'The production and use of audiovisual media for user education in UK academic libraries', *Audiovisual librarian*, **8**, 1982, 185–90.

82   Cullen, P. and Kirby, J., *Design and production of media presentations for libraries*, Aldershot, Gower, 1986.

83   Abel, M. *et al.*, 'The design and production of a multimedia presentation for library induction', *British journal of academic librarianship*, **7** (2), 1992, 91–100.

84   Thompson, A., *Guide to the production and use of audio-visual aids in library and information science teaching*, Paris, General Information Programme/UNISIST (Unesco), 1983.

85   Fothergill, R. and Butchart, I., *Non-book materials in libraries: a practical guide*, 3rd edn, London, Clive Bingley, 1990.

86   Andrusyszyn, M., 'The effect of the lecture–discussion teaching method with and without audiovisual augmentation on immediate and retention learning', *Nurse education today*, **10**, 1990, 172–80.

87   Thompson, G., 'Rhetoric and reality: the meeting of minds', *Audiovisual librarian*, **18** (4), 1992, 246–51.

APPENDIX: DIRECTORIES LISTING PRODUCERS/DISTRIBUTORS OF AUDIOVISUAL AIDS

UK sources

Audiovisual directory, Croydon, EMAP Vision, annual.

European multimedia yearbook, London, Interactive Media Publications, annual.

Grant, C. and Sarmiento, M. (eds.), *Distributors: the guide to video and film sources for education and training*, London, BUFVC, 1990. From 1994 onwards, *Distributors* is to be incorporated in *BUFVC handbook for film and television in education*, London, BUFVC, expected May 1994.

Health education index, 9th edn, London, Edsall, 1987.

Henderson, J. and Humphreys, F. (eds.), *Audio-visual and microcomputer handbook*, 4th edn, London, Kogan Page, 1984.

Jones, M., *International guide to locating audio-visual materials in the health sciences*, Aldershot, Gower, 1986.

McKeown, R., *National directory of slide collections*, London, British Library, 1989 (British Library Information Guide no. 12).

National Sound Archive, *Directory of recorded sound resources in the United Kingdom*, London, NSA 1988.

Oliver, E. (ed.), *Researcher's guide to British film and training technology*, London, Kogan Page, annual.

Osborne, C. (ed.), *International yearbook of educational and training technology*, London, Kogan Page, annual.

Whittlestone, K. (ed.), *Guide to software and resources for computer based learning in medicine, nursing, dentistry and veterinary science*, 2nd edn, Bristol, CTI Centre for Medicine, 1992.

US sources

AV market place, Ann Arbor, MI, Bowker, 1993.

Educational film/video locator of the consortium of college and university media centers and R. R. Bowker, 5th edn, Ann Arbor, MI, Bowker, 1990.

Ely, D. and Minor, B. (eds.), *Educational media and technology yearbook*, Littleton, Libraries Unlimited Inc., annual.

Healthfinder: locating audiovisual materials, Washington DC, National Health Information Clearinghouse, 1984.

National Library of Medicine, *Health sciences audiovisuals*, Bethesda, MD, National Library of Medicine, quarterly. Each issue some 80 microfiche.

National Library of Medicine, *National Library of Medicine audiovisuals catalog*, quarterly, with the fourth issue being the annual cumulation, Bethesda, National Library of Medicine.

NICEM, *Index to AV producers and distributors*, 7th edn, Medford, NJ, NICEM/Plexus Publishing, 1989.

Pemberton, J., *Policies of audiovisual producers and distributors: a handbook for acquisition personnel*, 2nd revised edn, Metuchen, NJ, and London, Scarecrow, 1990.

Searching online for health sciences audiovisuals, Baltimore, MD, Southeaster/Atlantic

14 Managing document delivery services

❖ *Sheila E. Cannell*

The process of document delivery involves the bringing together of users with the text of the document they want. The success of the management of this service will determine the success of the library for the user. It is of little use to have a page of bibliographic references ouput from a database if the library cannot quickly get the full article for the user to read and digest. Users' expectations for a fast and efficient document delivery service are rapidly increasing. They see how quick and easy it is to find information on databases. The actual delivery of the document, particularly if it is not in their own local library, is for many users frustratingly slow: yesterday would be best, the next day or within four days might be acceptable, but several weeks is too late. The purpose of this chapter is to look at how these services can be managed to improve the quality and speed of document delivery.

The fastest method of document delivery is to deliver material from the library's own stock, allowing the user to photocopy, consult or borrow the item. Maximizing the use of the library collection, in which there has been considerable investment, is the first challenge to the librarian managing document delivery systems, and the first part of this chapter looks at this.

However, in many cases, the library will not hold the item in stock. Decreasing budgets, spiralling publication rates and increasing prices, outlined in the *Coles report* on the scientific, technical and medical information system in the UK,[1] mean that no library, even the largest, can stand on its own. All are dependent on other libraries and on local and national networks, including electronic networks, to find material. The emphasis in health care libraries has shifted from ownership to access. The role of librarians has also changed, and is now about facilitating access to information, wherever that information is held, on behalf of their users. The users need not even be aware of whether the document is in the library stock or not. The process of acquiring it from another source should appear to the user as simple as acquiring it from the user's own library. However, for many practical and pragmatic reasons, this process is not – and is unlikely to be – seamless. The second part of the chapter concerns access through interlibrary lending, looking both at locating material in other libraries, and at the practicalities of the process. The chapter concludes with sections on the quality aspects and costs of document delivery.

MAXIMIZING THE AVAILABILITY OF LIBRARY STOCK

It is most satisfactory for both the user and the librarian if the requested item can be supplied immediately from the library stock, as a loan, for consultation, as a photocopy or as a printout from an electronic database. Library management in this area should be directed towards both maximizing the availability from library stock and encouraging use of the material already available within the library, by ensuring that the collection is appropriate to the users' needs. Availability depends on several factors: the stock acquisition policies, the quality of the access to the stock, and the efficiency of the loan and photocopy systems.

Central to the process of document delivery is the library's stock acquisition policy, and the librarian must strive to ensure that the core collection is appropriate to the use made of the library. Carrying out availability surveys on a regular basis can help the librarian to decide whether the stock acquisition policy is meeting the needs of users. Regular use surveys of periodicals can also indicate where changes are required. There is no place in the health care library of today for maintaining a periodical title just because the library has always taken it.

The requests for documents received for items not in the library can inform the librarian about the stock acquisition policy. The subjects of the requests may change subtly from year to year, and the stock acquisition policy should reflect these changes. The number of requests for one item may suggest that an item should be bought rather than repeatedly requested on interlibrary loan: if 20 requests are received in one year for a periodical, and the periodical costs, for example, £100, it may be appropriate to consider purchasing the periodical. However, before this decision is made, some questions must be asked: were all the requests by one user, who may shortly leave? Were all the requests for parts of the journal published some years ago? In the latter case the journal may no longer be of the same quality, or its emphasis may have altered.

The quality of access to the library stock is also important. A book catalogue that is easy to use and allows users to identify the material that the library holds on a particular subject may encourage use of an alternative item that the library has in stock rather than an item not in stock. Current awareness bulletins of recently acquired books and periodical articles will encourage the use of this material. Versions of the *MEDLINE* database, which allow the library to tag periodical references with their own holdings will also direct users to the more easily available material in the library stock. Good signposting, user education and regular shelf-checking to ensure that books and periodicals are correctly shelved will all make it easier for users to find the document they want.

Loan policies affect the quality of document delivery. Most, but not all libraries, allow the loan of some types of material. Lending material means that the book or periodical is not available in the library for other users, and the balance between satisfying the user who wants to take the item away for studying with the user who arrives wanting to find the item on the shelf is always difficult for the librarian to deal with. Not lending items which may be required for clinical reasons may be appropriate. An efficient and well advertized recall system is essential. Some libraries allow some material out on loan but restrict the loan period for certain types of publication, such as reference books, major textbooks and recent or unbound parts of periodicals. In this context it is worth noting that the highest use of a periodical is likely to be between 12 and 18 months after publication. Having material unavailable, through long loan or binding, at this time inconveniences users.

The management of lending is now usually automated, and there are many integrated library systems on the market for both small and large libraries.[2] These systems ensure the efficient management of the loan, return, hold and recall of items, and some also allow self-service issue for periods of time when a library is unstaffed. They will also usually allow imaginative use of loan periods to increase the availability of material to users. For example, if an item is in demand, its loan period can easily be changed from the library's normal four weeks to three days, to allow more users to have access to it in the same period.

For many users, however, photocopying, rather than lending, is the most important library service because it allows them to retain documents. Libraries usually provide self-service photocopiers for their users, and it is important to provide a machine which is simple to use, is robust enough to cope with the demands which the public put on photocopying machines, and appropriate for the copying of library materials such as large periodical volumes. This also implies some form of charging mechanism, usually based on a card operated system to minimize the amount of cash handling, since libraries are obliged by the provisions of the Copyright Design and Patents Act 1988 to recover all costs, including staff costs, in setting their charge for photocopying. There are several useful guides to this Act for librarians, who should be able to advise their users on the copyright regulations.[3]

Health care libraries are beginning to make available some material in electronic format so that users – either in the library or networked to their own desk – may look at, download to disk or print out selected documents. These documents may be on CD-ROM, on a local network, or on the Internet. Making available such material provides new challenges to the librarian. The librarian needs to provide appropriate equipment, and to plan new charging mechanisms and user education programmes. However, since authors and publishers are beginning to use these methods to publish material, the librarian must become involved and make these services available in the library. The biggest growth area in the next few years is likely to be the use of the Internet to publish material, either as an original publication or in parallel to print publication. Document delivery from the Internet will grow rapidly in importance. Health care libraries that do not have easy access to the Internet to assess what is available may have to depend on commercial services. Librarians are advised to keep abreast of the health librarianship literature to see what is and becomes available. The *Follett report* provides a useful summary of the position up to 1993.[4]

DOCUMENT DELIVERY FROM OTHER LIBRARIES
Access through interlibrary lending
If an item is not available from stock, the librarian can borrow or arrange to receive a photocopy of it from another library through the interlibrary loan (ILL) system. In order to do this, the librarian has to locate the material and ensure that arrangements are in place that enable it to be borrowed, usually by means of a local network, or a national or commercial scheme. In an ideal world, this process would appear to the user as an extension of document delivery from the library's own stock, but this is rarely the case.

Locating material
Librarians have built up many union lists of where to find items that they do not have in their own libraries. For periodicals, the first port of call will normally be to check the union list of their local or regional network. There are many types of local union lists: some NHS regions maintain lists of the holdings in each of their libraries, some voluntary organizations, such as the Association of Scottish Health Sciences Librarians or the Psychiatric Libraries Cooperative Scheme, maintain a union list of periodicals in their geographical or subject area; some large academic institutions maintain a local union list for their geographical area, sometimes backed up by a metropolitan van service for delivery. Some of the union lists only give information about the titles held, and the librarian will either have to help the user to arrange a visit to the other library to consult the material, or borrow the document from the other library.

However, many union lists also have a cooperative photocopy or loan scheme, which allows the user to get a photocopy or loan of the requested item. Until recently, many of these schemes were fairly informal and provided a free exchange of photocopies. Now these are having to become more formal, with membership, vouchers, cross-charging mechanisms and structures which ensure that the cooperative scheme members are not infringing the Copyright

Act. However, such schemes are the bread-and-butter of much of the ILL activity of health care libraries, and still provide a cost-effective service to their members.

In addition to formal union lists, through experience, librarians build up their own contacts and knowledge about what is available in other libraries. This is particularly important in the case of borrowing books from other libraries, since it is usually more difficult to find locations for books.

If the item is not available through a network, the librarian can try one of the other services, usually the British Library Document Supply Centre (BLDSC). In the *Coles report*, most librarians surveyed expected the BLDSC to remain the most important supplier of documents in the future.[5] The BLDSC is the most important resource in the UK for material in every subject area, including health care. The serials taken by the British Library and available for supply by photocopy or loan are listed in *Current serials received*.[6] The 1994 edition lists 65,000 titles. The BLDSC sells request forms and these now represent a form of currency for interlibrary lending in the UK. The BLDSC also uses a number of back-up libraries to supplement its collection.

Another important service, aimed specifically at health care libraries, is provided by the British Medical Association (BMA) Library.[7] To use this scheme, the library must become an institutional member of the BMA Library. The library can either buy BMA voucher stamps to put on request forms, or can make individual requests.

In the United States, the number of commercial document delivery services is growing and some of these services are now transferring their attention to the European and UK market. Since some of these have developed in response to the difficulties of document delivery in the USA, and others have developed in order to supplement their profit as database producers or periodical agents,[8,9] it will be interesting to see whether they gain a foothold in the UK, where the situation is different. These services will certainly be aggressively marketed. Examples of these services are OCLC Prism ILL Service and the Blackwell/CARL UnCover2 service. They usually offer delivery by facsimile and can be very fast. Some libraries, or their users, will be prepared to pay for the rapid delivery. Payment is usually at point of use by credit card, and the services may be aimed directly at the end user and will not necessarily be mediated by librarians.

Newer developments are exploiting electronic networks to deliver documents.[10] Such electronic document delivery, in the UK using the technology of the Joint Academic Network (JANET), SuperJANET and the Internet, looks promising. It will provide rapid document delivery direct to the user. There are, however, many technical, copyright and organizational problems to be solved before such access is appropriate for all libraries on a day-to-day basis.

One important development is the Ariel software, developed in the USA by the Research Libraries Group.[11, 12] Ariel is a software package designed to send, receive and print images of documents. The documents are scanned, compressed and stored on a microcomputer, and then transmitted via the Internet to the requesting library, which must also have a workstation with the Ariel software.

Practical issues in interlibrary loan document delivery

The practical management of the ILL service has often been treated as an independent function within libraries. It is now having an increasing impact on other library services, as libraries move from holdings to access policies. If document delivery is ever to appear seamless, the ILL process must become much more closely integrated with other services, such as loans and photocopying.

The ILL process has been one of the last library housekeeping functions to be automated, possibly because the manual systems served very well and the service itself could act independently of other library services. Now, there are a number of automated ILL packages, some standalone, others integrated into a library system, which allow the transmission, receipt, issue and return of each item to be recorded.[13] Although there are advantages to automating with a standalone system, such as improving the management information available, there are greater advantages to be gained by integrating the ILL module with other parts of the library systems package, where this is possible. Such an integrated system will allow users, after searching the online public access catalogue and finding that the item wanted is not available, to move immediately to make an ILL request. An integrated system allows all the circulation data for library loans and interlibrary loans to be recorded together. Automation of the ILL process certainly makes it easier to keep statistics and other management information about all types of document delivery, a powerful tool in the management and future planning of document delivery services.

To facilitate the ILL process, the librarian normally provides a form for the user to complete. The form should require the user to complete bibliographic information about the item requested, including:

- the source of reference (so that the librarian can check if the information is unclear)
- information about whether a photocopy of the item is acceptable
- the latest date the item will be of use
- information about the person making the request.

The back of the form can be used to track the progress of the ILL request if the process is not automated.

The processing of ILLs is dependent on the quality of the information provided by the user. The information is usually good if taken from a database, and it can be helpful to encourage the user to attach the printout to the request form. Librarians prefer the information they send elsewhere to be correct, and some librarians spend a lot of time verifying the bibliographic information before sending requests on. While it is obviously essential to check whether the library has the document in stock, further bibliographic checking may not always be necessary. Experienced ILL staff will usually pick up requests which look wrong. When the information looks complete and correct, the request can go through straightforwardly and more quickly if it is sent off immediately. The supplying library will return the form if it is incorrect, and the item can be checked at that stage. Less time will be spent on checking the occasional returned form than on routinely verifying bibliographic details of every single request before transmission.

Requests can be sent to the supplying library by post, telex, facsimile or electronic mail, and are usually sent on vouchers or with numbers that are bought in advance. Some of the commercial services are seeking payment by credit card at point-of-use. The BLDSC accepts requests by post, telex, fax, ART (automated request transmission), which includes ARTel (ART by telephone), and, in the future, by electronic mail. It also accepts requests via some database hosts, for example BIDS. Full information about using BLDSC services is available in the *UK customers handbook*.[14]

The slowest part of the ILL process is the supply of the actual document, and this is where the user will notice the difference between requested items that are in the library stock and those that are obtained on ILL. Documents are normally sent by post, although the commercial suppliers and the BLDSC, for an additional charge, will send items by facsimile. Future developments with facsimile transmission and electronic document delivery should speed up this part of the process.

Once the document is received as a photocopy or a loan, it has to be passed on to the user. Again, this part of the process can add significantly to the time delay between request and receipt by the user, if for example, the internal postal system of the hospital or institution is slow and causes delay in informing the user knowing that the item has been received in the library. Electronic communication within the institution, both for receipt of requests and informing the user that the document has been received, will improve this situation.

The librarian has a responsibility to care for loans from other institutions, and has to pass on this responsibility to the user. If the lending library places restrictions, for example allowing use in the library only, the end user may be dissatisfied, but the librarian must comply with the lending library's request. The librarian is also responsible for ensuring that a user returns the material in sufficient time to return it to the lending library by the due date.

QUALITY ISSUES IN DOCUMENT DELIVERY

All librarians should be concerned with ways of improving the quality of document delivery services, and the speed and efficiency with which documents are delivered to users. Carrying out surveys on the availability of materials in the library and how the users perceive the speed and effectiveness of the ILL service are valuable starting points. The recording of statistics of document delivery, including loans, photocopying and the success and failure of interlibrary loans, is also essential. Users demand a continually improving service. In a survey carried out in Edinburgh University Library, while most interlibrary loans for medical users arrived within seven to fourteen days, most users thought they should arrive within four to seven days, and a significant number thought they should arrive within one to three days.[15] Librarians will have to respond to these expectations by continually monitoring, re-examining and, where possible, improving–all the processes involved in document delivery, and perhaps by making it more clear to users how long they can expect to wait for their interlibrary loans to arrive. Developments in electronic document delivery are likely to have a major impact in increasing the speed of the receipt of items, but at a cost.

The librarian must also question the value of what is supplied. Every librarian knows about the recalled book or interlibrary loan so keenly sought, and then barely looked at because it is now no longer needed or is otherwise of little value. In a small survey of the quality aspects of the interlibrary loan service in Edinburgh University Library, 75% of Medical Faculty or NHS users found the interlibrary loans they had received very useful, 18% found them fairly useful, but 7% found them either not very useful of not at all useful.[16] It is obviously a concern that scarce time and resources are being spent on items of little value. The librarian needs to know why they are not useful: is it because they are received too late, or is it because the user did not have sufficient information to hand when making the requests? The number of requests for interlibrary loans decreased in Edinburgh University Library on the introduction of the *MEDLINE* on CD-ROM service, which gave users easy access to abstracts of periodical articles for the first time. It may be that the users could now more easily assess the value of items for which they had previously put in an interlibrary loan. An American study has looked in more detail at the use of documents obtained on interlibrary loan and at the reasons for requesting the documents.[17] This survey identified that some requested documents were not read, but affirmed the value and timeliness of the interlibrary loan service. Librarians may wish to look at carrying out such surveys in their own libraries to assess the quality of their own document delivery services.

COSTS OF AND CHARGING FOR DOCUMENT DELIVERY

The present pressures for greater accountability, tight budgets and the need to develop contracts encourages the monitoring of costs. Identifying the costs of document delivery services is particularly difficult, since they encompass almost all library costs and relate to several of the functions of the library – acquisitions, loans, photocopying, as well as the more traditional interlibrary loan function. However, much can be done to provide unit costs for document delivery services and this information can be used in several ways. For example, the unit cost, including staff costs, materials costs, direct costs (vouchers) and administrative overheads, of a loan or an interlibrary loan can be worked out for a library,[18] and this can be used in looking at the merits of acquiring an item for stock or on interlibrary loan.

For librarians who are developing contracts, knowing the unit cost of loans, photocopies and interlibrary loans is essential. Even when these services are defined as core or basic services in the contract, the librarian needs to know the number and unit costs of the services in order to develop a contract with a particular group.

Working out the unit cost is also essential in deciding whether, and how much, to charge users for the services. Charging users for document delivery is often based on historical precedent rather than on knowledge of the actual costs. Practically all libraries charge for photocopying of their own material, but not for loans. Some libraries charge for interlibrary loans and others do not. Those which do not tend to absorb the costs of the interlibrary loan service in the operating budget. Those which charge may charge a small flat rate sum, intended to act as a deterrent to the too casual request for an interlibrary loan, or, more rarely, the full cost. Some libraries charge users for items which they can retain but not for items they must return; this decision is often not in the hands of the user or the librarian and may not make much sense to the user who just wants the information. The whole situation of charges for document delivery can be confusing for users, who will be uncertain about which document delivery services they have to pay for and which they do not. The librarian should look at the pattern and costs of all document delivery services in determining charges.

Libraries using the newer commercial services and electronic document delivery services tend to be uncertain about charging for these new services. If the cost of the service can be controlled and is a flat payment in advance, the library is unlikely to charge for it and will absorb the costs; if it depends on use, the library is more likely to charge on the costs. The introduction of commercial services may cause libraries to look more rigorously at their costs and charging policies.

CONCLUSION

There have been several recurring themes in this chapter. The first theme is the need to view all document delivery services together as part of an integrated process. For the user, whether the item comes from the local or another library does not matter. For the librarian there are still many practical reasons to differentiate rather than integrate the processes, but it is a good discipline for the librarian to think as the user would and view the request as a request for information from whatever source. A second theme is the need to use information gathered as part of the ILL process for future planning to improve the management of the service. A third theme is the increasing expectation of users for a continually improving service, where documents are delivered more speedily. The final theme is the impact which electronic document delivery and commercial services are likely to have on the future of document delivery services. Librarians must be aware of, and manage, these trends on behalf of their users.

REFERENCES

1   Royal Society, British Library and Association of Learned and Professional Society Publishers, *The scientific, technical and medical information system in the UK: a study on behalf of the Royal Society, the British Library and the Association of Learned and Professional Society Publishers*, project directed by Professor B. R. Coles, British Library R&D Report No. 6123, London, Royal Society, British Library and Association of Learned and Professional Society Publishers, 1993.

2   For example, Leeves, J., *Library systems: a buyer's guide*, Aldershot, Gower, 1989. See also the periodical *Vine*.

3   For example, Clark, C., *Photocopying from books and journals: a guide for all users of copyright literary works*, London, British Copyright Council, 1990.

4   Follett, B. (ed.), Joint Funding Council's Libraries Review Group, *A report for HECFE, SHEFC, HEFCW and DENI*, Bristol, Higher Education Funding Council for England, 1993.

5   Royal Society, *op. cit.*, 196–8.

6   *Current serials received*, current edn, Boston Spa, British Library Document Supply Centre.

7   Bonnett, P, 'The development of interlending through the BMA's institutional membership scheme', *Assistant librarian*, **85** (12), 1992, 179–82.

8   Khalil, M., 'Document delivery: a better option', *Library journal*, **118** (2), 1993, 43–7.

9   Malamud, J. and Levine, L. (eds.), 'Symposium: Docushock: options for document delivery in the nineties'; *Bulletin of the Medical Library Association*, **82** (2), 1994, 161–87.

10   Braid, J. A., 'Electronic document delivery: a reality at last?', *Aslib proceedings*, **45** (6), 1993, 161–6.

11   Jackson, M. E., 'Using Ariel, RLG's document transmission system to improve document delivery in the United States', *Interlending and document supply*, **20** (2), 1992, 49–52.

12   Bennett, V. M., 'Electronic document delivery using the Internet', *Bulletin of the Medical Library Association*, **82** (2), 1994, 163–7.

13   Leeves, J., ' Automation of ILL management systems', *Interlending and document supply systems*, **21** (3), 1993, 12–17.

14   *UK customers' handbook*, current edition, Boston Spa, British Library Document Supply Centre.

15   Moon, B. E., 'Maintaining the quality', in Else, B. (ed.), *Forum for interlending: Interlend '92: assuring quality*, proceedings of a conference held at Bath University, 9–11 July 1992, 44–50, Forum for Interlending, 1993.

16   Ibid.

17   Lovas, I. *et al.*, 'Health professionals' use of documents obtained through the Regional Medical Library Network', *Bulletin of the Medical Library Association*, **79** (1), 1991, 28–35.

18   See, for example, Jones, L. and Nicholas, D.,'Costing medical libraries: the feasibility of functional cost analysis', *Health libraries review*, **10** (4), 1993, 169–201.

15 Developing resource sharing tools

❖ *Caroline Sawers*

No library can ever be self-sufficient. Even if resources of time, money, space and staffing were not in short supply, the size of the pool of subject matter from which information may be required by health care staff makes it impossible for the individual librarian to know where to find everything, or for the individual library to have a stock collection policy that will satisfy all demands made upon it. Efficient resource sharing gives the library user access to the whole knowledge base of health care.

Libraries within the health care field are small, normally between three and twenty staff, and their resources are limited. It is necessary for them to develop systems for resource sharing that are manageable and within their means to achieve (Table 15.1).

Table 15.1 Advantages and disadvantages of resource sharing

Advantages	Constraints
For users	
Wider choice of material	Time delay for document delivery
	Loss of 'browsing' capability on site; may mean travelling
For librarians	
Improvements in service within existing resources	Loss of autonomy in stock selection
Links formed with neighbouring libraries; knowledge of what's available nearby	Can feel less helpful to users
Take advantage of special collections	

Resources that can be shared include:
- 'free' resources over the Internet
- serial holdings
- books

- grey literature
- audiovisuals
- non-bibliographic resources.

HOW TO SHARE
Sharing without developing tools
As more and more libraries gain access to networks, in particular, JANET (the Joint Academic Network) and the Internet, the opportunities for 'free' resource sharing will increase by the use of remote library catalogues, and more opportunities to order interlibrary loans over the network. There are few restrictions on consulting remote catalogues, but, once connected, a multitude of interfaces to contend with. A number of tools are being developed to help navigate the Internet (Table 15.2) and sort out the useful from the less useful material to be found on it.[1] These tools are crude and still in their infancy, and as health care librarians gain access to the Internet, their traditional skills will be required to facilitate the resource sharing opportunities opening up worldwide.

Table 15.2 Internet tools

Gopher
(Developed at the University of Minnesota, home of the 'Golden Gophers'. Its function is to 'go fer' things, and the pun stuck).
- Menu driven method of finding and using resources on the Internet.
- American Library Association has one.[2]

Archie
- A method of searching through archives of files held on remote file-servers to find public domain and shareware software or other files.
- It relies on files being given a helpful name.

Veronica
(Very Easy Rodent Oriented Net-wide Index to Computerized Archives).
- Acts as an index to gophers

WAIS
(Wide Area Information Servers).
- A text searching system. Gopher looks through a sequence of menus, WAIS looks for words in files.

World Wide Web
(WWA)
- Uses hypertext links to get from one idea, document, file or other resource to the next.
- Each WWW is built to give a view of the Internet from a particular perspective. It relies on the designer having thought of the links that a user

might want, and built them in at the design stage. In contrast to the other tools described above, which are essentially text based, WWWs employ colour, graphics, graphical user interfaces, sound and moving images, and are consequently demanding of network resources.

- Most universities now have one, and very often the library has been heavily involved in designing it.
- NLM has several.[3]

Bulletin board services and mailing lists which individuals can join are available over the Internet. Two popular mailing lists are Lis-Medical (UK) and MEDLIB-L (USA). They both contain much useful information, and give librarians the opportunity to join in discussions and share their own knowledge.

The expected development of electronic journals is in its infancy, with many questions still unanswered about quality, the place of peer review in the electronic publishing business, and the editorial process.[4] The place of resource sharing within this area has yet to be developed. ADONIS, the most promising experiment up to now in full text journal publishing, is only available in CD-ROM format, and not yet networkable.

Several commercial services are beginning to appear which link current awareness services with document delivery. They are known under the generic name CASIAS (current awareness service – individual article supply) (Table 15.3).[5, 6] Although primarily designed for end user searching and use, they are used by librarians in a variety of ways for alerting or SDI (selective dissemination of information) services, but less often for routine document delivery as the prices are not competitive with the British Library Document Supply Centre (BLDSC). For items required urgently, the cost can be less than the BLDSC Urgent Action Service.

Table 15.3 CASIAS Services

Blackwells	Uncover
British Library	Inside information
EBSCO	Cas-ias
OCLC	First Search
SWETS	Swetscan

There are many opportunities for librarians to share one another's resources over the network. It is to be hoped that the capacity of the network will be able to support the volume of traffic it will be required to carry.

Serials

Some forms of resource sharing are easier than others, which is one reason for the proliferation of union lists of serials (Table 15.4). The items required are easily photocopied (subject to copyright regulations), posted or faxed. It has been said that wherever two or three librarians are gathered together there shall be a union list. Union lists are organized on a geographical, subject or institutional basis.

Table 15.4 Examples of Union Lists of Serials

Domain of List	List Owner	Coverage
Subject	(NHS) Management Librarians Group	Libraries in health authorities
	Psychiatric Librarians Cooperative Scheme	115 libraries throughout UK
	INFAH (Information Focus for Allied Health)	Union list of holdings in libraries in schools of occupational therapy and physiotherapy
Geographical	Most NHS Regional Library Services, or Regional Associations of Health Service	Sometimes including other sources for better coverage, for example including BMA holdings
Institutional	London University Librarians	Holdings on LIBERTAS, widely used system in the institutions making up London University

Union lists can save money at the time of use. O'Donovan[7] reported a saving to the Northern Regional Health Authority of £20,000 in 1988–9. This was based on a union list of 1500 titles in 34 libraries.

Another NHS regional library service's union list containing 4000 titles covering the stock of 47 libraries, formed the basis for 13,969 interlibrary copies in 1993–94, 37% of the total, which would otherwise have to have been obtained from the BLDSC.

The savings made by cooperative use of stock is offset by the costs of setting up and maintaining a union list. These overheads increase with the size and complexity of the list. When one NHS regional library service merged two large union lists, one list was supplied as a DOS conversion from a word processor. This contained a number of errors (2.5% of the total records) which had to be manually corrected. This error rate had to be counted into the costs of preparing the list and set off against future savings.

Union lists are also of use in collection planning. As serial prices increase faster than library budgets, it makes sense for neighbouring libraries to cooperate over planned journal purchases and cancellations. Subject to copyright regulations, shared contents pages help browsing at each site.

An experiment at Pennsylvania State University,[8] involving cooperative collection development, linked two libraries over 100 miles apart through the Internet. Some low use duplicate journals were identified for cancellation at each site, and only the contents pages made available. The ARIEL document transmission software system (integrating PCs, scanners, laser printers and communications equipment) was used for the document delivery.

The temptation to do something new, and precisely tailored to a particular situation, is always there, but the resources in staff time required for acquiring the information in the first place, and then keeping it up to date, are not cheap. It is always prudent to investigate the existence of a suitable alternative, or even a nearly suitable alternative, before starting on a task requiring a long-term commitment.

It is both quicker and more cost effective to use the British Library than to use more than one union list, and certainly cheaper to use the British Library than to make telephone calls to other libraries 'just in case', especially if the supplying library asks for a British Library form as payment for ad hoc requests.

Staff time must be dedicated to the process of collection and updating, as an out-of-date list wastes time (and therefore money), and lacks credibility. Getting the system right to start with and keeping it simple are always important, but particularly so in shared tools.

Whiffin,[9] in her draft guidelines for the production of union lists of serials prepared for IFLA in 1981, draws attention to the importance of interests held in common by participants, and a shared vision of the value and benefits to be gained. It is important that nobody feels victimized by the operation of a union list and that arrangements are made to compensate net lenders. If common standards and protocols are imposed rather than agreed there will be a lack of commitment to the scheme which may jeopardize its success. Resource sharing imposes constraints on participants, whose views should be sought during the planning process.

Speeding document delivery by using electronic mail and fax transmission between the participants in a union list of serials is in regular use in some regional systems, and many health care librarians use ARTtel or fax to send requests to the BLDSC.

Books

Books have been shared for many years and the development of tools to facilitate sharing have been helped by the programmes for Universal Bibliographic Control (UBC) and Universal Availability of Publications (UAP) of UNESCO and IFLA.[10] These programmes led to the development of the International Standard Bibliographic Description (ISBD).[11]

In the United Kingdom, the public library regional resource sharing cooperatives, of which LASER (London and South Eastern Library Region) is a good example, provide good models for book resource sharing. LASER's Viscount system, now heavily computerized, is being extended to sectors outside public libraries and actively marketed in the health sector. LASER is also involved with a European Union (EU) project ION (Interlending Open Systems Project), which links the interlibrary lending activities of the UK, The Netherlands and France by computer network.[12]

The *British national bibliography* (BNB) has just joined forces with a commercial company, Libris, to develop a major new union catalogue. Starting with the holdings of the North Western and South Western Regional Library Bureaux, there are plans to add the holdings of Ireland, Scotland, Wales, the North East and East Midlands.

Also within the public library sector, Marylebone Medical Library, now part of the Westminster system, developed an excellent medical collection as part of the metropolitan subject specialization scheme.

Sharing records of books among health libraries is becoming easier as technology improves. Health service libraries attached to academic institutions and medical school libraries are able to use the library catalogues available over JANET and the Internet.

Three NHS regional library systems have long-established cooperative cataloguing arrangements which grew out of systems designed to improve the quality of the cataloguing (Table 15.5). Another, currently being piloted, is building on this earlier experience and using the advantages of modern technology to enrich the data by downloading author affiliations and subject information from subject, abstract and contents fields of the BookFind CD-ROM. This is an example of cooperation between the health service and a commercial supplier. Apart from quality issues, these cooperatives save money on interlibrary loans, help with stock selection and collection planning, and add cohesion to the network. It is always up to the individual librarian to decide whether a particular item may be lent. Books can be expensive to post, but costs can be saved by using transport schemes where they exist.

Table 15.5 NHS Regional cooperatives

NHS Regional Library Service	Date started	
Wessex	1969	Card production, micro fiche, now telephone network to OPAC using UNICORN
South East Thames	1978	Card production, now telephone network using LIBRARIAN
South West Thames	1980	Card production, micro-fiche, now networked using INMAGIC
North West Thames	1994	INMAGIC/BookFind. Distributed via BookFind CD, only available to contributors via a password

Grey literature

Much valuable material is found within health organizations in unpublished or semi-published form. Librarians are involved in trying to improve access to it in three ways: by attempting to influence the producers of the material to improve its presentation, thereby making bibliographic control and thus access to the information contained in the material easier; by the traditional methods of collecting and documenting the material; and by recording its existence on databases which are then made widely available, but leaving the material *in situ*.[13-15]

In order to share grey literature, bibliographic control must be applied to the documents, but influencing their producers is not so easy. There is no lack of advice.[16] Minimum requirements for the document itself are for the addition of a title page containing:

- title
- author/department responsible for the document
- date of publication
- place of publication
- price
- statement of availability, e.g. 'further copies are available from . . . '
- copyright statement.

Advice is also given on how to obtain ISBN numbers, and recommendations are made for the deposit of copies with the Copyright Libraries, Departments of Health and Social Security Library Service and local libraries.

It is easier to control grey literature if librarians take responsibility for collecting, storing and recording whatever is produced within their own geographical or organizational patch.

Efforts to keep track of Health Service circulars, *Executive letters* and other health service guidance has exercized many health authorities and health service librarians, and there is a great deal of duplication of effort as they try to keep up-to-date collections and lists of the various series. The decision of Cambridge Health Authority to make its Circulars database available for sale on a subscription basis is to be welcomed. It is very current, and issued monthly in ASCII format which is easily loaded into a text retrieval or database management system.

A constraint on sharing grey literature can be the difficulty of replacing lost items.

Audiovisual material
In most health care libraries the audiovisual stock is integrated with the rest of the material held, and the software used for cataloguing has fields added to accommodate audiovisual items. Another model is that used in the Wessex Regional Library and Information Service, where a separate audiovisual library is maintained which acts as a resource for all the libraries in the network, publishing lists of its holdings from time to time. The advantages of separate provision are that expertise in collection, storage, use and promotion of the media can be built up, but integrated provision provides the user with access to the full range of material without differentiating between physical formats.

A constraint on resource sharing audiovisuals is the initial high cost and, again, the difficulty of replacing lost items. The range of formats, and consequently the different kinds of equipment required to use them, can also militate against easy resource sharing. As Stewart says in her chapter in this book, 'interlibrary loan of audiovisual materials is not universally well established'.

Non-bibliographic resources
It is also useful to consider sharing non-bibliographic resources such as contacts, registers, collections of projects, and all other material of the kind kept in a box of 5 in × 3 in cards on every librarian's desk.

An example of a non-bibliographic source which will usefully be shared is the register of research in progress commissioned by the Research and Development Directorate of the NHS Executive. It runs under BRS search software and has been distributed to regional directors of R&D, who are under an obligation to keep it up to date by including local research.

Another form of resource sharing is illustrated by an initiative of The Library Association which has set up a register of information technology expertise. A database is being formed which can be interrogated, and contacts given for help and advice on hardware and software problems.

SOURCES OF DATA

Before starting from scratch and committing staff time to manual input, it is worth considering whether it is possible to obtain machine-readable records and import them (Tables 15.6 and 15.7).

Table 15.6 Sources of data

Other members of cooperative	Quality assurance measures are crucial
Other similar libraries	If the data is very nearly right, use theirs, improve, and feed improvements back to the originator
Commercial CD-ROM	e.g. *Whitaker's books in print plus*, Book Data's BookFind
Internet	e.g. BNB, CURL
Online systems	e.g. OCLC, BNB, MEDLINE

Table 15.7 Criteria for choosing sources of data

Is it exactly what is needed?	Other libraries within a cooperative, or similar libraries are likely to have similar aims and requirements, and use compatible subject headings or class numbers.
Coverage	Does the data cover the full range of user's interests?
Is there more detail than is required?	Few health care libraries need the depth of cataloguing required by MARC.

Is there less detail than is required?	Minimal subject access provided by MARC. Extra subject enrichment provided in some newer services, e.g. BookFind CD-ROM.
How easy is the data to import?	This will depend on the export capacity of the originating software, otherwise data conversion software must be used.
Will there be much additional work to do to the data?	Error rates. Addition of local information.
Reasonable cost?	Not paying for detail that will be discarded. Compare rates for manual input with cost.

SYSTEM DESIGN FOR RESOURCE SHARING TOOLS

Resource sharing tools are part of the whole resource sharing system, which also includes interlibrary loans, circulation, transport and, where appropriate, copyright clearance.

It is likely that the tools will be databases developed on a computer. Computers are readily available, and suitable software for database production is reasonably cheap. It is tempting to suggest that a computerized database is always the right answer, but it may not be. The proposed database may be very small, the number of access points to the data required limited, there may be no suitable computer available, or the staff and users may not be computer literate. In this situation it is probably unwise to consider a computerized solution. However, these are extreme constraints, and in most cases a database developed on a computer will be the answer.

When developing a standalone system it can be done entirely to satisfy the needs of the primary user, but where there is more than one person or library system concerned, other factors should be taken into account (Table 15.8). The bigger the cooperative the more things are likely to go wrong, and the more important it becomes to plan ahead for problems and try to forestall them. It is probably impossible to satisfy each participant completely, but everyone's wishes should be taken into consideration. If the same people are both users and producers there will be a greater tolerance of faults such as duplicate entries. This may not be helpful to end users.

Table 15.8 Factors to consider in system design

Holistic	The tool should fit neatly into the whole resource sharing system
Flexibility of output	Will the system produce all the outputs required now, and easily produce more as they are required in the future?
Needs of the users	
Librarians	Are the needs of the disparate library systems within the cooperative taken into account?
End users	If the tool has a public interface, such as an OPAC, can the faults be kept to a acceptable level, or will naïve users be confused?
Keeping it up to date	Are the arrangements for keeping the system up-to-date such as will encourage the participants to do it?

DATABASE STRUCTURES

Some definitions follow:

- a **database** is a collection of records such as the bibliographical descriptions of books and their locations (a catalogue) or details of journal holdings (a union list of serials);
- each **record** is made up of a collection of fields into which the constituent parts of the record (author, title, publisher) are put;
- a **field** is a part of the record (author fields contain all authors, title fields contain all titles);
- **data elements** are the constituent parts of a record;
- a **database structure** is the framework, consisting of fields and decisions on indexing, designed to hold the data that makes up the records.

Librarians who have studied cataloguing should find this easy to grasp.

Table 15.9 incorporates suggestions for a protocol, developed by Carmel, to be adhered to by database producers in order to make data easily transferable from one database to another.[17]

Time spent at the planning stage thinking about the fields required will pay dividends later. It is easy enough to combine fields at the reporting stage, but if, for instance, all elements of an address have been put together in a field called ADDRESS, it will be difficult to produce useful lists under the street or postcode. If several subject headings are put into the same field, or authors are not separated from corporate authors, retrieval is made more difficult.

Table 15.9 Features of a good database structure

Separation of data elements	All separate elements of a record should be identified and put into appropriate fields within the data-structure.
Indexing	Appropriate for the data within the field, e.g. keywords for text, probably including stop words to stop the indexes becoming cluttered; special indexing for dates.
Reporting/flexible output	Ability to sort by any field in the record
Standard field names or field labels	Preferably mnemonic, for ease of use, e.g. AU for author, TI for title, PU for publisher.
Boolean fields	Should be avoided for ease of searching.
Coded data	Should be avoided, as it causes delay at the input stage for codes to be looked up, and confusion for the searcher.

When designing a data-structure, all the access points to the data that may be needed later should be incorporated. Especially when dealing with grey literature, careful planning for access points is vital. The greyer the document the more access points need to be provided to it, and the subject indexing must be done in greater depth. There are fewer rules and precedents to work on when dealing with this type of material.

It is a good plan to make sure that all related data-structures use the same names for fields as it makes the transfer of data from one database to another very easy. If several databases are in use, it can be confusing for people entering data if, say, DT is used as the date of entry in one database and the year of publication in another.

When looking for sources of data, if a good database structure is found it is worth considering using it, maybe improving it and feeding the improvements back to the originator, thereby raising the standards of both.

Control of data entry
All cooperatives or producers of shared databases impose some control over data entry on the members. Within the health care field, subject access is generally considered to be of primary importance. Authority files for other fields in the database, institutions, corporate authors, formats or publishers are helpful in aiding consistency.

Subject thesauri

Thesauri for subject headings abound in health libraries, the two most widely used being MeSH (Medical Subject Headings, the thesaurus used for *Index medicus* and *MEDLINE*),[18] and *DH/DSS-data thesaurus*.[19] Despite the existence of many thesauri, health seems particularly prone to the introduction of jargon terms, or common terms given a particular meaning within the service (e.g. purchasing intelligence, internal market, commissioning agencies), which must be accommodated within the thesaurus if the retrieval requirements of users are to be adequately served. Terms also fall out of favour (e.g. 'mental retardation', 'mental handicap' replaced by 'people with special educational needs', 'people with learning difficulties').

There is always a trade-off between responsiveness to subtle changes in the language of the subject and total control of the thesaurus. The Drug Information Pharmacist's Group *Pharm-line* database is an example of extreme control, on occasion causing a decision to be made between adding an abstract with an inappropriate indexing term or holding it back until the correct term has been approved. Most cooperatives choose a system of compromise and synthesis. Whatever method is chosen for dealing with the addition, deletion or change of terms must work fast. Several systems have an extra field in the database structure to accommodate terms that are candidates for later inclusion in the subject thesaurus. At the time of retrieval this field is searched together with the field controlled by the thesaurus. The contents of the field are regularly reviewed and decisions made about individual terms.

Training for data entry

People who are involved in data entry to cooperative databases must receive sufficient initial training for them to feel comfortable with the database they are contributing to. Revision courses or supplementary courses should be held as necessary. Checks of the data can reveal a need for remedial training of individuals. The training does not always need to consist of formal courses, often informal methods are more appropriate. In some places a mentoring or 'buddying' system has been tried with success. Recognizing the competence level of participants at an early stage and taking appropriate action is all important.

Documentation for data entry

Training needs to be backed up by good documentation. Librarians frequently complain about documentation produced by others, but it is difficult to do well.[20] Most cooperatives produce guides to help with data entry.[21-24] They should be clear and unambiguous, including plenty of illustrative examples, scope notes on what to include and what to exclude (for example, should tertiary indexes or free occasional newsletters be included in union lists of serials?), and should make sure that the guidance remains consistent from one edition to the next.

Quality control
Dealing with duplicate entries

Combining data from a variety of sources often results in duplicate records. A decision should be made on whether it is worth keeping them, or whether to find a cost effective method of identifying and removing them. Four models illustrate different approaches.

1   *Make a virtue of accidental duplication.* The producers of *Pharm-line* prefer to keep any duplicate abstracts in the database, as they consider the viewpoints of different abstractors give added value to the database. This will only work where the users and producers of the database are the same people.

2   *Include duplicates for subject enrichment.* CURL[25] (Consortium of University Research Libraries), comprising the libraries of Cambridge, Edinburgh, Glasgow, Leeds, London, Manchester and Oxford Universities, maintains a database, available over JANET, which deliberately keeps the records of each participating library and considers that different records for the same item give added subject enrichment. The consortium was set up with initial University Grant Council funding as a cost-saving collaborative method of combining the cataloguing efforts of the participants, all of whom made heavy use of MARC records obtained from the British Library or the Online Computer Library Centre (OCLC). The database also includes *British national bibliography* tapes, and may be used as a source for bibliographic data. The database is a pool of data rather than a shared catalogue.

3   *Identify duplicates using control numbers.* Townley[26] describes a 'link and merge' technique using Library of Congress card numbers or OCLC control numbers which reduced a large database, the holdings of 17 libraries (the Associated College Libraries of Central Pennsylvania), from 1,086,778 to 709,523 records, a reduction of 35%. The incidence of false merges was found to be insignificant. Duplicates still occur where there are no control numbers.

4   *Use the software.* Online hosts are working on algorithms to detect and remove duplicates following the introduction of their cross-file searching facilities, but it is not an easy problem to solve. OCLC, a major bibliographic database, has a commitment to removing duplicates by employing complicated algorithms which track and remove them but also has a team of people working on the database manually.

Most resource sharing initiatives rely on manual methods and casual observation to detect and remove duplicates.

Consistency of input

The main problem with any shared database is one of maintaining consistency in the application of controlled terms, subject headings or corporate authors (not helped by the frequency with which institutions change names). Inconsistency can be caused by differing levels of competence, differing interpretation of rules governing data entry, lack of training, lack of identification with the goals of the enterprise, or indifference.

Database producers have developed various techniques for dealing with inconsistency and trying to keep the data clean. A full quality control programme, such as that employed by the Drug Information Pharmacist's Group for their database *Pharm-line*, is an ideal to be aimed at, but is very time consuming. Elements from it can be utilized by most producers (Table 15.10).

Table 15.10 Pharm-line Quality Programme

Entry by one person, always checked by another	Each Drug Information Centre is staffed by two qualified pharmacists.
Annual meeting, abstracts sampled and scrutinized by experienced panel	The knowledge that one's own work might be scrutinized by one's peers in this way has a very beneficial effect on the quality of the abstracting.
Speed of entry monitored	Targets part of quality assurance process
Compliance with thesaurus monitored	The application of thesaurus terms is studied; the software only allows terms in the thesaurus to be entered.

Techniques of data sampling, looking either at the input from a particular library, at a particular subject area or at the indexes, are all very useful methods of checking the quality of the data.

Error reporting

Encouraging the members of a resource sharing scheme to report errors is helpful and encourages the members to feel that they have a stake in the finished product. At least one cooperative offers incentives for errors spotted, in the form of vouchers for interlibrary loans.

User group

A user group is another useful method of exerting peer pressure to help improve the quality of the data. It gives members a chance to influence corporate decisions within a cooperative. If the database is publicly available, consider two groups, one for end users and one for user/contributors.

All resource sharing systems managers know where the trustworthy input is likely to come from and where their efforts in checking are best directed.

Choosing software

Before starting to evaluate software packages, it is important to be very clear about what the output from the database is expected to be and to achieve. What comes out of a computer system is governed by what goes in. The expression 'garbage in, garbage out' is often used to cover a situation where the computer has been blamed for human inadequacies at the planning stage (Tables 15.11 and 15.12).

Table 15.11 Criteria to help make a sensible decision about which software to use

Ease of use	Appearance of the screen; command/menu searching to suit competence of different users.
Input	Templates to help with input; authority files for fields with controlled terms.
Output	A good report generator which can handle output in whatever form required, e.g. printed list, subsets on diskette.
Indexing	Term, keyword and specialist indexing, e.g. for dates.
Speed of retrieval	Should not deteriorate with increasing size of the database.
Reliability of developer/ supplier	Track record in the field. Frequency of new software releases. Responsiveness to suggestions from users.
Support	From supplier. From user group.
Training	Easily available. Moderate cost.

Documentation	Good software can be let down by inadequate documentation.
Helpdesk	Preferably in the same country. Enough lines for the telephone to be answered fast.
User group	Independent of the supplier, but enjoying a good relationship with it
All members of a cooperative use the same software	Mutual support. Data conversion kept to a minimum
Relationship to other packages	Should integrate with other software used. Same look and feel as other software used (less necessary with Windows applications).
Same software for all databases	Only one software program to learn. Chosen software should be flexible enough for different databases.

Table 15.12 Comparison between information retrieval systems and database management systems

Information retrieval systems	Database management systems
Good for textual information	Good for structured information Not so good for free text
Variable field length	Fixed field length, heavy on disk space
Inverted file indexing, updating can be slow if heavily indexed	Run-time indexing, slows retrieval time
Fast interactive retrieval Speed less dependent on database size	Slow retrieval from large files, often serial searching
Multistage searching Fuzzy searching	Queries best defined, because often 'whole field' indexing
Thesaurus and authority files can be built in	

Report generator

The report generator is a very important feature of software for resource sharing because it governs the physical appearance of the output. The flexibility
and ease with which reports can be produced will help with the fine tuning of
the output, as it is unlikely to be right first time. The software house will be
happy to write a new output format every time one is needed, but this will add
to the cost, and control over the system will be lost. It is also worth considering at this stage whether the software can export all, or a subset of, the data in
an ASCII text file which can be used for loading into another system if the need
arises.

Indexing and sorting

Retrieval of the data and ease of searching are helped, or hindered, by the way
the system handles the indexing. The data may be indexed by keywords or by
phrases, or by indexing every word (full text). All fields may be indexed or
only some. Full-text indexing of every field rapidly fills up hard disk space. If
full-text indexing is used, the techniques for searching should be more sophisticated than the usual Boolean AND, OR and NOT. Some form of term or relevance weighting is required to avoid redundancy and false drops when
retrieving information. It is important to consider the list of stop words, particularly with full-text indexing, and to find out whether it is possible to add to
or subtract from it.

The sorting capabilities of the software should be evaluated. If *Journal of the
American Medical Association* is required to file with the 'the' ignored, the software must be capable of handling it.

How the software handles numbers at the start of titles can be critical. Does
'1st . . . ' file before '1001 things to do . . .'?

Sorting, manipulating and retrieving dates must be provided for. Most software designed for library use has been programmed to accept dates in any
form, complete or incomplete (e.g. Sep 93, 12–9–93) and to distinguish between
the European and American forms (is 12-9-93 9 December, or 12 September?)

Size

The size of the proposed database is a factor to consider when selecting software. Some packages have a limit on the number of records within a database.
The time taken for searching or updating can be adversely affected by the size.
There is generally a trade-off to be made between the depth of indexing and
the space occupied on the hard disk. With well written software, depth of
indexing should not affect the speed of retrieval, but it is wise to check.

Thesaurus
Some library software has the ability to hold thesauri and other authority files online to use as look-up tables when entering data. If this feature is required, make sure a large enough file can be handled.

Take a look
It is prudent to visit a site where the software is up and running with a similar application to the one proposed. A user group or the software house is generally happy to provide a list of suitable contacts.

Particularly if the application is designed for end user interrogation, the look of the software is of prime importance. In an institution where Windows has been adopted as the common interface, the proposed software must run happily under Windows, or have a version written specifically for Windows.

Help with selection
Two good directories of software for library applications, both frequently updated, are those compiled by Dyer and Gunson[27] and Wood.[28]

The Library Information Technology Centre[29] provides various guides to selecting software, and has sample copies of software packages that can be tried out.

FUTURE DEVELOPMENTS
The electronic library without walls that has been heralded for some years is still some way off, although elements of it may happen faster than expected. EU sponsored experiments, such as IRIS in the Republic of Ireland and PICA in The Netherlands, both providing access to disparate databases through a common interface, point the way forward for the future.

A hope for the future is that a national database based on the existing NHS regional cooperatives, and with the participation of medical schools will be formed. Either the Internet or the proposed NHS national network[30] could be used to carry it. The technology is there, it remains to be seen whether we have the political will and can attract the resources to make it happen.

REFERENCES
1   Krol, E., *The whole Internet. User's guide and catalog*, 2nd edn, California, O'Reilly & Associates, Inc., 1994. ISBN 1-56592-025-2.
2   'ALA's got a gopher', (Internet news), *Computers in libraries*, **14** (6), 1994, 44.
3   'National Library of Medicine (NLM) Internet-accessible resources',. *National Library of Medicine news*, **49** (3), 1994, 1–2.
4   McKnight, C., 'Electronic journals – past, present . . . future?', *Aslib proceedings*, **45** (1), 1993, 7–10.

5   Brown, D. J., 'Current awareness and document delivery: the changing market', *Serials*, **6** (3), 1993, 29–39.

6   Rowley, J., 'Revolution in current awareness services', *Journal of librarianship and information science*, **26** (1), 1994, 7–13.

7   O'Donovan, K., *Library and information services for health professionals in the Northern Regional Health Authority*, Health information series no.3, Newcastle, Information North, 1990. ISBN 0-906433-09-6.

8   Dell, E. Y., 'A resource sharing project using ARIEL technology', *Medical references services quarterly*, **12** (1), 1993, 17–27.

9   Whiffin, J., *Guidelines for union catalogues of serials. 1st draft prepared for the IFLA section on serial publication*, Victoria, B.C., Canada, June 1981.

10 Line, M. J. and Vickers, S., *Universal availability of publications (UAP)*, IFLA Publications 25, Munich, K. G. Saur, 1983. ISBN 3-598-20387-X.

11 IFLA International Office for UBC. *Manual on bibliographic control*, Paris, UNESCO, 1983. PGI-83/WS/8.

12 LASER (London and South Eastern Library Region), *Annual report 1992–93*, LASER, 1993. ISBN 0-903764-34-2.

13 Faulkner, A. and Mullins, P., *Operational policies for recording unpublished reports in the South Western Region's health authorities*, Bristol, Health Care Evaluation Unit, University of Bristol, 1991.

14 Prior, P. and Faulkner, A., *A regionwide database of locally produced, unpublished documents in the South Western Region*, Bristol, Health Care Evaluation Unit, University of Bristol, 1991.

15 Wilson, C., *West Berkshire Health Authority libraries: grey literature project*, Reading, Medical Library, Royal Berkshire Hospital, 1991.

16 SCOOP, *Guidelines on the preparation of local authority publications*, Library Association, Information Services Group, Standing Committee on Official Publications, 1989 ISBN 0-9512011-2-3.

17 Carmel, M., *Reconciling microcomputer databases*, MSc thesis, University College London, 1990.

18 National Library of Medicine, *Medical subject headings*, Bethesda, MD, NLM, published annually.

19 Dua, E. D. (ed.), *DH/DSS-Data thesaurus: the thesaurus of the Departments of Health and Social Security Library Service*, 2nd edn, London, Departments of Health and Social Security Library Service, 1993.

20 Kanter, J., 'User guides for CD-ROMs: the essentials of good print documentation', *CD-ROM professional*, **5** (5), 1992, 31–4.

21 South West Thames Regional Library Service, *A quality library service: management manual for healthcare libraries*, Guildford, SWTRLS, 1993.

22 Drug Information Pharmacist's Group, Database Working Party, *Pharm-line: guidelines for contributors*, London, DIPG, 1992.

23 South Thames (East) Libraries, *Cataloguing guide*, STEL, 1994.

24 Wessex Regional Library and Information Service, *MARC cataloguing manual*, revised edn, WRLIS, 1994.

25 Motherwell, W. D. S., 'The CURL bibliographic database', *Aslib Information*, **18** (9), 1990, 278–80.

26 Townley, C. T., 'College libraries and resource sharing: testing a compact disc union catalog', *College and research libraries*, **53** (5), 1992, 405–13.

27 Dyer, H. and Gunson, A. (comps.), *A directory of library and information retrieval software for microcomputers*, 4th edn, Aldershot, Gower, 1990. ISBN 0-566-03628-2.

28 Wood, J. (comp.), *European directory of software for libraries and information centres*, Aldershot, Gower, 1993. ISBN 1-85742-092-6.

29 Library Information Technology Centre, *Introductory pack on information retrieval software for MS-DOS*, London, LITC, 1993 (continuously updated).

30 NHS Management Executive, *IM&T strategy overview*, Department of Health, 1992. ISBN 1-858-39-02-6.

16 Developing people

❖   *Rachel Cooke and Janet Holman*

In her book on health services management, Wendy Ranade summarizes critical changes in health care:

> Governments throughout the Western world are aware that they face a widening gap between what is possible and what is affordable in healthcare. This is leading to a much greater stress on evaluating the benefits and costs of healthcare interventions, new technologies and those already in use, and renewed interest in preventive strategies and health promotion.[1]

As a result, librarians working in a health care environment are experiencing an unprecedented rate of social, political and economic change. This has been dealt with in detail elsewhere in this book but is summarized here to highlight the staff development implications.

1   Changes are taking place in the delivery and management of health care, with greater stress on the benefits and costs of treatment and an emphasis on health promotion and preventive strategies. This raises the questions of accountability for the information which is provided and whether it represents current research and best practice. Librarians may find themselves in the situation of having to evaluate the information provided, assessing its accuracy and currency.

2   Changes in the roles of library staff are requiring them to develop and take on more business-like attributes. These have come about through an emphasis on value-for-money services, requiring accounting and business planning skills. There is also a focus on customer care and service quality, which requires customer service skills and the skills to evaluate services and information sources. The quality movement also means that more employers and more library services want to be able to state that their staff are fit for the job. One way of achieving this might be through a stated programme of training and development.

3   The pervasive influence of information technology for management and information sources requires computer skills and advanced searching skills,

including the knowledge to select appropriately from a growing number of databases.

4 Changes in the work contract which can mean the demise of the 'job for life' through the introduction of contract working, with all its implications for future prospects and pensions. Employers are beginning to value practical skills as well as academic qualifications. This has led to the movement for vocational qualifications and the development of skills portfolios which emphasize a personal responsibility for keeping up-to-date in the chosen area of information work.

RANGE OF LIBRARY STAFF REQUIRED

It does not matter whether the library is in a small unit of a health authority providing purchasing intelligence, a multidisciplinary library in an acute hospital serving a number of trusts, an academic library for health care students or an information unit in the voluntary sector, the majority of libraries in the health care sector stand alone for most areas of activity. These activities include stock and journal management, customer and information services, user education (including curriculum development) and library management activities. A group of libraries may work together because they are in the same region, have a specialist subject interest in common or are linked by academic institution, but still the librarian at the head of each library will be responsible for the majority of the tasks that go on in that library. For example, the cataloguing of library stock may be performed cooperatively with other libraries in the same region, but the staff of the library will select, order and process the stock and will also catalogue the item if it has not been catalogued by another library.

If the senior librarian is to ensure that all the tasks, from stock selection to CD-ROM user education, are performed effectively then the appropriate staff will be needed; in some instances they may be working alone, in others there may be 20 or more people.

All libraries needs to have a clear staffing structure, with the skills required and salary grade for each post stated in individual job descriptions. In the NHS there are no salary grades designed for library staff. Some hospitals have appointed library staff on their own locally created salaries, but in most cases in the NHS library posts are linked to the Administrative and Clerical grades (A&C) while senior library staff may be on the performance-related Senior Management pay scales (SMP). In the academic sector there are set salary grades for library work. The Library Association has produced a series of salary guides which are essential reading when trying to identify the correct grade for a post.[2-4]

CONTINUING PROFESSIONAL DEVELOPMENT (CPD)

'It is a professional responsibility of all librarians to be competent in professional activities and keep abreast of developments in librarianship'.[5]

In her book *Personal development in information work*,[6] Sylvia Webb explains that personal development is a broad process that can encompass training, and is also a constant process in which individuals seek to enhance their abilities, skills and knowledge and develop new ones in the process of realizing their full potential.

The health care environment is stimulating to work in, with a fast pace of scientific and technological change. There is a vast body of information relating to health care practice and in order to access this there has to be a firm reliance on the skills and currency of knowledge of the information worker; librarians must ensure that their skills match and anticipate the needs of the customer. Many health care libraries are small, and in these circumstances personal development, training and job skills can be very much an individual responsibility. Even in larger libraries and regional systems, where there may be formal schemes of staff development, there will still be a heavy emphasis on personal responsibility for developing skills for the job.

Many professions, including nursing, have schemes to ensure that their members keep up-to-date and maintain their skills, and most of these involve compiling a portfolio of skills and experiences. British information workers are encouraged to use the Library Association's *Framework for continuing professional development*[7] to record their job development and career history. The Framework was designed to guide individual members of The Library Association (which includes all grades of information workers) through the process of devising personal development plans related to their work and to wider aspects of their life. The Framework encourages people to take responsibility for their own professional development, but it emphasizes partnership with the employer and The Library Association encourages employers to use the Framework in staff review and development programmes.

The underlying principles of the Framework are:

* open access to continuing professional development for all staff
* joint responsibility between employer and employee
* importance of keeping a record or logbook.

The Framework continues the process of evaluating work experiences and skills, which starts for the new professional with the writing of a professional development report (see below). The Framework was adopted by the American Library Association in 1994. Continuing professional development and use of the Framework are regarded as highly advisable, but essentially voluntary. There is current professional debate on the real value of a voluntary scheme.[8]

For most of us, the major portion of our continuing professional development will be work based and, fortunately, health care libraries offer many development opportunities. Such libraries are often small and there is more chance to become involved in all aspects of the service, including:

- planning and reviewing the service
- representing the service at meetings and thereby learning more about the parent organization
- good opportunities to review and discuss the service.

The subject area itself is full of technological and scientific advances. Medical libraries pioneered the use of technology for managing information, for example, *MEDLINE.*

The realities of working life and the pace of change in health care information services necessitate regular professional updating for all. This is sometimes provided by in-service training or external courses, but it also requires commitment and personal contribution, such as keeping abreast with professional literature and sharing and receiving skills and knowledge from colleagues. By far the greatest source of professional development comes from day-to-day opportunities that occur in the workplace.

APPRAISAL AND STAFF REVIEW

One aspect of the rapid pace of change we have to deal with is that all organizations are being expected to do more with less. Therefore it is essential to maintain and develop the most important resource of all, the human resource. Staff appraisal forms the cornerstone for all training and development programmes, and the process of appraisal and the subsequent development programme are central to keeping and motivating staff.

Formal appraisal schemes are by no means widespread in the health sciences and few library staff are assessed and paid on results. The literature on personnel management acknowledges that most people are motivated by the recognition that they are doing their job well, whether or not this is linked to pay. To maintain motivation, it is good staff management practice to review the work of individuals annually. A systematic approach provides the following benefits.

Job holders have an opportunity to:
- know what is required of them in a job
- be told how they are doing
- receive praise and recognition
- be given support and guidance
- be given a chance to express their point of view

- have a say in their own development and future.

Managers have an opportunity to:

- think seriously what they expect of their staff
- discuss new ideas
- improve the relationship between the two parties
- strengthen their position as leader.

The library service benefits from:

- improved/good staff morale
- shared commitment to the aims of the service
- information and ideas for future planning
- identification of training or job development needs.

However the appraisal plan is structured, all staff should be included. It is sensible to link in with or use any schemes already in operation in the hospital, medical school or employing organization. Advice could be sought from the personnel department on how to do an appraisal, or inclusion in existing schemes requested. This could be followed up by linking in with training and development opportunities which may also be offered by the organization.

The Industrial Society publishes a short and practical guide[9] to the principles and practice of appraisal. The following basic principles for a good appraisal interview are taken from this guide:

- allow enough time
- ensure privacy
- both sides should prepare for the appraisal
- review the work of the past year and set objectives for the coming year
- set reasonable objectives, which are worth doing
- set dates at regular intervals to review work
- make sure the mechanics don't get in the way of the communication.

This publication also includes examples of documentation which can be adapted for individual use.

PLANNING AND DELIVERING TRAINING
The process of reviewing work and progress through CPD and appraisal will almost inevitably lead to identifying training needs. Training is likely to be concerned with that aspect of personal development which is work related; it will be the result of personal need and the needs of the library service. It may be required to combat poor performance, for general future development or for specific skills to do the job. The aim of training is clear and simple: it is to help people to become more effective in their jobs, and therefore fulfil the

objectives of the library service.

All too often we are forced to take an opportunistic approach to training – 'It's your turn this year', or 'who can we send to this?' – but to fulfil the two aims of training outlined above it is essential to take a planned approach, considering:

- what skills are needed to do the job
- who needs them
- what training can be done for those skills
- when is the right time to do it in terms of service and individual need.

The benefits of a planned approach are that training will be timely, appropriate and cost effective.

A training plan could begin with a training needs analysis.[10] This might sound like a very formal approach, especially with a small staff. However, it is important to be rather more analytical than simply asking staff what they think their training needs are, although this is an important component of devising a training plan.

The training plan should move the service along and the aims might include:

- to enable staff to cope with change
- to introduce new staff to the job
- to teach skills for the job so that the required level of performance can be reached
- to develop staff for the future needs of the service
- to prepare staff for further qualifications or develop them for a new job.

The programme should consider how training will be delivered. In house training could include on-the-job training, an in-house course, guided reading or a learning package. External sources include training run by the hospital or medical school. The benefits of this are that training may be at low cost, there is the chance to meet other health care workers and some courses could be better done, for example, word processing, time management and report writing. Training run by professional groups and associations provides the chance to meet other information workers, consider other kinds of information provision and contribute to the profession a whole.

The training programme might be included as part of an annual report or incorporated into a quality assurance programme. It could be published and circulated to staff or to the organization's training department.

The training programme for our own health care libraries network is a policy statement outlining our commitment to staff development for all grades of staff. It incorporates a mission statement about the library network and the overall aim of the training programme. It groups training activities into three strategic areas:

- introduction to the service, including induction and the programme for professional trainees
- skills for the job, including reference skills, computer skills and a variety of management skills
- service development, which includes new management approaches and the application of new technologies.

The strategy concludes with an annual programme of training events which demonstrates the training emphasis in any one year.

If you organize a training event, for one person or for a group, a large body of literature is available recommending how to do it. Daines *et al.*[11] outline the way in which adults learn and the steps to be followed in designing and delivering a training event for an adult audience, and suggest appropriate methods. The authors outline the elements which adult learners consider make a 'good' course.

1. Course design: This includes a clear statement of the purpose of the course (objectives). There is appropriate content which is pitched at the right level. The course includes a variety of learning methods, provides a chance to try things out and includes feedback on how participants are doing.
2. Teaching style and 'values': participants are treated in adult ways, with their experience and contributions being valued as a part of the learning. They want to feel comfortable in the learning group.
3. Efficient organization of the course, a good teaching environment (including refreshments), good teaching materials, time keeping and attention to detail.

INDUCTION: MAKING NEW STAFF WELCOME

The quality of the induction programme organized for new members of staff will affect their whole relationship with the library. If staff feel secure and comfortable in their working environment, and know that they are valued members of the team, then they will feel motivated to work. In reality, this means that before actual job training (induction level) begins, all new members of staff must be orientated to their surroundings; only after this has been achieved will they be able to mentally attune themselves to their job induction. Of course, if the job induction is not done properly, new recruits will not be able to do their job effectively and will yet again feel insecure.

Orientation

This covers very basic needs:

1   New staff should be shown where the following are located: lavatories; secure storage for personal effects; coat hooks; drink making facilities; canteen facilities; where their desk is (or their main work point, if they have one). If they do have a desk then it is important to ensure that it is ready for them, not piled high with everybody else's 'junk', and has the full range of stationery and equipment that they will require.

2   They should be introduced to all other members of staff in the library and relevant people from outside that they will come into regular contact with.

3   Their terms and conditions of employment should be given to them and important points should be explained to them.

4   New staff should be made familiar with the organization's health and safety policy, where the fire exits and alarms are located, and the fire drill.

To ensure that none of these items is missed out, a simple checklist should be drawn up. Such a checklist is often sent, with other details of the induction programme, to new recruits prior to commencing their employment.

Skills to do the job

As with orientation, a useful tool in basic job training is a checklist of items that need to be covered. By drawing up a checklist before the new member of staff starts work, the trainer can ensure that all the subjects that need to be considered have been covered and to what depth the new recruit needs to be informed. The trainer can also use the list to identify who should instruct the new recruit about what. After the induction period is completed, the checklist can again be used to review the training programme and to identify any gaps in the staff member's knowledge and skills. This should then enable the new recruit to be trained in a systematic and productive manner.

An induction programme should always be geared to the individual. It is sensible to have a standard checklist for particular jobs which can be adapted for different members of staff, as people come to a job with different knowledge and skills. Obviously, someone who will be working in a library for the first time will require a very different programme from someone who has worked in a medical library before.

Never assume knowledge. A new library assistant was once set the 'easy' task of tidying some non-fiction shelves of stock in a public library; after a few minutes it became apparent that although she regularly used the library she did not have any idea how the Dewey Decimal system worked. She had been in post for less than half an hour and had already been made to feel stupid.

Induction training should be well paced. Never try to cover all the items on an induction checklist in one day. Spread it out, give new recruits a chance to practice what they have been shown. People can only take in so much information at a time; too much theory can be daunting and cease to be relevant. For staff who will be working part-time, the programme should not be too spread out otherwise there is the danger that they will become bored with waiting to 'get on' with the job.

Where do I fit in?

All new members of staff need to know where they fit into an organization. In the health care sector this means knowing not only where in the scheme of things they belong, but also where the library fits into the whole organization (hospital, health authority, voluntary organization).

If the recruit has come from outside the health care sector, some background on the structure of health care delivery is useful. This will also enable the new recruit to get a clearer picture of the types of users the library serves and their information needs.

The Library Association has produced a useful series of *Library training guides*; Julie Parry has written the guide on induction.[12]

THE NEW PROFESSIONAL

Recruiting a newly trained librarian can bring a breath of fresh air and provide the seedcorn of a high quality workforce for the future of the library service. Above all the new professional needs a programme of development opportunities that provides practical work to underpin the academic, helping them towards professional maturity.

In the United Kingdom, the Library Association's scheme[13] for developing the new professional requires a structured, on-the-job training scheme which includes exposure to all aspects of the job, from the routine to decision making, and culminates in the submission of a professional development report to the Association. Employers submit a programme which must be validated by the Library Association; the approved programme prepares candidates for entry to the Library Association's register of qualified librarians and the achievement of chartered librarian status.

A health care library service can provide many practical training and development opportunities in a changing and challenging work environment, which also gives a good example of the challenges to be met in other library services. All health care libraries offer a highly focused service with a strong identification with the user group. A good range of information technology will be in use. John Hewlett has translated this in some detail into a checklist of development opportunities which a healthcare library can provide.[14, 15] Although this was prepared for newly trained registration candidates, it is a good checklist for all professionals new to health care library services.

In the United Kingdom, the majority of health care libraries are linked to regional networks which correspond to the organization of the health service. This provides good opportunities for the new professional to learn about cooperative services and the variety in library services, from universities to hospital libraries, from patient information services to information for hospital managers. South Thames (West) Regional Library Service, for example, offers opportunities for a regional trainee to work in a number of situations in turn: attached to one library, working directly with a chartered librarian; with distance supervision; or in central support services where they might be helping to maintain a cooperative catalogue or be responsible for a current awareness service.

In order to develop professional maturity, new professionals need opportunities for reflection and discussion with other librarians through their work or through attending professional meetings. In return, they can provide fresh ideas or a new slant, and are able to ask searching questions about the service.

ADVANCED COURSES

Staff should be encouraged to continue to improve their skills and widen their knowledge. For some this may mean gaining a Masters degree in library and information studies, or a related subject. Since the mid-1980s, the range of higher degrees and the methods of studying for them has increased greatly.

‑As well as traditional full-time courses available at most library schools, many courses are now available part-time. When allowing members of staff to study for a Masters degree on a part-time basis, managers need to remember that the course will take up a lot of the staff members' time and energy and that they will need to know that they have the support and backing of their manager. However they will probably be able to base a lot of their course work, and certainly their thesis, around the work of the library, which should prove to be of benefit to the library and the organization in which it is set.

A relatively new method of studying for library qualifications is by distance learning. The Department of Information and Library Studies, University of Wales Aberystwyth, has developed three such courses. Two of these courses are relevant to library staff in the health care sector: MLib Management of Library and Information Services, and MSc Information Systems and Services for Healthcare. Both courses are three years long and available only to those who already have relevant work experience. Studying by distance learning takes a high degree of commitment from students, as they will be studying on their own and so will have little contact with fellow students or tutors.

Apart from the course at Aberystwyth, the Department of Information and Library Studies at Loughborough University is currently (1994) seeking accreditation from The Library Association for an MSc in Health Information Management.

Library assistants may wish to study for a first qualification in librarianship, either for a first degree, or for a postgraduate diploma or Masters degree. Again, there are now a number of opportunities to study on a part-time basis. In the future, if staff do not have the necessary academic qualifications for entry to a course, they will be able to state the level of National Vocational Qualification that they have achieved to prove their competence to enter their chosen course of study.

The Library Association leaflet *Where to study in the UK*[16] is produced annually and lists all the higher qualifications currently accredited by The Library Association and those seeking to be accredited.

SCOTTISH AND NATIONAL VOCATIONAL QUALIFICATIONS
At present, a new, alternative type of qualification system is being set up in the United Kingdom. Scottish and National Vocational Qualifications (S/NVQs) enable people to gain recognition for their knowledge and experience without having achieved a certain academic level prior to entry. S/NVQs are being developed for a wide range of industries and professions. Within the health care sector there are a number of groups that have S/NVQs, such as care assistants and finance staff. S/NVQs can be achieved at five different levels, which have been agreed across the board; individual professions then work out the detail for each level.

S/NVQs are issued by approved awarding bodies, through assessment centres. Each candidate is appointed an assessor by the assessment centre. The assessor works with the candidate to decide what needs to be done before the candidate can be awarded an S/NVQ; for example attendance at a course may be required to fill a gap of knowledge.

S/NVQs are being worked out for the library sector, and it is planned that pilots should take place up to level four during the summer of 1995. Table 5.1 sets out the competencies needed to achieve each level, with a guide to the type of library job that a person aiming for that level of qualification might be engaged in.

Table 16.1 Guide to S/NVQ levels in the library sector

On levels . . .
The following is a very preliminary guide – 'at this moment in time' as the phrase goes – of job titles and possible S/NVQ levels. It is published here not as a hostage to fortune as it would be if it were not clearly signposted as *tentative*, but as a helpful guide to the way levels might work out. The final arbiter on levels will be NCVQ.

NVQ Level	Possible ILS job title
2 Range of activities, variety of contexts, some complex and non-routine, some teamwork.	Library Assistant, Counter Assistant, Clerical Assistant, Loans/Issues Clerk.
3 Broad range of varied work activities, mostly complex and non-routine. Working mostly autonomously, often controlling or guiding others.	Supervisor, Library Manager, Senior Records Manager, Assistant, Senior Library Assistant, Technical Indexer.
4 Broad range of complex, technical or professional work activities, using fundamental principles and complex techniques in often unpredictable contexts. Personal autonomy with responsibility for work of others and resource allocation.	Librarian, ILS Manager, Information Scientist, Technical Information Manager, Archivist, TIC Manager, Systems Librarian.
5 Use of significant range of fundamental principles and complex techniques across wide and often unpredictable contexts. Very great personal autonomy, significant responsibility for others and for resources and for strategic planning.	Director, Chief Librarian, County Librarian.

This table is produced with permission from *LIS-LB newsletter*, **1**, 1994, 3.

S/NVQs will be useful to library managers when recruiting new staff, as they will assist in identifying those who have the necessary skills and competencies to do the job; for example when appointing a new library assistant, the candidates may not have any library experience and few academic qualifications, but they may have a level three S/NVQ.

With the lack of specific salary grades for library staff within the NHS, S/NVQs will be useful when attempting to get library posts regraded, as the appropriate S/NVQ level for that post will be used for other positions within the organization.

The Information and Library Services Lead Body (ILS-LB) is responsible for developing S/NVQs in the field of library and information work. For further information about the progress of S/NVQs for the library and information sector, ILS-LB can be contacted by telephone on 0171 255 2271.

With the introduction of S/NVQs in the field of library and information work, there will be a significant advancement in the development opportunities for library assistants. Together with the longer BTEC, SCOTVEC and City and Guilds 737 certificates in library and information competence courses, more short, specific courses will be introduced to help library staff improve their competence.

With the S/NVQs structure in place there will be a system which ensures that all library staff can be given opportunities to follow courses that lead to qualifications. If this is backed up by a commitment to planned staff development through an appraisal scheme, the increased efficiency and effectiveness of staff will make a significant contribution to the quality of the library service.

REFERENCES

1 Ranade, W., *A future for the NHS?: health care in the 1990s*, London, Longman, 1994. ISBN 0 58205 987 X.
2 Library Association, *Health care sector library staff: Salary guide 2*, London, Library Association, 1994.
3 Library Association, *University library staff [Ex-UFC sector]: Salary guide 4*, London, Library Association, 1993.
4 Library Association, *Specialised library and information services: Salary guide 7*, London, Library Association, 1991.
5 Library Association, *Code of professional conduct*, London, Library Association.
6 Webb, S., *Personal development in information work*, London, Aslib, 1986, ISBN 0 85142 201 2.
7 Library Association, *Framework for continuing professional development*, London, Library Association, 1992.
8 Freeman, M., 'A sense of direction: librarianship and CPD', *Librarian career development*, **2** (3), 1994, 26–8.
9 Lawson, I., *Notes for managers: appraisal and appraisal interviewing*, London, Industrial Society, 1989.
10 Williamson, M., *Training needs analysis*, Library Training Guides, London, Library

Association Publishing, 1993. ISBN 1 85604 077 1.

11   Daines, J., Daines, C. and Graham, B., *Adult learning, adult teaching*, Nottingham, Department of Adult Education, University of Nottingham, 1992. ISBN 1 85041 065 8.

12   Parry, J., *Induction*, Library Training Guides, London, Library Association Publishing, 1993.

13   Library Association, *Routes to associateship: regulations and notes of guidance*, London, Library Association, undated.

14   Hewlett, J., 'Pre-registration training in health-care libraries. II. Progress assessment checklists', *Health libraries review*, 5, 1988; 234–45.

15   Hewlett, J., 'Training for Library Association chartering in health-care libraries', *Health libraries review*, 5, 1988, 181-8.

16   Library Association, *Where to study in the UK*, London, Library Association 1994.

FURTHER READING

Cooke, R., Gillespie, I. and Hartley, B., 'Training for Library Association chartering in health-care libraries; part III: exercises for pre-registration trainees', *Health libraries review*, 6, 1989, 25–8.

Baker, D. (series ed.), *Library training guides*, London, Library Association Publishing, 1993 onwards. A series of practical guides on aspects of training. Individual titles currently available are:

Bamber, T. (ed.), *Supporting adult learners*.

Fisher, B., *Mentoring*.

Lacey Bryant, S., *Personal professional development and the solo librarian*.

Levy, P., *Interpersonal skills*.

Morris, B., *Training and development for women*.

Nankivell, C. and Shoolbred, M., *Presenting information*.

Parry, J., *Induction*.

Parry, J., *Recruitment*.

Phillips, S., *Evaluation*.

Whetherly, J., *Management of training and staff development*.

Williamson, M., *Training needs analysis*.

ILS newsletter, 1, 1994, (whole issue) This issue provides the background information to the development of S/NVQs for library and information work. *Librarian career development*, 2 (4), 1994, (whole issue). This issue is devoted to the debate on CPD, the effectiveness of the LA CPD framework and S/NVQs in library and information work.

Library Association, *Financial assistance for study*, London, Library Association, 1994 (work is informative).

Library Association, *Getting started*, London, Library Association, 1994 (work is informative).

Library Association, *Qualifications for library assistance*, London, Library Association, 1993 (work is informative).

Library Association, *Where to study in the UK*, London, Library Association, 1994.

17 Issues in funding of health science libraries

❖ *Peter Morgan*

Information is not free. Every element of library and information services incurs a cost, though this may not be visible to the user, and the library's success in delivering what its users require therefore depends, in part, on its ability to obtain and apply an adequate level of funding. For health care libraries this elementary concept masks a peculiarly complex combination of factors, which the librarian will have to understand and cope with in order to manage the library effectively. Anyone can run a library if given sufficient funding, but it takes a skilful library manager to do the job when funds are scarce.

The task is not easy, not least because political and social pressures are bringing about a radical reappraisal of the extent to which library services can and should be subsidized from central funds, and procedures that appear to be well established may be totally superseded within a year or two. Nowhere is this trend more apparent than in the National Health Service (NHS). Moreover, the different governmental structures that apply in the various parts of the United Kingdom mean that what is true for England will not necessarily apply in Scotland, Wales or Northern Ireland.

Financial management involves two main tasks. First, the librarian must be able to present a case for a given level of funding. This involves

- forecasting users' needs
- planning services and facilities to meet those needs
- calculating the cost implications
- preparing a budget
- identifying the appropriate source of funds; and
- justifying the library's case to the body from which funding is sought.

Second, the librarian must be able to administer funds efficiently in order

- to achieve the desired purpose
- to obtain value for money and
- to account for the expenditure incurred.

To be able to handle financial responsibilities successfully, the librarian must be knowledgeable about the different sources of funding available, the channels through which they may be approached, when they may be approached, the types of financial provision they can make, and how to manage the money when it is received.

SOURCES OF FUNDING

Sources of funding essentially fall into two categories: external and internal. 'External', in this context, signifies that funding is provided through grants and other subsidies from bodies outside the library, such as government departments and parent organizations. 'Internal' funding is generated by the library from its own activities, through charging for services and sale of goods.

External sources have traditionally been the mainstay of library funding, with internal income generation seen as a useful supplement. These distinctions are becoming blurred by the movement towards service contracts and cost centre budgeting, through which the library secures most or all of its funding by selling agreed levels or types of service.

External funding

Most health care libraries are funded largely, often exclusively, from public sector sources. Within the NHS a number of different funding bodies are involved. NHS libraries are usually seen as an intrinsic part of the educational process and so draw most of their support from the various bodies responsible for medical, nursing and allied health professional education. Some libraries serve a specific user group, but an increasing number combine several such responsibilities into multidisciplinary libraries and thus have a more complex relationship with their funding sources.[1]

Historically, medical libraries, serving the needs of continuing medical education and based within postgraduate medical centres, have been the mainstay of library provision in hospitals. Since 1991, responsibility for postgraduate medical and dental education funding has passed from district health authorities to regional postgraduate deans, who now control medical library budgets. Each dean negotiates a contract with district postgraduate centres, through their parent trusts, for the provision of continuing medical education, and a part of each contract defines the role of the library and the contractual obligations it must meet in return for its annual funding.

Nurse education has undergone a similar change. The Project 2000 curriculum, announced by the United Kingdom Central Council for Nursing, Midwifery and Health Visiting (UKCC) in 1986, brought with it a shift away from self-contained hospital based nursing schools and their libraries, towards nursing colleges linked with institutions of higher education. Library provision for nurse learners now relies on contracts between regional health authorities and educational institutions, with no ring-fencing of library funding, to support resources both at the college and on the hospital site.

While the majority of NHS libraries rely most heavily on funding from educational sources, certain other NHS activities, such as clinical audit or the NHS research and development strategy, may also provide library funding for specific purposes. For some purposes, such as services to NHS managers and purchasing commissions, separate libraries may be funded.

The higher education sector is another important source of funding. It encompasses both the undergraduate and postgraduate medical school libraries of the traditional universities, and the complementary range of health sciences library services in the new universities. The Higher Education Funding Councils for the UK allocate block grants to universities on behalf of the Department for Education, supplementing what the universities obtain from student fees and other sources of income such as research grants, and leaving the universities themselves with considerable discretion as to how much of this income they distribute to libraries, and it is rare – though not unknown – for the Funding Councils to earmark library funding within the block grants. The Funding Council grants are increasingly calculated to reflect universities' assessed ratings for quality of research and teaching, but a highly rated medical faculty (and its library) will not necessarily benefit proportionately, as the individual universities may take the view that subject areas like medicine are privileged by virtue of their ability to attract more research income than others, and that they must therefore be prepared to see some of this income shared across the full subject range of university faculties.

Medical research is a further potential source of funding. The Medical Research Council (MRC) supports research not only in its own units, some of which include libraries, but also in universities and hospitals. Following changes in the dual-support system of university and research council funding, the overheads of MRC supported research projects, which may include an element for library costs, are met as part of the MRC's specific grants. However, the medical charities, another major source of support for medical research, continue to assume that a well funded library is already available in the institutions that will house their research projects, and therefore make no funds available for library costs.

Some health care libraries also receive grants, notably from the British Library, to support their research and development projects in the fields of librarianship and information science.

Internal funding

When we turn to consider internal funding we enter an area of much controversy. The debate over 'fee *versus* free' – that is, whether it is ethical and desirable to charge users for specific library services – has raged for years, and is an inevitable consequence of the widening disparity between, on the one hand, levels of recurrent library funding and, on the other, increases in the costs incurred by libraries both to maintain established services and to introduce newer, technology dependent services. The ethical arguments are complex, but it must be acknowledged that for many libraries the ability to generate income, by charging for access to facilities or for the provision of services, is and will remain an essential fact of life. In other words, the library must be prepared to embrace a mixed economy if it is to survive.

The pressures to adopt this policy frequently come from the parent institution which might, for organizational or political reasons, require the library to generate income. Sometimes they will originate from within the library itself, seeing this as the only way of maintaining certain services or of developing new ones.

THE LIBRARY BUDGET

A budget is a financial statement that estimates income and expenditure for itemized activities over a given period. Once approved, it provides a control mechanism to monitor activity and ensure that the library keeps within its agreed expenditure limits.

Budget and cost centres

There are two ways of defining the library for financial purposes: as a budget centre and as a cost centre. Most health care libraries have traditionally been treated as budget centres; they are regarded as a central concentration of shared resources, serving a broad cross-section of users in the organization and funded essentially from a single source as part of the organization's overheads, receiving a budget that can be defined and controlled. This method ensures that a central resource is maintained, but does not encourage it to be responsive to user needs.

By contrast, the cost centre model has been employed less frequently but is now being adopted more widely both in the NHS and in universities. The library is defined in terms of the services it provides, and these are demand-led by the users. Costs are apportioned to different departments throughout the organization in proportion to their usage of the service. Departments can use their purchasing power to exercise choice, by developing their own internal services or by using alternative services elsewhere. This method is more sensitive to user needs, but makes it more difficult to ensure that the essential core resource is maintained.

In practice, library services may be seen increasingly as hybrids of these two systems, combining a budget controlled core level of resources and services with a cost centred control of the more specialist or peripheral services.[2,3]

Managing change

The librarian's skill in preparing and obtaining an adequate budget is crucial to the success of the service. Often, funds are allocated to the library simply on the basis of what was provided for the previous year, increased by an amount which, to a greater or lesser degree (usually the latter), attempts to keep pace with inflation. This passive form of budget preparation, in which the librarian may be given little or no opportunity to contribute to the process by which a funding authority finalizes its library grant, creates two major problems. First, for many years the cost of printed books and journals has risen annually at a rate well in excess of the average rate of inflation, on which grant increases are likely to be based. As most non-staff costs are incurred by libraries in purchasing printed materials, the gap between the funds received and the funds needed to maintain the same level of acquisitions grows steadily.[4] Second, even if this system took full account of the true inflation rate in library costs, it would at best provide only for a steady-state service. In practice, libraries are under constant pressure to develop their services, responding to change in the organizations they serve and consequently in the needs of their users, extending the range and type of services offered, and implementing technological advances.[5] These developments may require funding over and above the steady-state baseline.

For the library to be a dynamic, relevant and integral part of the parent organization, the librarian must take every opportunity to influence budget preparation.[6,7] If the organization is undergoing a period of change, as has happened in both the NHS and the higher education sector in recent years, the opportunities may be considerable. In the NHS, for example, the evolution of the internal market has given rise to the purchaser–provider relationship: each aspect of health care delivery is bought by a purchasing authority from a provider unit on a contractual basis. This has combined with the shift in responsibility for medical libraries, from district authority to regional postgraduate dean, to create a new system of library funding.[8-10]

Change also brings risks. There is a danger that the library will be low in the order of priorities, and that the costs of implementing change elsewhere in the system will leave inadequate funds for library services. Such a situation arose with Project 2000, as some nursing colleges channelled their resources into other, higher profile areas of activity, leaving their libraries poorly supported.

At such times there should be a greater scope for asking fundamental questions about the library budget, and for reappraising established assumptions about its size and purpose. While the questions may originate from a higher level, within or outside the library's parent organization, the librarian should always be seeking to take the lead and to initiate action. This becomes particularly important when budget preparation becomes a matter not simply of fine tuning, but of radical reappraisal when the entire basis of a library's funding is under scrutiny.[11]

Funding models

At this stage, the librarian may wish to develop a model that can provide a framework for establishing the cost of different elements in the library, or of different libraries in an organization such as a regional library network. Various procedures may be adopted, but all will have a common objective: to present a model for funding a library or libraries at the level necessary to achieve and maintain an agreed standard of service.[12-15] It will be immediately obvious that 'an agreed standard of service' is a concept that itself embraces a range of complex issues, but there must be a clear understanding as to what is required of the library before any meaningful discussions can take place about the budget. Funding is a means to an end, not an end in itself.

Any funding model must employ methodology and data that are understood by, and acceptable to, those it is designed to influence. It must also be sufficiently flexible to accommodate at least some element of change in the assumptions and data on which it is based.

Models may seek to create a formula, incorporating indicators that may be permanent or variable: as the latter change, so the final picture is modified.[16-19] Key elements relating to the library service and its clientele are selected as significant indicators of scale and activity, and are combined to present an overall summary. The formula may cover elements such as library staff, stock, services and accommodation, and can also be weighted by taking account of factors such as the size of a potential user population (with variables such as the number of junior doctors in a district, or students in a medical school). A cost can be assigned to each indicator, and thus a budget prepared for the library as a whole. Where a number of libraries are part of the same organization, the formula can provide a consistent basis for the distribution of funds.

Formula funding is open to criticism as being a relatively crude device, discriminating against diversity. This can be countered, to some extent, by developing several versions of a formula for use in different contexts, where, for example, the distinctive circumstances of large and small libraries need to be fully acknowledged. Formula funding invites suspicion if the formula is not revealed to those who depend on its outcomes, but it can also be publicized, to demonstrate its objectivity and win acquiescence. In a situation where a library fails to receive as large a budget as it would wish, the morale of library staff may be better sustained if the allocation procedure is seen to be open and equitable.

An essential part of formula funding is the process of assigning costs to indicators. This assumes that the unit costs are known and agreed. They may best be calculated by the process of functional cost analysis, which seeks to identify all the costs of running a library – staff, stock and services – and to associate them with a set of library functions, thereby costing the library both in terms of input (the budget being provided) and output (the services by which users judge the library). The result is a series of unit costs for each activity, giving a baseline for monitoring changes from year to year and, for groups of libraries, for comparing their functional and unit costs.[20-22]

This form of cost analysis depends heavily on availability of the necessary operational statistics. These may be collected routinely as a standard management requirement, but for the most thorough analysis it may be necessary to collect additional data in order to achieve the required level of detail and accuracy. The collection of management data and the associated analysis of costs also have an important role in the development of performance indicators, where the emphasis shifts from quantitative to qualitative assessment.[23-25]

Analysis of costs has taken on a new significance with the move to contract based library services and competitive tendering. The library manager needs accurate information on costs in order to prepare a realistic tender for contracts, and the prospective purchaser of library services needs to be assured that value for money is being offered.

Another form of fundamental reappraisal involves the procedure known as 'zero-based budgeting'.[26] In simple terms, the budget for a new financial year is prepared without reference to previous levels of funding. Each element in the service is assessed, justified and costed without being constrained or guided by the practice of previous years. Its value lies in its potential for breaking free of inherited practice and starting afresh, through a detailed scrutiny of all the library's operations and costs.

Usually a less rigorous procedure will suffice, or it might be advantageous to apply the zero-base approach only to a specific aspect of library expenditure. Whichever approach is adopted, it must employ a sound methodology that is understood by, and acceptable to, the funding authority. While librarians might benefit from the knowledge they gain about the cost of the service they run, there is little point in spending much time and effort producing a budget proposal that is out of touch with current funding practices. The librarian will therefore need to become acquainted with the organization's financial procedures: these should include the financial planning criteria, timescales and jargon that are employed. Librarians also need to recognize those areas of finance over which they have little or no control, such as legal requirements, taxation, external and internal audit regulations, and salary levels.[27]

Above all, the library's budget must support activities that are consistent with the aims and objectives of the organization it serves. This means that the library must have its own objectives clearly defined and approved, so that its funding needs can be justified in terms of meeting those objectives.

Where a radically new budget is planned, as when a library has to negotiate a new contract with a purchaser of its services, it may be helpful to run it as a 'shadow' budget for a preliminary period alongside the existing budget. In this way many problems can be anticipated and resolved before they become a reality, thus easing the transition from the old system to the new.

Annual budget estimates

The analytical procedures outlined above are appropriate when major organizational changes are warranted, but not suitable as an annual exercise. For most libraries, the routine preparation of annual recurrent budgets will be a far less radical task, often still following inherited patterns of allocation and expenditure. Here too, though, the key to preparation of a budget is in the costing process. The library is, in effect, putting a price on its services and asking the parent organization or the purchasing authority to buy them. Although most parent organizations have in the past simply chosen to operate and pay for their own library on a budget centre basis, with budgetary negotiations confined to the level of service rather than to the more basic question of the existence of the service itself, an increasingly commercial approach is becoming more evident, linked to the concept of cost centres, and the parent body or purchaser may be willing to consider using alternative, external forms of library service. In calculating its costs and pricing its services, the library must therefore be sensitive to the existence of any competitors and to their prices.

The costing process will include areas of expenditure that deal with fixed or predictable cost items, and with others that are more variable. It will need to distinguish between those that represent recurrent commitments and those that are non-recurrent and therefore more controllable.

Central core resource expenditure will include

- staff costs, which are outside the library's control once an agreed level and grading of staff has been established
- books and audiovisual materials
- periodical and CD-ROM subscriptions
- administration (postage, telephones, computer networks, stationery, travel, training)
- equipment purchase
- service contracts.

Though these items are not demand-led and are controlled to a much greater degree by the librarian, expenditure is often affected by outside factors and thus difficult to estimate: periodical prices, for example, are vulnerable not only to the increase in publishers' cover charges, but to fluctuations in the exchange rates between sterling and other currencies.[28-30] Funds may be allocated to different areas of expenditure using agreed guidelines or formulas, as when apportioning the acquisitions budget among subject areas or departments.[31-33]

Demand-led expenditure will include

- interlibrary loans and other forms of document delivery; current awareness services
- online searches
- photocopying
- enquiry services.

Estimating the likely demand for a service is always a difficult task. If the service has existed for some time, past experience will provide a useful guide, though the web of interrelated services means that changes in one area may have unpredictable consequences elsewhere (thus, for example, periodical cancellations may stimulate interlibrary loan demand). New or reorganized services inevitably present even greater problems, even if introduced to meet an identified demand.

In producing estimates for all these expenditure heads, the librarian will need to draw on a combination of hard factual information, such as known price increases for periodicals, informed estimates, such as periodical agents' predictions of general levels of price increases or information from the parent organization on the number of staff or students that are expected as potential library users, and professional intuition.

External sources of funding may seem to be remote and ill-defined, and at the same time to have vast financial resources at their disposal. However impressive and irrefutable the library's case for funding might appear, it will be competing with other interests for a share of resources that are always ultimately finite. If the library is to secure a greater share, its success will be at the expense of some other department dependent on the same source. This may be a non-library activity or, if the external source in question has itself already determined the proportion of its funds to be made available for libraries, another library. In preparing and submitting a budget, the librarian must understand the organizational politics involved, and be sensitive to the existence of competitors.[34] The library's case may be assisted if it is endorsed by users, but efforts to form such alliances will be counter-productive if those same users see the library's ability to obtain funds as a threat to their own primary interests. Conversely, it will sometimes be possible to argue that when funds are limited, every member of the organization stands to benefit if the library is adequately supported as a central service, whereas those same funds, if channelled into other more narrowly focused departments, may have a divisive effect by provoking rivalries and jealousies.

Income generation

The budget will also be expected to show those areas where income – 'internal funding' – is to be generated by the library. It has already been observed that the introduction of charges for services remains a controversial issue. Bearing this in mind, a library that introduces charges must think carefully about how best to announce and justify such decisions to its users. The actual choice as to which services are subject to charges will depend on a variety of factors. If the rationale is the need to control demand by introducing a price deterrent, the service concerned will be self-selecting, though there will still be a further decision as to whether the charge represents full or partial cost recovery. If the rationale is to generate income, either to compensate for a shortfall in recurrent funding or to acquire 'new' money in order to fund a development, then expert judgment will be necessary in deciding where the burden of charges will fall in order to produce the income target. It may be tempting to select the most popular service, or that for which the administration of a charge is simplest, or that which is used predominantly by those thought to be best able to pay. At the same time, the librarian will be anxious to avoid penalizing vulnerable user groups, or threatening the viability of services by overpricing them. It is essential to establish at the outset that the library will be able to retain most, if not all, of the revenue it generates, after allowing for deductions such as VAT where applicable.[35-41]

Charges will sometimes prompt library users to seek access to alternative local libraries, where choice exists. For libraries which are members of a single organization or cooperative, it may be prudent to ensure that the other libraries are forewarned of any decisions on charging that might have a knock-on effect on demand elsewhere. In some circumstances it will be necessary for a common charging structure to be applied to all such libraries, and to be introduced in them all simultaneously.

New developments

Most organizations, in approving library budgets, draw a distinction between the recurrent budget – the input that maintains staff, stock and services at agreed levels – and other costs such as new developments, equipment and capital building programmes.

Budgets for new developments must include both non-recurrent start-up costs (equipment, documentation, training, accommodation, and so on) and recurrent costs (including staff). They should also take into account any predictable knock-on effects, such as increased demand for interlibrary loans following the introduction of online or CD-ROM bibliographic searching. Budgets for equipment may need to make provision for its depreciation, if a register of assets is maintained, and for its obsolescence and eventual replacement, especially where computer equipment is involved.

It will not always be possible to secure additional money to finance developments, and the library will then be faced with the decision as to whether the desired development takes a higher priority than some existing area of expenditure, thus warranting an internal transfer of resources. At a relatively modest level, this principle is seen at work when a new periodical subscription can be taken up only if the funds are released by cancelling other subscriptions. Of much more fundamental importance is the debate that may arise when a major development has to be funded in this way. The advent of electronic information services provides an example, as libraries consider how far they should transfer resources from more traditional, print-based services into electronic facilities.[42-44]

Monitoring expenditure

The organization will have its own accounting procedures and these will largely dictate how the library's accounts are processed. The librarian must monitor patterns of expenditure and income, compare them regularly with the expectations represented by the library's approved annual estimates, and take appropriate action if the variance in patterns of expenditure is greater than expected. If discrepancies between estimates and expenditure are more than temporary in nature, economies or additional income generation will have to be considered when the following year's budget is prepared. It is essential to plan cost saving measures as far ahead as possible, to allow time for consultation with users and other interested parties before decisions are made; and both internal and external deadlines (such as the organization's fiscal year, or renewal dates for subscriptions) must be taken into account.

The librarian who can demonstrate competence in managing estimates and accounts effectively is more likely to win a sympathetic hearing when presenting a case for additional funding.

REFERENCES

1   Stewart, D., 'Responsibility for funding NHS library services', *Health libraries review*, 9, 1992, 62–5.
2   Revill, D. H., 'Cost centres and academic libraries', *British journal of academic librarianship*, 4, 1989, 27–48.
3   Stirling, J. F., 'Devolved budgeting', *British journal of academic librarianship*, 7, 1992, 1–7.

4 Antes, E. J., 'More with less: library management in the face of budget constraints', Bibliotheca medica Canadiana, 11, 1990, 131–6.
5 Martin, M. S., 'The changing library environment', *Library trends*, **42**, 1994, 478–89.
6 Black, W. K., 'The budget as a planning tool', *Journal of library administration*, **18**, 1993, 171–88.
7 Robinson, B. M. and Robinson, S., 'Strategic planning and program budgeting for libraries', *Library trends*, **42**, 1994, 420–47.
8 Carmel, M., 'Management by agreement: contracting for library services in South West Thames', *Health libraries review*, **8**, 1991, 63–80.
9 O'Donovan, K. (ed.), 'Costing library services – towards a model for the NHS. Proceedings of a seminar and workshop held at the University of Newcastle upon Tyne 13 December 1990', *Health libraries review*, **8**, 1991, 120–41.
10 Rhodes, A., 'Costing contracts in the NHS', *Health libraries review*, **8**, 1991, 131–3 in O'Donovan, K., *q.v.*).
11 Campbell, J. D., 'Getting comfortable with change: a new budget model for libraries in transition', Library trends, **42**, 1994, 448–59.
12 Hall, J. T. D., 'New methods of top-slicing', *British journal of academic librarianship*, **7**, 1992, 9–15.
13 O'Connor, S., 'Editorial – Why the interest in library funding models?', *Australian library review*, **9**, 1992, 58.
14 Smith, K., 'Funding models: a special library perspective', *Australian library review*, **9**, 1992, 97–8.
15 Taylor, C. R., 'Library budget model developed for the South Australian Institute of Technology', *Australian library review*, **9**, 1992, 71–8.
16 Godbolt, S. and Hewlett, J., 'The funding of postgraduate medical education in NHS libraries – is a formula workable? A case study from the North East and North West Thames Regions', *Health libraries review*, **9**, 1992, 77–81.
17 Gove, S., 'Formula funding in a multidisciplinary medical library: a case study at St George's Hospital Medical School, University of London', *Health libraries review*, **9**, 1992, 81–2.
18 McIntyre, B., 'The paradoxes of our timidity: library funding models and advocacy for libraries', *Australian library review*, **9**, 1992, 59–69.
19 Morgan, P., 'Editorial – Formula funding: a prescription for improvement', *Health libraries review*, **9**, 1992, 49–51.
20 Jones, L. and Nicholas, D., 'Costing medical libraries: the feasibility of functional cost analysis', *Health libraries review*, **10**, 1993, 169–201.
21 Kantor, P. B., 'Cost and usage of health sciences libraries: economic aspects', *Bulletin of the Medical Library Association*, **72**, 1984, 275–86.
22 Kantor, P. B., 'Library cost analysis', *Library trends*, **38**, 1989, 171–88.
23 Hamaker, C. A., 'Some measures of cost effectiveness in library collections', *Journal of library administration*, **16**, 1992, 57–69.
24 Hewlett, J., 'Who uses NHS libraries? Preliminary results from a survey of post-graduate medical libraries in North East Thames', *Health libraries review*, **9**, 1992, 66–76.

25 Van Loo, J., 'Performance indicators in the Oxford Region Library and Information Service: first steps', *Health libraries review*, 5, 1988, 221–5.

26 Chen, C. C., *Zero-base budgeting in library management: a manual for librarians*, Phoenix, Oryx, 1980.

27 James, S. M., 'Costing library and information services – an overview', *Health libraries review*, 8, 1991, 120–33 in O'Donovan, K., q.v.

28 Barker, J. W., 'What's your money worth? Materials budget and the selection and evaluation of book and serial vendors', *Journal of library administration*, 16, 1992, 25–43.

29 Bonk, S. C., 'Rethinking the acquisitions budget: anticipating and managing change', *Library acquisitions: practice and theory*, 10, 1986, 97–106.

30 Hayes, S., 'Budgeting for and controlling the cost of Other in library expenditures: the distant relative in the budgetary process', *Journal of library administration*, 3, 1982, 121–131.

31 Burdick, A .J., Butler, A. and Sullivan, M. G., 'Citation patterns in the health sciences: implications for serials/monographic fund allocation', *Bulletin of the Medical Library Association*, 81, 1993, 44–7.

32 Harris, M., 'Division of funds within the library: allocation of the materials budget in the academic library', *Australian library review*, 9, 1992, 99–101.

33 Young, I. R., 'A quantitative comparison of acquisitions budget allocation formulas using a single institutional setting', *Library acquisitions: practice and theory*, 16, 1992, 229–42.

34 Hayes, S. and Brown, D., 'The library as a business: mapping the pervasiveness of financial relationships in today's library', *Library trends*, 42, 1994, 404–19.

35 Akeroyd, J., 'Costing and pricing information: the bottom line', *Aslib proceedings*, 43, 1991, 87–92.

36 Downing, A., 'The consequences of offering fee-based services in a medical library', *Bulletin of the Medical Library Association*, 78, 1990, 57–63.

37 Haynes, R. B., Ramsden, M. F., McKibbon, K. A. et al., 'Online access to MEDLINE in clinical settings: impact of user fees', *Bulletin of the Medical Library Association*, 79, 1991, 377–81.

38 Morgan, L. K., 'Fee-based services in health sciences libraries', *Science and technology libraries*, 5, 1984, 23–31.

39 Olaisen, J. L., 'Pricing strategies for library and information services', *Libri*, 39, 1989, 253–74.

40 Webber, S., 'Charging for library and information services in medical libraries: a review of the literature and a survey of current practice', *Health libraries review*, 10, 1993, 202–23.

41 Williams, T. L., Lemahu, H. L. and Burrows, S., 'The economics of academic health science libraries: cost recovery in the era of big science', *Bulletin of the Medical Library Association*, 76, 1988, 317–22.

42 Bierman, K. J., 'How will libraries pay for electronic information?', *Journal of library administration*, 15, 1991, 67–84.

43 Collins, A. M. K., 'Financing CD-ROM: the experience of a university medical library', *Program*, **23**, 1989, 443–6.
44 Cox, J. and Fletcher, A., 'Using new electronic information products to fund others', *Health libraries review*, **8**, 1991, 87–93.

FURTHER READING

Davinson, D., *Academic libraries in the enterprise culture*, Viewpoints in LIS, no. 2, London, Library Association Publishing, 1989.
Dow, R. F., 'Sustaining organization advantage in times of financial uncertainty: the context for research & development investments by academic libraries', *Library trends*, **42**, 1994, 460–6.
Dunn, J. A. and Martin, M. S., 'The whole cost of libraries', *Library trends*, **42**, 1994, 564–78.
Katz, R. N., 'Academic information management at the crossroads: time again to review the economics', *Serials review*, **18**, 1992, 41–4.
Leonard, B. G., 'The metamorphosis of the information resources budget', *Library trends*, **42**, 1994, 490–8.
Norton, B., *Charging for library and information services*, Viewpoints in LIS, no. 1, London, Library Association Publishing, 1988.
Roberts, S. A. (ed.), *Costing and the economics of library and information services*, (Aslib Reader Series, vol. 5, London, Aslib, 1984.
Roberts, S. A., *Cost management for library and information services*, London, Butterworths, 1985.
Roberts, S. A., 'Editorial (on costing, charging and information audits)', *Health libraries review*, **10**, 1993, 165–8.
Schauer, B. P., *The economics of managing library service*, Chicago, American Library Association, 1986.
Spyers-Duran, P. and Mann, T. W. (eds.), *Financing information services: problems, changing approaches and new opportunities for academic and research libraries*, New Directions in Librarianship, no. 6, Westport, Greenwood, 1985.
Wood, M. S. (ed.), *Cost analysis, cost recovery, marketing, and fee-based services: a guide for the health sciences librarian*, New York, Haworth, 1985.

18   The health libraries network of Zambia

❖   *Regina Cammy Shakakata*

To understand why a 'least developed country' such as Zambia should acquire a sophisticated telecommunication system such as HealthNet (see Figure 18.1) over and above telephone, fax or telex for communicating intra-nationally and internationally, one should have knowledge of the socio-economic standing of the country and appreciate the geographical setting of the country. Zambia has an area of 752,614 square kilometres, 90% of which is habitable. This implies that its 8.09 million habitants (data for 1990 from the Central Statistical Office) are spread all over the country except the 10% of the total area that is uninhabitable.

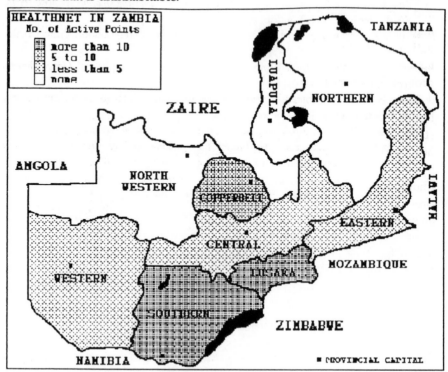

Fig. 18.1   HealthNet in Zambia

Zambia is surrounded by eight countries, namely Malawi, Mozambique, Zimbabwe, Namibia, Angola, Zaire, Tanzania and Botswana. Of these countries, Zimbabwe, Mozambique, Tanzania, Botswana, Malawi and Zambia are linked to some form of electronic network. Zimbabwe and Zambia both have reasonably developed electronic mail networks which link them to the outside world.

Administratively, Zambia is divided into nine provinces and 59 districts. The major towns and provincial centres are well served by all-weather roads, but access to the interior parts of the country is difficult, especially during the rainy season. The country enjoys a relatively good telephone infrastructure although at times lightning tends to disturb communication when it blows pieces of equipment.

Health care provision in rural areas is not easy because rural habitation is normally in hamlets. In Northern Province, Chilubi Island on Lake Bangweulu is serviced by the Zambia Flying Doctor Service (ZFDS) at monthly intervals. An orthopaedic surgeon in the School of Medicine operates a flying service called Flyspeci to rural hospitals supported by Churches Medical Association of Zambia. Although communication with the ZFDS and Flyspeci is by radio and telephone, respectively, there are definite inadequacies for passing information containing clinical data. Chilubi Island and other places in a similar situation need better communication systems to liaise not only with the ZFDS headquarters, but with other health institutions such as the central, general, provincial and district hospitals.

The trends in health facility networks show that Zambia has a fairly good health service infrastructure and a reasonable cadre of health personnel by standards of the developing world.[1] The health system, as it stands now, is heavily biased in favour of curative services rather than preventive services and it favours the urban over the rural population. This pattern is changing under the influence of the Alma Ata Conference recommendation in favour of preventive services and rural areas. These health services are not supported by an effective health care library service. Out of the 84 hospitals and several rural health centres, only 44 have access to libraries. Ten of these libraries are attached to health training institutions. The better endowed libraries can assist the less privileged libraries and the majority of the hospitals and rural health centres to access health care literature quickly and inexpensively by use of e-mail.

The health services and health status in all parts of the country are suffering from the declining economy and the negative impact of Economic Recovery Programmes under the International Monetary Fund and World Bank propelled Structural Adjustment Programmes. It is against the devastated economic background that e-mail usage, especially HealthNet in the health sector, has found ground in Zambia. Within the national framework, HealthNet is designed to serve as an important communication tool. The development of HealthNet follows the model of the National Health Reforms up to district level. The Ministry of Health and other health care institutions are major beneficiaries of the system, whereas the School of Medicine with its medical literature and a pool of consultants becomes an invaluable partner in the development of HealthNet.

ELECTRONIC MAIL SYSTEMS

An e-mail system (Zambia currently uses FidoNet) has many advantages over the telephone, fax or telex. Some of these advantages are that e-mail is inexpensive; the caller does not have to wait for the addressee to pick up the message, but messages can be left to be picked up when it is convenient for the addressee, e-mail messages can be prepared on relatively easy-to-use word-processors and imported for onward transmission. In the case of Zambia, the programme used for e-mail is a FidoNet compatible program called Frontdoor which can also be used to prepare short messages. It is, however, advisable to use word-processors to prepare longer messages that need to be presented in a certain format.

In addition, e-mail has the capability of sending a message to more than one recipient through its conference and bulletin board capabilities.

Conferencing facilities are some of the delights of e-mail. It is possible with e-mail to hold electronic conferences with people who share the same interests and objectives no matter where they are in the world as long as they are hooked to the same telecommunication system. For example, FidoNet users can have several conferences running according to user group interests. The advantage of a conference over other open messages is that messages contained in conferences are seen by subscribers to the conference only.

Bulletin boards are one form of contacting many users simultaneously without having to call or send the message several times. There may be time variations between the time the message is sent and the time all the persons for whom the message is intended receive it. These variations may be due to the number of computers that the message goes through before reaching its destination or the timing with regard to picking up messages.

In Zambia, e-mail has opened up avenues for communicating with the world cheaply and speedily. Although the Zambia FidoNet does not have direct access to the Internet, international messages are always sent through the Zonegate in South Africa or via GreenNet in the United Kingdom. These international connections will improve for Zambia once an Internet connection is installed.

An e-mail transmission is semi-automated in the sense that when a message is prepared for transmission, the sender is not required to sit at the machine until the message goes. The Frontdoor system is designed in such a way that it will attempt to send a message at least 30 times before it gives up. Therefore, the sender can do other jobs while the computer dials the number to which the message is being sent

INTERNATIONAL PERSPECTIVES

Electronic mail developed alongside microcomputers in the early 1980s in the USA and Europe. Computer-to-computer communication was first developed through a system called the International Research Network (Internet) some 20 years ago. The Internet started as a network system of the National Science Foundation of the United States of America. Later, the Joint Academic Network (JANET) of the UK joined the Internet and became the most prominent user of the Internet. Other users of Internet outside the USA and the United Kingdom are the governments of countries in Western Europe, as well as Canada, Japan, South Africa (through UNINET), Israel, Hong Kong and Australia. GreenNet, which is concerned with the conservation of the environment, PeaceNet working for disaster relief, and HealthNet for health information systems are some of the global telecommunication systems which have developed. The Internet has approximately 1000 networks hooked up to it and over 200,000 hosts throughout the world. The growth rate of the Internet is 100 additional hosts every year.[2]

Some networks are emerging at the regional level in Africa, e.g. the Pan Africa Development Information System Network (PADISNET) which is being coordinated from Addis Ababa. Under PADISNET, Africa is divided into four regions called the West African Development Information System (WADIS), East and Southern African Development Information System (ESADIS), Central African Development Information System (CADIS) and North African Development Information System. Zambia is coordinating 19 countries of ESADIS with its database at the United Nations Economic Commission for Africa–Multinational Programming and Operational Centre (UNECA-MULPOC). PADISNET aims to collect and index indigenous developmental literature, using e-mail connectivity to transmit the bibliographies to the coordinating centres and the member countries. The Africa region database is in Addis Ababa.

In East and Southern Africa, the end of the 1980s saw the establishment of the East and Southern African Networks (ESANET), an e-mail network linking the Universities of Zimbabwe, Zambia, Nairobi, Dar-es-Salaam and Makerere to enable these institutions to exchange research information. ESANET has resulted in the development of local area networks (LANs) in the institutions in which it operates. In Zambia, the LAN is called the University of Zambia Network (UNZANET).

The proliferation of e-mail networks in Africa has equally improved the methods of communication among non-governmental organizations (NGOs). In Nairobi, a network called NGONet is expanding at a considerable rate within Kenya and is spreading over its borders to other countries. In Harare there is MANGO (Microcomputer Access for Nongovernmental Organizations and a sister network, ZANGONET in Lusaka, Zambia, bringing the world of NGOs closer together and keeping in step with e-mail systems such as GreenNet.

Some critical meetings to decide on the development of e-mail took place in 1992. In 'Bringing it together: Africa 1992',[3] Barad discusses these meetings. The meetings took place in: Toronto, as a meeting of the Global Networking Workshop funded by Partnership Africa Canada and the International Development and Research Centre (IDRC); Dakar, the Regional Informatics Network for Africa (RINAF) project; Kobe, Japan was the INET '92 centre of activity; and two three-day workshops were held in Nairobi – the International Workshop on Digital Radio Technology and Applications, jointly organized by IDRC and Volunteers in Technology Assistance (VITA), and the Workshop on Science and Technology Communications Networks in Africa, which followed. They were cosponsored by the American Association for the Advancement of Science (AAAS) and the African Academy of Science (AAS).

In August 1993, the university librarians from East and Southern Africa who met in Harare under the auspices of the AAAS seriously discussed the possibility of using e-mail to promote library services. This information technology (IT), which is being developed and becoming affordable by users in Africa to promote the availability of literature in libraries, is seen as a means of sharing resources by developing countries. Although the meeting revealed that librarians are still hesitant to take up the IT to supply current literature, the steadily growing interest is evident in the achievements of the libraries that were represented. These university librarians are linked to one form of electronic network or another, but they need to define the sort of information that has to be put on the networks. In a similar vein, a network of Carnegie Grantees recommended the use of e-mail to coordinate network activities at their meeting which took place in April 1993 at Dakar, Senegal.

THE ZAMBIAN FRAMEWORK

There are three user categories of e-mail in Zambia – UNZANET, ZANGONET and HealthNet – which have the same host at the University of Zambia Computer Centre. As of November 1993, there are 31 users of UNZANET based at the University of Zambia Great East Road Campus, the Institute for African Studies and the School of Medicine. The usage of

UNZANET is mostly for international communication. Although the main university library is linked to UNZANET, its full potential has not yet been fully explored because automation of the library collection is only beginning.

ZANGONET has about 16 users from local NGOs, agencies of the United Nations and the World Bank. There is great potential for the system to expand as more and more NGOs discover the potential of e-mail as a communication tool over short and long distances. During the drought that hit Southern Africa during the 1991–2 rainy season, the World Food Programme and the United Nations Fund for Population Activity (UNFPA) used e-mail to communicate between Zambia and New York.

HealthNet, which is the most elaborate of e-mail systems in Zambia, had 65 users in November 1993. HealthNet communicates at two levels, first via a low orbit satellite travelling at a speed of 22,000 kilometres per hour at a distance of 700 kilometres above the earth's surface. The 45 kilogram microsatellite is a creation of the Surrey Satellite Technology of the United Kingdom. Although it does not have the capacity to load large library files and could offer less than 10–15 minute passes if more groundstations falling under the satellite's path tried to upload messages simultaneously, its current potential to transmit messages from one groundstation to another inexpensively is a great relief to the developing countries currently linked to HealthNet. The second level of communication at national level in Zambia is the terrestrial based e-mail system using the local telephone infrastructure which is set up by the Posts and Telecommunications Corporation. When messages are downloaded by satellite, they are forwarded to the host computer which connects to the local e-mail system. Users of HealthNet call into the host like any other e-mail users to pick up their messages. Similarly, when transmitting HealthNet messages by satellite, the messages will move by e-mail from the transmitting point to the host, from where the messages are uploaded to the satellite using packet radio technology. The e-mail's FidoNet system links into the Internet via South Africa. At the moment, both the terrestrial and satellite based telecommunication systems are inexpensive to use in Zambia because even when a telephone line is used to transmit a message all the way to Europe, the USA or Canada, the bill for transmitting such a message is low as the call is an incoming high-speed one. If such calls become more expensive, communicating by HealthSat will be the cheaper alternative for use by health care e-mail users. HealthSat is also an important back-up (and will shortly have its own Internet connection) as well as being the only way to communicate with certain other African countries who have no conventional e-mail.

As of October 1993, the other HealthSat groundstations (see Figure 18.2) were Yaounde in Cameroon, Brazzaville in the Congo, Accra and Navrongo in Ghana, Nairobi in Kenya, Maputo in Mozambique, Dar es Salaam in Tanzania,

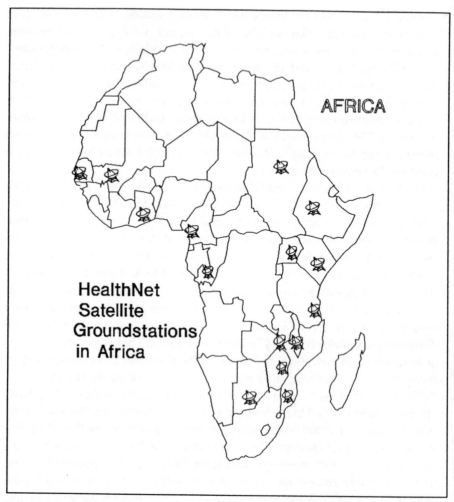

Fig. 18.2   HealthNet satellite groundstations in Africa

Kampala in Uganda and Harare in Zimbabwe. The non-African countries on HealthNet are Rio de Janeiro in Brazil, Havana in Cuba, St Johns in Canada, Tasmania in Australia and Cambridge, Massachusetts, which is the headquarters in the USA. Six further sites were waiting to be licensed and installed: Mali, Malawi, Botswana, Ethiopia, Sudan and the Gambia.

ILLUSTRATION OF SITES IN AFRICA
HealthNet in practice
HealthNet has been adopted as a communication tool by representatives of various health care institutions, who consulted and agreed at the HealthNet

Workshop for Physicians and Hospital Administrators held in October 1993, that HealthNet is the most cost effective and most secure and reliable means of communicating among health care workers that there is today. This is how the health care workers see the system helping in their work.

The University of Zambia Medical Library
The University of Zambia Medical Library is using HealthNet, as a communication tool with other libraries both at national and international levels. Within Zambia, the Medical Library communicates regularly with other health libraries to exchange and share health information and literature. These libraries are the Tropical Diseases Research Centre, Chainama Hills Hospital, Chainama College of Health Sciences and the World Health Organization (WHO), which have access to HealthNet and need to be encouraged to use the system to access health literature that is not held in their libraries. The remaining notable health sciences libraries at the Evelyn Hone College of Applied Arts and Commerce, where the paramedical personnel are trained, and the University Teaching Hospital, Schools of Nursing, Midwifery and Theatre Nursing, all based in Lusaka, still have to be linked to HealthNet. In the Copperbelt Province of Zambia are the Scully Medical Library at the Ndola Central Hospital and the ZFDS Library in Ndola. In Southern Province there is a self-contained, fully automated health sciences library at Monze District Hospital with an active HealthNet user clientele. Although these libraries serve key health training and service institutions, a large number of them are short of professionally trained manpower. By implication, this means that networking of these libraries using electronic media may be further delayed in spite of the small number of libraries involved.

At the international level, the Medical Library is using HealthNet in a library partnership programme. Under this programme, the Medical Library is twinned with the Health Sciences Centre Library at the University of Florida, Gainesville, USA. This service was actively used between June 1991 and July 1992, before the Health Foundation of New York purchased and installed a Hitachi multistack CD-ROM player at the Medical Library. This development saw the growth of CD-ROM databases from one (Compact Cambridge MEDLINE) to approximately 12 databases. The growth of this information centre prompted the Medical Library to share its resources with other libraries in southern Africa.

World Health Organization
The WHO office in Lusaka is using e-mail to communicate with Geneva. However, WHO would like to see HealthNet used more at the national level to transmit rural generated health information to and from the WHO office. It

is anticipated that HealthNet will improve liaison between the Ministry of Health and WHO to relay information on epidemics from the periphery. WHO suggests the further use of HealthNet to circulate information on health literature and other health information from Geneva.

Provincial Medical Officers

The Provincial Medical Officer in Southern Province is using the system to transmit messages to district hospitals. The district hospitals, on the other hand, would like to see a situation whereby there is more communication among themselves. Communication with the levels below the District Health Board, that is the rural health centre and community zones, will not immediately be achieved through HealthNet because the HealthNet infrastructure stretches down to the district level only. HealthNet is implementable at district level because the district hospitals are currently manned by medical officers or doctors who are likely to appreciate the use of HealthNet.

Churches Medical Association of Zambia

The Churches Medical Association of Zambia (CMAZ) is the largest single non-governmental organization (NGO) that offers health facilities throughout the country with its 31 well staffed hospitals and rural health centres. CMAZ uses HealthNet to communicate with its member hospitals, and is planning for substantive information to be transmitted over HealthNet.

Ministry of Health

The Ministry of Health (MOH) is the principal provider of health services and all the planning that goes with the services. The MOH runs nine provincial hospitals, five general and central hospitals, 56 district hospitals and numerous rural health centres. Although any health institution below the status of a district will not benefit from HealthNet immediately, nevertheless the MOH has adopted the system for communicating among health workers in Zambia and as a health information system. It is proposed and agreed that HealthNet will be used to communicate with districts and to transmit monthly returns of statistics from the district to the regions and quarterly reports from the regions to the Central Health Council and for instruction.

The MOH sees HealthNet as a vehicle for circulation and disbursement of funds information at various levels and for circulating staff registers for comparative purposes by districts. HealthNet is also to be used for resource mobilization. Other uses of HealthNet by the MOH include administration, policy decisions and technical development of delivery systems.

The University of Zambia School of Medicine

The University of Zambia School of Medicine sees HealthNet as a communicating tool between the School of Medicine and Master of Medicine (MMed) students who spend up to six months on placement in the district hospitals. They would at the same time be writing dissertations. Before the establishment of HealthNet, this meant repeated trips to and from the University Teaching Hospital (UTH). In future, the students' work and comments from the School of Medicine will be transmitted by e-mail. Once the system is fully utilized by both the students and teaching staff, it could save up to three weeks of student time in travelling between Lusaka and the districts.

Chainama College of Health Sciences

The students of the college are put on placement in the district hospitals of Livingstone, Sinazongwe, Chipata, Ndola, Chama, Samfya, Mongu, Kasama, Sefula, Kabwe and at the UTH. These students need current health information and literature to make their attachments meaningful. The Medical Library offers literature search services to hospitals that are linked to HealthNet from which these students can benefit.

Medical Stores Limited/Pharmaceutical Services

Plans are underway to circulate stock lists of their drugs via HealthNet. The current procedure for distributing drugs is that the district hospitals have to request drugs through the Provincial Medical Officers, who make the request to the Pharmaceutical Services who later forward the requests to the Medical Stores Limited. This procedure is very slow, and it sometimes takes about four to six weeks to deliver medicines. Consequently, many drug items are out of stock by the time the delivery lorry arrives. Even though kits for rural health centres and community health workers are supplied by Medical Stores Limited, supply is erratic. The preferred procedure is to cover the whole of a particular province with information on the availability of drugs. Considering that Medical Stores Limited has the monopoly of narcotic analgesics, resulting in some hospitals having no drugs at any given time, half the problem of drug supplies can be solved if lists of drug supply were circulated via HealthNet to enable hospitals to make drug orders by e-mail. Another solution under consideration is the bringing commercial pharmaceutical companies onto the HealthNet system.

Consultations

There are many consultants in general and central hospitals and UTH. In terms of numbers and types of consultants, the UTH has the largest reservoir in the country. Therefore, a large volume of clinical and medical consultations will be channelled through the UTH when the service is fully developed.

Referrals
It has been observed in the past that only 10% of referrals see the specialist in time. HealthNet is being used to ensure that all referrals are expected at their destination at a particular time. In this way, a patient is be admitted directly and the same system is being used to communicate to the originating hospital when the patient is discharged.

University Teaching Hospital Laboratory
Currently, the peripheral hospitals send in samples of specimens. When the results are analysed, they are typed into the computer on a purpose-designed form, imported into Frontdoor and sent by e-mail. This saves several weeks of communication time. Since the results are already computerized, the need to retype is not there once appropriate programs are installed and importation into Frontdoor made possible.

AIDS coordination
There are several organizations working in the areas of AIDS and related diseases. Some of these are: the national AIDS control programmes based at the WHO offices in Lottie House; ZAMBART I-LSHTM and ZAMBART II – TB related AIDS research; University of Texas – University of Zambia Research and Training Programme; AIDS counselling services at Kara Counselling; anti-AIDS education in Family Health Trust and WHO. All these organizations are beginning to be coordinated by use of the conferencing facility on HealthNet.

Optimization of HealthNet
The Medical Library is, in more than one way, the custodian of processed health care information. Therefore, the emerging status of the Medical Library as the most powerful single user of HealthNet is apparent. Consequently, the optimization of HealthNet will largely focus on the activities of the Medical Library. The Medical Library sees one way of optimizing HealthNet as the establishment of CD-ROM networks to take advantage of its 12 databases. Some services are already offered by the Medical Library through HealthNet, although library users request information offline. The Medical Library plans to provide remote access to library services and electronic resources 24 hours a day because as Bellamy et al.[4] put it, this does potentially save users' time and staff time too.

Unlike Internet, which has library catalogues and campus-wide information systems, taking up the lion's share of the growth and excitement in contemporary networking,[5] HealthNet in Zambia will initially carry literature searches from commercial and foreign databases because they are available at the Medical Library, followed by the bibliographic data from the *African index medicus* local database. The Medical Library anticipates networking CD-ROMs, using a LAN for the users of e-mail based in the University of Zambia and the UTH, and a wide-area network (WAN) for users of HealthNet outside Lusaka. The former is implementable if the technical and software problems are sorted out because the CD-ROM vendors allow LANs but not WANs.[6] CD-ROM technology is preferred because it is cheaper to run than online systems. The sort of databases referred to by Nickerson,[7] such as the Texas A&M, *Wilson's humanities index, Social sciences index, Easy and general literature index, Applied science and technology index, Biological and agricultural index* and *Business periodicals index,* which are accessed via the Internet, are equally expensive for Africa unless they become accessible using the CD-ROM technology which is finding ground in Africa.

National HealthNet policy

The Ministry of Health adopted HealthNet as a health information system for Zambia during the workshop held in 1993. To consolidate the status and role of HealthNet in health information communication systems, HealthNet is accommodated in the National Health Reforms. By implication, the persons manning HealthNet in the various hospitals are employees of the Ministry of Health. The HealthNet responsibility is assigned to the Health Information Officers at district level as a matter of policy. The HealthNet Planning Team will still constitute the School of Medicine, Computer Centre, CMAZ, UNICEF and Ministry of Health.

United States President Bill Clinton and his Vice President Al Gore (1993) said on the occasion of inaugurating e-mail at The White House:[8] 'As we move ahead into the twenty-first century, we must have a government that can show the way and lead by example'. They warned, however, that: 'We must be realistic about the limitation and expectations of the White House electronic system . . . As we work to reinvent government and streamline our processes the e-mail project can help to put us on the leading edge of progress'.

These statements could not have been made at a better time when we in Zambia have been in two minds over whether the introduction of e-mail was a wise decision when there were other national demands like poverty that required priority support. Now we know that we did the right thing to adopt HealthNet as a health information system and to allow the development of e-mail in the country, it is the only way for us to be 'on the leading edge of progress'.

REFERENCES

1   Zambia, Republic of, *Ministry of Health National Health Policies and Strategies (Health Reforms)*, Lusaka, Ministry of Health, 1991.
2   Krol, E., *The whole Internet users' guide and catalog*, Sebastopol, O'Reilly and Associates, 1992.
3   Barad, B., 'Bringing it together: Africa 1992', in *Internet Society news*, **1** (4), Winter 1993, 10.
4   Bellamy, L. M., Silver, J. T. and Givens, M. K., 'Remote access to electronic library. Services through a campus network', in *Bulletin of the Medical Library Association*, **79** (1), 1991, 53–62.
5   Peters, P. E., 'Networked information resource and services: next steps', in *Computers in libraries*, **12** (4), 1992, 46–52.
6   Leggott, M., 'LANS and CD–ROMs', in *OCLC micro*, **5** (4), 1989, 18–19.
7   Nickerson, G., 'Networked resources', in *Computers in libraries*, **11** (11), Dec 1991, 38–42.
8   Clinton, B. and Gore, A., 'White House electronic mail access', in *Internet Society news*, **2** (2), Summer 1993, 14.

FURTHER READING

Abba, L. G., 'RINAF: A network interconnection project of academic and research institutions in Africa', in *Electronic networking in Africa: advancing science and technology for development*, Washington, DC, AAS/AAAS, 1992, 11–23.
Bennett, M., *HealthNet in Zambia: improving communications for health*.
Bennett, M., 'Zambia links up to HealthNet', in *Computers in Africa*, **6** (5), Sept/Oct 1992, 60.
'Demystifying electronic mail', in *Computers in Africa*, **6** (5), Sept/Oct 1992, 50–7.
Hoehl, S. B., Local area network implementation: moving toward phase III', in *Special libraries*, **80** (1), Winter 1989, 16–23.
Kittle, P. W., 'Networking the light fantastic CD-ROMs on LANS', in *CD-ROM professional*, **5** (1), Jan 1992, 30–7.
Notess, G. R., 'Gaining access to the Internet', in *Online*, September 1992, 27–31.
Report of a Workshop for Physicians and Hospital Administrators held at the Commonwealth Youth Programme Africa Centre, Lusaka, Zambia, 1993, 21–22 October, 1993.
Sloan, S., 'Remote control of a CD-ROM LAN', in *Computers in libraries*, **10** (11), Dec 1990, 47–9.
Zambia country profile 1990–91, London, The Economist Intelligence Unit, 1990.

19 Health care library services in the USA

❖ *Michael Carmel*

American medical librarianship exerts a powerful and continuing influence over the development of the profession internationally, in part through its sheer size, but mainly because of the quality and value of the many professional tools and techniques developed at the National Library of Medicine and elsewhere.

HEALTH CARE IN THE USA

To appreciate the environment within which American health science librarians and informaticians work, it is essential to understand something of the complexity of American health care delivery systems, where both purchasers and providers of health care operate in a highly competitive marketplace dominated by the private sector.

The providers of health care

Health care is provided mainly by two mechanisms: physicians in private practice, and hospitals.

Private physicians work in offices and are reimbursed on a fee-for-service basis. Most are specialists. In general, insured patients choose which physician they wish to see at the time of need, although they may have a preferred provider, especially if they are members of a Health Maintenance Organization (HMO) rather than a standard insurance scheme. Many of these physicians are unaffiliated to any hospital or larger institution, so do not have right of access to a hospital library except by special arrangement.

Doctors are also directly employed by hospitals, as specialists ('physicians') or trainees ('interns and residents'). Some of these are known as general practitioners, but they bear little resemblance to a British or European family doctor service. They are closer to the British concept of a general physician working in an outpatient department.

There are almost 6000 hospitals in the USA, but many are very small. Dorenfest[1] estimates that there are 3300 acute care hospitals of over 100 beds. Ownership is varied: they may be private partnerships of the medical staff, shareholder corporations, charitable or religious foundations, state or local government establishments, or university owned. Size can also vary from a few dozen beds with no in-house medical staff, to the 900 doctor Cleveland Clinic offering specialist services worldwide.

Hospitals have no choice but to run their affairs as businesses.The main source of income for all hospitals is the same: fee-for-service billing of insurance companies, HMOs, government schemes or individuals. There is no top-down planning of health care provision at any level. Providers react to the availability of insurance income by expanding, contracting or relocating services. Hence the phenomenon of seriously under-doctored areas alongside over-provision and empty beds.

As in pre-NHS Britain, much of the primary and secondary care of the poor and uninsured is provided by hospital emergency rooms on a walk-in basis. The ability of the uninsured to gain access to expensive facilities in this way is a contentious issue, but the tradition that public, charitable or university hospitals never turn away the sick is still strong, at least in most big cities.

The Federal Government is involved in health care provision through the armed services hospitals and the Department of Veterans Affairs (VA). The VA offers service-related care to the USA's 27 million living service veterans. It administers 171 medical centres and employs some 12,000 physicians and 60,000 nurses, making it equivalent in scale to an English Region, or the whole of Scotland. The VA has played a pioneering role in many information, library and informatics initiatives, with effective coordination and resource sharing across the whole network.

Academic links

Most large hospitals cherish a university link which allows them to take students and interns, and attract high quality staff. In some hospitals, all physicians and some senior nursing and paramedical staff are honorary faculty, and therefore entitled to use the medical school's library service. One example is the University of Washington in Seattle, to which all medical staff in four states are affiliated. On the other side of the country, the Countway Library in Boston treats 12,000 Harvard-affiliated faculty as core users.

Both universities and hospitals compete in the affiliation business, and some hospitals prefer a distant to a local affiliation, not wishing to be linked to a clinical competitor. Academic Health Centers (university hospitals) nevertheless remain distinctive, and are the providers of choice for most tertiary care.

EDUCATION FOR HEALTH CARE

Most health care professionals, including nurses, are educated in universities to degree or higher degree level. Some large campuses are devoted entirely to health sciences education.

There are about 120 medical schools, excluding off-shore colleges. These divide broadly into the 'private' universities, often very federal in structure, and the state universities.

Some large state universities (New York, California) have several medical schools on geographically separate campuses, each with its own network of affiliated hospitals, and its own library service. Conversely, most large urban areas have more than one medical school.

Medicine and dentistry are generally taught on four-year postgraduate courses, with a clinical component from an early stage. The standard qualification is the taught MD, a concept unknown in the UK. Graduate entry means that American medical students are older than their British counterparts and enter the profession later and more indebted.

Many schools have revised their curricula into a problem-orientated format, with clinical and pre-clinical sciences, such as physiology or pharmacology, integrated around the larger systems and disease states. In a few schools, case work is the main teaching method, with academic and research staff seen as a learning resource, leading to an enhanced perception of the role of information resources and services.

THE NATIONAL NETWORK OF LIBRARIES OF MEDICINE

The National Network of Libraries of Medicine (NN/LM), formerly known as the Regional Medical Library Program, was set up under the Medical Library Assistance Act of 1965. It is a hierarchical network on four levels.

The base is formed by the local libraries, mainly in hospitals, used by doctors, nurses and other health care practitioners to support their clinical practice and continuing education. There are about 3700 of these.

Base libraries rely on the support of 131 resource libraries, mainly in medical schools or multidisciplinary health sciences teaching institutions.

At the third level are eight Regional Medical Libraries serving geographical areas of the United States. These regions are very large. Some have populations equivalent to the UK, while at least one – the Pacific North West – has a land area greater than western Europe.

At the apex is the National Library of Medicine (NLM), which administers the programme and budget and offers a wide range of supporting activities, as well as being a supplier of last resort and 'holder of record' for the knowledge base of health care.

Members of the network are self-selected, following certain simple criteria. They need not be 'medical libraries' as such, but must hold health sciences materials and must provide services to health care professionals.

Base libraries

It cannot yet be said that all health care workers in the USA have access to professionally managed library services. The NN/LM's efforts at encouraging local provision are limited by the independence and commercial imperatives of the health care providers. Nevertheless, there is a great wealth of resources overall, and most large hospitals have their own libraries, while some smaller organizations share facilities. Pressure is maintained by the Joint Committee on Accreditation of Health Care Organizations, which has recently tightened up the recognition criteria for information management.

A survey for the American Hospital Association (AHA) in 1990,[2] applying quite strict criteria (the ANSI standard Z39), identified 2167 hospital libraries. Reworking the data, applying the lower criteria typical of earlier surveys, 3410 hospital libraries were identified. Taken with Dorenfest's figure[1] of 3300 acute hospitals of over 100 beds, this would suggest that almost all hospitals of any size have some kind of library, but that only 65% have trained librarians.

In practice, these libraries are not unlike their counterparts all over the world. Working in often cramped quarters and under constant pressure from a demanding clientele in a climate of constant change, they are both challenging and exciting places to work. They are generally staffed by highly professional and responsive librarians, using pragmatically whatever technology they can lay hands on.

In 1993 Wiesenthal[3] conducted a survey of library managers in the VA to ascertain what developments they considered both desirable and likely. Their key desirables were familiar to hospital librarians everywhere:

- the concept of a user always having to come to the library will disappear;
- in-depth print collections will diminish;
- computer laboratories providing access to the latest technology, e.g. interactive video, CD-ROM, and computer-assisted instruction will be an integral part of the library service;
- library and media production services will merge to form a single learning resources service;
- the library service will establish an interface with other information systems within the medical centre such as patient files, clinical database management files and/or medical records;
- the demand for personnel with both information/library sciences and computer technology background will increase dramatically.

Society libraries

A library used to be a major feature of the work of many local and regional medical societies in the USA. In some areas (as in the UK) they provided the core or starting point of today's finest collections. Today the survivors are few since, in the USA as in the rest of the world, maintaining a local society library up-to-date, and in attractive quarters is no longer seen as economically viable.

Where they do survive, these libraries can still provide a vital link with the information network for many physicians and other health professionals without a hospital affiliation. One which prospers is the Allen Memorial Library in Cleveland, Ohio. Established and owned by the Cleveland Medical Library Association, it is today managed as a branch of the Case Western Reserve University's Health Science Library, but still has a character and charm of its own. The Massachusetts Medical Society has chosen a different model, by funding an important part of the outreach work of Harvard's Francis Countway Library and others in the area, for the benefit of its members.

Area Health Education Centers
Some individual states have taken their own action to ensure the availability of continuing education facilities to all health professionals. Usually this is done by establishing Area Health Education Centers (AHECs) which have good modern library services open to all users in the state. In North Carolina this has been taken several steps further with the development of thiNCnet, a comprehensive resource-sharing network, applying advanced systems, and based around the state's network of AHEC libraries, incorporating hospitals and several major academic health centres.

National societies
Faced with increasingly accessible local networks, some national societies have positioned themselves in the library market by emphasizing their specialist focus and skills. The American College of Obstetricians and Gynecologists (ACOG), for example, bases an active information service on a small collection in limited quarters, with almost no provision for in-person readers.

This library has a high profile and is deeply involved in the core activities of the organization. In the area of clinical guidelines, the library does much of the background research, and monitors and keeps the expert committees informed about patterns of enquiries. The library service supports member physicians in their clinical work, and also provides information to purchasers, and evidence to government on policy issues. With support from the NLM's Integrated Advanced Information Management System (IAIMS) Programme, ACOG has set up its own information system for members – ACOGNET – accessible by both modem and Internet.[4]

Medical school libraries
The 120 medical school libraries form the backbone of the cooperative net-

work. Hague[5] described visits to six of these in the eastern USA in 1986, selecting five features ('undimmed impressions') to mention in his concluding remarks: 'thorough professionalism'; 'sheer size'; 'sophistication of computer systems'; 'willingness to pass on costs to the consumer'; 'acceptance of – and adaptation to – end-user searching'.

These impressions remain equally valid today, although there is less contrast, one hopes, with equivalent libraries in Britain. One is learning to take for granted professionalism in library management and service. In automation, networking and end-user searching, the gap is rapidly closing. Charging and cost recovery are widely implemented in UK universities (as in Britain, US hospital libraries rarely charge). In size, however, the contrast has, if anything, increased, whether defined by journal collections, accommodation or staffing levels.

Collections

Some medical school libraries have journal collections similar to those in the UK, of between 500 and 1200 current titles, but collections of 2000 to 2500 are more common, while 3000 or more is not unusual. Several factors in the USA contribute to the different policies in the two countries:

- the absence of a reliable and fast source equivalent to the British Library Document Supply Centre
- a tradition of independence
- perception of interlibrary loans as a second-class service
- large distances between libraries
- the role of these libraries as resources for others
- more money.

There are signs of change in response to both new technology and economic circumstances. The resource sharing potential of the National Network, increasing reliance on the Docline request service, standardized charging and fax transmission (and more recently Ariel) are between them creating a viable alternative to large local holdings. At the same time, rising journal costs are coming up against severe cash limits, and in some cases cash reductions ('dollar cuts') in library budgets. Cuts in subscriptions are therefore real, much talked about, and far from painless.

Nevertheless, there are two factors that continue to sustain the demand for independent collections at a level higher than most British librarians would consider attainable or even desirable. First is the absence of a comprehensive and reliable national document supply centre. Alongside that goes the role of medical school libraries themselves as heavy net lenders within the NN/LM. One resource library, Cleveland Health Science Library, is quoted as supplying 40,000 documents in Northeast Ohio in 1992, against 4000 received.

Space
New library buildings form a regular feature in the *Bulletin of the Medical Library Association*. The accommodation of medical school libraries is often very spacious and architecturally imaginative. This applies both to older foundations such as The Countway in Boston and the Welch Library of Johns Hopkins University in Baltimore, and to new and exciting buildings such as the UCSF Library in San Francisco and the Washington University Library in St Louis. These last two have over 8000 square metres each of floor space, and appointments which combine luxury with high technology. At UCSF, the Library has not only developed part of its space as a Center for Knowledge Management, but has also made over space to other informatics-related departments to gain the benefits of closer working.

The new Eskind Biomedical Library at Vanderbilt University, Nashville, opened in 1994, accommodates the Center for Medical Informatics, authoring environments and instruction space, as well as the library itself. At a little under 6000 square metres it is hardly cramped by any standards, but perhaps it does suggest that the trend to ever larger buildings has peaked. It is arguably as imaginative in design, both functionally and architecturally, as any library in the world.

Staff
Administration of large collections, spacious accommodation and long opening hours dictate a need for high staffing levels. Twenty-five staff is rather modest among US medical school libraries, while staffs of over 40 are not uncommon – about double the UK equivalent at each end of the range. A few libraries have as many as 60.

Activities and services
Activity statistics collected by the Association of Academic Health Science Libraries Directors indicate that the use of these libraries is not much higher than in the UK, although self-service photocopying seems to be further along the same upward curve.

Libraries frequently use their resources to develop value-added facilities and services. One regular feature is a computer laboratory with hardware and software for individual and class use, including CAL programs, multimedia learning packages, network links, and working packages such as wordprocessing, spreadsheets and database management systems. These vary from about a dozen machines to 40 or more. At a growing number of institutions, the library staff have taken the opportunity to offer courses to students and faculty in the use of computers, or in areas such as problem solving or Internet use.

Two special examples of outreach deserve mention. First, there are still clinical librarians in a number of centres, although the concept has evolved since its 1970s origins and is now usually seen as librarians working with hospital doctors by attending clinical report meetings to provide information support. Secondly, the involvement of librarians as facilitators in the new style of curriculum has been taken to a new level at some schools, where students work as teams in a problem-solving approach to learning, and senior library staff share the responsibility of working with them.

Historical collections

Most American medical schools take great pride in keeping their collections of historical material in near-ideal conditions and with excellent facilities for study and research. It is often overlooked that many American medical schools are as old as most of their European counterparts and have been actively and judiciously collecting and conserving work of historical, scientific or aesthetic merit for several generations.

Regional Medical Libraries

Several Federally funded cooperative programmes are managed under contract by the eight specially designated Regional Medical Libraries (RMLs). As well as being a medical school/resource library, each RML takes on substantial training, user education, promotion and resource-sharing responsibilities.

A particular responsibility of the RMLs is to promote the use of NLM's searching and document request software, GRATEFUL MED and LOANSOME DOC, directly by end users and especially by unaffiliated physicians. Promotion incorporates marketing, user education and support, and is an example of the National Network's concern that all health professionals should have access to reliable information, irrespective of their affiliation.

One of the largest of the Regions is the Pacific North West, centred on the University of Washington at Seattle. Even without its RML responsibilities, this would be a very large medical library, with very large commitments. It takes about 4000 current journals and employs 70 full-time equivalent staff including student help (19 professional posts). There is a tradition of outreach service to the four 'WAMI' states – Washington, Alaska, Montana and Idaho – where a high proportion of all medical and health care staff are alumni. A resource development grant (1993) from NLM will enable all hospitals in the region to be linked to the resource libraries through the Internet.

The National Library of Medicine

The apex of the National Network is the NLM, whose mandate under the National Library of Medicine Act is to 'assist the advancement of medical and related sciences, and to aid the dissemination and exchange of scientific and other information important to the progress of medicine and to the public health'.[6]

Constitutionally, the NLM is one of the National Institutes for Health (NIH). With over 500 staff it is a large and complex organization, having three main divisions: the library itself, the Lister Hill National Center for Biomedical Communications, and the National Center for Biotechnology Information. Each of these has both in-house research projects and a programme of research grants and contracts.

In 1985–6 the NLM Board of Regents commissioned a far-reaching review, not only of the Library's own activities but of every aspect of information management in health care. The outcome was the *Long range plan*[6] which still structures the NLM's activities in preparation for 'the electronic world of the future' and underpins its commitment to 'improving the infrastructure for information transfer and facilitating the effective use of this infrastructure'.

There is no true equivalent to the NLM in any other country. It is well known in the medical and library worlds as the source of several vital tools of the information trade – the MEDLARS family of databases and products, MeSH and the NLM Classification – and of many innovations in information handling and knowledge management.

The NLM is the main channel for funding the National Network, and manages federal support for research in health informatics and communications. Current work includes the Unified Medical Language System and the Visible Human Project, and in 1994 it was announced that NLM will coordinate federally funded research into the electronic patient record. The NLM also provides financial help to individual health science libraries, principally through Resource Awards. The emphasis of these changes over time, and is currently (1995) on using technology for resource sharing and on creating the means to participate in the NLM's other programmes.

PROFESSIONAL ASSOCIATIONS

American health care librarians have a choice of four major associations, as well as numerous local societies – or none.

The American Library Association is widely seen as catering primarily for public and school librarians, and since it has no independent qualifications structure is thought to offer little to most health sciences librarians, although it does mention a hospital libraries section.

The Association of Research Libraries caters for the general academic library community and has an active medical membership.

The Special Libraries Association recruits actively in the health sector and is popular for its dynamic approach and excellent publications.

It is, however, to the Medical Library Association (MLA) that most professionally active US medical librarians, and many overseas, turn for professional support. It has 5000 members organized in 14 regional 'chapters', and 22 special interest groups ranging from international relations to informatics. It publishes the quarterly *Bulletin*, which until the 1980s had a virtual monopoly in the field (since dented by *Health libraries review* and *Medical reference services quarterly*).

The MLA has an active continuing education programme for its members, and has recently moved towards establishing practice-based and accredited qualifications in health science librarianship through the establishment of the Academy of Health Information Professionals.

Independence confers both advantages and disadvantages on the MLA as compared with the Health Libraries Group of The Library Association in the UK. Clearly, it has great freedom of action, which it uses to the full. On the other hand, the lack of a wider unified structure for all librarians weakens the profession as a whole, and there is much concern among leaders of the medical library community over their apparent inability to influence the content of library and information science education at Master's level, or more generally to regulate the qualification structure and entry to the profession.

CONCLUSION

US medical libraries may contain as much as half of the world's total medical library resources and personnel. They have contributed enormously to the development of the profession at large through the innovative application of technology over many years. They are responding dynamically to the double-squeeze of new challenges and budget cuts. Coverage remains uneven and there are unexpected gaps in service to clinicians and supporting staff. The year on year work of the National Network of Libraries of Medicine may well change these features out of all recognition over the next decade.

REFERENCES

1   Dorenfest, S. I., 'United States and England: a comparison of progress in automation', *Current perspectives in healthcare computing*, conference proceedings, Harrogate 15–17 March 1993, Weybridge, BJHC Ltd, 1993.
2   Wakeley, P. J. and Foster, E., 'A survey of health sciences libraries in hospitals: implications for the 1990s', *Bulletin of the Medical Library Association*, **81** (2), April 1993.
3   Wiesenthal, D., 'The future role of the health sciences library in the Department of

Veterans Affairs', *Bulletin of the Medical Library Association*, **81** (2), April 1993, 129–34.

4   DeGeorges, K., Van Hine, P. and Pearse, W. H., 'ACOGQUEST: the model phase of the IAIMS project of the American College of Obstetricians and Gynecologists', *Bulletin of the Medical Library Association*, **80** (3), July 1992, 276–80.

5   Hague, H., 'Recent developments in American medical libraries and at the ISI', *Health libraries review*, **4** (3), Sept 1987, 172–80.

6   National Library of Medicine, *Long Range Plan*, 1987. The full report is in seven parts. Besides the Plan itself and the Executive Summary there are five panel reports:
Building and organizing the library's collection
Locating and gaining access to medical and scientific literature
Obtaining factual information from databases
Medical informatics
Assisting health professions education through information technology.

20 Health library provision in the UK

❖ Margaret Haines

Since the last edition of this book, the National Health Service (NHS) has embarked on a series of major reforms which have revolutionized the pattern of health care delivery in the UK. During this same period, the higher education sector has also undergone significant change and the education of clinical professionals has been modified both in terms of its funding, and its fundamental philosophy. All of these changes have had a tremendous impact on health library and information services in the UK.

This chapter will begin by briefly discussing some of these changes to the environment in which health libraries operate, and the remainder of the chapter will describe these libraries and their efforts to meet the information challenges posed by the reforms.

CHANGES IN THE NHS AND HIGHER EDUCATION SECTORS
Changes to the NHS

Table 20.1 lists the major government documents which signalled the reform of the national health system. The seeds for major reform in health care began with a Royal Commission on the NHS which, in 1979, noted unacceptable variations in patterns of care with social and geographical inequalities.[1] Then, in the early 1980s, an NHS Management Inquiry led by Sir Roy Griffiths found an NHS lacking in precise management objectives, management information systems for evaluating performance against objectives, and control over professional groups.[2] In the latter part of the 1980s, Department of Health reviews of primary care and community care found a lack of standards, a lack of sensitivity to the needs of patients, including their need for information, and a lack of systems for evaluating effectiveness of care.[3,4]

The cumulative effects of these critical findings were policy changes which introduced a more managerial culture into the NHS through revised and strengthened management structures and through mechanisms for closer monitoring of the care provided by various professional groups. Contracts for both general practitioners (GPs) and dentists were implemented against much opposition.[5] Improved information systems were also on the agenda, and the

Table 20.1: Significant NHS Changes 1979–94

NHS event/policy	Impact on NHS
1979 Royal Commission on the NHS	Greater awareness of unacceptable variations in patterns of care and of geographical and social inequalities
1983 NHS Management Inquiry	The strengthening of management hierarchies and mechanisms for making clinicians more accountable to managers
1987 White Paper – Promoting Better Health	Improved standards, cost effectiveness and responsiveness of primary care; indicative
1988 Health and Medicines Act	Prescribing plans, medical audit, GP contracts, etc.
1989 White Paper – Caring for People	Increased choice for patients, better provision of information, more health promotion, purchasing of care by local authorities
1989 White Paper – Working for Patients (NHS Review)	Creation of internal market of purchasers and providers; introduction of GP fund-holding and NHS trusts; extension of medical audit, reorganization of NHS management tiers; improved waiting times; improved NHS information management etc.
1991 Health of the Nation	Set targets for improved health and called for Public Health Information Strategy
1991 Patients Charter	Guaranteed waiting times, better complaints procedures, more information about local services
1992 IM&T Strategy	Person-based information systems strategy, training initiatives; NHS wide network, etc.
1993 R&D Strategy	Better resourcing and targeting of NHS research money in context of a national framework; information systems strategy including dissemination through libraries; three new information resources
1994 Functions & Manpower Review	Abolished RHAs, centralized some functions and devolved others, precise roles and explicit targets, strengthened accountability

implementation of the recommendations of an earlier steering group on health services information led to increased data gathering and analysis at district and regional level.[6]

The move to a more business-like NHS was firmly established in 1989 with the unveiling of the most significant revision of the NHS since its inception.[7] Whilst the basic principles of tax-funded health care and free care at the point of use remained untouched, the major change was the creation of an internal market of purchasers and providers. Purchasers, either district health authorities, family health service authorities (FHSAs) or some larger GP practices (GP fund-holders) were given the resources to buy health care for their clients through contracts negotiated with providers. Providers, mostly self-governing public hospitals, called NHS trusts, were given control over their budgets and the freedom to develop service packages attractive in the marketplace. Other changes from this 1989 NHS Review included initiatives to improve waiting times, reduction in size and reorganization of the NHS management tiers, the extension of medical audit, and improved management information systems and networks.

What can be said about the implication of this rapid period of change within the NHS for libraries? All the reviews mentioned the need for better management information, for better clinical research and audit information, for information on outcomes of clinical treatment, for better patient information, for better information about health needs. However, few of the reform documents specifically mentioned the fact that libraries can and should play a major role in gathering and disseminating this information. Traditionally they were seen only to serve the research and education needs of clinical staff. The NHS of the 1980s with its emphasis on managers, quality management and management information systems tended to equate information with data, not textual information, and data handling with computer units, not libraries. Librarians themselves, however, recognized the importance in the new 'managerial' NHS of setting standards and guidelines for NHS libraries and took it upon themselves to develop documents such as *Providing a district library service.*[8]

Of all the NHS changes, the emergence of the purchasing function has probably had the most impact on the library and information profession. Not only do purchasers require a whole range of information resources, from data to text to soft information, described collectively as purchasing 'intelligence', but purchasing intelligence officers also require a range of skills, some of which are not traditionally associated with librarians, such as the handling of numeric data. The result has been the development of new training programmes for health information professionals who wish to take on these posts, and also the emergence of a variety of models of purchasing intelligence units.[9, 10] Guidelines for purchasing intelligence units produced by the NHS

Management Executive were among the first NHS documents to explicitly recognize the role of libraries in supporting the purchasing function.

Several other key events occurred following the NHS Review. In 1991, the government released a health strategy, called *Health of the nation*[11] which set targets for improvement in key health areas, and a *Patients charter*[12] which guaranteed maximum waiting times, proper investigation of complaints and more information about local health services. The former resulted in increased demands on some libraries for information to support the interpretation of national targets for local areas, and the latter resulted in the creation of a new type of health information service – regional health information services, targeted at the general public.

Then, in 1992, the long promised *IM&T strategy* (information management and technology) was released, which was designed to support the business plans of the NHS Management Executive.[13]

The *IM&T strategy* should have had the most impact on libraries as it was formulating a national strategy for health information, including a national network for the dissemination and exchange of information. There has been some concern within the library community that the *IM&T strategy* overemphasized the need for the NHS's wide-area network to handle numerical and statistical information and ignored the importance of textual information resources.

1992 also saw the unveiling of the Department of Health's research and development (R&D) strategy, launched as the first attempt by any country to establish a coherent R&D infrastructure.[14] The R&D srategy was accompanied by an information systems strategy, a comprehensive programme of initiatives for disseminating R&D information to users and for establishing research based practice. This information strategy not only advocated better use of libraries but it also established three new information resources:

- the Projects Register System, a national register of NHS and DOH funded research;
- the UK Cochrane Centre, which prepares, collects and disseminates systematic reviews of randomized controlled trials (RCTs); and
- the NHS Reviews and Dissemination Centre in York, which commissions reviews of available research beyond the area of RCTs and disseminates the findings to NHS managers, clinicians and the general public.

All three R&D initiatives have produced new databases, all have involved libraries in their consultation phases and all plan to use libraries to disseminate their resources.

Since 1993, the NHS has been coping not only with the implementation of the reforms but also with the streamlining of the top tier of management brought about by the Functions and Manpower Review of the Management Executive. When an early consultation document suggested that the regional tier of the NHS would not need libraries, the Regional Librarians Group actively and successfully lobbied on behalf of these libraries.[15] This lobbying appears to have been effective as the final document contained the following commitment: 'ensure that information and research findings – the "knowledge base of health care" – are effectively transmitted via libraries and other means', and to allow regional offices to retain libraries to meet their own needs.[16]

In summary, the introduction of a more managerial culture into the NHS in the 1980s and the major reforms of the 1990s have placed new demands on health libraries. Whilst there are opportunities opening for libraries in the NHS, particularly in supporting the R&D programme, there is still inadequate funding for many libraries and for librarians training in the new roles; there are new competitors for these roles; there is still a lack of integration of text based information services with NHS information technology (IT) systems; and the level of duplication and fragmentation caused by lack of coordination between and within regions is still of major concern.

Changes to the education of health professionals
During the same period, there have also been major changes in higher education. The expansion which began with the new universities in the 1960s accelerated with the transformation of polytechnics into universities in the 1990s. This has resulted in increased student numbers, but also some serious financial constraints.[17] Yet the academic sector appears to be ahead of the health sector in the use of information networks and has one of the most advanced and comprehensive wide area networks, the Joint Academic Network (JANET) in the UK. Against this background, there have been fundamental changes in the education of all health professionals. Table 20.2 lists some of the changes at both undergraduate or pre-registration level and at postgraduate and post-registration level for nurses and doctors.

The major change in pre-registration training for nurses was due to a shift to more research based learning requiring self-study.[18] These changes in the Diploma in Nursing Studies curriculum required greater resources and, as a result, some nursing colleges merged and others were incorporated into institutions of higher education. Before the end of 1995, all nursing colleges will be incorporated into university departments and nursing libraries will be the responsibility of the academic libraries. These mergers are often complicated due to different expectations from the university and the colleges about the need for hospital based library services for nursing students who are located many miles away from the main university campus.

Table 20.2 Changes in education of health professionals , 1981–94

Specific Reform	Sector	Changes introduced
Project 2000 (1986)	Nursing – Pre-registration	Change in emphasis in pre-registration training from ward-based skills training to research-based self-directed learning; closer links with higher education
PREP (1990)	Nursing – Post-registration	Statutory requirement to provide evidence of continuing education through courses, study leave and other professional development activities
Medical Act (1983)	Medicine – Undergraduate	Relaxation of statutory require-ments imposed upon medical school curriculum in terms of preparing doctors to undertake any form of medical practice
GMC review (1993)	Medicine – undergraduate	Substantial reduction in burden of factual information in under graduate curriculum; emphasis on research-based learning and critical appraisal of evidence; introduction of systems drawing on wide range of technological resources
NHS Review (1989–90)	Medicine and dentistry – postgraduate and continuing	Protected PME budgets devolved to postgraduate deans to cover study leave, traineeships, post-graduate medical centres and libraries; regions allowed to apportion costs of multidiscip-linary libraries between professional groups or leave in medical budget

Post-registration nursing education also changed when new statutory requirements for post registration education and practice (PREP) were issued by the UKCC in 1990.[19] Again, the major impact of this change was to require more independent study and research based continuing education. Graduate nurses are entitled to have their continuing education needs met at the workplace, but not all hospital libraries are resourced to support them. The emergence of NHS educational consortia, with remits to purchase resources on behalf of NHS staff, may assist in ensuring that nurses' information needs are met by multidisciplinary libraries in NHS Trusts.

Undergraduate medical education has also undergone a shift away from an apprenticeship system which required students to memorize a large quantity of information so that they would graduate with enough knowledge and skill to practice any form of medicine, surgery and midwifery. In the 1970s and 1980s, several changes were introduced to relieve the burden on the undergraduate curriculum, such as the introduction of a pre-registration training year and a relaxation of the statutory requirements imposed upon the curriculum.[20] In 1993, the education committee of the General Medical Council (GMC) issued a new set of guidelines recommending research and technology based learning to reduce the emphasis on the uncritical acquisition of facts.[21] These recommendations are quite new and it is unclear what their impact will be on medical school libraries. However, experience in North America has shown that students in medical schools with a problem based learning curriculum are significantly more active users of library resources and require more user education and IT training than medical students in traditional schools.

The NHS Review also affected the training and education of NHS staff as pre-registration training of non-medical staff was devolved to regions and postgraduate medical education was devolved by regions to postgraduate deans to administer for traineeships, study leave and postgraduate medical centres and libraries.[22, 23] As many postgraduate centre libraries are multidisciplinary, regions have the option of apportioning the costs between professional groups or leaving all the money for libraries in the medical budget.[24] The involvement of deans in postgraduate medical centre funding has resulted in greater regional coordination and more attention to the importance of the role of regional librarians in managing regional library networks.[25]

Continuing medical education (CME) funding is handled differently from postgraduate medical education in that it remains within the NHS market and is arranged through purchaser–provider contracts. This does not appear to be working well because providers are not building the cost of CME into the cost of contracts and thus funds for library support of CME are not protected.[26]

In conclusion, the net impact of all these changes to education and training of health professionals, both within the NHS and within the higher education sector, is to place increased demands on all health libraries, not only for more print and electronic resources, but also for staff with skills in managing all types of resources and in teaching the end-user.

HEALTH LIBRARIES AND NETWORKS IN THE UK

There are nearly 1000 health libraries in the UK representing many different sectors and types. It is essential to have directories and guides to these resources and a standard reference work is the *Directory of medical and health care libraries in the United Kingdom and Republic of Ireland.*[27] In 1994, the British Library commissioned a report on special library statistics which covered NHS, medical school, medical research, professional association, royal society and pharmaceutical libraries.[28] Other sources of information include statistical data published by groups such as the Regional Librarians Group and the University Medical School Librarians Group, and descriptive reviews in books and journals.[29-32]

Table 20.3 attempts to classify the types of libraries listed in the *Directory*[27] by parent organizations such as hospitals, institutions of higher education, government departments, foundations and research institutes, professional societies, NHS commissioning agencies, pharmaceutical companies, and consumer organizations. The rest of this section offers brief descriptions of these types of library, with some examples and comments on how they have fared under the reforms.

Table 20.3 Health libraries by organization and type

	Total	Multidisciplinary	Medical	Nursing/PAMs	Other
Hospital	355	205	143	5	2
Nursing/PAMs college	104	17	0	86	1
Commissioning agency	21	0	0	0	21
University/higher education institute	96	45	28	8	15
Government	19	7	3	0	9
Research institute	34	2	23	0	9
Royal College/Society	25	3	12	2	8
Pharmaceutical company	23	3	0	0	20
Consumer health information service	20	0	0	0	20
Other	44	8	7	1	28
Total	741	290	216	102	133

Libraries in the health service

As Table 20.3 shows, the majority of health care libraries in the UK (nearly half the total libraries in the *Directory*) are part of a hospital or postgraduate medical centre attached to a hospital. Whilst these libraries are usually quite small, their numbers make them the most important collective information resource in the NHS. It has been estimated that current investment in NHS libraries is approximately £20 million per annum.[33]

In the past, library services were the responsibility of hospitals and were divided along rigid disciplinary lines, often with separate libraries for medical staff and other staff, resulting in unnecessary duplication of resources.[34] After the publication of *Providing a district library service* in 1985, attempts to help libraries share resources were largely coordinated at district level but there was still uneven provision of library service. In six regions, regional librarians were appointed to provide professional advice to libraries on staffing, training and use of technology, and to coordinate library resources in the region. Largely as a result of the regional librarians' efforts, the majority of NHS libraries became multidisciplinary, usually serving all clinical staff in the hospital in which they were based and often other health professionals employed in their district. Given the numbers of medical and non-medical direct care staff in the NHS (estimated at 550,000 in 1992),[35] this is a sizeable audience, many of whom have continuing and postgraduate information needs. Increasingly, these libraries are also serving the non-direct care staff such as managers and support staff. Extending limited resources to satisfy all client groups has proved to be a major problem for hospital libraries, and there is still great variation within regions in the resources made available for libraries, especially in those regions without full-time regional librarians.

As mentioned earlier, the 1990 reforms devolved the funding arrangements for most NHS libraries to postgraduate deans. Where postgraduate deans work closely with regional librarians on funding of libraries, there have been improvements such as mergers of libraries into viable units with professionally qualified staff, more consistent access to libraries for all disciplines, reduction in duplication of resources, etc. Where the deans have devolved library budgets to clinical tutors, or have made other arrangements, there has been a tendency to re-establish disciplinary barriers. The fact that many hospitals are now autonomous trusts and not part of a district infrastructure may also create barriers to library access. This makes the need for regional coordination even greater, but it has also put new pressures on the regional librarian by adding the role of purchaser of library services on behalf of regions, which they do through 'negotiating and monitoring contracts to ensure continuous improvement in the accessibility, quality and reliability of information services'.[36] Recently, the Regional Librarians Group issued a position paper calling for more co ordination and resource sharing at regional level and for leadership and policy direction at national level.[37]

Typical cooperative arrangements in NHS regional networks include interlibrary loan agreements, union lists and databases, study days, shared purchase of software, participation in electronic networks, etc. A similar type of network is AWHILES, the All Wales Health Information and Library Extension Service. It provides central support from the University of Wales

College of Medicine to postgraduate centres and hospital libraries in Wales.[38]

Schools of nursing libraries, many based in hospitals, used to be among the most numerous in the NHS. In 1978, there were 299 such libraries listed in the *Directory* but only 104 appear in the latest edition and it is expected that there will be none by the next edition. The decline in numbers is due to the mergers of colleges of nursing into higher education institutions. Some of the universities which have taken over the library services for nursing students have been located many miles from the site of nursing training. These geographic constraints and the general under-estimation of information resources required to support the new Diploma in Nursing Studies curriculum have led to many problems, including inadequate library service provision for both faculty and students.[39, 40]

Various studies have looked at the resourcing of nursing libraries due to both Project 2000 and to the revised continuing education requirements for nurses under the PREP system. They have concluded that there was a need for: standards specifically for nursing libraries and national monitoring of library provision against these standards; improved funding and greater support from national nursing bodies; and greater cooperation through better regional strategic planning of library and information services led by a regional librarian.[41, 42]

Several recent developments have addressed some of these concerns. The English National Board (ENB), which is responsible for the infrastructure required to support the continuing education of nurses, commissioned management guidelines for developing libraries and information services.[43] New models of commissioning library services for the nursing profession have also emerged, and it is likely that NHS educational consortia will in future 'purchase' library services on behalf of all NHS nurses. The impact on libraries of this change to continuing education of nurses is still being realized and some believe that it is more challenging than the impact of Project 2000.[44]

Other NHS information resources include the libraries and information units in the new commissioning agencies. Most of these are new to the health library community, although some have developed from former district health authority management libraries. Some of the new purchasing intelligence units have staff with enhanced information handling skills, particularly in the area of statistical data. There are less than 20 commissioning agency libraries/information units listed in the *Directory* but this is probably due to the fact that not all staff in these units are aware of the value of a listing in the *Directory*.

Not all forms of regional cooperation involve just NHS libraries. Health information plans (HIPs) were designed to improve forward planning of libraries through voluntary and constructive partnerships involving private, voluntary and public sector libraries and information services.[45] Whilst HIPs are emerging in several counties and regions, the best documented HIP is the Health Information Plan in the Northern Region, which is a partnership of many different health information providers. The aim of the HIP is that 'every person in the Northern region should have access to health and social care information resources through an integrated system of partnerships among all types of information provider'.[46]

Libraries in higher educational institutions

University medical schools hold some of the largest and most important library collections in the UK. There are over 30 medical schools in the United Kingdom and Ireland although, due to the rationalization of medical education resources and facilities in London, some independent medical schools are being incorporated into large multifaculty institutions.[47]

Many medical school libraries not only serve the needs of undergraduate students and faculties but also fulfil a key role in supporting continuing clinical training and health information provision for local NHS staff. For example, some have contracts to supply library services to clinical staff in local health authorities, most offer services to hospital medical staff and postgraduate researchers, and some have dual responsibility, such as the medical library at Queen's University in Belfast which also incorporates the library of the Department of Health and Social Services in Northern Ireland.[48] Funding for these NHS services may be as much as 60% of the total medical library budget.[49]

Medical school libraries are also increasingly taking over responsibility for students in other health disciplines such as nursing and the professions allied to medicine (PAMs) as their colleges are merged into higher education. However, some nursing and health college libraries are integrated into the university library system as faculty libraries. The *Directory* actually lists 96 libraries which are part of universities but only 31 of these are medical school libraries. The remainder are teaching and research libraries associated with faculties of nursing, allied health, veterinary medicine, pharmaceutical science, etc.

Funding of university libraries generally is a major concern and various studies have indicated that it is inadequate to meet current information support needs of education and research.[50, 51] Recently, the Joint Funding Councils commissioned the first major review of libraries in the higher education sector since 1967.[52] Led by Professor Sir Brian Follett, the review group noted several disturbing trends: the decline of spending on libraries as a percentage of total institutional expenditure, the decline in library spending per capita; and the decline in book purchases per capita. The group expressed concern over the implications for libraries of the recent growth in student numbers, the role of libraries in supporting research, the disproportionate increase in the cost of print resources, and the failure to take advantage of new opportunities with developments in information technology. The Follett review group issued 45 recommendations, including the development of information strategies in each institution, pump-priming for library cooperation, library provision funded through the block-grant process, recurrent non-formula funding for specialized collections provided that free access is given to bona fide researchers, and funding for a variety of electronic information transfer projects. The Follett review concluded that there needed to be a 'sea-change' in the way institutions plan and provide for information needs of those working within them and that institutions must take urgent action to address serious shortfalls in library and information resources. It is hoped that the initiatives planned under the Follett review will address some of the problems facing medical, nursing and other academic health libraries.

Other health libraries

There is no national library of medicine in the UK. Instead there is a group of national and quasi-national libraries and information services which collectively offer a national health information resource equal to that of any other nation. The principal libraries are the British Library, which includes health materials in its collections and information services, the Department of Health (DoH) Library, which provides services to employees of the DoH in England, and several independent libraries from the Royal Colleges and societies, foundations and charities, research institutes and quangos. These will only be discussed briefly but comprehensive listings of these libraries are available.[53-55]

The British Library is a national centre for reference, study and bibliographical and other information services to support institutions of education and learning, and libraries and information centres in industry.[56] Of major relevance to health libraries is the British Library Document Supply Centre (BLDSC) which is located in Boston Spa, West Yorkshire. BLDSC is devoted to the supply of documents to other libraries, both nationally and internationally, and it is estimated that biomedical requests account for over 40% of the usage made of its collection of over 60,000 journals. Located within BLDSC is the Medical Information Centre which indexes British journals for *MEDLINE* and produces CATS, a series of current awareness services covering complementary medicine and allied health subjects. A London based section of the British Library, the Science Reference and Information Service (SRIS), has one of the largest public access life science and medical collections in the UK.

The DoH Library serves staff working for the DoH and the NHS Executive in both London and Leeds. The Library's catalogue is available online through

Datastar as *DHSS-Data* and is considered to be the major UK resource covering the management of health care. As a result of the reorganization of the regional health authorities into regional offices of the NHS Executive, the DoH Library will have closer ties with these regional office libraries. The DoH Library also works closely with two quasi-national health care management libraries based in the King's Fund, a health charity, and in the Nuffield Institute for Health, part of the University of Leeds. Both of these libraries include large collections of grey literature, offer public enquiry services, produce their own databases, and act as World Health Organization (WHO) Documentation Centres. The King's Fund also manages the SHARE network, a national information service on health and race, and the Nuffield Institute manages three information services, including the UK Clearinghouse for the Assessment of Information on Health Outcomes, the Community Care Innovative Practices Project and the European Clearinghouse for Health Service Reforms.

These three libraries operate their own network – the Healthcare Management Information Consortium (HMIC). The first of its kind in the UK, it has been established to promote the coordination and development of health care management library and information services. In particular, HMIC's objectives are to ensure the comprehensive coverage of all non-clinical subjects relevant to the NHS between the three constitutent information centres, to facilitate the most efficient use of information resources within these centres, and to encourage the development of national health care information strategy, which is responsive to local and regional information needs. Specific projects include shared collection analysis and development, setting of standards for exchange of bibliographic records, and agreed protocols for thesaurus development.[57]

There are over 20 professional association and over 40 other medical research libraries in the UK situated in the Royal Societies, the Royal Colleges, the Postgraduate Medical Institutes, etc. Some of the major resources include the following.

The British Medical Association (BMA) Library is a private library providing research facilities, enquiry and document delivery services and dial-up access to Medline for over 80,000 individual members of the BMA. The BMA also offers an institutional membership service which provides, among other services, a document delivery service for other health libraries.

The Royal Society of Medicine Library in London is one of the largest postgraduate medical collections in the world outside North America, with over 600,000 volumes and over 2000 current journal titles. It is the principal back-up collection for the British Library Document Supply Centre.

The Royal College of Nursing Library is the largest nursing library in

Europe and serves a large client group of student and graduate nurses in the UK and overseas. Its extensive holdings include a special collection of nursing research theses.

Several of the Royal College libraries have extensive historical collections, such as the Royal College of Physicians and the Royal College of Gynaecologists and Obstetricians. However, the finest historical medical library in the UK is the Wellcome Institute for the History of Medicine, which has 300,000 volumes including many manuscripts and incunabula.

Many of these independent libraries are situated in London and have formed a discussion group which meets informally once or twice a year. This is the Independent London Librarians Group whose members are primarily the Royal College libraries. It is difficult to say how the NHS reforms and educational changes have affected this group, but it is certainly true that they are no different to other health libraries in terms of financial pressures brought about by increased journal and book prices. Those open to the public are also experiencing pressure due to increased use from NHS staff and students unable to satisfy their information needs in their own libraries.

Pharmaceutical libraries are another group of research libraries with significant collections and resources, but which generally operate quite independently of other health sector libraries due to the proprietary nature of the business. Whilst these large companies fund a sizeable proportion of clinical research done in universities and research institutes, their libraries are usually reserved for their own research and management staff. There are two types of information units in pharmaceutical companies: research libraries which support the internal R&D and marketing needs, and medical information services which respond to internal and external enquiries about the drugs manufactured by that company.

There is a growing network of consumer health information services, some of which are provided by public libraries such as the Westminster City Libraries and Hertfordshire Arts and Libraries, by the regional health information services established under the terms of the Patients Charter, by hospital libraries such as the Health Information Services at the Lister Hospital in Stevenage, by independent trusts such as Help for Health in Winchester, and by national charities such as the Aids Helpline or by local community health councils (CHCs) and advice bureaux.

Finally, there is also a large number of libraries which defy classification into these major types, but include medical reference libraries in the public library system such as Westminster Libraries' Health Information Library, health promotion libraries in quangos such as the Health Education Authority, libraries in the Poisons Units, and many others.

LOOKING FORWARD

As mentioned in the first section of this chapter, the policy changes and reforms in health and higher education have undoubtedly put pressure on libraries for new resources and services. Until recently, these pressures were not recognized by senior officials in either sector. However, concerted lobbying by health librarians, in many different types of health libraries, has finally brought attention to their concerns.

In 1992 and 1993, two seminars were organized by a consortium which included the British Library, the Department of Health, the Regional Librarians Group and representatives from other health library constituencies such as consumer health information services, academic libraries, the independent libraries, etc.[58, 59] These seminars were designed to raise awareness amongst senior health managers, researchers and educators of the need for better management of the country's health information resources and of the important contribution which libraries could make to this process. With the support of the Chair of both seminars, Baroness Cumberlege, the Parliamentary Under-Secretary of State for Health (Lords), senior NHS officials made a commitment to look at what could be done at national and at local level to improve the quality of and access to the knowledge base.

Two important developments have happened as a result of these seminars. First, the Department of Health has appointed an NHS Library Adviser to advise the NHS Executive on a national policy to ensure effective coordination of health care information provision and dissemination of the knowledge base, and to devise a national library and information strategy for health care. Second, the success of the group organizing the Cumberlege seminars highlighted the value of a single voice speaking for the health library community. The Library and Information Cooperation Council (LINC) for the UK, asked this group to propose the formation of a Health Panel whose members would include all the health library professional associations and networks. In future, the LINC Health Panel will represent the interests of the health library community to local and central government and can thus ensure that the library and information implications of major health policy changes will be addressed.

REFERENCES

1   Royal Commission on the NHS, *Report*, Cmnd 7615, London, HMSO, 1979. 2 National Health Service Management Inquiry Team, *NHS management inquiry*, London, Department of Health and Social Security, 1983.
3   Department of Health and Social Security, *Promoting better health: the government's programme for improving primary healthcare*, Cm 249, London, HMSO, 1987.
4   Department of Health and Social Security, *Caring for people: community care in the*

next decade and beyond, Cmnd 849, London, HMSO, 1989.

5 Department of Health and Social Security, *Health and Medicines Act*, London, HMSO, 1988.

6 Steering Group on Health Services Information, *First report to the Secretary of State*, London, HMSO, 1982.

7 Department of Health, *Working for patients*, Cm 555, London, HMSO, 1989.

8 *Providing a district library service*, London, King's Fund, 1985.

9 Hepworth, J., 'Staffing intelligence services', *Health libraries review*, **9**, 1993, 52–61.

10 Smith, C., 'Purchasing intelligence: the role of the library', *Health libraries review*, **9**, 1992, 97–100.

11 Department of Health, *Health of the nation*, Cmnd 1986, London, HMSO, 1992.

12 Department of Health, *The patient's charter*, London, HMSO, 1991.

13 National Health Service Management Executive, Information Management Group, *IM&T strategy: an overview*, London, Department of Health, 1992.

14 Department of Health, *Research for health: a research and development strategy for the NHS*, London, DOH, 1993.

15 NHS Regional Librarians Group, *Functions and manpower review 1993–94. Management of library services in the proposed new structure. NHS Regional Librarians Group evidence*, January 1994.

16 National Health Service Executive, *Managing the new NHS: functions and responsibilities in the new NHS*, London: NHS Executive, 1994.

17 Edwards, C., Day, J. M. and Walton, G., 'Key areas in the management of change in higher education libraries in the 1990's: relevance of the IMPEL project', *British journal of academic librarianship*, **8** (3), 1993, 139–77.

18 United Kingdom Central Council for Nursing, Midwifery and Health Visiting, *Project 2000: a new preparation for practice*, London, UKCC, 1986.

19 United Kingdom Central Council for Nursing, Midwifery and Health Visiting (UKCC), *The report of the post-registration education and practice project*, London, UKCC, 1990.

20 Department of Health and Social Security, *The Medical Act*, London, HMSO, 1983.

21 General Medical Council (GMC), Education Committee, *Tomorrow's doctors: recommendations on undergraduate medical education issued by the education committee of the General Medical Council in pursuance of section 5 of the Medical Act 1983*, London, GMC, 1993.

22 Department of Health, *Working for patients: working paper 10*, London, HMSO, 1989.

23 National Health Service Management Executive, *Postgraduate and continuing medical and dental education*, EL(90) 179, 12 September 1990.

24 Bayley, T.J., 'Libraries, postgraduate medical education, and the management of change', *Health libraries review*, **10**, 1993, 3–9.

25 Morgan, P., 'Editorial – health libraries under review – are we in the picture', *Health libraries review*, **8**, 1991, 205–9.

26 Easmon, C., 'Postgraduate and continuing medical education in North West Thames', *Medical library bulletin of the Thames Regions*, **100**, 1994, 6–9.

27   Wright, D. (ed.), *Directory of medical and health care libraries in the United Kingdom and Republic of Ireland*, 9th edn, London, Library Association, 1994.

28   Berridge, P. J. and Sumsion, J., *UK special library statistics: a consultation report on research commissioned by British Library Research and Development Department*, Loughborough, LISU, 1994.

29   Holdsworth, J., *The provision of health care information in the U.K.: a summary report*, BLR no. 98, London, BLRDD, 1991.

30   MacDougall, J. and Brittain, J. M., *Use of information in the NHS*, London, BLRDD, 1992.

31   Holdsworth, J., 'Health science libraries', in *British librarianship and information work, 1986–1990*, (Bromley, D. and Allott, A. (eds.)), London, Library Association, 1992.

32   Morton, L. T. and Godbolt, S., 'Medical libraries and their use', in *Information sources in the medical sciences*, 4th edn, London, Bowker-Saur, 1992.

33   NHS Regional Librarians Group, op. cit.

34   Ibid.

35   *NHSME news*, (79), 11 March 1994.

36   Carmel, M., *Library services in the internal market: a policy discussion document*, Guildford, South West Thames Regional Library Service, 1991.

37   NHS Regional Librarians Group, op. cit.

38   Lancaster, J., personal communication, 1994.

39   Snell, J., 'Brought to book', *Nursing times*, 88 (7), 1992, 26–31.

40   Thompson, C. and Bullimore, A., 'The implications of Project 2000 for nursing libraries', *Health libraries review*, 7, 1990, 125–35.

41   Childs, S., 'A survey of nursing libraries in the Northern region', *Health libraries review*, 11, 1994, 3–28.

42   Capital Planning Information (CPI), *Library and information services to support Project 2000; NURLIS phase 1: a report to the Royal College of Nursing and the British Library*, Stamford:CPI, 1992.

43   Ashcroft, M., *Provision of library and information services to nursing professionals; NURLIS phase II; management guidelines*, London, English National Board for Nursing, Midwifery and Health Visiting, 1993.

44   Crane, S. and Urquhart, C., 'Preparing for PREP: The impact of change in continuing education for nurses on library provision of journals and current awareness services: a case study', *Health libraries review*, 11, 1994, 29–38.

45   Office of Arts and Libraries, Library and Information Services Council, *The future development of libraries and information services: progress through planning and partnership*, London, HMSO, 1986.

46   Childs, S., *Health information in the north*, Health Information series no. 7, Newcastle upon Tyne, Information North, 1993.

47   Department of Health, *Report of the enquiry into London's health service, medical education and research*, London, HMSO, 1992.

48   Crawford, D. S., 'Regional health library provision in Northern Ireland', *Bulletin of the Medical Library Association*, 78 (4), 1990, 364–9.

49 Holdsworth, 1992, op. cit.
50 Walton, G., Bissessur, R. and Cooper, R., 'Survey of library and information use by health-care students', *Health libraries review*, **10**, 1993, 57–74.
51 Holdsworth, 1992, op. cit.
52 Follett, B. (ed.), Joint Funding Council's Libraries Review Group, *A report for HECFE, SHEFC, HEFCW and DENI*, Bristol, Higher Education Funding Council for England, 1993.
53 Morton and Godbolt, op. cit.
54 Tabor, R., 'Biomedical libraries and information services in Great Britain', *Health libraries review*, **3**, 1986,21–7.
55 Association of Scottish Health Librarians, *Directory of health information resources in Scotland*, Edinburgh, Motherwell/ASHSL/Scottish Library Association, 1993.
56 *Strategic objective for the year 2000*, London, The British Library, 1993.
57 Haines, M. P. J., 'Developing HMIC: the Healthcare Management Information Consortium', *Library management*, **14** (3), 1993, 22–7.
58 Feeney, M. (ed.), *Healthcare information in the UK. Report of a Seminar held on 1st July 1992 at the King's Fund Centre, London*, BLRDD Report 6089, London, The British Library, 1992.
59 Feeney, M. (ed.), *Managing the knowledge base of healthcare: report of a seminar held on 22nd October 1993 at the King's Fund Centre, London*, BLRDD Report 6133, London, The British Library, 1994.

21 Health informatics: a new dimension for health care librarians

❖ *Michael Carmel*

The fundamental aims of informatics and library services are identical: to ensure that providers of health care have access to reliable, relevant and up-to-date information, enabling them to enhance the quality of care. This chapter explores some of the common ground between the two and the possible advantages of shared understanding and joint working, and draws some conclusions for librarians about the opportunities presented.

Because this is new territory for most librarians, the chapter is largely descriptive. It draws heavily on American examples because it is in the USA, and particularly in the Integrated Advanced Information Management System (IAIMS) programme of the National Library of Medicine (NLM) that these issues have been most effectively raised, but the lessons to be learned are of universal application.

'THE VIRTUAL LIBRARY'

Harley introduced the concept of 'the virtual library' in 1980.[1] Its essence lies in the fact that it provides a complete and seamless library service in a manner which is transparent to the user. To its providers, it may be a complex interaction of people, organizations and paper-based systems; computers, software, databases and networks; referrals, lendings and borrowings. To the users it is simply their library, and a gateway into the limitless world of knowledge.

Harley's concept owes nothing to later hyperbole about 'virtual reality'. The virtual library need not, in theory, be electronic at all. It is not so much a replacement for library services as they currently exist, as the fulfilment of their aspirations.

In this sense, George Gould's vision, enunciated almost 100 years ago and rediscovered by Lois Ann Colaianni[2] is an excellent definition of the virtual library:

> I look forward to such an organization of the literary records of medicine that a puzzled worker in any part of the civilized world shall in an hour be able to gain a knowledge pertaining to a subject of the experience of any other man in the world.

But of course it is the availability of electronic tools for information handling that has focused attention on the realistic feasibility of a virtual library service, virtually anywhere.

Librarians exploit computer systems to provide electronic access to the library and open access to literature searching facilities; to create and deliver specialist databases; to make available electronic books and hypertext learning systems; to receive and deliver document images; and to offer access to other 'libraries'. They are also engaged in helping their users to come to terms with the technology.

MEDICAL INFORMATICS
This working definition is offered by the NLM in its *Long range plan*:[3]

> Medical Informatics attempts to provide the theoretical and scientific basis for the application of computer and automated information systems to bio-medicine and health affairs. . . . (It) is oriented toward the invention and dissemination of powerful information management tools. These include frameworks for organizing and encoding medical knowledge, methods for acquiring and representing judgmental knowledge based on experience, computer networks to permit efficient communications among health personnel, and systems to provide customized advice . . .

It goes on to define six 'fundamentally important issues and methodologies': cognitive processes; medical decision making; the human–machine interface; knowledge representation; knowledge acquisition; and information storage and retrieval.

Greenes and Shortliffe[4] define medical informatics (MI) more broadly as 'the field that concerns itself with the cognitive, information processing and communication tasks of medical practice, education and research, including the information science and the technology to support these tasks'.

Of the many areas of development work in informatics, the three which attract most current interest are: the electronic patient record (EPR); the storage, retrieval and transfer of images; and the development of decision support systems (DSS) for clinicians.

The electronic patient record (EPR)
The potential clinical advantages of a well structured, accurate, accessible and shareable health record for each individual user of the health care services are too obvious to need spelling out.[5] They were spotted long ago, and if it were easy it would have been done:

> . . . the next generation of patient care systems . . . will go a long way

towards automating all patient care functions with a fully automatic patient record available for all patients . . . but today the health care industry is faced with information systems that are far from this vision. . . . we must change our approach . . . Past difficulties have resulted from oversimplification and improper definition of user requirements.[6]

Large-scale government-funded research programmes are under way in the European Union under the Advanced Informatics in Medicine programme,[7] within the UK as part of the NHS Information Management and Technology Strategy,[8] and in the USA.[9] It has to be admitted that these programmes are motivated as much by the need for reliable exchange of information between purchasers and providers as they are about clinical quality, but for the moment, at least, the two are seen as mutually reinforcing.

There are many synonyms for the electronic patient record:

computerized		
computer-based	patient	database
automated	health	view
electronic	medical	record
virtual		
online		

as well as acronyms such as CMR, CBMR EMR, OMR and EPR.

In terms of applications and use, probably the most successful EPR systems to date are in Europe, among general practitioners in The Netherlands[10] and the United Kingdom.[11] It has to be said, however, that these are comparatively simple systems involving clear ownership, few users, restricted sources of data, and relatively easily identified patients. Attempts to develop comprehensive hospital record systems reveal ever greater levels of complexity and ambiguity in all these areas. Two effective and pragmatic systems are MARS at Pittsburgh and OMR at Boston.

The Medical Archive Retrieval System (MARS),[12] system developed at the University of Pittsburgh, exhibits many of the features of a clinical database moving cautiously towards the notion of a full EPR. It is a very large database into which is transferred all the clinically relevant information from university hospitals, which is already available in electronic form. This includes not only laboratory data (updated every 15 minutes) but also all word-processed reports such as X-ray reports, histories and discharge summaries (updated daily). The database is networked to all wards and departments. An important feature is that each user can have predetermined formats for viewing the data relevant to their usual needs. *MEDLINE* is also available on MARS, searchable through the same software, and there are plans to integrate Pittsburgh's own

Decision Support System, QMR.

The Outpatient Medical Record (OMR) database developed at Beth Israel Hospital, Boston, has been equally pragmatic.[13] It is not as comprehensive as MARS but is in some respects closer to a true EPR. One important feature is the incorporation of a (voluntary) 'problem list' feature, encouraging direct input by clinicians. Dr Safran has commented that the development team were taken by surprise at the high level of use of this feature, and the tendency of clinicians to enter substantial amounts of information. It is a 'live' system used during consultations.

It will be quickly seen from these two examples, among many, that the issues around the creation of an effective shared clinical record require a combination of theoretical clarity, detailed analysis and pragmatism, which can only come with team effort. The comparison also demonstrates that even the definition of a patient record is problematic, or as the MARS team say 'the patient record is in the eye of the beholder'.

Managing images

Modern medicine has come to depend on the image as the key component for teaching, research and clinical practice. . . . Whether we are talking about pathology teaching slides, fluorescent markers in research, or CT scans in clinical practice, the viewing, study and analysis of images has become an all-pervasive part of medicine. Thus in any attempt to improve information management in medicine, the transport and control of image data must be of prime concern.[14]

Images have become both an exciting and a confusing field of work, as technology has created ever more effective means of looking at, and into, the human body. Many of these use digital computers in the image creation or enhancement process, suggesting that computerized management should be feasible. It has to be remembered, however, that the primary purpose of most images is for immediate clinical use – to take a look – and that optimizing that function will always take precedence over management considerations.

Computerization of image management does seem to offer advantages:

- more efficient organization and retrieval
- accessibility at the time of need by use of the network
- integration of information from different visual sources
- integration with textual and numeric information
- security and conservation
- creation of three-dimensional browsers, analysis tools and multimedia teaching tools.

At the same time there are many gritty problems to be solved along the way, not least those of storage and network capacity and interface design, where the ambitions of the developers always seem able to outrun the currently affordable technology.

Decision support systems

It is over 30 years since the earliest diagnostic 'expert systems' were devised, and 20 years since publicly available systems were first announced. Yet there are few, if any, such systems in widespread clinical use today, despite enormous progress in the design of the underlying knowledge bases, the algorithms and the user interfaces.

The use of the term 'expert system' for medical applications of so-called 'artificial intelligence' is unfortunate. It has tended to generate both hopes and fears which are quite unrealistic, and to lead to unreasonable disappointment (or relief) when the benefits, although real, are found to be limited.

This danger has been recognized within the informatics community, as by Miller and Masarie[15] in a paper entitled 'The demise of the "Greek Oracle" model for medical diagnostic systems'. They charge earlier developers, including themselves, with incorporating 'an ambitious model for diagnostic decision support that contributed to the current lack of widespread acceptance of diagnostic expert systems'.

These systems no longer attempt to emulate the decision making skills of an expert, nor do they attempt to provide definitive answers. They offer either: timely reminders for busy clinicians who may have overlooked an important fact or deadline (alerting systems); or a method for interrogating a knowledge base to retrieve the likely or possible solutions to a given problem (usually diagnostic), ranked by probability. Developers have switched from trying to beat the human diagnostician on his own ground, and are using the specific advantage of the computer – that it never forgets.

THE COMMON GROUND

Librarians and informaticians share a common purpose of delivering accurate and up-to-date information to the clinical practitioner at the time when it is needed. From this arise inevitably a whole range of shared issues.

Quality of information

High among these is the questionable quality of much of the information in the literature, in knowledge bases, and even in clinical guidelines. This is even more of a problem to practitioners than to scientists, given their need for quick and authoritative answers. Under the flag of 'evidence based health care'[16] this has become a major issue in every country, among providers, purchasers, educators and consumers of health care, but inevitably it belongs in a rather special way to those developing and managing services designed to deliver information to practitioners who will be applying it to individual patients.

Users
Health care practitioners are often perceived as reluctant users of information systems of all kinds. Whether this is fair, or reflects poor system design, is a moot point. But in either case, users need encouragement and help to define their needs, which are themselves constantly changing. Librarians have become rather good at this, and in recent years have also become better at other aspects of marketing, such as winning trust, promotion of services, and training end-users in existing systems. It could be argued that we have both much to teach and to learn from informatics specialists in these areas.

Infrastructure
At the infrastructure level there are shared issues of network capacity (especially for image management and transmission), connectivity and architecture, and software and operating system compatibility, especially where investment in existing systems cannot be written off. It is perhaps surprising that as the capacity and quality of hardware on every front (storage, processing, networking) goes on rising, and costs falling, information systems nevertheless continue to come up against capacity and system constraints.

Still more important is the need for common interfaces and workstations which will simplify the procedures for the user without undermining functionality.

> It has become apparent that for the future systems to be useful in the consultation they have to be one step ahead of the clinician and present clinically relevant information and decision support at different stages in the consultation process (i.e. differential diagnosis, producing a list or evaluating hypotheses; selecting a course of action; managing continuing problems; and anticipatory care). This requires an effective interface, a knowledge base, decision support software and management guidelines all packaged into a patient orientated workstation.[11]

Language
Language is often a major hidden barrier to effective access to information. We need more than one standardized language, because each is based on different usages and a different frame of reference. The core users of each language often see their own as general, or at least generalizable, and cannot see the need for other frameworks. This has been a viewpoint expressed at various

times by supporters of ICD-10 (epidemiology), SNOMED (pathology), MeSH (clinical research) and Read codes (clinical practice).

We also need a common language system for all aspects of health care, but one which will not damage the integrity of the many special purpose nomenclatures and thesauri already in use. The NLM is making a major contribution to a solution by its term-mapping Unified Medical Language System (UMLS). In Europe, the GALEN project is attempting a multilingual equivalent.

Librarians tend to have a very pragmatic approach to thesaurus construction, looking for something that works well enough for its purpose without undue complexity. We also like, pragmatically, to combine natural langauge and controlled thesauri in a complementary way. This will not work for every clinical application, some of which require extreme accuracy, but there is undoubtedly scope for the pragmatic approach in many informatics applications, and for a more analytical and structured input to library systems.

There is therefore scope at least for joint working and a sharing of skills and perspective between library services and informatics departments. The next section, however, looks at a brave attempt to go much further than this and develop totally integrated systems.

INTEGRATED ADVANCED INFORMATION MANAGEMENT SYSTEMS (IAIMS)

IAIMS is a programme of the National Library of Medicine which has long been encouraging designers to adopt an integrated approach to information systems. It had its origins in a report by 1982 Matheson and Cooper[17] and a 1984 Symposium sponsored by the National Library of Medicine.[18]

IAIMS encourages institutions to integrate all clinical and academic information to the benefit of patient care, research, education and administration. Matheson[19] stresses that 'The crucial, indeed pivotal, concept is Integration . . . (which) at the information level means relating information from one source to another'. Seventeen institutions have received grants, including many outstanding centres of medical informatics research.

The ideal of a fully integrated system still lies in the future. The great success of the IAIMS program has been not in solving one 'grand challenge' but in mapping the many smaller but gritty challenges on the road to integration, and in solving at least some of them.

One of the keys to its success has been the involvement of clinicians, librarians and information technology specialists working together on shared problems of information management.

IAIMS is a highly successful programme, even though it seems not to have achieved its early rather simplistic aims. Certainly there is no single centre or product to which one can point and say 'There is IAIMS, working'. IAIMS can be judged successful in that it has:

(a) significantly influenced the culture of the institutions involved and their corporate attitudes to sharing of information, resources and skills;

(b) begun to change the cultures of the main professional groups involved, breaking down tribal barriers;

(c) begun to create a new breed of multiskilled professional, with some level of 'mix and match' training at a high level (MSc, PhD) for doctors, librarians and computer specialists;

(d) mapped the main problems of integration in detail, and stimulated work on some of the solutions and products required;

(e) identified the critical success factors in integration;

(f) created a sufficient range of specific products and services to act as exemplars for future work.

The next great challenge for IAIMS will be to find ways to disseminate the attitudes knowledge and skills that have been acquired or developed in a small number of centres.

The process is as important as the product. It will not therefore be possible for other centres to easily 'buy-in' to the benefits of IAIMS. This applies even more to other countries and cultures, who will have to go through their own learning and development process.

LESSONS FOR LIBRARIANS
The development of libraries and informatics over the past 20 years shows a great deal of common ground and shared interests, not only in technology, where the same facilities are critical to both, but even more in areas related to the quality of information – its accessibility, interaction with users, including marketing and training, organizational issues, and economic issues.

There is little interaction between the two outside North America. The interaction which exists in the USA has proved extremely lively and productive for both sides. Interaction is nevertheless hard work for both sides, and requires constant effort and goodwill. Interaction is still far from universal, even in the USA and where successful is almost invariably the result of direct and conscious action by the NLM and its many library and informatics development programmes. IAIMS is at the heart of this process.

Other countries would benefit from a research programme adapting the IAIMS principles to their own patterns of health care, research and teaching. The main missing element in the UK and in Europe is a strong leadership focus equivalent to the NLM. We should indeed try to develop such a focus.

In the meantime, many opportunities are arising for day-to-day cooperation at the grass roots level wherever clinicians, information technologists and librarians are interested enough and enterprising enough to be prepared to work together for common goals.

FURTHER INFORMATION

Health informatics is a fast moving field of research and practice. One of the best ways of tracking developments is through the Y*earbook of medical informatics*,[20] which reproduces each year key papers from the literature. The British Medical Association Library runs an invaluable Medical Informatics Information Service.[21]

ACKNOWLEDGEMENT

The author would like to thank the Fulbright Commission, the British Library R&D Directorate, the Cleveland Health Sciences Library and his employers for facilitating the substantial study on which this chapter is based.

REFERENCES

1   Harley, A. J., 'Towards the virtual library', in *The nationwide provision and use of information – report of the proceedings of the Joint Conference of The Library Association, Aslib and the Institute of Information Scientists 15–19 Sept 1980*, Library Association, 1981.

2   Colaianni, L. A., 'That vision thing' (Janet Doe Lecture), *Bulletin of the Medical Library Association*, **80** (1) Jan 1992.

3   National Library of Medicine, USA, *Long range plan*, 1987. The full report is in seven parts. Besides the Plan itself and the Executive Summary there are five panel reports:
    Building and organizing the library's collection
    Locating and gaining access to medical and scientific literature
    Obtaining factual information from databases
    Medical informatics
    Assisting health professions education through information technology

4   Greenes, R. A. and Shortliffe, E. H., 'Medical Informatics: an emerging academic discipline and institutional priority', *JAMA*, **263** (8), 23 Feb 1990, 1114–20.

5   Weed, L., *Knowledge compiling*, New York, Springer-Verlag, 1991. ISBN 0 38797 537 3.

6   Dorenfest, S. I., 'History, benefits, past problems and future directions in efforts to computerise the patient record' (abstract of paper) American Medical Informatics Association, 1993 Spring Congress; St Louis, 1993, 56.

7   Rector, A. L., Nowlan, W. A. and Kay, S., 'Foundations for an electronic medical record', *Methods of information in medicine*, **30**, 1990, 179–86.

8   NHS Management Executive, Information Management Group, *An information management and technology strategy for the NHS in England. Handbook for IM&T specialists*, London, HMSO, 1992. ISBN 1 85839 019 2.

9   Institute of Medicine, *The computer-based patient record: an essential technology for health care*, Washington DC, National Academy Press, 1991.

10 Van der Lei, J., 'The use of computer based patient records by Dutch general practitioners', (abstract of paper), American Medical Informatics Association, 1993 Spring Congress; St Louis, 1993, 55.

11 Purves, I., 'Implications for family practice record systems in the USA: Lessons from the United Kingdom' (abstract of paper), American Medical Informatics Association, 1993, Spring Congress, St Louis, 1993, 54.

12 Yount, R.J., Vries, J. K. and Councill, C. D., 'The Medical Archival System: an information retrieval system based on distributed parallel processing', *Information process management*, **27** (4), 1991, 379–89.

13 Safran, C. *et al.*, 'Outpatient medical records for a teaching hospital: beginning the physician computer dialogue', in American Medical Informatics Association, *Fifteenth annual symposium on computer applications in medical care (SCAMC) proceedings*, New York, McGraw-Hill, 1992, 114–18.

14 Eaton, E. K. (Principal Investigator), *IAIMS grant application on behalf of Tufts University*, unpublished.

15 Miller, R. and Masarie, F. E., 'The demise of the "Greek Oracle" model for medical diagnostic systems', *Methods of information in medicine*, **29**, 1990, 1–2.

16 'Theme issue on evidence based practice', *Health libraries review*, **11** (4), Dec 1994.

17 Matheson, N. W. and Cooper, J. A. D., 'Academic information in the academic health sciences centre: roles for the library in information management', *Journal of medical education*, **57** (10), Oct 1982, Part 2 (whole part).

18 National Library of Medicine, USA, *Planning for integrated academic information management systems. Proceedings of a symposium*, Bethesda, Maryland, NLM, 1985.

19 Matheson, N. W., 'Symposium on integrated academic information system (IAIMS) model development', *Bulletin of the Medical Library Association*, **76** (3), July 1988, 221–67 (descriptions of six projects).

20 *Yearbook of medical informatics 1992– . Advances in an interdisciplinary science*, Stuttgart, Schlattauer Verlagsgesellschaft, 1992 (comprises selected reprints of journal articles).

21 The Medical Informatics Information Service, The Library, British Medical Association, BMA House, Tavistock Square, London WC1H 9JR. Tel. 0171 383 6452.

22 Professional associations for librarians in the health sector

❖ *Margaret Haines and Judith Palmer*

Health care librarians are often the only information professional in their organization. This can mean that their professional development needs are not well supported by in-house education services. Fortunately, there are many library and information professional bodies which offer this support to health librarians. Most professional associations, especially those operating at national or international level, offer a range of services to members. These include publications such as journals, newsletters and directories, annual meetings and conferences, continuing education courses and other training events. Some also offer career and recruitment services, scholarships and research grants, and consultancy services.

Membership of professional associations can be personal or institutional. Some professional associations allow both types of membership but with different rights and benefits. Some associations will restrict their membership, e.g. to *ex officio*. Also, associations may vary in scope, i.e. their remit may be certain subjects or they may reflect the views of librarians working in one particular sector.

An excellent source of information about professional bodies in the UK is Peter Dale's *Directory of library and information organizations in the United Kingdom*, which gives a detailed description of over 200 professional bodies, including geographical scope, contact addresses, membership criteria, activities and publications, etc.[1] Whilst it is not confined to the health care sector, it does include descriptions of many health related special interest groups of larger associations. A comprehensive listing of health sector associations is also available in *MHWLG newsletter*.[2] Some of the professional associations open to health librarians or libraries in the UK are described below.

NATIONAL GROUPS

The Library Association (LA) is one of three major information professional bodies in the UK, the other two being the Institute of Information Scientists (IIS) and the Association for Information Management (Aslib). The Library Association is the British professional association for the regulation of the profession of librarianship.[3] The LA represents over 25,000 people working in all sectors of the profession and acts as a single voice for the profession in dealing with central and local government. It has 12 branches and 23 special interest groups including the Health Libraries Group (HLG). HLG unites over 2000 LA members working in the health and welfare sector and provides opportunities for discussion and exchanges of views on issues relevant to these sectors.[4] HLG has three sub-groups: Libraries for Nursing (LfN); IFM Healthcare (IFM); and the Community Care Network (CCN). The sub-groups also have their own elected officers and run their own meetings and continuing education events. LfN provides a communication and education network for all interested in the provision of library and information services to midwives, nurses, health visitors and community nurses, and makes representation to professional nursing and library bodies and organizations. IFM's members include librarians and intelligence officers working in the NHS to serve the information needs of managers. The objective of this sub-group is to facilitate the flow of relevant, timely and accurate information between providers and users in the management of health care. CCN has only recently formed from a merger of two former sub-groups: the Reading Therapy Sub-group and the Domiciliary Services Sub-group. Again, it is focusing on the needs of librarians working in the community care sector.

While HLG is open to members throughout the UK, Scotland and Wales also have their own national associations for health librarians, the Association of Scottish Health Service Librarians (ASHSL) and the Association of Welsh Health Librarians (AWHL), respectively.

The Institute of Information Scientists is another UK based professional body which is open to librarians and other information professionals. It 'aims to promote and maintain high standards of information work, to establish qualifications for those in the information profession and to initiate and maintain contacts between information scientists . . . It promotes the existence and value of the information professional to employers and creates awareness among senior management of the benefits of organized information management'.[5] IIS has branches and special interest groups but none are specific to health.

Aslib differs from the LA and IIS in that it is primarily an association for corporate organizations. However, its special interest groups are open to individual members with an interest in the subject. There is an Aslib Biosciences Group (ABG) which promotes the exchange of information in the fields of agriculture, biology, medicine and the environment. It has often cosponsored events with other health information associations.

Aslib, IIS and the LA are professional associations with sub-groups which could be described as subject specific groups. Other subject specific groups which are not part of major professional bodies include the Dental Librarians Group (DLG), the Cancer Libraries in Cooperation (CLIC), the Psychiatric Libraries Cooperative Scheme (PLCS), the Consumer Health Information Consortium (CHIC) and the Information Focus for Allied Health (InFAH).

In contrast, there are other library bodies which are limited to members from specific sectors. An example is the Standing Conference of National and University Libraries (SCONUL) which was created to assess the implications of developments in higher education on libraries and to represent the views of these libraries to policy making bodies. SCONUL members include libraries in postgraduate institutions and universities and national libraries. There is a SCONUL Advisory Committee on Health Services (ACHS) which assesses the impact of developments in the health service on libraries and advises on all matters related to the acquisition and control of library materials needed for students in medicine, nursing and the professions allied to medicine.

Another group operating in the academic sector is the University Medical School Librarians Group (UMSLG) which began in 1983. It was formed by medical school librarians in the UK and the Republic of Ireland to provide an active national forum through which to exchange views, coordinate action and raise their political profile.[6] Membership of the group is *ex officio*, being restricted to the librarian in charge of each library. Besides regular meetings of members, this group sponsors seminars and workshops, makes submissions to national bodies, conducts surveys and collects statistics on member libraries, and operates two electronic discussion lists on JANET (the Joint Academic Network), one of which is open to any JANET user.

A third group operating in the same sector is the University Health Sciences Librarians (UHSL). This was constituted in 1994 to provide a more accessible association for all librarians in this sector.[7] Although membership is open, only members from university affiliated institutions can hold office. This group acts as a forum for discussion of issues relating to libraries in higher education and for providing rapid responses at national level for matters of concern to members.

This division between *ex officio* and personal associations also exists in the pharmaceutical sector, where there are two groups providing support to librarians and information officers. Information Managers in the Pharmaceutical Industry (IMPI) is a group of the managers in charge of information functions of 12 research based UK pharmaceutical companies. IMPI provides them with an informal forum for discussion of issues relevant to information handling, as well as a focal point of contact with suppliers of information products, services and software.

On the other hand, the Association of Information Officers in the Pharmaceutical Industry (AIOPI) is open to all those engaged in medical, scientific or technical information work in the pharmaceutical sector and opens its meetings to non-AIOPI members. It runs a one-year training course for members on all aspects of medical and research information.

An important group that could be described as sector-specific is the NHS Regional Librarians Group (RLG). Membership is by invitation only and is restricted to the five full-time NHS Regional Librarians and to those who fulfil the role of Regional Librarian in the other NHS regions in England and in Wales, Northern Ireland and Scotland. Recently, the RLG invited a few librarians whose responsibilities have a direct impact on NHS libraries to participate as observers. RLG provides 'a national focus in the representation of library services to the NHS'.[8] It provides advice on library management and the development of national policies, coordinates activities of the various regional library and information services, negotiates with non-NHS resources nationally, and publicizes libraries and their value throughout the NHS. There are active sub-committees which address specific issues such as standards, statistics, information technology and liaison with other groups. Of all associations in the health care field, it operates with the broadest remit and speaks for the majority of NHS librarians.

One particular group of NHS librarians, those working in regional health authorities, which are now known as regional offices, formed their own support group and network in 1973. This group has limited its membership to NHS Executive regional office librarians and two librarians from each NHS region, in order to protect its ability to share ideas and concerns more informally.

One of the newest groups operating in the NHS sector is ASSIST – the Association for Information Management and Technology Staff in the NHS. This group arose from the need for a professional association representing the growing community of NHS staff responsible for planning, implementing and managing information systems. ASSIST includes many different types of information workers and whilst librarians are in the minority, they are already represented at both branch and national council level. Besides providing opportunities for the exchange of ideas and for responding to national information policy, ASSIST is developing professional standards and is working with the NHS Training Directorate and on a professional certification programme for its members called the Statement of Recognition.

Finally, a unique group amongst the professional information bodies in the health sector is the cross-sectoral and cross-disciplinary group known as the Medical Information Working Party (MIWP). MIWP was set up by MHWLG, the Publishers Association and the Association of Subscription Agents to provide a forum for the exchange of views between medical booksellers, librarians and publishers.

Whilst some may feel there is a need for groups which cater to specialist interests, the sheer number of associations for librarians in the health sector, many of which have overlapping interests, can be confusing both for librarians and for other professional groups or statutory bodies wishing to communicate with them. Presently, there is no coordination amongst groups lobbying on behalf of librarians in the health sector. Senior officials in the government have commented publicly about the need for an umbrella group which would act as a 'single voice' for this community. In 1994, the Library and Information Cooperation Council (LINC) was approached by representatives of the Regional Librarians Group about this problem. LINC, which is charged with promoting library cooperation throughout the UK, offered to consider the creation of a Health Panel which could be composed of representatives of all the health library groups in the UK and which could coordinate their views and act as a vehicle for communication with central and local government and other official bodies. If this panel receives the support of the groups listed above, it could reduce the fragmentation which characterizes the health library profession at the moment, which would result in a much stronger professional lobby.

Table 22.1 displays the national professional bodies discussed in this section in subject vs. sector and personal vs. institutional cells.

LOCAL/REGIONAL GROUPS:
The associations listed in the previous section cover all of the UK, with the exception of the Welsh and Scottish Associations. Health librarians, however, may find it difficult to find the resources to attend meetings of these UK bodies or may find the variety and the size of the groups or the geographical spread of members unhelpful in terms of finding support. Local or regional library groups often provide the opportunity for more regular contact, for discussion of local issues, and for concentration on practical matters. Some of these groups are formal library networks with interlending agreements and union lists and catalogues. These are described in the chapter on the UK Health Library Network. However, there are other groups which operate in much the same way as the national bodies, with elected executive, personal and/or institutional memberships, newsletters, etc. Examples are the Yorkshire Regional Association of Health Care Libraries and Information Services (YRAHCLIS) and the Trent Regional Association for Health Care Libraries and Information Services (TRACHLIS). Others are even less formal, such as the Independent London Librarians Group (ILLG) which serves a group of London based medical and health research libraries based in the Royal Colleges, other health professional associations, quangos and charities. ILLG has no elected executive and meets informally to discuss issues of mutual concern.

INTERNATIONAL ASSOCIATIONS

There are several important international associations in the health care field which are open to UK health librarians. Of most relevance to the UK is the European Association for Health Information and Libraries (EAHIL) which aims to improve cooperation amongst health librarians in Europe, to raise standards of provision and practice, to inform health librarians and information officers, to encourage mobility and to represent the interests of health librarians at European level, especially at European institutions and at the World Health Organization. EAHIL has a membership of nearly 500 European librarians, including those from the newly independent states and the former Yugoslavia, plus members from the USA, Canada, China and Australia.

The largest health library association in the world is the Medical Library Association (MLA) founded in 1898. This is based in the United States but has members in the USA, Canada, Australia and many other countries including the UK. It has a membership of over 5000 institutions and individuals. MLA 'fosters excellence in the professional achievement and leadership of health sciences library and information professionals to enhance the quality of health care, education and research'.[9] MLA has 14 geographical chapters, 23 sections including one on international cooperation, and 11 special interest groups. In 1989, it established the Academy of Health Information Professionals (AHIP) which is the only peer-reviewed certification programme for professional development and career achievement in the health library sector.

The Special Libraries Association (SLA), founded in 1909, is another international, professional association serving more than 14,000 members who work in special libraries, including those in industry, government, academic institutions and research facilities. It is organized in a similar way to MLA and has 55 chapters, including a European chapter, and 27 divisions, including a pharmaceutical division. SLA also offers conferences, continuing education events, self-study programmes, career and employment services, scholarships and research grants.

Many other countries have specialist health library associations which are worth joining if only for their journals and publications. For example, the Canadian Health Libraries Association (CHLA), which aims to improve health and health care by promoting excellence in access to information, produces *Bibliotheca medica Canadiana* a quarterly journal committed to assisting the worker in the small and isolated library.

Importantly, there are associations of associations which support professional development of health librarians. A key organization, the International Federation of Library Associations (IFLA), is open to national library asociations, institutional members and personal affiliates, and runs an annual conference which is held in a different country every year. Whilst IFLA's activities tend to focus on its core programmes – advancement of librarianship in the Third World, preservation and conservation, universal availability of publications, etc. – the annual conference usually includes a section on biomedical information and libraries. IFLA also sponsors the organizing committee for the International Congress on Medical Librarianship (ICML) which is held every five years. The 8th ICML will be held in London in the year 2000.

REFERENCES:

1   Dale, P. (comp.), *Directory of library and information organizations in the United Kingdom*, London, Library Association Publishing, 1993.
2   Palmer, J., 'Professional associations in health information', *MHWLG newsletter*, **11** (2), 1994, viii–xiii.
3   Dale, op. cit.
4   Willis, A., 'The Library Association Medical Health and Welfare Libraries Group, 1978–1992', *Health libraries review*, **10**, 1993, 111–18.
5   Ibid.
6   Morgan, P., personal communication.
7   Walton, G., personal communication, 1994.
8   Forrest, M. and Carmel, M., 'The NHS Regional Librarians Group', *Health libraries review*, **4**, 1987, 160–3.
9   Medical Library Association, *MLA Directory 1994/95*, Chicago, MLA, 1994.

❖ Index